MEDIATING NATURE

Mediat   Nature provides a history of the present nature of mass mediation.
It exan   the ways in which a number of discourses, genres, institutions and
techno   of observation have historically shaped the current ways of imagining the   re of nature, and the nature of mass mediation. Where much of the
existing   ch treats mass mediation as a matter of media technologies, texts,
audien   institutions, the current book adopts a somewhat different approach
that br   own the conventional boundaries between these elements: it considers 'ma   ediation' as a historical process by means of which the members of
audien   d indeed publics more generally have been taught to be observers of,
if not i   ture. As part of this approach, the book offers an investigation of the
historic   interrelation of a number of social genres and their characteristic techniques   bservation. These include landscape paintings and gardens, modern
zoos, p   phy, early cinema, nature essays, disaster and 'animal attack' films,
as well   documentaries on television. An integral aspect of the investigation in   what Lindahl Elliot describes as a 'social semeiotic' methodology
that co   semeiotic theory of Charles Peirce with a historical sociology of
cultura   ions. This enables the book to challenge some of the assumptions
of natu   also of culturalist and postmodern discourses about the nature
of natu   the nature of mass mediation.

Top   timely, this fascinating book will be of great interest to students
and res   rs in the fields of media, sociology, cultural geography and environmental   es.

Nils I   hi Elliot is a researcher in cultural and environmental studies. His
researc   ialism is in the social semeiotics of nature.

To

INTERNATIONAL LIBRARY OF SOCIOLOGY
Founded by Karl Mannheim

Edited by John Urry
Lancaster University

AFTER METHOD
Mess in social science research
John Law

BRANDS
Logos of the global economy
Celia Lury

THE CULTURE OF EXCEPTION
Sociology facing the camp
Bulent Diken and Carsten Bagge Lausten

VISUAL WORLDS
John Hall, Blake Stimson and Lisa Tamiris Becker

TIME, INNOVATION AND MOBILITIES
Travel in technological cultures
Peter Frank Peters

COMPLEXITY AND SOCIAL MOVEMENTS
Multitudes acting at the edge of chaos
Ian Welsh and Graeme Chesters

QUALITATIVE COMPLEXITY
Ecology, cognitive processes and the re-emergence of structures in
post-humanist social theory
John Smith and Chris Jenks

THEORIES OF THE INFORMATION SOCIETY, 3RD EDITION
Frank Webster

MEDIATING NATURE
Nils Lindahl Elliot

HAUNTING THE KNOWLEDGE ECONOMY
Jane Kenway, Elizabeth Bullen, Johannah Fahey and Simon Robb

MEDIATING NATURE

Nils Lindahl Elliot

Routledge
Taylor & Francis Group

LONDON AND NEW YORK

First published 2006
by Routledge

2 Park Square, Milton Park, Abingdon, Oxon OX14 4RN

Simultaneously published in the USA and Canada
by Routledge
270 Madison Ave, New York, NY 10016

Routledge is an imprint of the Taylor & Francis Group

Typeset in Galliard by
Prepress Projects Ltd, Perth, UK

Printed and bound in Great Britain by
Anthony Rowe Ltd, Chippenham, Wiltshire

British Library Cataloguing in Publication Data
A catalogue record for this book is available from the British Library

Library of Congress Cataloging in Publication Data
A catalog record for this title has been requested

ISBN10: 0–415–39177–6   ISBN13: 978–0–415–39177–1 (hbk)
ISBN10: 0–415–39325–6   ISBN13: 978–0–415–39325–6 (pbk)
ISBN10: 0–203–08724–0   ISBN13: 978–0–203–08724–4 (ebk)

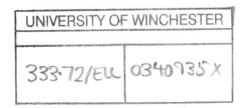

CONTENTS

ACKNOWLEDGEMENTS

I would like to begin by thanking John Urry for inviting me to submit a proposal to the Routledge International Library of Sociology Series, and for providing comments on a draft of the book. John's generous support has made it possible for me to publish this book in its present form. Carmen Alfonso, Ben Highmore and Hans Lindahl also provided detailed comments on drafts of the book, and I am very grateful for their input. It goes without saying that any misinterpretations that remain are entirely my own.

Constance Sutherland and Gerhard Boomgaarden at Routledge provided generous support and advice for which I am also very grateful. The same is true for the kind assistance provided by Andrew R. Davidson and the team at Prepress Projects.

I developed the ideas and the research for this book at the School of Cultural Studies at the University of the West of England, Bristol. The School provided research leave and constituted a lively place in which to study and teach some of the subjects found in the following pages. I am particularly grateful to Jane Arthurs, who has been a generous and supportive head of school. I'm also very grateful to the students who participated in my undergraduate and postgraduate courses, and who encouraged me to clarify the ideas presented in the following pages. I used an early draft of parts of the book in one of my undergraduate courses in 2004/5, and would like to thank the especially attentive reading and helpful questions raised by Dorothea Brueckner, Pascale Yasmine and Simon Steadman.

The research leave provided by the School was more than matched by grants awarded over the last five years by the Arts and Humanities Research Board of England and Wales (1999–2000) (now the Arts and Humanities Research Council); by the British Academy (2000); and by the Economic and Social Research Council of England and Wales (2002–2004).

I wish finally to acknowledge the patience and the support of my friends and family, who understood my absences from non-academic everyday life. It is my hope that the publication of the book will mark the beginning of the end of the *askesis* that preceded its completion.

I dedicate this book to F. Stanley Glynn, from whom I first learned about the imaginary institution of culture.

INTRODUCTION

Mediating Nature offers a history of the present nature of mass mediation. The ambiguity of the phrase 'the present nature of mass mediation' is deliberate: the history in question is both a history of the present nature of mass mediation, and a history of the mass mediation of nature. I shall suggest that such a history goes some way towards explaining the nature of modern environmentalism.

Each of the terms used in this account – 'nature', 'mass mediation', 'modern environmentalism' and a 'history of the present' – calls for critical scrutiny, and in the following pages I shall consider some of the problems that each raises.

Nature

I should like to begin with the notion of 'nature'. Some readers may be surprised that I use 'nature', and not 'the environment'. Does the word 'nature' not suggest the kind of old opposition between human and non-human nature, between the city and the country, between nature and culture, that is arguably the philosophical (and not so philosophical) underpinning of the current environmental crisis? Surely 'the environment' would provide a more up-to-date understanding of 'nature', i.e. one that recognizes that the so-called 'human' and 'non-human' natures are ineluctably intertwined, parts of a proverbially inseparable whole? If so, why stay with 'nature'?

The first answer is that nature has stayed with us. Just in 2004 and 2005, in a tsunami that killed hundreds of thousands of people across and beyond the Indian Ocean, in an earthquake in the Kashmir region that may have killed as many as 100,000 people, in a hurricane that destroyed a modern city in the United States, but also in the everyday death of life, nature has reminded us that, as Terry Eagleton (2000) puts it, it has the last word.

To be sure, it is not only in death that nature continues to live; a dialectic of culture and nature arguably shapes all aspects of human practice in so far as there remains a nature that is, in Kate Soper's terms, 'independent of human activity (in the sense that [it is] not a humanly created product)', but 'whose forces and causal powers are the necessary condition of every human practice' (Soper 1995: 132–3).

A second answer is that, whether such a nature continues to shape human life or not, this is the nature that is preferred by the mass media. Over the last thirty or so years, the complex accounts of ecosystematic relations that can be found in ecology textbooks, and the increasingly baroque accounts of 'hybrid' natures found in academic texts such as this one appear to have been ignored by the producers of most genres of mass communication. Indeed, the nature represented in such genres remains, for the most part, the 'extreme nature' seen in Steve Irwin's *Crocodile Hunter* or in *The Day After Tomorrow,* or perhaps the 'Edenic' nature seen in posters spread out on the concourses of many shopping malls as well as in the wallpapers of untold millions of computer screens.

A third answer is that this nature – the 'non-human' nature – also informs many representations of the modern environmentalist movement, understood in a broad manner that includes conservationist organizations and environmentalist activists but also everyday environmentalist sensibilities. For example, a quick search towards the end of 2005 of the websites of a number of mainstream – and even 'not so mainstream' – environmentalist organizations suggested that the discursive opposition between human and non-human nature remains very much a part at least of their public *raison d'être*. The WWF, whose acronym once stood – and in the US still stands – for the World Wildlife Fund, changed its name to the World Wide Fund for Nature. The organization suggested that this change was meant to reflect its concern with conserving what it described as 'the environment as a whole'. But, aside from maintaining the word 'nature' in its name, the WWF described its 'ultimate goal' as being 'to stop and eventually reverse environmental degradation and to build a future where *people live in harmony with nature*' (http://www.panda.org/about_wwf/who_we_are/index.cfm, accessed 15 September 2005, emphasis added).

For its part, Friends of the Earth, a non-governmental organization (NGO) generally identified with a 'social ecological' form of environmentalism, described itself as an organization whose '1.5 million members and supporters in 70 countries campaign on the most urgent *environmental and social issues* of our day, while simultaneously catalyzing a shift towards sustainable societies'(http://www.foei.org/about/index.html, accessed 15 September 2005, emphasis added). Its mission statement suggested that its first aim was to 'protect the earth against further deterioration and repair damage inflicted upon the environment by human activities and negligence' (http://www.foei.org/about/mission_statement.html, accessed 15 September 2005).

Even Reclaim the Streets (RTS), an organization (or as it described itself, a 'disorganization') whose campaigns had been based on a refreshingly urban politics, included an essay in its website titled 'Ecology and the Social City' which suggested that 'With the *environment and social impact* of contemporary city life increasingly evident in pollution, destruction, poverty, stress and crime, a critical and reconstructive look at *the city and its' [sic] relations with the natural world* seems not only timely – but urgent' (http://rts.gn.apc.org/socialcity.htm, accessed 15 September 2005, emphases added).

In each case, the human–nature, culture–nature divide could still be seen to be structuring, however tacitly, the environmentalist groups' own discourses. The point of this brief analysis is not to suggest that such groups (or indeed the producers of the mass media) *ought* to have moved on from the 'old' discourse of nature. Rather, it is to note firstly the continued relevance of the category, and secondly to begin to suggest with Kate Soper (1995) that it is virtually impossible to *avoid* some kind of a human–nature distinction in the context of modern cultures. This does not mean that 'naturalist' or, as Soper puts it, 'nature-endorsing' activists are right, let alone that 'nature-sceptical', or what I shall describe as 'culturalist', scholars are wrong. It *does* mean that the politics of nature are, from the start, remarkably complex and slippery, and require careful scrutiny and elucidation. This is as true for those whose discourse starts from biologism – the doctrine that everything in human affairs is ultimately a matter of nature – as it is for those whose discourse starts from – or indeed arrives at – *culturalism*: the doctrine that 'everything in human affairs is a matter of culture' (Eagleton 2000: 91).

Mass mediation

I shall return to the question of the nature of nature in this and later chapters. I now want to turn to the question of the nature of *mass mediation*.

Mass mediation – and its subset, mass communication – is commonly reduced in everyday discourses to 'the mass media'. In so doing, such discourses frequently conflate it with the institutions, and/or the instrumental technologies of television, the printed press, film, the internet and so forth. In the following pages I would like to suggest that these institutions and technologies are only a part of a process – the process of mass mediation – that entails an order which is both more than a matter of institutions and less than a matter of technology.

It is more than a matter of institutions in so far as institutions are defined in the narrow sense of 'organizations' (I shall suggest a broader definition of the notion of institution below). Mass mediation involves institutions such as the BBC, but it also involves their audiences, the messages that the institutions produce or circulate, and indeed the broader socio-cultural context in which all of these exist. In turn, mass mediation is *less* than a matter of technology, at least in the instrumental sense of this term, in so far as mass mediation is generally not effective in the way that media technologies are commonly assumed to be: children, for example, do not simply go out and murder other children after observing one child killing another in a video. (Such 'media effects' were taken for granted by many media critics after the killing of Jamie Bulger in the United Kingdom.) If this *were* the case, one might expect to find rather fewer children on the streets. One might also expect to find rather more gorillas in the rainforests: people do not 'save gorillas' simply because someone tells them, on television or elsewhere, that they ought to do so. This does not mean that the notion of media 'effects' – understood from the perspective of what I describe in Chapter 1 as 'secondness' – has no validity. It does mean that the order of 'effects' is mediated by social practices that cannot themselves be *reduced* to a matter of 'effects'. As this last point begins to make clear, mass mediation is also *more* than a matter of technology in the sense that the development, deployment, and social appropriation of any given technology of communication – and not just of *communication* – is always part of a much broader cultural dynamic.[1]

How, then, to re-conceptualize mass mediation? In the following chapters I shall suggest that mass mediation is better understood as a historical process that has involved, and to this day continues to involve, a panoply of *pedagogies of massification*. This somewhat inelegant expression requires two sets of clarifications. First, I take it with Basil Bernstein (1990; 1996) that pedagogic practices are an integral aspect not just of formal schooling, or even of informal educational contexts, but of cultural reproduction. In addition to formal and informal pedagogies, it is perhaps therefore necessary to speak of 'non-formal' pedagogies. Non-formal pedagogies involve teaching and learning practices where nothing is taught – nothing is *deliberately* taught – but where something is nonetheless *learned*.

Second, what I describe as pedagogies of massification entail the manifold non-formal pedagogies whereby the members of a cultural group or set of groups are taught to be part of an agglomeration; in particular, part of *mass culture*. In some respects, the notion of a mass culture may seem like something of an anachronism, in the pejorative sense.[2] In the era of post-Fordism and neoliberal 'consumer choice', the notion of a mass culture may seem peculiarly outdated. And yet it is clear that what I describe as massification goes on in any number of everyday contexts where people are routinely transformed into parts of agglomerations: into audiences, visitors, publics or indeed *consumers* who are bought and sold by advertisers, mobilized by politicians or persuaded by environmentalist campaigners to support one or another campaign. As I also hope to explain, the forms of agglomeration associated with mass culture have a history, and one that is intimately related with the history of the representation, and indeed experience, of nature.

While the phenomenon of massification goes far beyond the experience of nature, in subsequent chapters I shall suggest that, historically, the spaces and times associated with nature came to play a key role both in producing massification, and in providing what was, paradoxically, a kind of prophylaxis for massification. For example, during the nineteenth century visits to nature (or a geography associated with it) became a form of mass tourism, but they also came to be regarded by urban reformers as a kind of treatment for a variety of real or imagined ills suffered by the working classes in the US and Europe – most notably those associated with industrialization and living in crowded urban areas. To be sure, maintaining the health of the masses served functions that went far beyond the people's health; a key concern was to maintain the health of the *workforce*, and thereby, of the economy. The mass mediation of nature became an integral aspect of a reformist discourse of, and on, capitalism.

As this account begins to make clear, *mass mediation* involves rather more than the mass media. In addition to the study of the conventional media, it involves the consideration of social processes that are not necessarily those associated with the 'headline' mass media, or indeed with the 'media' at all. I argue that the mass mediation of nature must be explained with reference to all those practices that have served as a *medium* for the pedagogy of massification 'via' 'nature'. The category of 'media' thereby includes city parks and national parks, but also zoos, natural history museums, the different means of transport employed in the context of mass tourism, and more recently, the campaigns of environmental activists.

Modern environmentalism

The expression 'modern environmentalism' is commonly used to refer to the so-called 'ecological revolution' that followed the publication of Rachel Carson's *Silent Spring*. It is also identified with the activism of groups like Greenpeace and Friends of the Earth, and more generally with the green sensibilities associated with their interventions. While this understanding is not wrong in itself, I shall argue in the following chapters that modern environmentalism needs to be reinterpreted in two fundamental ways.

First, and as my earlier analysis of environmentalist websites began to suggest, it is necessary to adopt a rather more historical perspective on the nature of modern environmentalism. This is literally true – we need to explain the nature of modern environmentalism's nature (or *natures*) – but also true in the sense that forms of environmentalist, or at least proto-environmentalist, protest have taken place since at least the eighteenth century, if not earlier. At that point, and as has been documented by the environmental historian Richard Grove (1995), doctors, natural historians and other observers combined empirical observations with an idealized conception of nature – the nature of the 'Edenic' isles – to protest that the deforestation of certain island colonies was leading to a local version of what is now called 'climate change'.

The second reinterpretation is somewhat more difficult to explain. Having suggested that modern environmentalism may have much older precedents than is generally assumed, I also want to suggest that the protests mentioned above were different from the present forms of environmentalism in two respects. First, there was still no category of the environment as we know it today. But second, and crucially, the activities were not based on what I describe as the mass mediation of risk politics and the risk politics of mass mediation.

This point requires some clarification. If we can say that Rachel Carson inaugurated modern environmentalism, it was not because she discovered and communicated the dangers of DDT or other pesticides. That work had already been begun by other scientists, who as early as 1945 began to suggest that the new pesticides ought to be used with caution. Rather, what made Carson's work remarkable was that it engaged in, and indeed *was engaged by*, a dynamic of mass mediation which produced a new kind of environmentalist pedagogy.

I shall describe this pedagogy in the last chapters of the book; here it suffices to highlight two aspects. First, and as part of the process of massification that I began to describe earlier, the new category of the environment itself became the object of a certain pedagogic process. Environmental activists believed that people needed to learn about threats to the environment, about environmental threats but also about the very notion of the 'environment' itself.

Second, teaching informally and non-formally about these aspects did not simply involve an instrumental use of the media of mass communication. I shall argue that, especially in the case of Greenpeace, this pedagogy meant that the environmentalist groups *themselves* became 'mass media' in both the institutional-instrumental sense of media producers and the sense of mass mediation described earlier. It is no coincidence, in this sense, that today advertisements for director-ships of Greenpeace typically place media expertise and experience at the top of the list of requirements for the post. By this account, groups like Greenpeace did not just 'use' the media; in key respects, they *became* media as well as mass mediators, even as their own practices were made possible by broader practices of mass mediation.

A history of the present

I have now provided an introductory account of what I mean by 'the nature of mass mediation' and 'the mass mediation of nature'. I have also begun to explain the relation between these two and modern environmentalism. But what about the notion of a *history of the present* nature of mass mediation? This notion raises more explicitly methodological questions, and in the remainder of this chapter I would like to provide a somewhat more technical account of this aspect of the book.

I should begin by noting that what follows is not, strictly speaking, a history, and indeed, a majority of the subjects covered by the following chapters are not developed on the basis of my own archival research. My use of the expression 'history of the present' is meant to signal that the following chapters are better described as a *problematization* of the nature of mass mediation in the sense of problematization defined by Michel Foucault. As Foucault puts it, 'I start with a problem in the terms in which it is currently posed and attempt to establish its genealogy; genealogy means that I conduct the analysis starting from the present situation' (Foucault in Castel 1994: 238). According to Foucault, the subject mat-ter of such a genealogy is not the study of representations of pre-existing objects, or indeed of discursively produced objects. Instead, it entails the study of 'the totality of discursive and non-discursive practices' that bring it into 'the play of truth and falsehood and [set] it up as an object for the mind'[3] (Foucault in Castel 1994: 238). The purpose of considering this 'play' is to investigate the production of seemingly incontestable claims and their practical repercussions (Castel 1994: 238).

In the first instance, engaging in such a problematization involves a critical examination of 'headline' genres such as natural history documentaries, feature-length fictional ecopics, news and current affairs, and so forth. I refer to the media institutions most obviously associated with the representation of nature as the 'nature media' in recognition of the fact that a small number of them – most notably the BBC, the National Geographic, Disney, Animal Planet and the Discovery Channel – have played a highly significant role when it comes to establishing the parameters for what I shall describe in Chapter 2 as the classification and framing of nature. But, for the reasons explained earlier, I shall also consider the more general process of *mass mediation*, and thereby 'non-traditional' media such as zoos and nature theme parks, national parks and city parks. These may seem less important today, but have historically played – and indeed still play – a key role in the mass mediation of nature.

But I shall also consider a number of practices that may seem to have little or no relation to the mass mediation of nature: for example, the emergence of rail travel, the rise of the modern business organization, and economic and political institutions associated with the rise of mercantile, industrial and then managerial forms of capitalism. The justification for including these is that, as Foucault explains, a history of the present, a genealogical investigation, is a form of inquiry that records 'the singularity of events outside of any monotonous finality' and seeks them 'in the most unpromising places, in what we tend to feel is without history' (Foucault 1998: 369). Although the different practices I have mentioned clearly *do* have a history, I suggest that contemporary forms of the mass mediation of nature may seem to be without *these* histories. One of the objectives of this book is to show that there are a series of 'nocturnal connections' between practices apparently not related to nature or to the mass mediation of nature, but which have arguably played a significant role in establishing the parameters for the play(s) of truth and falsehood of the nature of mass mediation.

Now the problematization of the nature of mass mediation requires another parallel problematization, a problematization of a dualism that I mentioned when I justified the continued use of the concept of nature, and which cuts across discourses about the nature of mass mediation, and the mass mediation of nature. The dualism in question is one that opposes 'nature naturalists' and 'nature culturalists' and allows scientists, media professionals and researchers alike to speak of a 'human' and a 'non-human' nature, or indeed of *culture and nature*.

From the perspective of many physical scientists and media practitioners involved in science and environmental communication, the existence of nature as a 'mind-independent' entity can be taken for granted. Nature, by this account, exists in the way that the rainforest or the gorilla does. In so far as they accurately represent such a nature, the empirical and factual grounding of natural history documentaries, zoo displays, news features and a variety of other media can be regarded as being unproblematic.

But, from the perspective of many academics in the humanities and in the critical social sciences, the opposite is true: nature is first and foremost a concept, and one that is premised on a problematic opposition between nature and culture.[4] In so far as this is the case, it is necessary to critique any practice that fails to question the nature of nature – not least, the TV documentaries and other mass media genres that carry the opposition. At a time when global warming appears to be transforming life on Earth; when traces of deca-bromodiphenyl ether (deca-BDE) can even be found in the fat of polar bears in the Arctic circle (Pearce 2004)[5] and when cyborgs and genetic modifications are making it more difficult than ever to establish neat boundaries between what counts as the 'natural' and the 'unnatural', advocates of this discourse suggest that it is necessary to develop a new, more critical discourse that leaves behind the dualistic opposition between culture and nature.

The tension between these two stances comes to a head in a variety of practices in which nature, or something associated with it, is, in effect, made to present itself even as it is represented. An obvious example of this phenomenon may be found in zoos, where real animals are put on display, ostensibly in order to present themselves, but also to represent something else: the species or a principle of conservation. Further examples may be found in parks, landscapes and any other context where the geography is essentially ambiguous from the point of view of its classification as a matter of presentation or representation. To cite another example, in the case of the geographies found in national parks, the landscape is at once a matter of 'land-*scaping*' – privileged viewing areas in some respects *produce* the landscape by suggesting that it ought to be viewed as such – but also a physical geography that cannot be reduced to a matter of human or cultural intervention. Such phenomena might well be described as involving not just 'representations' but '*re/presentations*' – at once 'representations' *and* 'presentations', or what Charles Sanders Peirce (1931–58) describes as the phenomenon of entelechy: simplifying somewhat, perfect, or seemingly perfect, signs. A less than perfect version of this phenomenon also may be found in the technologies for the mechanical (and now electronic) reproduction of nature: photography, sound recording, cinematography and any other technology of representation in which an 'index' of nature coexists with a conventional way of representing it. According to Pierce, indexes are signs which are in a real or 'causal' relation to their objects of representation.

The signs of entelechy (or 'entelechian signs') are part of a phenomenon that I describe as the 'dedoubling' of nature as a sign of nature and as a physically material entity. By 'dedoubling' I refer not just to the fact that objects have both a semiotic and an 'empirically verifiable' reality, but to the tension that results when it can be suggested, equally validly, that an object is more a sign, or more the 'object-in-itself'. I would like to engage in a genealogical investigation of the nature of mass mediation that traces the history of this ambiguity but does so in a manner that avoids the temptation of resolving it in favour of either the nature-naturalist or the nature-culturalist discourse. If it is true that the predominant modern cultural institutions have long attempted to eliminate the ambiguity in favour of a naturalistic account of such phenomena, I shall suggest in Chapter 1 that many forms of academic research in the humanities and the social sciences have incurred the opposite error by offering a radically culturalist account of the sign-objects in question.

I have provided a 'thumbnail' sketch of the problematization from which the present study begins. I would now like to qualify my appropriation of the methodology of genealogy.

As I noted earlier, a 'present problem' serves as the point of departure for what Foucault describes as a genealogical investigation. Foucault's notion of genealogy is premised on a methodology of historiography that is rather different from that adopted by traditional forms of historiography. A genealogy, and thereby a 'history of the present', forgoes a 'progressivist' form of historical inquiry, i.e. one that is based on the assumption that the march of time is just that: a *march* that departs from one clearly defined place and finishes in another, planned, place. Foucault alerts the researcher to the trap of an essentialist history, that is to say, one that takes for granted that meanings and practices have an essence and neat origin and remain largely unchanged across contexts. Instead, he suggests that the task of the researcher is to isolate certain *scenes* and to consider, as I suggested earlier, the changing play of truth and falsehood as it accrues to an ensemble of both discursive and non-discursive practices relating to the problem in question.

It is perhaps a testament to Foucault's influence in the humanities and the critical social sciences that many readers/writers – myself included – will not regard this as a particularly new or different way of engaging in social inquiry. Foucault has, in this sense, succeeded in making many traditional forms of historiography suspect, even as he suggests, perhaps with a twinkle in his eye, that '[g]enealogy is grey, meticulous, and patiently documentary' (Foucault 1998: 369).

This does not mean, of course, that his methodology should be appropriated uncritically; in the context of the present investigation, Foucault's approach raises a number of problems, not least those involving the scope of the study. As begins to be evident from my examples, the scope of the practices in question is too vast to be researched in any one book, or by a single researcher. It is thus necessary, on the one hand, to engage in the production of what Stuart Hall (1992a) has described as 'historical generalizations': accounts that abstract, of necessity, from the detail of complex events in order to provide a broader perspective of the contexts. But it is also necessary to reduce the scope of the present inquiry, and I shall do so in two main ways. First, and still within a relatively Foucaultian frame, I shall focus on the institution of some of the mass-mediated *techniques and technologies of observation* that have posed most radically the question of the nature of nature, and of an ostensibly non-interventionist *observer* of nature. I take it that the problem of observation – the nature of observation and the observation of nature – is fundamental to the understanding of the nature of nature, and the nature of mass mediation.

When I refer to techniques and technologies of observation, I refer to techniques and technologies such as those found for example in photography and cinema, but also in single-point perspective in painting and design, in landscape gardening and, to a degree, in the more recent simulacra of habitats in zoos. In all of these examples, and as I explain in forthcoming chapters, it is tempting to think of observation and indeed of the observer in terms of an individual passively *looking* at something. But building on the insights of Jonathan Crary (1990), I will argue that there is rather more to observation than meets the eye: the observer for any given context works to conform to – to 'observe' – social rules. By this account, the observer is, *as observer*, both the producer and the effect of a heterogeneous system constituted by discursive, social, technological and institutional relations. It follows that the manner in which someone observes nature in one place may be determined, at least in part, in another 'place', and with respect to the logic of other social contexts.

As I noted above, Foucault suggests that a genealogical inquiry is patiently documentary. But documenting the practices outlined above by way of archival research would almost certainly require not one but many lifetimes of work, and so my second reduction involves the rather more modest method of engaging in a patient *rereading* of some of the existing historical narratives; this with the aim of producing a 'creative synthesis' based on a somewhat different logic of recontextualization (Bernstein 1990) than is usually found within any one of the disciplines or interdisciplines in which any of the original texts was produced. By 'creative synthesis' I mean a study that recontextualizes existing scholarship in a manner that allows the articulation of new (or newer) questions and narratives. Of course, all syntheses are, by their very nature, 'creative'. In this book I'd like to develop this process by bringing together a range of academic and non-academic discourses and subject matters that are normally kept quite separate, but which arguably need to be considered together if one is to problematize the nature of mass mediation in the manner I described earlier. I take it that creativity is largely a matter of an unusual recombination of existing discourses or practices.

I have focussed thus far on what might be described as problems of scope. But there is a rather more fundamental problem with adopting Foucault's conception of problematization in the current inquiry, one that some readers may have noted by virtue of my earlier critical realist comments about the nature of nature. Foucault famously 'detested nature', and made a somewhat theatrical point of 'turning his back' to landscapes that a friend tried to show him (Éribon 1993: 46).[6] It seems clear that this dislike is related to Foucault's more general antipathy for the discourse of essences; Foucault might well be characterized as the high priest of the critique of essentialist forms of research, a critique that is now paradoxically widely treated as an essential canon of critical research practice. This is arguably part of what led him to suggest that the task of a genealogical inquiry is *not* to consider the representation of pre-existing objects (Foucault 1984).

In the pages that follow, I nonetheless want to argue that a history of the present nature of mass mediation *must* involve the consideration of the representation of pre-existing objects (and, to be sure, not just 'objects'). As I started to suggest at the outset of this chapter, I also want to argue that it must take seriously the possibility that there *is* such a thing as material nature, as defined earlier by Kate Soper. The most obvious justification for this may be found in the events that took place during the last year that I was writing this book – the tsunami in the Indian Ocean, the hurricanes in the Caribbean, the earthquake in the Kashmir region. A somewhat more subtle justification may be found in a critical examination of the excess of culturalism; were Foucault alive today, he might perhaps smile wryly and propose a genealogy of the current vogue of culturalism. To be sure, it might be argued that doing so would be to engage in research in a truly Foucaultian *spirit* (*sic*): if a history of the present really is about considering the 'play of truth and falsehood' by means of which something is transformed into an 'object for the mind', then there can be no better 'something' for this purpose than 'nature', particularly at a time when a 'telluric' nature vies with the nature of cyborgs, genetic modification and, indeed, flame-retardant polar bears.

Given this last problem, I have decided to develop my history of the present with reference to the phenomenology and semeiotic (this spelling is deliberate) theory of Charles Sanders Peirce. In Chapter 1, I explain that in Peirce's work we find a way of articulating what I described as the phenomenon of 'dedoubling'. I also suggest that Peirce's theory may constitute a way of moving beyond the opposition between so-called 'representational' and 'non-representational' (Thrift 1996) theories – an opposition that, in my view, has come to institute an unproductive opposition between semioticism – the tendency to reduce all phenomena to a matter of signs – and what might perhaps be described as a new wave of empiricism or even romantic sensualism.

A 'propaedeutic' approach

Two rather different groups of readers constitute the readerly horizon for this book. On the one hand, I hope to engage with researchers interested in the problematization I have outlined in this introduction. I am however aware that, given the range of issues and subjects that will be covered, readers may well approach the book from the perspectives of a relatively heterogeneous ensemble of theories, vocabularies and reading styles. These include, in principle, those found in relatively realist forms of environmental studies, those found in relatively culturalist forms of cultural studies and cultural geography, and of course all those who either cannot be described in terms of, or themselves refuse, this classification. This is one reason why I have tried to write the book in a relatively 'propaedeutic' manner: in a manner that assumes that it is necessary to explain why a problem is significant, and why it deserves to be studied with reference to a certain set of theories. To this end, I have included two initial chapters and an appendix on Peirce that provide an introductory account of several aspects of the theories that both guide, and result from, the following problematization.

But I have also written the book in a propaedeutic manner because I would like to engage in dialogue with readers who are not themselves primarily academic professionals, but who might be interested in the issues raised in the following chapters. I have in mind environmental activists, but also all those whose work involves, in one or another way, the representation or interpretation of nature. Such readers may well find that much of the book is premised on what will seem like arcane distinctions and rather difficult theoretical perspectives. It is however my hope that the use of examples, the explanation of key concepts, and the inclusion of a glossary of Peirian terms should make the book more accessible than it might otherwise be.

With these different readers in mind, the book is divided into two parts. In Part I, Chapters 1 and 2 offer an extended introduction to the theory and methodology employed to engage in the problematization that follows. Both chapters also construct a certain present – a present mass mediation of nature – by referring to a recent series of mass media representations of the Ndoki rainforest in the Congo.

The rest of the chapters make up Part II. Each chapter within this part of the book is constructed as an ensemble of scenes. I employ this word not so much in the visual sense but in the drama sense of segments organized in a sequence that, taken together, constitute not the, but a play of 'truth and falsehood' as it pertains to the nature of mass mediation and the mass mediation of nature. The sequence, which is structured as a chronology with some analepses and prolepses (flashbacks and flashforwards), considers the antecedents and the actual emergence of the nature of mass mediation during a period that stretches from the fifteenth century to the early twenty-first century. While many of the scenes focus on practices in the United Kingdom and the United States, it is clear that globalization – to be sure *changing* forms of globalization – has both made possible and itself been made possible by the mass mediation of nature. The investigation must thus be rather more wide-ranging than might otherwise be the case, and the reader will find that at times I engage in the analysis of scenes that take place – take play – far from the physical geographical boundaries of the US and the UK.

I should note finally that this wide-ranging character, and indeed the methodology I have identified, require numerous ellipses and a relatively open logic of concatenation. I take it that my task is not so much to eliminate the silences between the scenes, but to remain attentive to the changing logics of the different contexts.

Bristol, January 2006

Part I

1

THE NATURE OF NATURE

Nature has the final victory over culture, customarily known as death.

Terry Eagleton

Ndoki (I)

In its 13 July 1992 edition,[1] *Time* magazine published what was to be the first in a series of major media representations about the 'discovery' of the Ndoki rainforest in the Republic of Congo.

The familiar red-bordered cover of *Time* magazine – first used in the 3 January 1927 edition to frame a drawing of the British imperialist, Leopold Charles Maurice Stennett Amery – featured a picture of a Western Lowland Gorilla. As the gorilla stared out at the magazine's readers, its head partly covered the 'M' of *TIME* even as a dramatic headline covered part of the right side of the gorilla's torso: 'INSIDE THE WORLD'S LAST EDEN'.

In the cover story itself, Eugene Linden, an environmental journalist, described an expedition to the Ndoki rainforest led by J. Michael Fay, an ecologist working with the Wildlife Conservation Society (WCS).[2] At the time that the expedition took place, the WCS was promoting the transformation of the Ndoki into a national nature park in order to preserve what the cover story described as the 'pristine' Ndoki rainforest. 'Pygmies,' Linden wrote, 'have crisscrossed central Africa for thousands of years' (Linden 1992: 63); but there was 'no evidence that they have entered beyond the fringes of this 3 million-hectare (7.5 million-acre) expanse of virgin forest,' a forest 'about the size of Belgium' (Linden 1992: 63–4). As far as Linden was concerned, this was a place that no human had ever seen before, 'the rarest treasure on this crowded planet: an ecosystem as pristine today as it was 12,000 years ago, before humans began to transform the earth' (Linden 1992: 63).

Three years after *Time* published its cover story, the *National Geographic* devoted the cover of its July 1995 issue to what was by then the newly established Nouabalé-Ndoki National Park. Echoing *Time*'s cover, the *National Geographic*

15

chose an image of one of the region's charismatic animals and framed it with a dramatic headline: 'NDOKI: THE LAST PLACE ON EARTH'. But, where *Time* chose a rather conventional medium shot of a gorilla, the *National Geographic* selected a blurred image of an elephant whose eyes were transformed into silver and red dots by the photographer's flash. The image was reportedly taken at the very moment when the elephant charged at Michael 'Nick' Nichols, the *National Geographic* photographer. There was, however, an additional motive for choosing this form of representation: as Nichols puts it,

> I'm just so bored with pretty pictures of wildlife. The last thing I would do is say go to the Serengeti and shoot a bunch of pictures of just beautiful wildlife. But I would like to go there and shoot a lot of pictures of lions killing things, and crocodiles killing things – as long as the edge is there. For me, the edge can be a combination of graphic elements, which is why I have a lot of movement in my pictures, and then the edge of survival, and what that means. So I strive and I shoot a lot of bad frames trying to get tension and movement and an edge. That's all graphic stuff, and colors, and underlying that is some kind of actual theme that's about conservation.
>
> (Nichols in http://www.michaelnicknichols.com/article/
> philosophy/, accessed 25 September 2005)

Like Linden before him, Douglas Chadwick, the author of the *National Geographic* cover story, narrated the woes and wonders of visiting what he described as a kind of hellish paradise: a place teeming with gorillas and golden cats, forest elephants and 'first encounter' chimps, trigoni bees and leeches, toona flies and 'nameless' fevers (Chadwick 1995: 6). Chadwick's expedition was also led by Mike Fay, whom Chadwick described as 'a modern version of the 19th century Congo explorer Henry Stanley, the unstoppable force whom the natives called Bula Matari, "breaker of the rocks"'(Chadwick 1995: 10).

In 1998, the WCS took a more direct role in the mass mediation of the Ndoki region by opening a 6.5-acre simulation of the Congo rainforest in New York's Bronx Zoo, its own 'flagship' park. The zoo's website described the exhibit as a 'lush mosaic of shady forest, treetop lookouts, rock promontories, stream sides, bamboo thickets, sunny meadows, forested pathways, wading pools, and retreats' that provided the animals with 'a great variety of habitat' (http://congogorillaforest.com/congointro/congohabitat, accessed 16 August 2005). A walk through this space was designed to emulate a walk through the Congo rainforest itself; and indeed, during a visit to the display, I helped to reassure a young family that a snake lying close to the walkway was make-believe and would not attack their children.

The *Congo Gorilla Forest* website eventually added a link to a *National Geographic* website, established a few years after the Bronx Zoo opened its new display, which described another of J. Michael Fay's expeditions. The website described a 15-month trek – the 'Megatransect' – taken in 1999–2000 by Fay across central Africa, during which he used digital cameras and a lightweight computer system to document his travels with dispatches to the website. Amid the sounds of a rainforest, a headline in the *Congo Trek* website quoted J. Michael Fay as saying 'I literally want as many people on Earth as possible to see this place and fall in love with it'(www.nationalgeographic.com/congotrek, accessed 16 August 2005).

Some two years after Fay began his trek, the BBC broadcast the *Congo* trilogy, an award-winning series produced by the independent TV production company Scorer Associates. The first two episodes of the series echoed the discourse of the representations found in *Time*, the *National Geographic* and indeed the Bronx Zoo: the Congo was described as one of the world's last great wildernesses and the programmes included a wealth of stunning footage of the flora and fauna of the region.

But the third episode had a surprise for its audiences. It reported that the Ndoki region might not be what it appeared to be. Whilst flying over the region in a small aircraft (presumably the 'air cam' built especially for the *National Geographic* article, and which the magazine noted that it had donated to the park), Mike Fay discovered ancient crop marks south of Lac Telle, north of the Ndoki River. He also discovered remnants of pottery along the beaches in several rivers in the region. If any doubt remained, Fay reported that several of the rivers in the region had large numbers of oil palm nuts lying at the bottom of their beds. As Fay put it whilst wading through one of the streams on the edge of the Nouabalé-Ndoki Park,

> [picking up some of the nuts]: It's kind of strange because you think what are these palm nuts doing here . . . cultivated species, and there's not a palm tree for miles and miles and miles around, so you think, what's going on? And then, we started collecting them, and we found that the oldest are 2300 years old, and the youngest ones are 900 years old, and nothing's younger. Thousands of creeks have them, just about every single one has them, immediately as you walk into the creek, you don't have to look, you don't have to excavate, you just look down and there they are in abundance, so it's not elephants bringing them in or birds.
>
> (Fay in BBC *Congo* documentary, Episode 3, 2001)

Fay's research into the history of the oil palm in Africa suggested that the dates of the oldest palm nuts coincided with a time when migrating farmers might well have introduced the palms to the region. This prospect, along with the other evidence mentioned above, made it clear to him that, far from being an 'untouched' rainforest, the Ndoki had been inhabited in ancient times. If the Ndoki ever was an Eden, it was, by the time it was 'discovered', very much a garden gone wild.

Naturalist, culturalist and postmodern natures

In the introductory chapter, I suggested that the problematization of the nature of nature constitutes a central aspect of the problematization of the nature of mass mediation. In that same chapter, I began to suggest that two general stances – the 'nature-naturalist' and the 'nature-culturalist' – establish the grounds for a dualistic interpretation of the nature of nature. In this chapter I shall provide a more detailed account of each of these stances, which I shall characterize as *discourses* of nature. This characterization – and indeed the introduction of a third discourse – will serve as a prolegomenon to the consideration of the nature of mass mediation.

I shall begin with what I describe as a naturalist discourse of nature. From the perspective of this discourse, nature is the collectivity of the non-human natural objects and processes, that is to say those objects and processes not produced by humans. It is also the nature whose sheer presence – whose absolute *present* – cannot be doubted: the nature that scratches and bites, the nature that grows and flows, the nature that gives birth and kills. It is, finally, a nature that is premised on a separation between the human and non-human nature, between nature and culture. This separation or insulation is what allows conservationist photographers such as the *National Geographic*'s Michael 'Nick' Nichols to specialize in the representation of nature, and to describe themselves as 'wildlife' photographers. More generally, it is a classification that has long justified the distinction between the social and the natural sciences. Social scientists deal with the social (human) world, and natural or physical scientists – the expression is telling – deal with the non-human world.

It is nonetheless the case that this *discontinuity* between culture and nature is contradicted by a certain continuity between the two categories, at least on the level of representation. An examination of the language used by Nichols to describe the nature of his photography reveals that his discourse is structured by metaphors that suggest an ontological or 'existential' *continuity* between human and non-human nature, or at any rate, between representation and what is represented, between the observer and what is observed. The practice of taking pictures is commonly described precisely as a matter of *taking* pictures, or of *capturing* a certain image with the camera. And indeed, as Nichols explains in his website, 'the lust for *capturing* the images has got to be what drives you' (www.michaelnicknichols.com/article/adventure, accessed 25 September 2005, emphasis added). I shall consider the gendering and sexualization of nature in due course. Here I simply wish to note that the notions of 'taking' and 'capturing' pictures suggest that representation is a matter of grasping a material object, in much the way that Nichols – or indeed a gorilla – might grasp a walking stick.[3] Where the human/non-human nature distinction suggests a fundamental *discontinuity* between nature and culture, the metaphor of *capture* suggests that, at least from the point of view of representation, there is, by contrast, a fundamental *continuity* between the two categories. Representation is – however paradoxically from an environmentalist perspective – a matter of setting metaphorical 'traps'.[4]

Such a discourse may seem to be appropriate in the context of photography; as I shall explain in a later chapter, photography has long been represented as a matter of the production of *indexes*: representations that, in the manner of weathervanes, have a real and physical link to reality. But the metaphor of capture is also widely employed by scientists describing the epistemological basis for – the 'theory of knowledge' that underpins – their work. For example, E.O. Wilson, a renowned myrmecologist, begins his Pulitzer prize-winning *The Diversity of Life* with a moving account of a storm breaking over a part of another great rainforest, the Amazon. As Wilson describes the extraordinary beauty of the setting, he ruminates on the problem of finding ideas that might 'capture' the processes at work in what he calls 'the nonhuman world' (1992: 9). Paraphrasing the ideas of the nineteenth-century chemist Berzelius, Wilson suggests that:

> We search in and around a subject for a concept, a pattern, that imposes order . . . We hope to be the first to make a connection. Our goal is to *capture* and label a process, perhaps a chemical reaction or behaviour pattern driving an ecological change, a new way of classifying energy flow, or a relation between predator and prey that preserves them both, almost anything at all. We will settle for just one good question that starts people thinking and talking: Why are there so many species? Why have mammals evolved more quickly than reptiles? Why do birds sing at dawn?
>
> (E.O. Wilson 1992: 8, emphasis added)

In the following paragraph he adds:

> These whispering denizens of the mind are sensed but rarely seen. They rustle the foliage, leave behind a pug mark filling with water and a scent, excite us for an instant and vanish. Most ideas are waking dreams that fade to an emotional residue. A first-rate scientist can hope to *capture* and express only several in a lifetime.
>
> (E.O. Wilson 1992: 8, emphasis added)

This statement maintains a degree of ambiguity about the site where concepts are to be 'captured'. But elsewhere Wilson makes it clear that he is referring to the mind. He also makes it clear that all human minds are utterly determined by material nature. Wilson is the founder of sociobiology (see Wilson 1980), arguably the most positivist form of naturalism, and in an interview with fellow sociobiologist Steven Pinker he suggests that 'everything that's in the body, including the brain and the action of the mind, is obedient to the laws of physics and chemistry as we understand it [*sic*]'. According to Wilson, 'there is a unity of the sciences' – a 'consilience' – 'through a network of cause and effect explanations in physics, biology and even the lower reaches of the social sciences.' In the same interview, Wilson suggests that he is intent on conducting a re-examination of 'the basic theory and contents of socio-biology, beginning with insects and eventually coming back to humans' (Wilson in www.edge.org/3rd_culture/wilson03/wilson03/wilson_p3.html, accessed 28 July 2005).[5]

As Wilson's account begins to make clear, the contradiction noted in the context of photography also permeates the discourse of sociobiologists. In *The Diversity of Life*, Wilson speaks of the 'nonhuman world'. But in the interview, he also makes it clear that, in some if not most respects, ants are very much like humans. From this perspective, it makes about as much sense to speak of the 'nonhuman world' as it does to speak of the 'non-ant world'.

The naturalist discourse of nature thus takes nature, in some if not all respects, for granted: nature is a 'first principle' that can be observed, studied and indeed questioned in a 'scientific' sense, but not in a 'metaphysical' sense: nature not only exists, but *is*.

I shall now consider a second discourse on the nature of nature, a discourse that is premised on what might be described as a culturalist perspective, and indeed a 'meta-discourse': a discourse that is explicitly *about* another discourse. By this account, nature is first and foremost a cultural concept, a *discourse* of nature. Nature was formed not billions of years ago, but in the seventeenth century, when European natural philosophers started to treat the term as an abstract singular: as a term that accords a single, universal, essential quality or character to an otherwise diverse group of elements (Williams 1983: 220).

From the perspective of a culturalist discourse, it can be said that Ndoki is a paradigmatic instance of nature in so far as it is a myth: far from being 'untouched', it is 'touched' by the (discursive) act of being declared 'pristine'. Whatever else the Ndoki is, it is the figment of what I shall describe in Chapter 2 as a modern cultural imaginary, whose subjects conceive nature on the basis of a binary opposition that dissimulates the 'interested' nature of nature, i.e. the *socially* interested nature of any *representation* of nature. Although aspects of his theory can hardly be called 'culturalist', the following passage, written by Ulrich Beck, exemplifies this discourse when it denounces what Beck describes as the naturalistic fallacy, a fallacy that he suggests pervades the environmentalist movement:

> with his [*sic*] internalized conception of nature, man [*sic*] abolishes, rescinds his own role of creator, discoverer, ruler, destroyer – more still, man cultivates it in opposition to his role of creator and destroyer, upholding it as the extreme of non-alienation, of non-civilization. Recourse to the concept of nature gives the appearance of an outer limit . . . The concept of nature does not betray the model its utterer associates it with – neither to himself/herself, nor to the addressee – in any event, not at first glance.
>
> (Beck 1995: 38)

In so far as this is the case, Beck suggests that:

> Whoever utters the word 'nature' deserves to be needled by the question, 'which nature?': Naturally fertilized cabbage? Nature as it is, i.e. industrially lacerated? Country life during the 1950s (as it is represented in retrospect today, or as it represented itself in days gone by to countryfolk, or to those who dreamed of country life, or whoever)?
>
> (Beck 1995: 36).

A culturalist discourse goes a long way in explaining how it is that different cultural groups can have a very different experience of the 'same' nature. It tends not, however, to be able to explain the nature–culture nexus in anything other than dualistic terms. Tim Ingold (1997) has suggested that it is now a matter of convention for social anthropologists – and social scientists more generally – to engage in the production of theories of the social that reproduce the human/non-human classification in several ways and levels. Humans are, on the one hand, more than organisms; but non-human organisms are less than persons. Humans have a History (with a capital H) whereas non-human organisms have a history. Humans transform nature into material objects, but are not themselves undergoing any transformation by nature. The list of dualisms goes on and on; to this we might add the opposition between *representations* and nature: representations are cultural, while nature is, in itself, a-representational. The signs that constitute the representations either are entirely cultural in themselves or involve a kind of absolute projection upon material objects such as landscapes, which this discourse argues are themselves, as land-*scapes*, cultural entities. It follows that the process of observation is itself cultural: the cultural 'mind' selects, on the basis of a certain cultural imagination or 'imaginary' (see Chapter 2), what should be observed, and in so doing filters out anything that does not conform to this 'template'.

Perspectives such as Ingold's constitute a third discourse, a third perspective on the nature of nature. This discourse, which I characterize as a postmodern discourse in the strict sense that it attempts to move beyond the characteristically modern nature–culture divide, suggests that nature is neither itself (as suggested by a naturalist discourse), nor a discourse (as suggested by a culturalist discourse): it is a 'hybrid' in the sense that it involves mutually imbricating elements, some of which are 'other than human' or 'more than human', and whose proverbial 'sum' is something other than the 'parts', which are in any case themselves 'hybrid'. Indeed, at least in Ingold's account, the very discourse of 'parts', 'sides', 'dimensions' or clear-cut boundaries more generally is discarded in favour of metaphors of relationality, fluidity and context-specific development.

From the perspective of this discourse, the discovery that the Ndoki is not as wild as it seems is not so much a matter of myth as of the realization that nature – or in this case 'wildlife' – involves what Sarah Whatmore (2002) describes as a 'hybrid geography', 'a relational achievement spun between people and animals, plants and soils, documents and devices in heterogeneous social networks which are performed in and through multiple places and fluid ecologies' (Whatmore 2002: 14). By this account, culturalist accounts are limited by their failure to animate

> the creatures mobilized in these networks as active subjects in the geographies they help to fashion. Their constitutive vitality is acknowledged not in terms of biological essences but as a confluence of libidinal and contextual forces. Here, the multi-sensual business of becoming, say, antelope or wolf and the inscription of these bodily habits in the categorical and practical orderings of human societies are interwoven in the seamless performance of wild-life.
>
> (Whatmore 2002: 15)

Accordingly, the Ndoki shows up not one, but two fallacies: the naturalistic fallacy, but also what might be described as the 'culturalist' fallacy, which continues to reproduce the nature–culture dichotomy in a world that not only is 'more than human', but has 'moved on' or, one might say with Whatmore, 'performed on' from the discursive opposition between nature and culture which the expression 'more than human' is meant to transcend.

Clearly, my threefold characterization reduces some of the 'internal' heterogeneity of the discourses involved, even as it amplifies the heterogeneity *between* them. Moreover, some researchers might well contest aspects of this (discursive) classification: for example, those that I suggest are associated with a certain form of postmodernism might well deny this classification. The point, however, is not to employ a simplified characterization to discredit the discourses, but rather to highlight a certain truth that each discloses, and that cannot quite be denied by the subjects of the other ('othered' and perhaps 'othering') discourses. It would be rather foolish to deny that there is a referent beyond the word 'nature' that is itself not human, and that is not in itself simply 'a referent'. In the case of the Ndoki, doing so would be to deny that there is indeed a nature (or something like it) that, as noted earlier, bites and scratches, gives fevers or perhaps even kills, and which is animated by the forces of the cosmos. As I noted in the introduction, in the year that this book was being completed, evidence of such a nature existed far beyond the Ndoki: a 'naturalist' nature killed an estimated 300,000 people across the Indian Ocean and destroyed large parts of the city of New Orleans. More generally, at the beginning of the twenty-first century, nature still has, as Terry Eagleton (2000) puts it, the upper hand: people across the world still die, whether they are hit by a tsunami or not.

But these selfsame examples arguably attest to the need for a critique of ideology of the kind that is generally integral to a culturalist analysis. In the case of the Ndoki, the explorers initially failed to observe what was, by Fay's account, abundant evidence of past (human) inhabitation. To be sure, the notion of a 'virginal' nature has long been critiqued by scholars as evidence of a masculinist and patriarchal conception of nature (see for example Merchant 1980), one that is quite evident in Michael 'Nick' Nichols' website. A number of historians have also noted some of the roles that seemingly 'wild' 'wildernesses' have played in reaffirming the 'own' values of modern cultural institutions (see for example White 1978).

More recently, critics have suggested that the levees in New Orleans had not been strengthened thanks in part to the US's so-called 'war on terror'. George W. Bush's suggestion during a speech given on 15 September 2005 in New Orleans that 'We're going to review every action and make necessary changes, so that we are better prepared for any challenge of nature, or act of evil men, that could threaten our people' (http://www.whitehouse.gov/news/releases/2005/09/20050915-8.html, accessed 9 October 2005) vividly exemplified a discursive logic that conflated the response to the hurricane with the mentioned war. Although at the time of the disaster in the Indian Ocean there was no early *tsunami* warning system in place in the Indian Ocean, the US Geological Survey's National Earthquake Information Centre, whose mission is to 'rapidly determine location and size of all destructive earthquakes worldwide and to immediately disseminate this information to concerned national and international agencies, scientists, and the general public' (http://neic.usgs.gov, accessed 2 October 2005), might well have played a more effective role than it did in preventing at least some of the deaths. In both cases – Katrina and the Indian Ocean tsunami – a different distribution of resources, and a different political economy of risk priorities, would doubtless have saved many lives.

Of course, nature, or something not unlike it, *did* have an agency in each of the examples, and this very interweaving of 'natural' and 'social' agency provides strong arguments for a postmodern discourse about 'hybrid' natures that moves 'beyond' *nature* and introduces vocabularies that reflect the fundamentally 'mixed' nature of nature.

The last point might seem to carry such weight as to force the researcher to abandon any talk of nature, and indeed, any talk of culture. And yet, as noted by Kate Soper (1995), this is more easily written than done. Soper argues that, however much it is necessary to question the divide between nature and humanity, the conceptual distinction remains indispensable:

> Whether . . . it is claimed that 'nature' and 'culture' are clearly differenti-
> ated realms or that no hard and fast delineation can be made between
> them, all such thinking is tacitly reliant on the humanity–nature antith-
> esis itself and would have no purchase on our understanding without it.
> (Soper 1995: 15)

The human/nature antithesis is as much a problem for what Soper describes as 'nature-endorsing' responses as it is for the 'nature-sceptical' stances. 'Arguments that would assimilate nature to culture by inviting us to think of the former always as the effect of human discourse presuppose the humanity–nature dichotomy as the condition of their articulation' (Soper 1995: 39). But equally, 'Those who insist on human affinities with other animals, or would have us view humanity as belonging within the order of nature, must admit that they are speaking of an affinity or continuity between two already conceptually differentiated modes of being' (Soper 1995: 40). What is at issue, Soper suggests, is not so much the distinction itself but the way in which it is to be drawn, and whether it is to be conceptualized as one of kind or of degree (Soper 1995: 41).

Soper's arguments are not easy to dismiss. They can, moreover, be employed to raise some uncomfortable questions for those who would deny any nature–culture boundary whatsoever. To begin with, one might ask whether the notion of hybridity accepts any boundaries. Would it be accurate to argue that all structures and processes – all 'structurings' – on Earth are now 'hybrid'? If so, how would, say, a volcanic eruption be a matter of 'hybridity'? To be sure, what about the nature that exists beyond the planet? Should one adopt the stance that the presence of humanly produced radio waves emanating from the planet themselves render the entire cosmos 'hybrid'?

Last but not least, if it is problematic to adopt an essentialist stance vis-à-vis the nature of nature – nature as a matter of certain natural *essences* – then surely this is also a risk when theorizing the hybridity of nature and the nature of hybridity. Is it not being argued that the environment is, or has become, 'essentially' hybrid?

First, second and third nature

The representations of the Ndoki and the brief account of some of the competing discourses about nature begin to explain why it is necessary to problematize (in Foucault's sense of the term) not just the nature of mass mediation but, before that, the nature of *nature*. Any problematization of the nature of mass mediation must be based, however tacitly, on some problematization of nature. Forthcoming chapters will consider the possibility that the opposite may, in some respects, also be true: that the problematization of *mass mediation* eventually also requires us to reconsider the problematization of *nature*. But for now it suffices to reiterate that the conceptualization of nature is not merely a matter of a 'local' conceptualization in the sense that it only affects nature as an 'object for the mind'. It also affects the way in which 'mind' is conceived and, thereby, the relation between 'object' and 'mind', or the manner in which a subject observes, represents, conceives and more generally experiences whatever is regarded as being nature, or a part of nature.

In so far as this is true, the researcher is obliged to take a stance with respect to this problem. Doing so nonetheless presents her/him with a doubly formidable task: the extension of the notion of nature – not to speak of its potentially infinite referents – is as vast as the use of the term is, paradoxically, context-specific. Moreover, the researcher wishing to problematize the nature of mass mediation is caught, even before s/he has begun to consider the nature of *mass mediation*, in a kind of double bind: nature, regarded in Kate Soper's (1995) terms as material nature – 'those material structures and processes that are independent of human activity (in the sense that they are not a humanly created product), and whose forces and causal powers are the necessary condition of every human practice' (1995: 132–3) – is in principle *everything*. But nature, regarded in Raymond Williams's (1983) terms as an 'abstract singular' – a term that accords a single, universal, essential quality or character to an otherwise diverse group of elements (1983: 220) – is in principle *nothing*.

I suggest that this remarkably sharp 'fluctuation' or, to use a more precise word in Spanish, this *desdoblamiento* in the 'play' of truth and falsity – a kind of simultaneous unfolding and splitting – is one of the characteristic features of a nature that must be regarded as *both* material nature *and* a symbolic form or, as I shall suggest later, as a *sign*. This aspect, which I shall describe in terms of the notion of 'dedoubling', needs to be at once accounted for theoretically and historicized. How is it that nature can be *nature* and so *not* nature? How has the dedoubling of nature come to be just that – a 'dedoubling' – in modern culture and, indeed, what are the cultural formations that have played central roles in its emergence?

There are a number of ways of addressing this question. In the following chapters I shall do so with reference to a social semeiotic understanding of the nature of nature, and the nature of mass mediation. The spelling of 'semeiotic' is deliberate, and refers to the theory of the nature of signs of the nineteenth- and early twentieth-century philosopher, Charles Sanders Peirce. For its part, the notion of a 'social' semeiotic problematization builds on the insights of social semioticians (without the 'e') like Michael Halliday (1978), Robert Hodge and Gunther Kress (1988) and Basil Bernstein (1990; 1996), who argue, in different ways, that the process of semiosis must be explained from the perspective of the cultural production, construction, circulation and reception of representations or *signs*. In effect, a semiotic analysis must be a part of a broader sociology of culture.

In Chapter 2, I shall engage with the more explicitly sociological dimensions of my approach. In this chapter I shall introduce a semeiotic conception of the nature of nature that is based on Charles Sanders Peirce's philosophy. Readers unfamiliar with this philosophy may now wish to turn to the Appendix ('The Nature of Peirce'), where I provide a detailed introduction to the pertinent aspects of Peirce's philosophy, to his phenomenological categories of firstness, secondness, and thirdness, and to his semeiotic grammar and typology. In the account that follows, I shall assume that the reader is acquainted with Peirce's phenomenological categories. These provide the basis for my own phenomenology of the perception of nature.

Central to this phenomenology is a distinction between three interrelated natures.

I call the first of these natures 'first nature', or the *nature of firstness*. This nature is well illustrated by the possibility that the Ndoki is indeed 'pristine'. This is, or appears to be, a nature that it is not yet determined, an immediate nature or, better yet, an 'i-mediate' nature. It is in this sense a *virtual* nature; not in the sense that it exists only on the Internet or in narratives, but in the sense that it is a matter of positive possibility: something that might well be something, something that might well become something else, but also something which has not (yet) done so or is just about to do so.

This kind of virtuality is the one experienced by the explorer-journalists when they first reach the Ndoki. They are apparently the 'first' to go in, and so partake of the firstness of *being* 'first'; but also experience the virtuality of the unknown: there is a promise, a hope that new things might be found in a context that appears to be 'as it always was'. Of course, upon reflection, the Ndoki never 'always was' – 'the Ndoki', or anything else. But this does not contradict, initially at least, the powerful sense of firstness, the powerful sense of virtuality: when entering entirely unknown territory, what will the explorers find?

The nature of firstness is, by this account, a nature that has not been determined, a nature of possibility. The metaphors of Eden used repeatedly to describe such a nature are appropriate in so far as they emphasize the promised *and promising* nature of the context. This discourse is of course heavily inflected by the discourse of Christianity. But one might also note that it carries the more general force of *expectation* of a promise. Far from being virtual in the traditional sense of the word, promises are, precisely by virtue of being virtual, very real.

Now this first sense of the firstness of nature is both complemented by, and can be translated into, another: a firstness of *feeling* such as is repeatedly expressed in the various representations. Douglas Chadwick provides a good example of the nature of firstness as a 'quality of feeling' when he says that one evening

> something reached out of the gloom and grabbed the lower part of my face. I yelped and milled my arms until the thing went away. I have no idea what it was. Maybe it was just an insect; the forest was full of huge moths, six-inch-long mantises, and nine-inch-long walkingsticks. My subconscious was still roiled by the images of the leopard that had been in the camp the night before.
>
> (Chadwick 1995: 8–9)

It is easy to imagine that in the split second when this happened there was sheer incomprehension, a sheer feeling of 'grabbed-ness', which was a matter of absolute firstness in so far as it was an immediate *feeling*. But this same example begins to illustrate another nature, one that almost instantly would have displaced, or rather re-placed, the nature of firstness: Chadwick *was* 'grabbed' – or at any rate, somehow 'touched' – and almost as soon as this happened the nature of firstness became second nature, or the *nature of secondness*.

Where the nature of firstness is a matter of the univocal, of the 'momentlessness', of the 'timelessness' of 'absolute' feeling, the nature of secondness is a matter of action and reaction. It thereby marks the coming of the moment, the emergence of place and the beginning of time in the sense of a *sequence*. A certain *action* on the part of 'the bug' leads Chadwick to *experience* something, and this *produces* a *sensation*, which in turn prompts a *reaction* by Chadwick: he 'yelps' and 'mills' his arms until 'the thing' goes away.

This is the nature associated with the (lower) body, the nature of bodily effort (or, as Peirce puts it, 'energetic interpretants') in the sense of the nature that bites the journalists, makes them sweat, gives them malaria, but also allows them to *move*. This is a 'dyadic' nature, the nature of the ant that bites the explorers, of an oil palm nut that falls into a river, of an elephant that charges at Michael 'Nick' Nichols, of the light that reflects off the surface of that elephant and enters Nichols' camera. It is what Peirce also and tellingly describes as 'the element of Struggle' (CP 5.45).[6] It might be assumed that this is a nature of 'cause and effect'. But there are several different *models* of causality, and models – understood as modality (model-ality) – imply interpretation and thereby what will be described as the nature of thirdness.[7]

In keeping with Peirce's phenomenology, this last nature, the nature of thirdness, is the nature of signs, that is to say words, images, thoughts and, more generally, all the media by means of which nature might be represented, and/or might be *made to present itself*: nature re/presented. In keeping with Peirce's semeiotic theory, this mediation involves a relation between three entities: (1) signs (or representamens) of nature; (2) whatever nature is represented and presents itself by way of such representamens; and (3) the interpretation of nature, and of signs of nature, by way of *interpretants*: the translation of the representamen into other signs. The Ndoki is not just the Ndoki: it is a rainforest, a pristine rainforest, an untouched wilderness and so forth. Any given representation of the Ndoki only makes *sense*, *semeiotic* sense (the sense of meaning), in so far as it invokes an imaginary matrix of representations such as I describe in the next chapter.

This is, of course, the nature of the Ndoki found in *Time*, the *National Geographic*, the BBC or, indeed, the Bronx Zoo. It might be thought that the last of these examples contradicts the rest. But in so far as the displays in the Congo Gorilla Forest can be said to be representamens of *habitats*, and in so far as the gorillas in the zoo are made to represent 'their' *species*, then they too, partake in – or are taken into, unto – thirdness. More generally, in so far as it is also a sign or a 'thought' – and thoughts or 'mentalities' are for Peirce themselves signs – then any aspect of material nature may be said to be in this sense a 're/presentation', and an instance of entelechy: the sign object – in this case the gorilla in the Congo Gorilla Forest – is at once its 'own' representamen and interpretant.

In so far as thoughts *are* signs, then even before the environment correspondent writes an article or takes a photograph, looks at a landscape, an animal or any other aspect of material nature (and of course the social world), s/he transforms it into a sign merely by virtue of thinking about it. This, however, does not mean that nature is all thought, in the idealist sense of the expression. On the one hand, nature, in the sense of second nature or the nature of secondness, can 'impinge' itself on the senses, regarded now not just as the semiotic senses, but as the *semeiotic* senses: the senses of meaning, but also the senses of sensation, the senses of action and reaction. On the other hand, firstness 'persists' 'in' the signs of nature

27

in several ways and forms: the signs may convey a sense of the firstness of feeling, but they may also involve forms of representation which themselves seem immediate: a photograph, for example, is more an instance of firstness than is a word in so far as it is more what Peirce describes as an icon than it is a symbol.

As this last point begins to suggest, two general sets of clarifications need to be made with respect to this account of the nature of nature. The first concerns the 'internal' logic of this phenomenology, while the second concerns the metaphysical problems raised earlier.

To begin with the first set of clarifications: each of the natures is qualitatively different, but all three are interwoven. The nature of secondness is more than the sum of its parts, and the nature of thirdness cannot be reduced to the nature of secondness. Put differently, the nature of thirdness, the nature of representation, is different from the nature of action and reaction, bodily effort, which is in turn different from the nature of firstness, the nature of possibility or positive virtuality. For example, an ant bite is quite different from a representation of an ant bite, and both are different from the possibility that an ant might bite.

But the three natures are by no means mutually exclusive. From Peirce's phenomenological perspective, firstness is always becoming secondness is always becoming thirdness. Put differently, degrees of the natures of firstness are always found in the nature of secondness, and of the nature of secondness in the nature of thirdness. And, crucially, the representational process itself involves firstness and secondness in so far as there is an object of representation (a 'first') that is represented by a word or any other sign (a 'second') that is mediated by other signs (a 'third', or 'thirds'). As Peirce puts it, 'The first is agent, the second patient, the third is the action by which the former influences the latter. Between the beginning as first, and the end as last, comes the process which leads from first to last' (CP 1.361). A photograph of an elephant charging at the camera is at once a photograph (thirdness); an elephant charging *at* the camera, or indeed light 'hitting' the camera's film or digitizing surfaces (secondness); and *an* elephant, in the double sense of its individuality and the momentary immediacy of its charge, as *felt* by the 'speechless' photographer (firstness). As begins to be clear from this example, and as I explain in some detail in the Appendix, this phenomenological organization extends to Peirce's semeiotic categories: any sign is a matter of firstness, secondness and thirdness; what varies is the 'emphasis' or significance of each of these elements. So it is, for example, that for a given sign-using community a photograph is primarily an icon (closer to firstness), whereas for another it might well be regarded as a matter of convention, and thereby a symbol (closer to thirdness).

The second set of clarifications follow on, in part, from the first. The above account is based on Peirce's *phenomenology*, and is meant to describe how nature 'comes to (human) *consciousness*'. It is, however, also based on a metaphysics that is at once idealist and realist, and is so in two interrelated ways.

From a semeiotic perspective, Peirce's theory is 'idealist' in the sense that it accords primacy to thirdness.[8] But it is also 'realist' in so far as it recognizes that 'indexicality', or a 'real connection' between the object of representation and the representamen, can determine the interpretant. This is particularly true, but not *only* true, for signs such as weathervanes and thermometers, in which nature can be 'seen' to determine the sign. All signs, he argues, entail at least a degree of indexicality, and thereby of secondness, but also of iconicity, and thereby of first-ness.

If Peirce's semeiotic theory is an instance of 'ideal-realism', so too is his phenomenology, and more generally, his cosmology, which has been described as being 'pansemeiotic' (Nöth 1990). A detailed account of this cosmology is beyond the scope of this book. Peirce toyed, characteristically dialectically, with the possibility that natural objects might have triadic relations amongst themselves:

> Possibly there may be Representamens that are not Signs. Thus, if a sunflower, in turning towards the sun, becomes by that very act fully capable, without further condition, of reproducing a sunflower which turns in precisely corresponding ways towards the sun, and of doing so with the same reproductive power, the sunflower would become a Representamen of the sun. But *thought* is the chief, if not the only, mode of representation.
>
> (CP 2.274)

Peirce was also an advocate of the theory of evolution; his interest in the question of firstness and chance relates in part to this advocacy of what is nonetheless perhaps the materialist theory *par excellence*. And yet his evolutionary cosmology was based on what he described as a 'Schelling-like'[9] idealism: if the universe is 'perfused with signs, if it is not composed exclusively of signs' (CP 5.448, fn), it is because matter is 'mere specialized and partially deadened mind' (CP 6.102). For Peirce, the mind by no means begins and ends in the cranial cavity; if thoughts are signs, and if signs involve the infinite concatenation of interpretants, then 'mind', regarded as semiosis, is at least as extended as humanity itself.

By way of a conclusion to this chapter, I would like to return to the three discourses on nature considered earlier, and to the methodology of problematization. How does Peirce address the three natures constructed by the naturalist, culturalist and postmodern (or 'hybridist') discourses? And what does Peirce contribute to a 'history of the present' of the nature of mass mediation?

I shall begin with the first question. Peirce's phenomenology articulates at least some of the aspects proposed by each discourse. It recognizes, to begin with, the 'firstness' of nature that is the *sine qua non* of naturalism. But it also recognizes the significance of a 'factual' nature that takes the form of dyadic relations and has a certain capacity to determine its own representation. Such a factual nature – what I describe in a later chapter as a nature of 'indexes' – is the nature favoured by scientific empiricism.

The phenomenology nonetheless goes a long way in recognizing the cultural-ist concern with the conventional and habitual nature of nature, the nature of thirdness. The concept of thirdness allows the semeiotician to suggest that signs of nature are in principle a matter of 're/presentation', i.e. that such signs continue to involve elements or dimensions of secondness and firstness.

This insight is, finally, what brings Peirce's work closer to the concerns of the advocates of a postmodern discourse: signs of nature, Peirce suggests, are by no means just signs, but signs are by no means just nature: nature is, in the discourse of hybridity, an energetic 'mind'. For any given phenomenon of nature, nature is always to some extent a matter of firstness, secondness and thirdness; but for that same phenomenon, at least as perceived by an observer, it is likely to be *more* a matter of firstness or of secondness or of thirdness.

What, then, does this articulation contribute to a 'history of the present' of the nature of mass mediation?

From a Peircian perspective, semeiotic methodology is, in theory at least, not bound by history. Or, if it is, it is, paradoxically, bound to a naturalistic conception of history in so far as it adopts the long term history of evolution. Chapter 2 will nevertheless indicate how Peirce's theory may actually provide part of the basis for a *social* semeiotic conception of mass mediation, and therein of observation. Here I shall simply note first that Peirce aids this book's problematization in so far as it serves to produce a preliminary articulation of the present nature of nature. As I have just explained, this articulation preserves the dimension of 're/presentation' and of dedoubling mentioned earlier by maintaining a tension between a realist and an idealist stance vis-à-vis the nature of nature. Nature is, to the observer, a matter of varying degrees of firstness, secondness and thirdness. Signs, in turn, are a matter of semiosis, but semiosis maintains 'in itself' an element of 'pre-semiosis' (firstness), and energetic determination (secondness). The problem, from this perspective, is not to leave semiosis behind, nor to choose between 'representationalist' and 'non-representationalist' approaches, but to discern the presences of firstness, secondness and thirdness in what are constantly becoming (and in some cases ceasing to be) *signs* of nature.

In so far as this is the case, a Peircian semeiotics can be said to have a heuristic value for the current inquiry: it moves the investigation forward by allowing us to ask: what is the history of signs of nature, thus understood? In particular, what is the history of a certain 'economy' of signs of nature, whereby nature moves from being treated explicitly as being a sign (as is the case in the early modern period), to being treated as being not a sign at all (as comes to be true from the nineteenth century onwards, at least in the context of modern scientific institutions)? As part of this process, how do particular institutions, discourses, techniques and technologies for the observation and representation of nature attempt to close down the play of the 'dedoubling' of truth and falsity in favour of one or another 'ism' (realism, idealism, nominalism, rationalism and so forth)?

A similar point can be made with respect to the nature of *mass mediation*. As will become apparent in the next chapters, naturalist and culturalist discourses about nature have played a significant role in accounts of the nature of mass mediation. Even at the beginning of the twenty-first century, many journalists might still describe their role in naturalistic terms. I have noted, for example, how the discourse of Mike 'Nick' Nichols echoed that of the naturalist E.O. Wilson. A similarly naturalistic, and indeed instrumental or 'indexical', account of the nature of mass mediation might be found amongst science and environmental correspondents and documentary filmmakers. How then, if at all, does the play of truth and falsity in regard to the nature of mass mediation echo, amplify or indeed change that of discourses regarding the nature of nature?

two dimensions – space–time – themselves presuppose a certain *corporeality*: the observer observes 'from' a certain body, a body which is one, and just one. We can say in this sense that the commonsense notion of observation privileges the firstness of the observer: in effect, the observer is treated as a monad, a single and indivisible entity but also an entity for which any observation – and the observation of anything – is possible.

Of course, the observer as observer always observes *something* and, in so far as this is the case, the monadic firstness of the observer is interrupted or broken by the secondness of the observational *relation*. From a commonsense perspective, the relation between the observer and the observed entails a two-way relation that is conceived in naturalistic terms, that is to say in terms that privilege the dimension of secondness: the observer engages in the kind of 'capturing' process described by Wilson in Chapter 1, but some aspect of nature may also direct the attention of the observer by generating what might be described as 'natural' indexes. These work to trigger the observer's attention: for example, when Chadwick is bitten by driver ants, this action, as mediated by Chadwick's physiological response, forces him to attend to the ants.

Now it is possible to critique this account with a theoretical approach such as that found in Jonathan Crary's (1990) *Techniques of the Observer*. As I began to explain in the introductory chapter, Crary suggests that observation is best understood not as a process of spectatorship, but as an instance of the Latin verb *observare*: '"to conform one's action, to comply with," as in observing rules, codes, regulations, and practices' (Crary 1990: 6). Crary suggests that '[t]hough obviously one who sees, an observer is more importantly one who sees within a prescribed set of possibilities, one who is embedded in a system of conventions and limitations' (Crary 1990: 6). Crary clarifies that such conventions entail far more than representational practices. If, he suggests, it can be said that there is an observer that is specific to a particular historical period, 'it is only as an *effect* of an irreducibly heterogeneous system of discursive, social, technological, and institutional relations. There is no observing subject prior to this continually shifting field' (Crary 1990: 6).[1]

It is possible to both explain and develop this critique by returning to the commonsense understanding of observation. Crary is suggesting firstly that observation is not a matter of individuality understood as 'personality'; he is suggesting that the individual observer inhabits, and is inhabited by, a complex subjectivity that is the 'effect', as he puts it, of a heterogeneous ensemble of discursive, social, technological and institutional relations. From this perspective, Fay's failure to observe the evidence of inhabitation can be reinterpreted as being not so much a personally subjective 'oversight' (though clearly it is that too) but a kind of cultural '*über*-sight': even though, and indeed precisely *because*, Fay is a trained ecologist, his form of observing the Ndoki conforms to a discourse that 'sees for him' in so far as it directs his gaze towards some aspects of the rainforest and not others.

More generally, critical historians might argue that, by virtue of exploring the Ndoki, Fay follows in the footsteps, literally and metaphorically, of all those predominantly white, European, male explorers who have instituted a tradition whereby rainforests and tropical geographies have come to be regarded as so many 'blank spaces' waiting to be colonized by European institutions and by their subjects' instituting imaginations.

I shall consider the notion of an 'instituting imagination' below. The two key points that I wish to make initially are that observation entails a collective and social process and that, by this account, the observer observes in a manner that is in some way unconscious or, at very least, never entirely self-conscious. In so far as this is true, the observer's observations conform to something – in this case a discourse, or a discursive formation (Hall 1992b) – that comes from *beyond* her/him and *abstracts* from the immediate context. Peirce himself speaks of 'abstractive observation' (CP 2.227): a process whereby what is seen is considered, 're-viewed', or somehow compared, however unselfconsciously, to what is already known, to what has already been observed and to what has already been represented. In so far as this process takes place, it is necessary to adopt the theoretical and methodological stance associated with the 'decentring of the subject'; that is to treat the individual not as an autonomous observer who observes 'on her/his own', but with, and indeed thanks to, a collective social observational process. This entails a paradox: in some respects at least, even though it seems that no one has set foot in some parts of the Ndoki before, what Fay sees in the Ndoki has already been observed *for* him by previous explorers, by other ecologists and by all those practices that in one way or another shape the manner in which he observes the Ndoki.

Having recognized this ineluctably social dimension of observation, I would now like to make what is, if not the opposite argument, then certainly one that tempers the incipient culturalism of its stance. Extrapolating from Peirce's theory, we can say that, along with what we might describe as a 'normal' or *habitual* form of observation, it is possible to conceive of the possibility of both an *immediate* form of observation and also a *dynamic* form of observation. What I am calling immediate observation involves observation that both is guided by and produces what Peirce describes as an 'immediate interpretant': the object is observed in a rhematic fashion or, as Peirce puts it, the observer 'leaves [the] Object, and *a fortiori* its Intepretant, to be what it may' (CP 2.95). This is observation considered from the perspective of firstness, and must have constituted an aspect of Fay's own observational process: Fay must have 'seen without seeing' the nuts in the bottom of the streams. Even if we argue that what I am calling an immediate or 'rhematic' form of observation is ultimately displaced by normal or habitual forms of observation that *are* guided by discourses, institutions and so forth, the possibility remains, must remain, of a form of observation that is not utterly determined by social codes. To argue otherwise would be to suggest that the observer always knows, consciously or unselfconsciously, what it is that s/he is observing.

For its part, dynamic observation entails a form of observation that relates to the 'dynamic interpretant' – the 'effect on the mind' actually produced by (and with) the sign (CP 8.343). We can say that, on this level, there is the beginning of a process of recognition, the object is observed in a 'dicent-ical' fashion: the observer observes in a manner which distinctly indicates a subject (CP 2.95), but experiences a degree of indetermination from the perspective of the intepretant. This is what happens when something is observed and questioned, or when a 'hypothesis' is formed but not confirmed with respect to an observation. This is observation considered from the perspective of secondness, and might well be expected to be the most significant form of observation in all those instances where some phenomenon of nature impinges itself on the mind (and/or is 'apprehended' by the mind) in a manner that calls forth some interpretation but defies easy classification. At some point, Fay must have begun interrogating the oil palm nuts, without yet knowing why they were there, or what their significance was. Once this significance was established, then a new order of 'normal observation' would have been instituted.

I would now like to return to Crary's account of the nature of observation. Crary's account constitutes the beginning of a critique of another aspect of the commonsense notion of observation: the notion that observation is not only individual but homogeneous, and indeed 'homo-geneous' in the sense of 'anthropogeneous'.

Each of these points requires some elucidation. It is easy to assume that seeing is entirely a matter of one's humanity, or that, if it is aided by technology, the technology, defined as a purely instrumental matter (i.e. machines or equipment), is entirely external to the perceptual process. From a constructivist and indeed a culturalist perspective, this way of understanding the relation to technology is problematic on at least two counts.

First, technology is always more than a matter of instrumentation; technology is better understood as a nexus of instrumentation and technique, where technique is itself understood as both 'applied' and socially situated 'knowledge', or better yet a 'way of doing' which, like craft, is itself embedded in a particular social and thereby moral and economic set of relations. Second, once a technology has become a part of habitual practice for the members of a certain culture, there is no neat boundary – or, as I call it below, 'classification' – between the technology, so defined, and the *sensorium*, the human sensory complex. From this perspective, a subject learns to observe in ways that are themselves 'technological'. So it is, for example, that the visitor at the Congo Gorilla Forest display (mentioned in Chapter 1) might well expect to see the gorillas 'close-up' or at varying distances because that is the way that s/he has always seen wildlife on television. If, as I suggested in the introduction, mass mediation entails a pedagogy, then this is one of the many ways in which it is instituted: mass mediation 'teaches without teaching' certain expectations about the proximity at which wildlife will be observed.

It can thus be argued that observation is thus by no means simply 'homogeneous'. On the contrary, at least for modern observers in the early twenty-first century, phenomena such as I have just described suggest the possibility that

observation entails the production of a cyborg-like 'hybrid' of organism and machine. A similar point has been made by Donna Haraway, who argues famously
– and we might say from a radically postmodern perspective – that 'By the late
twentieth century, our time, a mythic time, we are all chimeras, theorized and
fabricated hybrids of machine and organism; in short, we are cyborgs' (Haraway
1991: 150).

I shall return to this notion, which might well be described as a form of cyber-
culturalism, in due course. Here I wish to consider another way of problematizing
the idea of the homogeneity of the observer. It might well be assumed that the
person who observes does so from the perspective of the homogeneity of her/his
own biographical experiences. But such a notion must be mistaken in at least one
way: being a person is necessarily being a *social* person and, in so far as this is true,
being oneself is always to some extent a matter of being an other. This principle
of the heterogeneity (or 'alterity') of the self becomes more complex when it
is considered that the maturational process usually takes place in the presence
of multiple others, all of whom shape in various ways and to varying degrees
the own self and the own sense of self. But observation becomes extraordinarily
complex when it is considered that a modern cultural context involves exposure to
an ensemble of social spaces and times which are mediated by an array of institutions, discourses and technologies. In so far as this is true, then every individual
– and every individual's observational process – is potentially constituted by and
subjected to a wide variety of discourses, techniques and technologies.

Let us, for example, consider in more detail the manner in which a visitor
may observe the gorillas in the Congo Gorilla Forest display at the Bronx Zoo.
Let us assume that, before the visitor has gone to the Bronx Zoo, s/he has read
the *National Geographic* article on the Ndoki and seen the BBC documentary.
Let us further assume that the visitor has used the Bronx Zoo's website and has
seen the link to the *National Geographic*. As the visitor stands and watches the
gorillas, the visitor might well compare, more or less selfconsciously, the different
representations. The visitor might, for example, arrive at the conclusion that the
Zoo has achieved an extraordinarily realistic effect. Or, on the contrary, the visitor
might well be disappointed by the lack of realism of the zoo display. Whether the
visitor adopts the former stance or the latter, s/he brings to the zoo and articulates
a number of discourses, technologies and the social relations that go with them.
These include the discourses of naturalism, of conservationism, of tourism; what
I describe below as the different technologies of observation and displacement
associated with each medium and each genre (e.g. TV, internet, zoo); and the
remarkably complex social relations associated with each of these: relations, for
example, to the different media, and to the people or non-human animals represented by them; relations to conservationist organizations that attempt to 'sell'
a certain form of conservationism; or, indeed, relations to any friends or family
members who also partake in the visit and who contribute their own mediations.
Each of these may affect, and *will* affect, in one way or another, the observational

process. And not just 'affect': Crary (1990) goes so far as to suggest that the observational process is actually *constituted* by such relations and by the complex interrelation of spaces and times which they at once enact and presuppose.[2]

From this perspective, an observer, and indeed a *form* of observation associated with any given context and any given historical period, is best regarded as a culturally specific but also essentially heterogeneous entity: as the confluence of multiple forces which may and must be conjugated by the individual, but which cannot be reduced to the individual or to the individual observational episode.

It follows that a history of the present of such an observer must engage in a genealogical process that, as suggested in the introductory chapter, considers a wide ensemble of discourses, technologies, institutions and the relations associated with them. This raises once again the question of corpus: what discourses, which technologies, what institutions and which relations? But it also raises questions of theory: namely, how are we to explain the nature of institutions, technologies and social relations?

In the following sections of this chapter, I begin to address these questions by providing an outline of some of the aspects that I shall be considering in writing a history of the present of observation, regarded as an aspect of the mass mediation of nature. The description of these aspects will serve a dual purpose in so far as it will also introduce some of the major themes that will guide the problematization that I develop in the following chapters.

Imaginary nature

As I began to note earlier, it is possible to 'stare blankly' at something, that is to say, to engage in a form of observation that is, however momentarily, *not* determined by culture, by somehow pre-existing signs or 'normal' forms of observation. It is also possible to observe something in a manner that finds itself at a loss to provide a 'normal' interpretation.

A naturalistic account of observation also makes the strong point that, in some cases, some aspect of nature may act as an index that triggers, if not a process of observation, then certainly a degree of *attention*:[3] something is noticed, something 'turns heads'. In a context such as the Ndoki, we might go so far as to say that this kind of 'trigger', this nature of secondness, is constantly and indeed painfully inflicting itself on the sensuality of the observers. The Ndoki reminds the researcher that it is only possible to take for granted one's corporeality, and to dissolve this corporeality into the substance of semiosis – or indeed cyborg-like ensembles – when the own body is not constantly under physical threat from objects that are hardly best described as being 'hybrids', let alone 'cyborgs'. If it is true that any account of any process, social or other, is always socially situated, we can also say that any account of any *body* is also always *corporeally* situated.

This firstness of the corporeal experience – and, in the case of the Ndoki, the firstness of what seems like an exceedingly invasive secondness – nonetheless fails to explain how it is that Fay manages, despite the corporeal 'insults', to observe the Ndoki in a way that is consistent with the general pattern of representation that explorers – in particular white, European, male explorers – have used over the centuries to explain geographies unknown to themselves. With the benefit of critical distance, these patterns or regularities seem rather clear in the case of the different Ndoki representations considered in Chapter 1. Their regularity is made all the more remarkable by the fact that they inform the work of different explorer-producers who use different media and do so over a period of many years: approximately a decade separates the article in *Time* magazine from the BBC *Congo* series.

What are these patterns? The following are some of the most obvious.

First, and as I have already noted, the dominant narrative frame in all of the representations emphasizes the 'untouched' and 'pristine' qualities of the Ndoki – in effect, its firstness – and this serves in turn as the unspoken – indeed un-questionable – justification for engaging in a campaign to 'save' the Ndoki. The articulation of these two presuppositions is so much a matter of habitual practice that even the BBC series, which ultimately undermines aspects of this discourse, plays on the 'untouched' qualities of the Congo region during the first two of its three episodes. We can say in this sense that the firstness of nature constitutes a key aspect of the rhetoric of the different representations.

And yet it is also apparent that secondness too plays a significant role, both as a kind of confirmation of the wild, 'first' qualities of the Ndoki and as a source of dynamic and dramatic struggle between the explorers and the various 'hostile' elements of the environment. The Ndoki is as sublime as it is terrible; it is a place to be saved for its firstness, but also a place to be conquered in its secondness.

Third, all of the media representations privilege – and for that matter ignore – more or less the same species, more or less the same features of the geography. As a rule of thumb, the larger mammals are the object of the most sustained atten-tion, while the flora is virtually ignored. The ecosystemic features of the habitat tend to be under-represented while, by contrast, the organismic ecologies – if they can be called that – of certain 'charismatic' animals are over-represented. Even if some of the organisms in question are at the apex of a predatory 'pyramid', this criterion can in no way justify, for example, the virtual absence of the representa-tion of the significance of the *trees* to this habitat.[4]

Fourth, all of the representations construct the people that live in the Ndoki re-gion in ambiguous manners: the local inhabitants are, on the one hand, described as being more familiar with the geography and better able to travel through it, and by implication 'closer to nature', than the white explorer-journalists. But the repeated use of the word 'pygmy' reveals another side of the selfsame discourse: 'pygmy' is a colonial term that is derived from the Greek word for 'dwarf'. As such, it carries the colonial assumption that the height of white explorers is normal, in the sense that it is the norm. Moreover, some of the representations portray at least some of the local inhabitants as poachers. There is, in this sense, a dualistic account of local people: there is the 'good local' and the 'bad local', where the normative criteria are derived from the explorers' own conservationist inter-ests. As the *National Geographic* article puts it, quoting a French expatriate 'with three Pygmy wives', 'The Pygmy way is to hunt a little bit here, a little bit there, *institution* of nature, and it is this process that I now wish to consider in more detail.

In the first instance, the imaginary *institution* of nature involves the sedimentation of matrixes of values such as I have just described. Put differently, the qualities, or what with Peirce we might describe as *qualisigns* – any quality in so far as it is a sign – become part of habitual practice. With Peirce, it is possible to define habit or habitual practice as 'a readiness to act in a certain way under given circumstances and when actuated by a given motive' (EP 2.207). If a certain imaginary nature, if a certain way of imagining nature is to become an integral part of the cultural process, it must become a matter of habit, and to do so it must be explicitly or tacitly acknowledged, repeated and *co-responded* by similar practices by the members of a cultural group acting in certain contexts and in relation to certain motives.

This to the point of paradoxical firstness: a practice is iterated to the point that it becomes an unanalysed present. In contemporary modern culture, for example, rainforests are regarded almost *a priori* as a matter of nature, while cities are regarded as a matter of culture. As a kind of corollary of this value, it is often assumed that those geographies furthest from metropolitan centres are also the 'wildest'. This assumption is perhaps part of what leads Fay and the rest of the explorers to initially observe the Ndoki as an 'untouched' nature. It may also explain why the oil palm nuts remain unobserved or a matter of a rhematic or immediate form of observation: the palm nuts 'disappeared' into the expectations generated by way of the (habitual) imaginary.

When a habitual practice reproduces a certain imaginary, it also works to produce or reproduce what I describe as *circuits of anthropomorphism and cosmomorphism*. This process constitutes a central aspect of the imaginary institution of nature, and thereby requires some elaboration. When someone observes nature, or something that passes for nature, s/he cannot but project human and thus cultural forms onto it (Lindahl Elliot 2001). This humanizing projection may be described as anthropomorphism. An anthropomorphized nature may then be the selfsame nature with which an individual or social group identifies, and this in such a fashion that it helps to construct a sense of self, and indeed of 'others'. This second aspect of the process, this identification with nature, may be described with Edgar Morin (2001) as *cosmomorphism*.

The cultural production and reproduction of the two dynamics – anthropomorphism and cosmomorphism – comes to institute a cycle or circuit in so far as human forms are projected onto a nature that, humanized, paradoxically serves to identify, express or 'confirm', apparently with no human intervention or mediation, the anthropomorphic subject's beliefs, culture or politics.[5]

Such circuits involve a silent drawing and redrawing of symbolic boundaries as to what constitutes the properly human, the non-human and the 'in-between'. With Basil Bernstein (1990; 1996) we may describe this process in terms of the concepts of classification and framing. According to Bernstein, classification and framing constitute two analytically distinct aspects of social codes, that is, the that explorers – in particular white, European, male explorers – have used over the centuries to explain geographies unknown to themselves. With the benefit of critical distance, these patterns or regularities seem rather clear in the case of the different Ndoki representations considered in Chapter 1. Their regularity is made all the more remarkable by the fact that they inform the work of different explorer-producers who use different media and do so over a period of many years: approximately a decade separates the article in *Time* magazine from the BBC *Congo* series.

What are these patterns? The following are some of the most obvious.

First, and as I have already noted, the dominant narrative frame in all of the representations emphasizes the 'untouched' and 'pristine' qualities of the Ndoki – in effect, its firstness – and this serves in turn as the unspoken – indeed unquestionable – justification for engaging in a campaign to 'save' the Ndoki. The articulation of these two presuppositions is so much a matter of habitual practice that even the BBC series, which ultimately undermines aspects of this discourse, plays on the 'untouched' qualities of the Congo region during the first two of its three episodes. We can say in this sense that the firstness of nature constitutes a key aspect of the rhetoric of the different representations.

And yet it is also apparent that secondness too plays a significant role, both as a kind of confirmation of the wild, 'first' qualities of the Ndoki and as a source of dynamic and dramatic struggle between the explorers and the various 'hostile' elements of the environment. The Ndoki is as sublime as it is terrible; it is a place to be saved for its firstness, but also a place to be conquered in its secondness.

Third, all of the media representations privilege – and for that matter ignore – more or less the same species, more or less the same features of the geography. As a rule of thumb, the larger mammals are the object of the most sustained attention, while the flora is virtually ignored. The ecosystemic features of the habitat tend to be under-represented while, by contrast, the organismic ecologies – if they can be called that – of certain 'charismatic' animals are over-represented. Even if some of the organisms in question are at the apex of a predatory 'pyramid', this criterion can in no way justify, for example, the virtual absence of the representation of the significance of the *trees* to this habitat.[4]

Fourth, all of the representations construct the people that live in the Ndoki region in ambiguous manners: the local inhabitants are, on the one hand, described as being more familiar with the geography and better able to travel through it, and by implication 'closer to nature', than the white explorer-journalists. But the repeated use of the word 'pygmy' reveals another side of the selfsame discourse: 'pygmy' is a colonial term that is derived from the Greek word for 'dwarf'. As such, it carries the colonial assumption that the height of white explorers is normal, in the sense that it is the norm. Moreover, some of the representations portray at least some of the local inhabitants as poachers. There is, in this sense, a dualistic account of local people: there is the 'good local' and the 'bad local', where the normative criteria are derived from the explorers' own conservationist interests. As the *National Geographic* article puts it, quoting a French expatriate 'with three Pygmy wives', 'The Pygmy way is to hunt a little bit here, a little bit there, always changing around to let the forest rest. . . . But the Bantu villagers come, and they hunt and hunt and supply markets up and down the river. They hunt to make money, and it is that which kills the forest' (Chadwick 1995: 40). We are reminded in this sense of the point made by Richard White (1996) that, for many environmentalists, the categories of nature and work are mutually exclusive: in nature there can be no labour, at least no 'modern' labour.

One way of explaining these regularities – and I have only touched on a few – is in terms of the anthropological category of the cultural imaginary, and in terms of what I describe below as the imaginary institution of nature. We can say that the different journalists observe and represent the Ndoki in similar ways because they share more or less the same cultural imaginary, and work to institute more or less the same imaginary of nature.

Now the cultural imaginary is not the 'make-believe' or something fantastical; it is what *makes one believe* in a certain sense of reality, and thereby in a certain sense of nature. More than a 'fiction', the imaginary is a *fictio*, in the Latin sense of something that is to some extent formed, contrived, constructed, but also something that enables its subjects to produce more *fictiones*. Peirce provides a useful way of starting to explain the notion in so far as he suggests, as part of his pragmatist philosophy, that the meaning of signs is always found in other signs, in a chain or what might be described as a *matrix* of 'interpretants'. One first way of defining the cultural imaginary and its 'subset', imaginary nature, is precisely as a matrix of interpretants that has become a matter of habit over time and provides elements for a recurring way of representing and observing some aspect of the world. In time, and for a certain cultural group, a matrix of interpretants becomes the habitual way of interpreting the nature of nature, or the nature of a certain nature.

For example, an analysis of the different representations of the Ndoki suggests the following matrix: the nature of the Ndoki is 'nature itself' in so far as it is:

- *non-human* (or at any rate not a matter of *modern* humanity);
- *untouched, virginal* and thereby tacitly *female* (as opposed to 'un-penetrated', in what we shall note is historically a sexual metaphor that formed part of the 'domestication' of women in the early modern period);
- *the fundamental condition* for human existence, in the sense that it not only determines human practices but establishes a space in which such practices can take place in the first place; this principle in the case of the Ndoki is 'negative' in the sense that the nature is so fierce as to make it almost impossible to survive in the Ndoki;
- *wild* (as opposed to domestic, despite the fact that it could arguably be portrayed as being 'domestic' by those who live in or near it);
- *remote* (as opposed to being 'local', again taking for granted the perspective of one who lives or far away views from afar);
- *abundant* or 'teeming with life' (as opposed to an ostensibly 'scarce' and 'dead' or less lively nature closer to home);

- *'sensational'* or intensely 'sensual' in the double sense that the rainforest and other habitats are capable of enervating all of the bodily senses (as opposed to modern, urban contexts that are ostensibly unremarkable, and depress or flatten sensorial experience);
- amenable to *objectification* and *reification*, if only for the purposes of its own conservation (as opposed to something that is so immanent to experience that it cannot be transformed into a 'thing', let alone be exploited);
- but, despite all of the above values, nevertheless *continuous* with 'naturalistic' forms of observation, that is to say that the Ndoki can be faithfully observed and represented provided that the observer is 'methodical', patient, detailed and so forth.

Such a matrix of interpretants works not just as a network but as a kind of *'womb'* of cultural practice, as per the much older sense of matrix (*matrice*). One makes meanings by way of, and with reference to, this matrix. In this preliminary sense, the cultural imaginary is what Paul Ricoeur describes as 'the ethico-mythical kernel, the kernel both moral and imaginative which embodies the ultimate creaturely power of a group' and which is expressed in all the 'concrete representations by which a group represents its own existence and its own values' (1974a: 280–1).

Earlier, I suggested with Jonathan Crary (1990) that observation is not just a matter of a passive 'seeing' of something; it is an active 'observing of rules', conforming to certain prescriptions, to the rules for certain 'ways of seeing'. One way of articulating the relation between observation and the imaginary is by conceiving the imaginary as one such set of rules, perhaps the 'über-rules' by means of which the subject of a given culture observes an aspect of nature. By this account, Fay observes at once the Ndoki 'itself' and the Ndoki as 'filtered' by a matrix of signs such as I have just outlined. This account suggests that the two aspects – the subject of observation and the imaginary of observation – are distinct. In fact, if Fay 'sees without seeing' some aspects it is at least in part because the observer observes in a manner that blurs the two together.

The matrix of interpretants that I outlined above may seem timeless. However, one of the tasks of the history of the present that follows will be to relate the emergence of this imaginary nature to changing forms of observation and vice versa: just as we might well expect a changing imaginary to lead to changing forms of observation, certain observations – 'key' observations such as those performed by Galileo Galilei or centuries later by Henry Fox Talbot – might well lead to changes in the imaginary.

The imaginary institution of nature

I have thus far bracketed the question of power from my analysis. The account offered in the previous section nonetheless begins to suggest that nature becomes imaginary nature in so far as it undergoes a process that I describe as the imaginary *institution* of nature, and it is this process that I now wish to consider in more detail.

In the first instance, the imaginary *institution* of nature involves the sedimentation of matrixes of values such as I have just described. Put differently, the qualities, or what with Peirce we might describe as *qualisigns* – any quality in so far as it is a sign – become part of habitual practice. With Peirce, it is possible to define habit or habitual practice as 'a readiness to act in a certain way under given circumstances and when actuated by a given motive' (EP 2.207). If a certain imaginary nature, if a certain way of imagining nature is to become an integral part of the cultural process, it must become a matter of habit, and to do so it must be explicitly or tacitly acknowledged, repeated and *co-responded* by similar practices by the members of a cultural group acting in certain contexts and in relation to certain motives.

This to the point of paradoxical firstness: a practice is iterated to the point that it becomes an unanalysed present. In contemporary modern culture, for example, rainforests are regarded almost *a priori* as a matter of nature, while cities are regarded as a matter of culture. As a kind of corollary of this value, it is often assumed that those geographies furthest from metropolitan centres are also the 'wildest'. This assumption is perhaps part of what leads Fay and the rest of the explorers to initially observe the Ndoki as an 'untouched' nature. It may also explain why the oil palm nuts remain unobserved or a matter of a rhematic or immediate form of observation: the palm nuts 'disappeared' into the expectations generated by way of the (habitual) imaginary.

When a habitual practice reproduces a certain imaginary, it also works to produce or reproduce what I describe as *circuits of anthropomorphism and cosmomorphism*. This process constitutes a central aspect of the imaginary institution of nature, and thereby requires some elaboration. When someone observes nature, or something that passes for nature, s/he cannot but project human and thus cultural forms onto it (Lindahl Elliot 2001). This humanizing projection may be described as anthropomorphism. An anthropomorphized nature may then be the selfsame nature with which an individual or social group identifies, and this in such a fashion that it helps to construct a sense of self, and indeed of 'others'. This second aspect of the process, this identification with nature, may be described with Edgar Morin (2001) as *cosmomorphism*.

The cultural production and reproduction of the two dynamics – anthropomorphism and cosmomorphism – comes to institute a cycle or circuit in so far as human forms are projected onto a nature that, humanized, paradoxically serves to identify, express or 'confirm', apparently with no human intervention or mediation, the anthropomorphic subject's beliefs, culture or politics.[5]

Such circuits involve a silent drawing and redrawing of symbolic boundaries as to what constitutes the properly human, the non-human and the 'in-between'. With Basil Bernstein (1990; 1996) we may describe this process in terms of the concepts of classification and framing. According to Bernstein, classification and framing constitute two analytically distinct aspects of social codes, that is, the largely tacit 'rules' that structure any given form of practice. Classification involves the process of producing, but also of more or less strongly *insulating*, all kinds of categories: for example, what counts as nature and non-nature, the human and the non-human, what one may or may not eat, where one may or may not travel, or what counts as an acceptable or unacceptable environmental risk. Classification is, by this account, the fundamental moment of power in so far as it tacitly defines the limit between what something is and is not, but also the limit between what can and cannot be legitimately practised in a given context. The possibility of change or transformation is preserved within any given schema of classification by the very fact that there is always a 'gap' between the categories; this gap at once constitutes the potential for change and is what requires dynamics of control and disambiguation.

The last requirement explains the dimension of framing. Framing refers to the discursive, generic, communicational and more generally *practical* means by which a certain order of classification is produced, disambiguated or otherwise policed and eventually transformed. If classification involves the production of social categories, framing involves the institution of a combination or concatenation of such categories by way of the production of statements, discourses, but also, and more generally, all manner of genres of social action and interaction.

This aspect of the imaginary institution of nature can be illustrated with reference to the Ndoki. The Ndoki is classified by the different explorers and by the media representations as a kind of sacred space that is bounded off from all other spaces in so far as it is 'the last place on Earth', the last 'untouched', 'pristine' nature. The 'bounding off' is the classification. This classification is 'carried' by the different forms of representational practice considered in Chapter 1: wildlife photography in the case of the *National Geographic*; environmental journalism in the case of *Time*; a natural history documentary in the case of the BBC; a naturalistic display in the case of the Bronx Zoo. Each of these practices constitutes a certain way of *framing* the classification, where framing includes the particular sequence of signs used for the social practice; the way in which the sequence positions and opposes the viewer/reader/visitor in relation to what is represented and to the representational practice; and, more generally, the social context in which the practice, representational or other, takes place.

Two points need to be clarified with respect to these concepts. First, any instance of social practice entails some form of framing and, by implication, some form of social classification. The two dimensions of coded practice are only distinguishable by way of analysis; in practice, the two are completely intertwined. Indeed we can speak of *codes* when certain modalities of classification and framing coexist in a durable way, i.e. when they become a part of habitual practice thanks to everyday repetition and generally unselfconscious activities in one or more social contexts.

Second, in so far as Bernstein's theory takes it for granted that this is an utterly cultural and conventional process, it is necessary to attenuate the culturalism of this stance. With Peirce, it is possible to suggest that some classifications are at least partly a matter of *indexical* relations between the classification and what is classified: some classifications may be the result of a real link to material nature, as is the case when, for example, a weather forecaster uses a weathervane to indicate (and thereby classify) the direction of wind. It is also the case that classification involves not just a two-way, but a three-way relation and boundary: between the object of classification, the classification itself, and its interpretant.[6]

Bernstein's approach nevertheless allows us to specify the nature of circuits of anthropomorphism, and also what I described earlier as habitual or 'normal' observation. Where the first aspect is concerned, we can say that both anthropomorphism and cosmomomorphism must entail a process of classification and framing. Where anthropomorphism entails the projection of (human) classifications onto the non-human, cosmomorphism entails the identification with such classifications, or rather, with whatever semeiotic relation results from the juxtaposition of the classification and the classified object. In order for a certain circuit to 'sediment' and become a matter of habitual practice over time, it is necessary for the members of a culture to repeatedly frame their relations to nature in accordance with a certain schema of classification.

In turn, such systems or schemata of classification begin to determine what can and cannot be observed, even as certain habitual patterns of framing determine the manner in which something may be *legitimately* observed. Again, the observational process must not be *reduced* to a matter of purely conventional social classification and framing. But here again, Chadwick's experience with the 'thing' that grabs him (as described in Chapter 1) stands as an example of the continued relevance of indexical relations and, more generally, of immediate and dynamic forms of observation. To be sure, Fay's initial failure to engage in dynamic observation of the oil palm nuts equally proves the opposite case: that, even in the 'wildest', least studied, least 'normalized' contexts, the observational process may and must be at least partly instituted by social codes.

One of the tasks of the following chapters will therefore be to trace some of the changing ways of classifying and framing nature, and the consequences that such processes have had not only in the institution of particular circuits of anthropomorphism but also in the institution of particular forms of observation. Perhaps one way of underscoring the significance of this dimension of the analysis is by returning to a point that I began to make in Chapter 1: that one of the hallmarks of the modern discourse on nature involves the transformation of nature into an abstract singular. As I noted with Williams (1983), such a process involved according a single, universal, essential quality or character to an otherwise diverse group of elements. But it also involved insulating, that is, classifying, nature from other abstract singulars, not least that of 'humanity' itself. One of the aims, and indeed themes, of the following chapters will therefore be to trace the emergence of such a classification, to note its transformation over time and across contexts, and to consider its implications for the development of particular techniques and technologies of observation.

The space of observation

Thus far, I have taken for granted that observing involves seeing. As part of this process, I have also abstracted observation from the question of the nature of corporeality, and indeed from the question of the nature of space. But one of the aspects of the different narratives of the Ndoki that make them particularly fascinating is the manner in which they undermine both of these abstractions. In the narratives, the 'rest' of the human body, which is so easily taken for granted as a kind of observational *sine qua non*, becomes the subject of both attack and scrutiny. For example, Douglas Chadwick, the author of the *National Geographic* article, explains that his arms were 'crosshatched with infected thorn scratches that refused to heal. The bites of ants and *toona* flies showed red in between. Bee stings had raised lumps on my stomach and neck, and I had larvae wriggling through the surface tissues of my feet. Most of us were plagued as well by painful little ticks that favored parts of the body supposed to be very private' (Chadwick 1995: 8). As I began to suggest earlier, these and numerous other accounts remind the reader of the impossibility of taking the body for granted in relation to the observational process, not least in contexts such as those found in the Ndoki. In so doing, they invite the researcher to question the origin of what Crary (1990) has described as a certain 'decorporealization of vision' – a tendency to regard vision, and, by implication, observation itself, as being a matter of a relatively disembodied practice.

I shall argue in the forthcoming chapters that this question is in turn closely related to the problem of the nature of space. One way of explaining the 'decorporealization' of vision is with reference to the construction of a certain space by means of particular technologies of observation. I refer not just to so many 'instruments' for observation, such as photographic or film cameras, barometers or sound recording devices, but to their development in relation to *techniques* of observation that, as I explained earlier, involve craft-like forms of knowledge that both guide the use of instruments and may be embedded in the instruments' very design. Crary (1991) offers a good example of the relation between space, corporeality and the development of such techniques when he suggests that, from the sixteenth to the nineteenth century, the camera obscura constituted an *assemblage* with which to observe, but also with which to explain the nature of observation (Crary 1990). I shall consider this example in some detail in Chapter 3; here I wish to suggest that such technologies and the techniques associated with them institute at once certain models and experiences of observation, but also a certain conception, and eventually a certain experience of space.

Returning to the *National Geographic's* account of the Ndoki, we might for example note that Chadwick must in effect 're-corporealize' his experience by way of detailed descriptions of his bites, scratches and other corpereal 'insults' for at least two reasons: first, because the written technology of observation employed for the genre routinely excludes the non-visual senses as well as the lower corporeality, and so brackets key aspects of the intensely multisensual, and indeed polysemeiotic experience found in the natural space of the Ndoki; but second, because he prob-ably expects that a majority of his audiences will be unfamiliar with this aspect of the space, and/or that the same audiences will relish the experience of *reading and seeing*, with the benefit of distance, about the 'horror' of the Ndoki's bodily secondness. Either way, the article and the technology of observation presuppose a certain construction not just of the observational process but of space itself.

Now this raises the question: what exactly is meant by the notion of the 'con-struction' of space? Is space not itself a 'natural' entity?

We may provisionally adopt the distinction made by Henri Lefebvre (1991) between natural space, and social or cultural space: in effect, the equivalent in spatial terms of the 'dedoubling' process I have described with respect to material and symbolic or semeiotic nature. Social space is the space 'made' by humans, while natural space is the spatial category and analogon for what Soper describes as material nature. In its 'pure' form, natural space is the space of the magma of volcanos, a space that humans have thus far not affected.

Within the category of social space, Lefebvre proposes a further distinction be-tween *spatial practice*, the *representation of space* and *representational spaces*. Lefebvre establishes a homology between this slippery and unfortunately named triad and another triad which is easier to remember and employ: respectively, 'perceived' space, 'conceived' space and 'lived' space.[7] Perceived space involves social relations of production and reproduction and, in Lefebvre's terms, embraces 'the particular locations and spatial sets characteristic of each social formation' (Lefebvre 1991: 33). In the case of the Ndoki it involves, for example, the organization of the Ndoki's natural space into a park, with park ranger stations, trails and so forth. Conceived space is a matter of planned or conceptualized space, the space of a park planner's first proposals, or of an engineer's proposed grid for a transport system. As Lefebvre suggests, it involves the order that a certain relation of production imposes or attempts to impose. It is a matter of knowledge, signs, and codes (Lefebvre 1991: 33). For its part, lived space involves, as this name suggests, the manner in which a perceived and conceived space is actually *used* in everyday life. While Lefebvre suggests this is a matter of clandestine activity, with Michel de Certeau (1984) it is possible to suggest that it involves more generally the *tactical* ways in which subjects 'make do' with the spaces they appropriate. Returning to the Ndoki, we can say that the lived space of the Nouabalé-Ndoki Park is as much a matter of poaching (a clandestine activity) as it is the ways in which journalists, local inhabitants and all the park users actually circulate through and/or live in the park.

From a spatial perspective, the observation of nature marks the coming to-gether of social and natural space. This conjugation of spaces is therefore at least partly a matter of the cultural imaginary, and of the imaginary institution of na-ture by way of the circuit of anthropomorphism. If we consider, for example, the predominant way in which the different representations of the Ndoki classify and frame their visual images, we find that the images are as much a matter of

indexical signs as they are of the codes of linear perspective (I will consider these codes in Chapter 3). In turn, linear perspective arguably entails, at least in its conception, what Lefebvre (1991) describes as the 'double illusion'. The double illusion involves, as its name suggests, two fallacies with respect to the nature of space. On the one hand, the *illusion of transparency*, traditionally associated with idealist forms of philosophy, makes space appear *luminous*, a substance that, like the air it is modelled on, gives action 'free rein'. This illusion assumes that space is innocent and devoid of 'traps'. As the commonplace metaphors of transparency suggest, space, free of the contamination of opacity, is open to the observer and to the mind. By implication, this illusion is the beginning of a model of observation: to observe is to cast a 'ray' of knowledge (or of 'questioning') through something like a window by means of which the observer can readily see the world. But the notion of *contents* leads to the obverse illusion, the *realist illusion*, the illusion of 'natural simplicity', of 'things' having a natural reality in a space that then becomes an ordering of so many of those things (Lefebvre 1991: 27–9). From this perspective, things have more substance than the perceptual process, and so the direction of the 'ray' is, at least in an ontological sense, inverted: it is the things themselves that determine the nature of observation.

It might be thought that each of these illusions cancels out the other. But according to Lefebvre the opposite is true: each 'refers back to the other, reinforces the other, and hides behind the other' (Lefebvre 1991: 27). 'The shifting back and forth between the two, and the flickering or oscillatory effect that it produces, are thus just as important as either of the two illusions considered in isolation' (Lefebvre 1991: 30). In so far as this is the case, it is possible to begin to characterize a modern conception of observation whose space is, precisely, a matter of this oscillation: the observer casts 'rays' at so many objects in an empty space, and the objects respond by virtue of interrupting the progress of the rays, or perhaps even by sending their own rays back.

This account raises further questions for the history of the present: when and how do the 'double illusion' and its corresponding spatiality become instituted? And how are they related to the development (and transformation) of techniques and technologies for the observation of nature?

Heterotopias of nature

I have spoken thus far of *the* construction of space, but, as I suggested earlier, modern techniques of observation entail a multiplicity of spaces and times. As I also noted earlier, any given observational practice in modern cultures (and indeed not just in *modern* cultures) involves the transposition of forms of observation across contexts. This dynamic, which I describe in terms of the concept of transmediation, presupposes a practice, and requires a theory, of the multiplicity of spaces and times.

Foucault offers such a theory by way of the concept of *heterotopia*, which he first developed in *The Order of Things* (1970) but developed quite differently in some lecture notes published posthumously (Foucault 1986). In this book I make use of the latter formulation, in which Foucault defined heterotopias as

> real places – places that do exist and that are formed in the very described of society – which are something like counter-sites, a kind of effectively enacted utopia in which the real sites, all the other real sites that can be found within the culture, are simultaneously represented, contested, and inverted. Places of this kind are outside of all places, even though it may be possible to indicate their location in reality.
>
> (Foucault 1986: 24)

Foucault used the concept of heterotopia to describe discrete places that work to juxtapose 'in a single real place' several sites 'that are themselves incompatible'(Foucault 1986: 25) and which have a temporal dimension in so far as they include 'slices of time' or 'heterochronies' that are structured as 'absolute breaks in traditional time' (Foucault 1986: 26). According to Foucault, the concept includes cinemas, cemeteries, brothels, gardens, ships, prisons, boarding schools and even holiday villages – in a word, all those spaces that have in common 'the curious property of being in relation with all the other sites, but in such a way as to suspect, neutralize, or invert the set of relations that they happen to designate, mirror, or reflect' (Foucault 1986: 24).

The Bronx Zoo, which I referred to in Chapter 1, serves as a good example of a heterotopia: it contains, within its clearly demarcated boundaries, a sample of what might be taken to be 'all the animals in the world' and, in many cases, the habitats in which they live. All of these are collected, assembled and represented in one place, but this in a manner that arguably *inverts* at least some aspect of their original spatiality. For example, if animals are said to be 'free' beyond zoos, then in zoos a naturalistic order of representation can be said to dissimulate the fact that this 'freedom' is lost.

While this conceptualization is useful in itself, I shall extend it by making a distinction between heterotopias, *sensu stricto*, and what I describe as *heterotopic practices*.[8] Heterotopic practices work to (re)produce 'virtual' heterotopias in sites that do not necessarily entail the kind of physical geography envisaged by Foucault. Here I have in mind, for example, mass media news genres that are themselves constructed as a kind 'world of news' and 'news of the world'. We might also include scientific reports about the global effects, for example, of the eruption of a volcano, such as I consider in Chapter 7. I suggest that modern cultural formations – and modern forms of observation – are modern not least in so far as they involve such a heterotopic spatiality. As this point begins to suggest, unlike Foucault, I regard heterotopias, and indeed heterotopic practice, as being both culturally specific and a matter of *modern* cultures. Far from being universal, heterotopias involve a comparatively recent form of globalization and, as part of this process, constitute a central aspect of the mass mediation of nature.

This raises some additional questions for the forthcoming chapters: how does globalization – or what we might describe with Mary Louise Pratt (1992) as a 'planetary consciousness' – emerge in relation to the imaginary institution of nature, and vice versa? As part of this question, when and how do the first heterotopias of nature emerge? When and how do the first heterotopic *practices* appear, and how do they relate to the process of mass mediation? Last but not least, what effects do these practices have on the nature of observation, in the twofold sense of the 'character' of observation but also the nature that can be observed?

Now heterotopias, and indeed heterotopic *observers*, are made possible by diverse forms of *displacement*. Fay travels to the Ndoki; the Ndoki is 'taken' to audiences throughout the world. Heterotopias involve this 'physical' spatiality of displacement in so far as they involve empirical displacements on the part of the observer and, indeed, the observed; but also in so far as they articulate such displacements with displacement of a more virtual kind: 'symbolic' or semeiotic displacements. We can further note that displacement is about *moving* something from its 'original' place or position, but may also entail the *removal* of someone or something, in the sense of an enforced departure, thanks to, or as part of, a social process. I refer to the production of apparatuses and techniques that articulate all these forms of displacement – physical and social semeiotic displacement, but also 'voluntary' and enforced movement – as *technologies of displacement*. When displacement – or any other social process – occurs as part of a relation of domination, that is, a relation that involves an asymmetrical, indeed a *durably* asymmetrical, relation of power between or within social groups, then it is possible to speak of an 'ideological' relation (Thompson 1990) and of an 'ideological' technology of displacement.

I shall have more to say about such relations of power at a later stage; here I simply wish to suggest that it is only possible to begin to understand the social and environmental impact of mass mediation, and its characteristic technologies of observation, when these aspects are conceived in relation to such technologies of displacement. It follows that such technologies, and the social relations they enable, enact, or presuppose, must themselves be historicized, and especially the later chapters in the book will engage in such a process. In particular, I shall be concerned with historicizing contemporary technologies of displacement that are both produced and reproduced by way of film and other technologies of observation. How is it, for example, that modern environmentalists have come to take for granted the possibility of acting on behalf of environments far removed from the own?

Mass mediation and mass communication

And so I turn, finally, to the problem of the nature of mass mediation. In the introductory chapter, I suggested that I wished to move beyond theories of mass mediation and mass communication that reduce the mass media to so many 'instrumental' technologies or institutions.

The point is not to deny the significance of the instruments, technologies or institutions of mass mediation. On the contrary, we might well begin by recognizing the fundamental contemporary significance of media institutions, defined now not as habitual practice or as codes, but with John B. Thompson as 'specific and relatively stable clusters of rules and resources, together with the social relations that are established by them and within them' (Thompson 1990: 149).

From this perspective, the more recent forms of mass mediation of nature have been affected by the characteristic forms of organization of specific institutions like the BBC or the *National Geographic*. More generally, they have also been affected by generic institutions such as those involving the state, the family, schooling and, of course, the modern business organization. It is for this reason that the following chapters will analyse this dimension of the imaginary institution of nature and its consequences for the nature of observation. Amongst other aspects, I shall be concerned with analysing the manner in which such institutions engage in the commodification of nature, where nature is regarded now not just as a 'good' but as what John B. Thompson describes as a '*symbolic* good': nature as a *sign* that acquires an economic valorization, and which is made publicly available, in principle at least, to a plurality of recipients.

As I began to explain in the introductory chapter, I am nonetheless interested in problematizing mass mediation and mass communication from a more distinctly historical perspective: mass mediation in relation to what I described as pedagogies of 'massification'. If it is true that the observer is an 'effect' of a complex and heterogeneous ensemble of institutions, technologies, discourses and their social relations, then the phenomenon of mass mediation must be one of the most significant determinants of modern forms of observation.

In order to begin to explain how this is the case, it may be useful to return one last time to the examples of the Ndoki. In the Congo Trek website, which I mentioned in Chapter 1, Fay is quoted as saying that 'I literally want as many people on Earth as possible to see this place and fall in love with it' (www.nationalgeographic.com/congotrek, accessed 16 August 2005). We may presume that Fay does not literally mean that he wants as many people on Earth as possible to *visit* the Ndoki. Instead, he wants people to have access to the Ndoki by way of what we might describe with Peirce as a series of iconic replicas of the Ndoki; signs that, in Peirce's terms, offer the possibility of a seemingly immediate form of observation of the Ndoki.

Several aspects of Fay's idea make it an instance of mass mediation. There is, on the one hand, an appeal to large numbers or 'masses' of people. But there is also a double, if not triple, pedagogy of 'massification'. First, Fay's idea transforms people who would not normally regard themselves as being part of a mass, let alone *the* mass, *into* a 'mass' by virtue of being hailed as *people*. The expression 'people' fulfils an analogous function to the older notion of a 'mass' in so far as it unites a real diversity under one 'heading' or category; just as the notion of 'nature' is an abstract singular (Williams 1983), so too are expressions such 'mass' and 'people'.

Second, Fay says that he wants 'people' to see the Ndoki in large numbers *so that they might fall in love with it*. Such an expression presupposes a circuit of anthropomorphism in so far as the category of love is generally one reserved for human relations. We may however speculate that this invitation to engage in an explicit form of anthropomorphism and cosmomorphism has an ulterior motive; one that goes beyond a sentimental form of romanticism, or Fay's undoubted enthusiasm for the region. Fay may well expect, for example, that if he manages to mobilize enough people he will secure the long term financing and security of the park. Any such aspiration constitutes a second pedagogy, or at any rate a second pedagogic aspect of massification, in so far as it entails constituting an agglomeration for a certain political purpose. I should perhaps explain that here 'political' – with a small 'p' – refers to the fact that massification occurs in relation to certain interests. Such interests are themselves both informed and constituted by discourse, and are made more complex in so far as they involve not just the media of mass *mediation* but also media of mass *communication*.

This distinction requires some clarification. The media of mass mediation may be described as technologies of observation that entail a pedagogy of massification in one actual 'physical' (if not only *physical*) space that is shared, however momentarily, by both the mass mediators, or their specific institution, and the recipients, or all those who are the object of the process of mass mediation. This is true, for example, of zoos, natural history museums, national parks and so forth. The media of mass communication may be treated as a specialized 'subset' of these in so far as they involve a significant change in this spatiality and temporality. The recipients are at one remove from the production of the messages of mass mediation. They can nevertheless appropriate the messages – what Thompson describes as symbolic goods – thanks to the goods' extended availability in space and time (Thompson 1995: 26–31). This 'gap' between the production and the reception of the messages of mass mediation is what makes mass communication a specialized form of mass mediation. It is also what institutes a degree of indeterminacy in the process of mass mediation, one that institutions like the *National Geographic* attempt to overcome by way of audience research and other increasingly sophisticated technologies of audience surveillance and participation.

Returning to Fay's appeal, we can say that it is thanks to the Internet's extraordinary capacity to reach millions of users that he can engage in his pedagogy of (mass-mediating) conservationism. But the 'gap' between the production and reception of such messages establishes a certain ambiguity, distance and the possibility for lack of communication between producers and audiences. This in turn makes it both possible and necessary for Fay – and, as I note in later chapters, for groups such as Greenpeace – to assume that he can 'represent', in the political sense of the term, 'his' audiences' interests. This constitutes the third form or aspect of massification. Fay – or the producers of the website – must imagine their audiences, and in so doing have recourse to abstract singulars such as I mentioned above.

The audiences will, in turn, have to imagine and produce images of the producers (or at least of the production process). They will have to do so, initially at least, by way of what I describe, with Gianfranco Bettetini (1984), as the *subjects of enunciation*: semeiotic 'puppeteers' 'within' complex signs such as books, TV programmes or films that metaphorically pull the 'strings' of the different semeiotic processes that might be mobilized by any given sign. In the case of the *Congo* series, for example, TV audiences may observe the Ndoki thanks to a complex process of narration that involves not one but several 'subjects'. There are, on the one hand, what we might describe as actual or empirical subjects of enunciation: people like Fay who are shown on the programme, and who directly and explicitly invite viewers to observe the Ndoki in a certain way. But there is also a complex narrational process that occurs in so far as the 'camera narrator' shows or 'ocularizes' the Ndoki in a manner that cannot be simply reduced to any one empirical subject's point of view. Last but not least, the documentary involves not just the empirical subject or an actual narrator, and indeed not just camera 'views', but an ensemble of audio-visual media: camera, *in situ* sounds and added sound effects, music, voice-over narration, titles etc. What I am describing as the subject of enunciation is the 'puppeteer' – we might equally speak of a ghost – that articulates all of these media within one single programme, one single complex sign.

This account allows me to raise some final questions: when and how do the media of mass communication emerge, and how do they constitute such complex technologies of observation and displacement? Moreover, how do they affect the observation of nature and, eventually, the emergence of the practices associated with *modern environmentalism*? I shall suggest that modern environmentalist practices, at least as embodied in the campaigns of groups like Greenpeace, at once presuppose, identify with, and enact the forms of observation and mass mediation that are made possible by mass communication. As these two 'propaedeutic' chapters begin to suggest, and as the following chapters explain, this process has entailed far more than the instrumental use of one or another medium of mass communication. It also involved a rather longer history than might be imagined, and it is to this history that I now turn.

Part II

3

THE NATURE OF *MATHESIS*

I do not mean by beauty of form such beauty as that of animals
or pictures, which the many would suppose to be my meaning;
but . . . understand me to mean straight lines and circles, and
the plane solid figures which are formed out of them by turning-
lathes and rulers and measurers of angles; for these I affirm
to be not only relatively beautiful, like other things, but they
are eternally and absolutely beautiful, and they have peculiar
pleasures, quite unlike the pleasures of scratching.

Socrates in Plato's *Philebos*

The book of nature

In Europe at the crossroads of medieval and modern cultures, nature was a book:
an earthly appendix to the Bible. It was, however, a strange book: it had no covers and apparently required no reading skills. Its 'words' were to be found in the
ground and in the skies, in plants and in animals, in the great chain of being created by God.

This chain of being was anthropomorphized in terms of vitalist principles.
As noted by Carolyn Merchant (1980), Renaissance cosmologies were premised
on organic imaginaries that had their roots in the ancient Greek notion of the
cosmos as an intelligent organism. There were at least three different models of
an organic cosmos during the Renaissance, all sharing a vitalist principle in so far
as all regarded the cosmos as something that was essentially alive, that is, as an
interconnected, interrelated and above all *living* unity (Merchant 1980: 103).

In so far as nature was God's creation – in so far as nature was 'Nature' – and
in so far as God's signature could be found in all that He (*sic*) created, then
Nature could ostensibly be read by one and all at once as universal icons and
dicents of His presence. As described by Sir Thomas Browne, himself very much
a figure at the crossroads of modernity, the Book of Nature was 'that universal and
publick Manuscript, that lies expans'd unto the Eyes of all' (Browne in Eisenstein
1979: 455).

In fact, the Book of Nature was arguably as closed as the Bible was open. The Bible was open in so far as its each and every sign was a sign by virtue of being part of a celestial chain of *interpretant*: a holy matrix of meanings on which the clergy and all those able to read the Bible had to draw and were able to draw in order to interpret the symbolism of its each and every passage. Meaning in this great book, like the meaning in all books, by no means resided exclusively within its covers. But conversely, far from being utterly 'publick' and transparent, the reading of the Book of Nature required certain semeiotic skills that were not necessarily acquired as part of one's everyday life.

According to Michel Foucault (1970), until the seventeenth century these skills involved a logic of resemblance. During the Renaissance *epistéme* – what Foucault describes as a kind of 'meta-code' or 'code of codes' in the sense of code introduced in Chapter 2 – there were four predominant modalities of resemblance. The first involved what Foucault characterizes as resemblance based on *convenience*, whereby things were thought to resemble each other by virtue of the fact that they were located in the same place. Foucault offers, amongst other examples, that of moss growing on a rock: the moss was thought to 'resemble' the rock because it was next to it. A second form of resemblance involved 'emulation' and entailed a kind of 'convenience' that had broken the moorings of place and allowed things to imitate each other from afar and without motion: what Foucault describes as a sort of 'natural twinship existing in things' (Foucault 1970: 19–20), which he exemplifies with reference to the human mouth. The mouth was thought to be like Venus in that it gave passage to words and kisses of love. A third form of resemblance involved 'analogy' and entailed the superimposition of the first two forms of resemblance – 'convenience' and 'emulation': the relation, for example, between the stars and the sky was also thought to be found in the relation between plants and the earth. The plant was to earth what the star was to the sky. A fourth form of resemblance involved 'sympathy' and was a kind of transformative power of assimilation: for example, roses that had been used in funeral rites had the power to render melancholy those who later smelled them. The roses both carried the funeral's sorrow and subsumed those who smelled them in its sadness.

But how did subjects in the Renaissance – Foucault's subjects in the Renaissance – *discern* any of these icons?

Foucault suggests that what he describes as a *hermeneutics* of resemblance – the interpretation of resemblance – was corresponded by a *semiotics*: by the ability to discern the icons that might be interpreted, to distinguish their location, to know what constituted them *as* signs, and to know by what laws they were linked to certain forms of resemblance. From a Peircian perspective, both of these dimensions (the hermeneutic and the semiotic) are ineluctably woven together in any semeiotic process, but from Foucault's perspective 'the sixteenth century superimposed hermeneutics and semiotics in the form of similitude' (1970: 29). If the hermeneutic involved knowledge of relations of resemblance, the semiotic involved the ability to discern the 'marks' or 'signatures' that signalled similitude, that made the resemblances visible.

Foucault quotes Paracelsus – an exponent of vitalist theories of the cosmos – as saying that, even though God as creator 'has hidden certain things', 'he has allowed nothing to remain without exterior and visible signs in the form of special marks – just as a man who has buried a hoard of treasure marks the spot that he may find it again' (Paracelsus in Foucault 1970: 26). The knowledge of all living beings for those who appropriated this rule was the knowledge of the 'signatures' that were peculiar to each thing. 'A knowledge of similitudes', Foucault suggests, was 'founded upon the unearthing and decipherment of these signatures' (Foucault 1970: 26). Although the essence of every living creature, like the essence of the god that had created each and every one, was 'invisible', those with the knowledge saw the world as a 'vast open book', a book that 'bristle[d] with signs' (Foucault 1970: 27), signs that made the invisible *visible*. In a wonderful example, Foucault refers to Paracelsus' analysis of the signature of the aconite, a plant thought in the Renaissance to have curative powers for the eyes. The affinity or 'sympathy' between the two elements might well be read in the aconite's seeds: 'they are tiny dark globes set in white skinlike coverings whose appearance is much like that of eyelids covering an eye' (Paracelsus in Foucault 1970: 27).

Now Foucault's account makes it clear that, even if material objects of nature were icons, they were nevertheless treated as *signs*. To observe nature was, in this sense, to engage in what are by today's standards quite explicitly semeiotic procedures. The observation of signs of Nature required certain *reading* skills. However, these skills were rather different from those that might be taken for granted today. First, and most fundamentally, the chain of interpretant, that is to say the imaginary with which they were interpreted, was utterly different from the one that predominates today. As I noted earlier, nature was regarded as being not only the work of God but essentially alive. Second, what Foucault describes as the 'play' of resemblance and similitude meant that the classification of signs *as* signs was not only different, but premised on much weaker boundaries than is the case today. It can be suggested, quite paradoxically, that, at least in the world constructed by Foucault's account, observers were happy to live by the principle that semeiosis involved not so much mutually exclusive categories as a logic of equivalences in which something could be something else provided it was interpreted 'on a different level'. Foucault illustrates this principle, which he takes to be unique to the time, when he asks: 'What form constitutes a sign and endows it with its particular value as a sign? – Resemblance does. It signifies exactly in so far as it resembles what it is indicating (that is, similitude).' 'But what it indicates,' Foucault suggests, 'is *another* resemblance, an adjacent similitude, one of another type which enables us to recognize the first and which is revealed in its turn by a third.' Even if each resemblance receives a signature, this signature is no more than an intermediate form of the same resemblance; the second 'circle' of resemblance, the one involving the semiotic 'signature', would be an exact duplication of the first 'were it not for that tiny degree of displacement which causes the sign of sympathy to reside in an analogy, that of analogy in emulation, that of emulation

in convenience, which in turn requires the mark of sympathy for its recognition'
(Foucault 1970: 28–9).

Linear perspective

When and how did Nature stop being a book? How did nature stop being a matter of the play of resemblance and similitude? Perhaps most significantly, when
and how was a form of subjectivity produced for which there were thought to be
absolute differences *between* different kinds of signs, between the different 'circuits'
– of resemblance, but also, we might add, of anthropomorphism?

There is no single answer to these questions: no single site, no one philosopher
of genius, indeed no single cultural group provides a modern 'solution' to these
questions. It seems clear that in Europe and elsewhere the changes took place in
a manner that was fragmentary, discontinuous, uneven and always provisional:
there was no grand, overarching plan and, as will become clear in some of the
examples, some practices could frequently be 'modern' and 'not modern' at the
same time.

With the benefit of hindsight it is nonetheless possible to isolate some scenes
and to single out some events – even individuals – with which one can observe
the emergence or concretion of the discourses – and the non-discursive practices
– associated with the early modern forms of anthropomorphism. One such scene
involved the 'discovery' of linear perspective in scenography and painting in fif-
teenth-century Tuscany. This scene suggests that, as early as the fifteenth century,
the nature of a certain conceptualization of painting, and indeed of visuality more
generally, had begun to coexist with the nature of the Book of Nature.

Now legend – in the Medieval Latin sense of *legenda*, something to be read
– has it that early in the fifteenth century Filippo Brunelleschi, the Tuscan sculp-
tor, architect and 'artisan-engineer' who designed and built the dome in Florence
Cathedral, famously stood at the west door of the unfinished cathedral and performed a remarkable experiment. Brunelleschi had made a perspectivally 'correct'
drawing of the San Giovanni baptistery on a *tavoletta* or panel; as he stood facing
the cathedral's baptistery, he turned the *tavoletta*'s painted side towards the baptistery and then used what has been described as a 'lentil-sized' hole in it to peer
at the building. The hole opened 'pyramidally' to the other side – the painted side
–widening to the size of a *ducat* or coin. As Brunelleschi peered through the hole,
he held up a mirror that faced both him and the front of his small painting. By
this means, he reportedly discovered that the painting seemed a part of the real
object of representation, and in so doing confirmed that he had mastered what is
now known as the technique of single-point perspective. To be sure, the sky in the
painting itself reportedly had a reflective silver colour, so that when Brunelleschi
held up the *tavoletta* and the mirror on a partly cloudy day he would have seen the
motionless baptistery surrounded by clouds being 'pushed by the wind' – clouds
in motion.

Many textbook accounts of the origin of perspective not only assign it a neat origin – this experiment – but interpret it as a kind of coming of geometry to art: by this account, linear perspective, and single-point perspective in particular, is in effect the application of Euclidean geometry to provide a 'correct' spatial ordering of solids in a visual plane. Henri Lefebvre (1991) begins to provide an alternative to this story of origins when he suggests that the discovery of single-point perspective was part of a much broader social process that involved the transformation of the relation between town and country.

According to Lefebvre, from the thirteenth century onwards, Tuscan merchants and burghers transformed their *latifundia* or lordly domains into *métayons*, institutions in which the serfs of the medieval system became *métayers*. The *métayers* received a share of what they produced and, according to Lefebvre, this set in motion a series of changes that led to the transformation of the Tuscan landscape. In so far as the urban bourgeoisie needed to draw on the rural territory to feed town-dwellers and to obtain leather, wool and other goods, they transformed the country, and the countryside, in the logic of a new model, as Lefebvre explains:

> The houses of the *métayers*, known as *poderi*, were arranged into a circle around the mansion where the proprietor would come and stay from time to time, and where his stewards lived on a permanent basis. Between *poderi* and mansion ran alleys of cypresses. Symbol of property, immortality and perpetuity, the cypress thus inscribed itself upon the countryside, imbuing it with depth and meaning. These trees, the crisscrossing of these alleys, sectioned and organised the land. Their arrangement was evocative of the laws of perspective, whose fullest realization was simultaneously appearing in the shape of the urban piazza in its architectural setting. Town and country – and the relationship between them – had given birth to a space which it would fall to the painters, and first among them in Italy to the Siena school, to identify, formulate, and develop.
>
> (Lefebvre 1991: 78)

In effect, Lefebvre suggests that what he describes as a certain spatial practice (the organization of the *poderi* and the mansion, the cypresses and, eventually, the piazzas in the towns themselves) enabled a certain representation of space (a certain *conceptualization* of space) and this in turn resulted eventually in a certain 'lived' space, or what Lefebvre somewhat unhelpfully describes as representational spaces. Lefebvre makes the case that a changing mode of production resulted in a changing social production of space, and thereby in new perceived, conceived and lived spaces.

Lefebvre makes it clear that the three spaces should be 'interconnected, so that the "subject", the individual member of a given social group, may move from one to another without confusion' (1991: 40). He nonetheless recognizes that 'Whether they constitute a coherent whole is another matter. They probably do so only in favourable circumstances, when a common language, a consensus, and common code can be established' (1991: 40). 'It is reasonable to assume,' he adds, 'that the Western town, from the Italian Renaissance to the nineteenth century, was fortunate enough to enjoy such auspicious conditions' and that, during this period, the social construction of space came to be dominated by the representation of space and, in particular, by the code of linear perspective. If Lefebvre's account is valid, Brunelleschi's 'discovery' and the treatises on perspective that formalized the principles of linear perspective were only part of a much broader process. Even so, they clearly played a key role in transforming not only a representational space of religious origin but, thereby, the predominant techniques and technologies of observation. To put it in Lefebvre's terms, a 'multitude of intersections' came to be driven by the representations of space offered by the theories and theorists of linear perspective. It follows that such theories must have been, to begin with at least, anachronistic with respect to the older social ways of organizing space.[1]

This is a seductive account, and one that appears to acquire credence in so far as a number of fifteenth- and sixteenth-century textual sources during the period acknowledge the work of Filippo Brunelleschi. One of the earliest of such sources is Leon-Battista Alberti's treatise, *De Pictura* (On Painting, also written as *Della Pittura*). Alberti completed the treatise in 1535 and published it some five years later, dedicating it to Brunelleschi even as he ascribed to himself the discovery of the technique. Alberti was a painter, but he was also a learned man who was determined to use his knowledge of mathematics to establish a more objective footing for the principles and practice of painting. As he explained in the first book of *De Pictura*, he wished to make his discourse ('*oratio*') clearer by taking from mathematicians 'those things which seem relevant to the subject. When we have learned these, we will go on, to the best of our ability, to explain the art of painting from the basic principles of nature' (Alberti 1972: 37).

These 'basic principles of nature' amounted to a theory of vision that Alberti expressed in terms of Greek geometry, and its corresponding spatiality. The power of vision, he argued, was a matter of 'visual rays', 'ministers of vision' ('*visendi ministris*'), by whose agency 'the images of things are impressed upon the senses'. 'These rays', Alberti suggested, stretched

> between the eye and the surface seen, move rapidly with great power and remarkable subtlety, penetrating the air and rare and transparent bodies until they encounter something dense or opaque where their points strike and they instantly stick. Indeed amongst the ancients there was considerable dispute as to whether these rays emerge from the surface or from the eye.
>
> (Alberti 1972: 41)

Alberti skirted this 'truly difficult question' – a question that in some respects continues to be significant to this day – and invited the reader to imagine instead the rays as 'extended very fine threads gathered tightly in a bunch at one end, going back together inside the eye where lies the sense of sight' (Alberti 1972: 41). The threads' extension in the opposite direction might be described as being organized as 'a triangle whose base is the quantity seen, and whose sides are those same rays which extend to the eye from the extreme points of that quantity'; 'it is perfectly true,' Alberti stated, 'that no quantity can be seen without such a triangle' (Alberti 1972: 41). This triangle, he suggested, was in fact better understood as a kind of pyramidally shaped field of vision whose apex was found in the human eye. In what was to become the predominant metaphor of representation in modern cultures, Alberti proposed that the painter should begin by drawing a rectangle that itself represented a *window*: 'Let me tell you what I do when I am painting. First of all, on the surface on which I am going to paint, I draw a rectangle of whatever size I want, which I regard as an open window through which the subject to be painted is seen' (Alberti 1972: 55).

Again, it is easy to interpret this account as one of several 'firsts' – originary narratives. Alberti's work nonetheless begins to reveal the problems of what I described as 'textbook' accounts. While it is true that this was to become the modern visual metaphor par excellence, as noted by Hubert Damisch (1994), Alberti's spatiality continued to be at least partly rooted in an ancient Greek representation of space in so far as it was constructed with reference to the limits of the human figure. This becomes evident in the rest of Alberti's instructions: once a rectangle had been drawn, the painter should decide how large the human figures should be, and should divide the height of one of them (presumably the central figure) into three parts, using the measurement known as the *braccio* (a measurement meaning 'arm's length'). Three *braccia*, Alberti suggested, were about the 'average' height of a man's body. With this measure, the painter should then divide the bottom line of rectangle into as many parts as it would hold, and this bottom line should be proportional to the next transverse equidistant quantity seen on the pavement. His following instructions nonetheless formalized some of the basic principles of single-point perspective:

> Then I establish a point in the rectangle . . . and as it occupies the place where the centric ray strikes, I shall call this the centric point. The suitable position for this centric point is no higher from the base line than the height of the man to be represented in the painting, for in this way both the viewers and the objects in the painting will seem to be on the same plane. Having placed the centric point, I draw straight lines from it to each of the divisions on the base line. These lines show me how successive transverse quantities visually change to an almost infinite distance.
>
> (Alberti 1972: 55)

Now the fact that the first treatise *followed* the experiments of Brunelleschi, and that it was itself constructed in terms of a theory that was not quite that of 'fully' modern perspective, contradict the textbook accounts of 'discovery'. It also forces the analyst to adopt a more complex reading of history than is suggested by Lefebvre when he speaks of an 'auspicious' interconnection between perceived, conceived and lived space. With Damisch and André Chastel, it is possible to suggest that technique (in this case of linear perspective) is better understood as 'a knowledge contained within the figurative structures that administer it'[2] (Chastel in Damisch 1994: 79). In so far as this is the case, it becomes possible to conceive of single-point perspective not simply as a *discourse* of, or *on*, space – in Lefebvre's terms, a representation of space – but as a kind of practice, performance or 'enunciation' of a 'theory': one that only really becomes 'theory' *afterwards*. Damisch's (1994) central argument is that it was not that Brunelleschi *applied* geometry to painting (or scenography), but that his 'pre-geometric' practice began to give to the visual sense, and to 'illustrate', a modern conception of space, and thereby to prepare the ground for future developments in geometry. We can only say, in this sense, that his work, like the later theory of Alberti, was a step in the direction of Lefebvre's double illusion.

How was linear perspective to become an instance of the double illusion? It would be two more centuries before the fully Cartesian notion of space as 'empty' and 'homogeneous' was produced. However, with the benefit of hindsight, certain signs of modernity can be read into the work of both Alberti and Brunelleschi. Erwin Panofsky's classic essay, *Perspective as Symbolic Form*, begins to explain the multiple transformations of physical space – and one might say *optical* space – that are performed by the 'prototype' they develop. Panofsky argues that the metaphor of the window denied the material surface upon which individual figures or objects were to be drawn, and instead interpreted it as a 'picture plane' (Panofsky 1997: 27). He further argues that the theory suggests that humans see with a single and immobile eye, and that vision is a matter of geometry. Accordingly, it constructs humans as both geometers and Cyclopes: 'cyclopedal' geometers. These and other transformations performed by the model mean that, as far as Panofsky is concerned, linear perspective clearly constituted a *symbolic form*: it was, and remains, in the terms of the philosopher Ernst Cassirer, not just a sign – in Peirce's sense of the *legisign,* a convention or 'law' – but 'a peculiar and independent, self-contained world of meaning according to an inherent formative law of its own' (1955: 383). It was not, for this same reason, a sign that achieved 'its value from an outward, transcendent existence that is somehow "mirrored" in it' (Cassirer 1955: 383). On the contrary, and in the manner explained by Lefebvre with respect to the 'double illusion', it was a technique that allowed architects, engineers and painters to construct at once a 'transparent' space and a space 'filled' with 'real' objects.

Damisch himself takes this argument further, but does so in a way that distances itself from the problematic of symbolic forms *per se*. In a magisterial study of a variety of intricately detailed aspects of the history of the emergence of single-point perspective, he mounts a withering assault on what he describes as the 'representationalist hypothesis' (1994: 263), and on those who are 'prisoners of the referential prejudice' (1994: 283). Damisch is contemptuous both of any effort to ground single-point perspective in any narrowly semiotic account and of any naturalistic appeal to an objective, empirical and external referent. Instead, Damisch wishes to demonstrate that single-point perspective was, and today is still, better thought of as an epistemological 'system' not just for representing but also for 'thinking' and 'doing' a certain space. It was, in this sense, one of the earliest modern media of transmediation; that is, the transposition of modes of observation from one medium, one context, to another.

Now it might be assumed that transmediation entails discontinuity, and discontinuity only, between media. But of course transmediation must involve *both* continuity and discontinuity. In the context of representations of material nature, there must be, if nothing else, an element of continuity in the dimension of reference, the object of representation. This raises the question: have Damisch and Panofsky gone too far down the road of constructivism? This question, like my more general analysis of linear perspective, merits a particularly detailed analysis in so far as it raises some of the most fundamental challenges for a theory of 're/presentation', and for an ideal-realist epistemology more generally.

In one of several remarkable analyses, Damisch returns to Brunelleschi's experiment and engages in a line-by-line analysis of Antonio Manetti's biography of Brunelleschi, in particular its account of Brunelleschi's experimental procedures (Brunelleschi himself does not describe these, so it is necessary to consider 'second hand' accounts). Two aspects of the analysis suggest that Damisch *has* erred too far on the side of culturalism. The first of these involves Damisch's invocation – despite his general critique of this approach – of a remarkably conventional notion of representation. Damisch sets up an opposition between the image of Christ on Veronica's veil – an image which Damisch acknowledges involved the production of an index in Peirce's that of the term – and Brunelleschi's model or 'prototype'. The latter presupposed, 'of necessity', that it 'be absent from its place: the very structure of the tradition,' Damisch suggests, 'dictates this, as it could not have constituted itself as such except through the attempt to reactivate its traces' (1994: 91). 'Such is the case,' Damisch adds, 'with dreams, whose images, like this painting, are accessible to us only retrospectively' (1994: 91). If the painting on the *tavoletta* is taken as a stand-alone painting, this point seems difficult to refute. But Damisch seems to overlook the fact that the experiment, which was the context for the narration about Brunelleschi's experiment, did involve the co-presence of Brunelleschi, the painting on the *tavoletta, and the baptistery.* Brunelleschi was standing in the piazza. Unless he was sleepwalking (or rather 'sleep-standing'), any reference to dreams would have to be to day-dreaming. But of course this was no reverie: it was a determined, 'attentive' and 'calculating' mode of observation. By Damisch's own methodology, we cannot simply abstract from this fact, or indeed from the fact that the painting was produced for *scenographic* purposes. The experiment worked – or it was seen to work – because the painting, the baptistery and Brunelleschi's conception of each of these 'lined up'. To suggest, as Damisch does, that what really mattered was that Brunelleschi's position as painter 'could be deduced' from the painting is to miss the point, or rather the 'space': the spatial practice, the perceived space.

The second aspect involves what Damisch evocatively describes as 'the problem of the sky' (1994: 93). As noted earlier, Brunelleschi's painting made use of a silver colour burnished in such a way that 'natural air and sky were reflected in it, and even clouds that one saw pass by in this silver pushed by the wind, when it was blowing' (Manetti in Damisch 1994: 89–90).[3] Damisch's primary concern with this aspect of Brunelleschi's experiment is to use it as evidence of the *limits* of linear perspective, and indeed of its *exclusive* character: linear perspective must exclude all those aspects that it cannot neatly subsume within its (then) pre-geometric technique (here pre-geometric must really be read as 'geometric'). This is a central theme in Damisch's *A Theory of/Cloud/* (*Théorie du/Nuage/*) (2002), and one that leads him to state that:

> The new idea of the painting at the center of perspective's origin myth called for inclusion in the demonstration – on its margins, it would seem, and in the form of a reflection – of this unmastered, unmasterable background element, one that had to be *shown* but could not be except by use of a mirror – that is, paradoxically, by resorting to a *di-mostratio*. Thus the cloud mirror functioned as the index (narrowly construed) of a discontinuity between the order of that susceptible to representation by the means of *perspectiva artificialis*, and another element which, admitting of no term and no limit, seems to escape capture, demanding that it be presented 'in its natural form' (*l'aria e'cieli naturali*).
>
> (Damisch 1997: 94)

Damisch speaks of the 'referential prejudice', but here we seem to have, if anything, an example of an 'anti-referential prejudice'. Damisch is so concerned with explaining that clouds cannot be 'captured' by the cyclopedal geometry – a point that might itself be contested thanks to the fact that the clouds *were* included, in their wondrous ephemerality, *in* the painting – that he misses what was arguably its greater significance: here was, admittedly from a genealogical perspective, a 'prototype' of 're/presentation': a painting that was *both* legisignical in Peirce's sense of the term – there clearly *was* a transformation on the basis of newly formed convention – *and* explicitly indexical. With Peirce, we can say in this sense that Brunelleschi's perspectival technique, as embodied in the replica of the *tavoletta*, constituted a rhematic indexical legisign: as defined by Peirce, 'any general type or law, however established, which requires each instance of it to be really affected by its Object in such a manner as merely to draw attention to that object. Each Replica of it will be a Rhematic Indexical Sinsign of a peculiar kind' (CP 2.259). A rhematic indexical sinsign, it might be added, to the point – to the space – of full motion, the motion of the clouds themselves. Brunelleschi's *tavoletta*, if not the techniques recommended later by Alberti, Dürer and others, was in this respect an early forerunner of the kinds of photographic technologies that today most certainly *are* capable of capturing, albeit in a rather different way, the nature of clouds, if not the sky.

The printed book

Alberti's and other early treatises about art and nature only existed in manuscript form. Their circulation was thus drastically limited. Albrecht Dürer, for example, may have learned about Alberti's (and indeed Leonardo da Vinci's) theoretical work via Leonardo's friend Pacioli (Wöfflin 1971: 285). Much of the work in manuscript form was, in any case, a matter of trade secrecy: artisans were concerned to control the knowledge that frequently took them a lifetime and not a little suffering to acquire. By the time that Dürer himself produced his own treatise on painting (his *Manual of Measurement*, 1523), Johann Gutenberg's printing press had been adopted across many European capitals, and had begun to revolutionize the communication of knowledge. Dürer himself had his essay printed in 1525, and this would have secured a wider readership than Alberti could have dreamt of – or perhaps would have wished for – when he first produced his own treatise.

If it is necessary to critique a history of inventive genius in the context of single-point perspective, the same is true of the world of printing. To speak in this sense of 'Johann Gutenberg's' printing press is misleading in so far Gutenberg is better credited with the *assembly* of a series of technologies, some of which had been known for centuries. For example, block printing had been known in Europe and parts of Asia long before Gutenberg assembled his invention, and indeed a Buddhist book produced with metal movable type was produced in Korea as early as 1377.[4]

Be that as it may, Gutenberg began by printing his now famous Gutenberg Bibles from 1455 onwards. While the choice of the Bible reminds us of the pre-eminence of Christianity in early modern Europe, the development of the printing press was arguably an integral aspect of the rise of a capitalist economy in late medieval and early modern Europe. Printed books were bought and sold on a market, and constituted what John B. Thompson describes as 'symbolic' goods: signs or, as Thompson describes them, *symbolic forms* subjected to economic valorization (Thompson 1990: 13).[5]

As Thompson (1995) explains, the growing trade itself both generated and was made possible by new political and cultural networks. These were by no means a simple superstructure to the emerging capitalist infrastructure. Nor were they simple media for Catholic propaganda: the networks stood in ambivalent relationships with the Church and with emerging nation-states. Although it is true that the Church and State stood to benefit from the possibilities of communication opened up by the new printing technologies, the proliferation of printers and the dissemination of a growing number of texts meant that it became more difficult to control the dissemination of subversive materials. This was famously illustrated by the publication in 1517 of Martin Luther's 95 Theses, which became known within weeks in Germany, and within two months in the rest of Western Europe.

As appropriated in the contexts of the networks mentioned, the printing press was to have wide-ranging consequences. Until the development of printing technologies, large collections of books tended to be found in a few centralized 'great libraries' of the world such as the one once found in Alexandria. The adoption of printing presses in various European cities by the end of the fifteenth century began to change all of this. Lucien Febvre and Henri-Jean Martin (1976) note that, after the 1480s, the book trade became better organized and the unitary price of books fell to a fraction of what it had been, and by the close of the fifteenth century some of the biggest publishers produced 1500 copies of the more popular books. By the sixteenth century, 1000 to 1500 copies had become the average (Febvre and Martin 1976: 218). As suggested by Elizabeth Eisenstein (1979), this meant that, for the first time, many scholars across Europe had access to libraries whose collections equalled or eventually surpassed those of a few great libraries that were scattered across Europe.

If books became far more widely available than they once had been, this was partly because the time it took to produce each book was dramatically reduced. Until the advent of the printed book, all knowledge had to be copied by hand. This process, an integral aspect of what Eisenstein describes as 'scribal culture' which was replaced by 'print culture', was laborious and time-consuming. It had the effect not only of limiting the availability of books to medieval scholars but of forcing them to spend lifetimes making copies of their own and other scholars' work. As noted by Eisenstein, 'The lifetimes of gifted astronomers were consumed, right down to Regiomontanus himself, making copies, recensions and epitomes of an initially faulty and increasingly corrupted twelfth-century translation from an Arabic text' (Eisenstein 1979: 464). The institution of a 'print culture' now made it possible, in principle at least, for existing and new academic communities to accumulate knowledge and to circulate ideas at a far greater speed than was possible in the context of the 'scribal culture'. In this as in the following centuries, the speed of dispersion had social consequences. In cultures increasingly dominated by the measurement and commodification of clock time (see below), but also in societies where the life expectancy of scholars was twenty to thirty years below those of the early twenty-first century, knowledge was time.

Eisenstein suggests that another key change associated with 'print culture' was a greater accuracy in the texts. Until the advent of the printed press, such technologies were notoriously unreliable. Copying existing books by hand was not just laborious; it was also inexact, and the writing and images produced were prone to deterioration. As noted by Eisenstein, 'When it came to distributing hundreds of copies of a work containing long lists of numbers, or diagrams, maps and charts, or even precise detailed verbal reports, hand-copying was vastly inferior to print' (Eisenstein 1979: 461).

While this last assessment might be accurate in some respects, it overlooks a significant dimension of the social semeiotics of the printed books – one that I began to describe in Chapter 2 when I referred to the instituted 'break' (Thompson 1990) between the production and the reception of signs that characterizes mass communication. In *The Nature of the Book*, Adrian Johns (1998) underlines the significance of this dimension when he suggests that, far from standardizing and improving the quality of books, the printed book opened up a veritable Trojan horse of forgeries and editions of poor quality. Johns also shows how, even when printed editions did remain under the control of scholars, they continued to be produced under the aegis of courtly traditions, a fact that partly contradicts the notion of a neat transition from 'scribal' to 'print' culture. In one of several remarkable examples, Johns argues that Galileo Galilei's success was as much a matter of his ability to favourably position his book in the Medici court as it was of his astronomical theories. Johns explains that, like Alberti before him, Galileo worked to earn the patronage of the Medici, who had by now become one of the most powerful families in Europe and who identified iconographically with the figure of Jupiter. Galileo, who paid for the printing of *Sidereus Nuncius* (*Sidereal Messenger*, published in 1610) himself, named his Jovian satellites accordingly. The 'Medicean stars' constituted the centrepiece of his new book and, even though some difficulties arose when Galileo was informed that his choice of the name 'Cosmian' (after the Medici patriarch, the absolute prince, Cosimo II de' Medici) would not meet approval, a combination of last-minute changes, distribution to key princes and cardinals throughout Europe, and the eventual support of the Medici court guaranteed a positive response. This same logic later worked against Galileo when his ally and patronage broker in Rome, Campioli, fell from grace and thereby failed to secure a positive reading of Galileo's later *Dialogo Sopra i Due Massimi Sistemi del Mondo* (*Dialogue Concerning the Two Chief World Systems*) (Johns 1998: 24–7).

It might be argued that these events suggest that there was *no* 'instituted break' between the production and reception of Galileo's books. But, of course, Galileo worked to secure a favourable reception of his books precisely because there *was* such a break. And indeed, even if the *Dialogo* remained banned by the Church until 1822, its contents did become widely known and the 'Medicean stars' were transformed by astronomers into 'Galilean satellites': the *Dialogo*, like other books, did break with its immediate 'moorings'. While this process was clearly not a dyadic function of the printing technology *per se*, it seems doubtful that the work of Galileo, and indeed of the natural philosophers that followed him, would have achieved the status that it did were it not for the emergence, if not of a 'print culture', then certainly of a culture with print.

Mathesis in time

Galileo's name conjures up another scene, one from which many histories of science begin. The scene involves another cathedral, this time in Pisa, and another *legenda*. According to Vincenzo Viviani, Galileo began to develop his theory of the isochronism of the pendulum whilst at Mass at the cathedral. By Viviani's account, Galileo used his pulse to time the swing of the candelabra in the church, and by this means reportedly discovered that the period of the swing of a pendulum is independent of its amplitude – the notion of the isochronism of the pendulum. This discovery constituted part of the basis for Galileo's development of the technology of chronometric time. Paradoxically, it also provided Galileo's friend, the physician Santorio Santorio, with a technique to measure his patients' pulse. If the human body was the measure for Alberti's early theory of linear perspective, the beating heart was now at once the beginning, and the beginning of the end, of its own measure.

Strictly speaking, the pendulum clock was first invented by Christiaan Huygens, who patented the design in the mid-seventeenth century. But, if Viviani's *legenda* is accurate in this respect, the clock that began to tick in Pisa was of a different order from the mechanism developed by Huygens. Whereas the older circuits of anthropomorphism promoted a vitalist conception of the cosmos and a cosmomorphic identification with the vital possibility of both living and suffering, Thomas Hobbes, Francis Bacon, René Descartes and other philosophers began to conceive the world in the terms of a mechanistic cosmology, one that took the clock as its model. In the seventeenth century, the universe conceived and increasingly lived by the learned men and women of Europe began to tick. One of the earliest expressions of the birth of this dead nature is found in Hobbes' *Leviathan*, whose introduction famously began with the following words:

> Nature (the Art whereby God hath made and governes the World) is by the *Art* of man, as in many other things, so in this also imitated, that it can make an Artificial Animal. For seeing life is but a motion of Limbs, the begining whereof is in some principall part within; why may we not say, that all *Automata* (Engines that move themselves by springs and wheeles as doth a watch) have an artificiall life? For what is the *Heart*, but a *Spring*; and the *Nerves*, but so many *Strings*; and the *Joynts*, but so many *Wheeles*, giving motion to the whole Body, such as was intended by the Artificer?
>
> (Hobbes 1968: 81)

The mechanists reduced the cosmos to a matter of secondness, that is, to a universe that, once set in motion by God, was driven by mechanical relations of action and reaction. But action and reaction, after the to-ing and fro-ing of Galileo's pendulum, came to be regarded as being essentially a matter of measurement, that is to say, of measurable matter. In response to the ancient question, 'How might we know the world truthfully?', Galileo offered a very modern answer: he argued that the essential qualities of objects, the 'primary' qualities, were those that could be measured: those that involved the positions of bodies relative to others, but also their size, weight and motion. These qualities, he suggested, remained whether a human thought about them or not. In contrast, qualities such as taste, odour and colour –the 'secondary' qualities – were no more than 'mere names' and existed only in human consciousness.

This suggestion – in some respects an instance of *auto*-suggestion, and certainly the beginning of a radically anti-semeiotic discourse – both gave rise to and expressed a discourse of *mathesis*: the mathematical reasoning that began to make itself known in the work of the first theorists of linear perspective, but which now became a 'universal' principle, the objective foundation of the predominant form of modern rationality.

In fact, *mathesis* was, and to this day continues to be, based on a radically arbitrary principle of reasoning, on what Cornelius Castoriadis (1987) has described as an *identitary* logic and, therein, on *'legein'*. Identitary logic is the thesis that being is being something *determined* (*einai ti*), and speaking is saying *something* (*ti legein*). From a Peircian perspective, we can say that identitary logic does away with firstness, that is to say, indetermination. While mechanism seems to and indeed does privilege secondness, *legein* is premised on a *circular*, if not tautological, form of reasoning that proceeds by classifying *sets* of elements. Sets, suggests Castoriadis, *presuppose their own positing*: sets can be constituted only by presupposing that they have already been constituted (1987: 223). The key principle is that *a set is a set because it is defined as a set*: *x* is part of set *A* because *A* is $\{x, y, z\}$.

Far, then, from being based on some absolute 'external' reference, *mathesis* begins, now as in the early modern period, from an arbitrary principle of reasoning. Indeed, we can describe *mathesis* as one of the purest forms of thirdness, in the sense that mathematical reasoning proceeds, in theory at least, by way of the production of a *symbolic* logic. As defined by Peirce, symbols are representamens 'whose Representative character consists precisely in its being a rule that will determine its Interpretant' (EP 2.274). They are signs that are 'fit to serve as such simply because they will be so interpreted' (EP 2.307). Symbols are a matter of convention or habit, and are most obviously exemplified by words, sentences, books and other conventional signs such as numbers. By this account, *mathesis* is in some respects the opposite of mechanism: if mechanism explains the world in terms of action and reaction or secondness, *mathesis* does so not only in terms of signs, or thirdness, but in terms of the types of sign that are arguably the furthest removed from 'brute' secondness.

How, then, was this difference historically reconciled? One technique involved what I describe as the development of technologies of observation (and eventually institutions and fields) devoted to 'empirical' transmediation. From a semeiotic perspective, one of the tasks of the natural philosophers was to devise experiments and technologies by means of which symbols could be transformed into indexical signs and vice versa. As I began to explain in the Introduction, Peirce defines indexes as signs that are 'in real reaction with the object denoted' (EP 2.307); an index is 'a sign which refers to the Object that it denotes by virtue of being really affected by that Object' (EP 2.291–2). As Peirce puts it elsewhere, an index is forced to correspond to its object 'by blind fact' (CP 7.528).

Although indexes in the form of weathervanes and other similar instruments had existed for centuries, the late sixteenth and early seventeenth centuries witnessed the introduction of some of the earliest modern *numerical* indexes. I have already noted that Santorio Santorio developed a device that used the principle of the isochronism of the pendulum to measure the human pulse – the 'pulsilo-gium'. In the mid-seventeenth century, Envangelista Torricelli constructed, again under the influence of Galileo's knowledge, the first mercury barometer and, as noted earlier, Christiaan Huygens perfected the first pendulum clock. What I am describing as 'empirical' transmediation involved trying to establish an 'absolute' link between knowledge, regarded as a symbolic entity, and the world, regarded as an iconic entity, by way of measured, and measuring, indexes. We might speak in this sense of the technologies in question as devoted to the production of dicent indexical legisigns, as Peirce puts it, 'any general type or law, however established, which requires each instance of it to be really affected by its Object in such a man-ner as to furnish definite information concerning that Object' (CP 2.260).

The thermometer was the paradigmatic example of this process. But the pen-dulum clock also partook of this semeiotic in a more explicitly legisignal form. On the one hand, as noted by a number of scholars, clock time is utterly arbitrary, and is based on a kind of circular reasoning: the clock *tells* time because it *makes* time. Duration, following *legein*, is posited, counted and *told*; the second, the minute, the hour, the day and so forth, which *as numbers* do not have any 'natural' basis of their own, *become* time, even as time becomes a number. From this perspective, and contrary to the tacit pedagogy of modern institutions, if the universe 'ticks', it is because modern cultures came to 'clock'.

Far from being a neutral measure, timekeeping, so defined, became the subject of explicitly normative discourses among first Catholic and then Protestant elites. Indeed, time, increasingly and paradoxically conceived along the lines of a mod-ern conception of *space*, eventually displaced the more 'natural' time of the seasons and of the cyclical times of popular cultural and artisanal activities. This time was to be the time of production; a time that, as noted by Jesús Martín-Barbero (1993), was to replace the dichotomy of everyday life/festival with the dichotomy of work/leisure, with the homogeneous time of production: 'By abstracting time from the rhythms of human life, the time of production socially degrades the time of subjects – both individual and collective subjects – and transforms time into segmented homogeneous units – the time of objects – time which is mechanically fragmented and unrelated to context' (Martín-Barbero 1993: 90).

As in the case of Brunelleschi's experiments, it would nonetheless be a mistake to overlook the *indexical* dimension of this process. While there can be no doubt that linear or clock time, like linear perspective, eventually did become a matter of *legein*, it had a 'real' basis by virtue of the fact that it harnessed the secondness of the forces of gravity as they affected pendular movement, and as this movement came to be related to celestial orbits. Of course, even today, in the time of atomic clocks, it is necessary to adjust this time to allow for the fact that time, thus measured, cannot homogenize the celestial cycles. But such transformations do not deny, in and of themselves, the fact that there remains a link, in Peirce's terms a 'physical connection', between the measurement of time and something that is itself neither measured nor measurement.

Mind, body and *askesis*

Earlier, I noted that Damisch suggested that clouds were marginalized by Brunelleschi's experiment. Damisch argued that this was the result of the inability of linear perspective to incorporate bodies that did not readily submit to the geometric or pre-geometric ways of determining the nature of space. One of the ways in which painters such as Alberti and Dürer attempted to overcome this 'problem' was by developing instruments for what I described as technologies of observation in Chapter 2. Alberti, for example, used the grid method, or what he called a *velo* (a 'veil'), in order to impose a geometrical grid on human bodies. Dürer developed additional 'perspective apparatuses', which he described towards the end of his *Manual of Measurement*; the very last one shows a painter using what Dürer describes as 'a frame with a grid of strong black thread' with quadrangles 'about two fingers wide' and a pointer for 'scanning' at eye level (1977: 434–5) in order to draw a naked woman whose body is arranged in such a manner that her genitalia constitute the 'horizon' of the drawing.

Over the past ten or so years, questions regarding the 'difficulties' posed by the human body – and more generally by all 'natural' bodies – have become a focus of interest for cultural theorists, and the theorists pursue, however paradoxically, a problem that is now centuries old. How to represent a body that *both* resists *and* persists 'in' representation? In the seventeenth century, one answer to this question involved a radical classification of mind and body. Although the distinction between mind and body can be traced back as far as ancient Greek philosophy, there can be little doubt that it was Descartes' formulation in the *Discourse on Method* and other essays that most strongly classified the relation. Descartes famously suggested that matter was 'in and of itself' to do with, not sensory experience, but mathematically calculable extension (hence his expression *'res extensa'*). In contrast, he argued, the mind, or rather, thinking, was a fundamentally different substance by virtue of the fact that it had no extension, no materiality: the thinking mind was *res cogitans*. Thoughts, he argued, were not located in a particular place in the way that phenomenal objects were. Mind and matter were thus essentially different.

But it was not just that mind and matter were different. Descartes introduced a hierarchical principle into the classification by suggesting that the mind was that from which rationality began, and that the body could be studied by the mind and its (scientific) methods. His famous *cogito ergo sum*, 'I think, therefore I am', sought to ground this hierarchy in unassailable fact by suggesting that, whatever else might be doubted about the nature of the cosmos, he could not doubt that he doubted.

This mind–body dualism arguably became one of the discursive pillars of the predominant modern rationalities, and indeed of the modern opposition between 'man' (*sic*) and 'nature': Descartes and his followers defined nature in opposition to a 'mankind' whose essence could now be articulated in terms of the *cogito*. Eventually, this classification constituted a discursive justification for the modern *domination* of nature in so far as it effectively placed 'mind', and thereby a rational model of humanity, *above* 'nature', a category that forthwith would include not just the cosmos but also the lower human body. The threefold intellectual movement of objectifying, exteriorizing and 'killing' nature described by Carolyn Merchant (1980) was in this sense reflected by the objectification, exteriorization and metaphorical slaying of the *lower body*. This even as the mind was subjectified, interiorized and given apparently independent, that is, *essential*, life. This reduction and 'downgrading' of the lower body was itself conceived by way of machine metaphors, and paved the way for new visual technologies of observation and transmediation.

Indeed, just as the clock provided a metaphor for the cosmos, the historian of art Jonathan Crary (1990) has argued that a technology of observation called the *camera obscura* provided a metaphor for a model of *knowing* the cosmos that was based on this discourse. The camera obscura works by allowing sunlight reflected off objects to enter a chamber via a small hole, and to project their image on a flat surface within the darkened chamber. In the sixteenth century, lenses were added to correct the inversion, and mirrors allowed the lenses to project the image onto a horizontal surface, thereby allowing for a certain projection.

The camera obscura constitutes another example of what I have described as a technology of 'empirical' transmediation, albeit one that did not involve measurement. By the seventeenth century, several different uses were given to this device: natural philosophers regarded it as a model of reason and vision, but it also provided entertainment for the aristocracy by projecting an 'external' world, in full movement, onto a screen in a dark room (or later, in a portable box-like chamber). One of the more famous uses for the camera obscura was that it allowed artists to draw scenes and objects by projecting and then tracing their forms onto a canvas.

Beyond providing a conceptual metaphor, the camera obscura also provided an experiential model, a kind of 'practical' metaphor that was to have far-reaching effects. Indeed, Crary suggests that the significance of the camera obscura lay in its status as an assemblage. Far from having an exclusively metaphorical significance, or indeed being a machine used only for entertainment or for drawing, the camera obscura was 'without question the most widely used model for explaining human vision, and for representing the relation of a perceiver and the position of a knowing subject to an external world' (1990: 27). 'For over two hundred years it subsisted as a philosophical metaphor, a model in the science of physical optics, *and* was also a technical apparatus used in a large range of cultural activities' (1990: 29).

The philosophical model was premised on what Crary describes as 'an operation of individuation', a kind of '*askesis*'. The first term refers to the fact that the *camera obscura* was used to conceive the observer as an isolated, enclosed and autonomous being within the darkened chamber. In turn, *askesis* refers to a 'withdrawal from the world', one that occurred 'so as to regulate and purify one's relation to the manifold contents of the now "exterior" world' (Crary 1990:

39). Crary argues that, far from being a historical accident, this disposition both produced and reproduced the figure of an observer who was, in principle at least, a 'free sovereign individual' and a 'privatised subject' who was 'confined in a quasi-domestic space, cut off from a public exterior world' (1990: 39).

But this observer – this mode of observation – had another function, which was to separate the act of seeing from the physical body of the observer. This is what Crary describes as the decorporealization of vision. The observer's physical and sensory experience was replaced by the relations between the camera obscura, as mechanical apparatus, and an 'external' world that came to be regarded as a pre-given and objective reality (Crary 1990: 39–40). Just as Hobbes, Kepler and others used the clock to describe the cosmos, Crary quotes passages from Newton and Locke that suggest how indebted their philosophy was to the camera obscura. In particular, Crary quotes Locke as suggesting that human reason 'is not much unlike a closet wholly shut from light, with only some little opening left . . . to let in external visible resemblances, or some idea of things without; would the pictures coming into such a dark room but stay there and lie so orderly as to be found upon occasion it would very much resemble the understanding of man' (Locke in Crary 1990: 42).

For Locke as for Newton, Descartes and other natural philosophers, the camera obscura offered a way of knowing that could dispense with the 'sensationalism' of the lower body. It apparently allowed the mind, and the mind 'directly', to apprehend the primary qualities of what now came to be conceived and indeed perceived as an 'external' world. Nature was now made external not just to mind but, crucially, to the process of *observation itself*.

I shall revisit this theme in subsequent chapters. Here I wish to note that Crary's preoccupation with the discourse of natural philosophers must not allow us to overlook the fact that the sensational deaths of the lower body and embodied observation were not universally implemented or accepted. A variety of popular cultural forms resisted the rationalistic realism of the Cartesian discourse *and* the empiricist realism of Newtonianism. One of these forms involved what, with Mikhail Bakhtin (1984), Jesús Martín-Barbero (1993) has described as *grotesque* realism. According to Barbero, this realism presupposed a coding orientation for which the ultimate and essential reality was not that of the mind, as for Descartes, but that of the grotesque, the 'body-world and the world of the body' (1993: 65). The grotesque, Martín-Barbero suggests, 'is a world view which gives value to what are commonly considered the lowest elements – the earth, the belly – posed in direct contrast to the higher things – the heavens and the human countenance. The grotesque valued the lower regions because "the lowest is always a beginning"' (1993: 65–6). Martín-Barbero adds that, in contrast to a rationalistic realism that emphasized the completeness and isolation of objects, grotesque realism presupposed a world for which the essence of the body lay precisely in those parts that opened up communication to the world: the nose, the mouth, the genitals, the breasts, the phallus and, of course, the anus. 'An obscenity is so valuable precisely because through it we can express the grotesque:

the realism of the body' (1993: 66). I shall suggest in subsequent chapters that, even as elite groups within western European society attempted to institute rationalized experiences of nature premised on a strong classification of nature and of natural objects, many subaltern groups continued to experience nature in terms of 'rude' nature, one that was all about 'grotesque' lower body, sensation and, more generally, 'excess'.

Engendering nature

The conjunction of techniques, technologies and institutions that I have described in this chapter is associated with the 'birth' of a nature that was, in effect, dead. As Carolyn Merchant (1980) puts it in her classic *The Death of Nature*, 'The mechanists transformed the body of the world and its female soul, source of activity in the organic cosmos, into a mechanism of inert matter in motion, translated the world spirit into a corpuscular ether, purged individual spirits from nature, and transformed sympathies and antipathies into efficient causes. The resultant corpse was a mechanical system of dead corpuscles, set in motion by the Creator, so that each obeyed the law of inertia and moved only by external contact with another moving body' (Merchant 1980: 195).

The simultaneous birth and death of this nature marked the beginning of the end of the predominance of ancient circuits of anthropomorphism, and the emergence of an imaginary that was strongly indebted to emergent bourgeois values and to new forms of patriarchy. While Sir Francis Bacon protested that the new ways of knowing were to be for the benefit of 'mankind', this was clearly an instance of utopian reasoning with what today seems like an explicitly ideological role. On the one hand, it is quite clear that the new mechanistic imaginary helped to pave the way for the individualism that was to be associated with societies dominated by bourgeois classes; it is no coincidence that in *Leviathan* Hobbes described not just a 'mechanical' society, but a society whose mechanism was meant to keep in check the individuality of subjects whom Hobbes regarded as being naturally greedy: while Nature 'hath made men so equall, in the faculties of body, and mind' (1968: 183), 'she has also made them competitive, diffident, and vainglorious' (Hobbes 1968: 185). 'Hereby it is manifest, that during the time men live without a common Power to keep them all in awe, they are in that condition which is called Warre; and such a warre, as is every man, against every man' (Hobbes 1968: 185).

On the other hand, as Carolyn Merchant (1980) has documented, the discourse of nature was articulated in the language of an early modern form of patriarchy. During this period women became at once the object of a kind of instituted wrath and the unwitting protagonists of the new circuits of anthropomorphism. Whereas earlier organic cosmogonies had long gendered nature with images of a benevolently maternal figure, the discourse of mechanism gendered nature with images of sexual violence and exploitation. Merchant reveals, for example, how the narratives of Bacon and other philosophers of the time mixed metaphors for

other hand, as will be described in this chapter, the rise of modern formations, in particular those associated with what I have described as the new economy, and with the emergence of the nation-state as the other means of cultural centralization.

From this perspective, Newton played a key role in establishing a new form of occultism that was to constitute the cornerstone of a more distinctly *hegemonic* form of capitalism: one that involved not the philosopher's stone but, rather, what Karl Marx would eventually describe as the fetishism of commodities. The imposition of this form historically required precisely the mixture of brute force and seduction that today underpins capitalism more strongly than ever. As theorized by Antonio Gramsci (1971), modern culture has been shaped by the cultural imaginary of dominant groups, but this does not mean that such groups have been entirely successful in imposing their perspectives on subaltern groups. On the contrary, from a historical perspective, the dominant institutions of modern cultures have been successful thanks in no small part to their subjects' capacity to exercise intellectual leadership. But this has been by 'negotiating' with the subaltern groups, by recognizing some of their needs, desires or interests, and by incorporating aspects of their (competing) imaginaries. While physical coercion has always remained an option, and indeed one that has been employed frequently and brutally, it has been, more often than not, a last resort.

The emergence of mass mediation

Until the end of the seventeenth century, European societies were still organized predominantly on the basis of what some historians describe as 'parochial' societies. Most people lived in villages or small market towns and derived their livelihoods from agricultural or related activities. Governance was a matter of a multiplicity of groups and subgroups based on ancient classes, lineages, corporations, fraternities and age groupings (Martín-Barbero 1993). As I noted in Chapter 3, social relations were structured around the cyclical times of the harvest and the festival, and relations to nature were based on 'organic' cosmogonies.

These were by no means ideal societies. In *The Country and the City*, Raymond Williams (1973) rightly warns about the danger of idealizing forms of social order on the basis of a nostalgia for an ideal, and ideally receding, past. In Europe, pre-modern social formations involved the brutal exploitation of the peasantry. As Williams notes, it was in the fourteenth century, and not in the eighteenth or nineteenth, that members of the Great Society said 'We are men [*sic*] formed in Christ's likeness, and we are kept like beasts' (Williams 1973: 42). It is nonetheless true that significant changes to this order occurred over the seventeenth, and especially the eighteenth century. As noted by Raymond Williams (1973), by the eighteenth century some 5000 families owned nearly half of the cultivated land in England, but of these some 400 families, in a population of between seven and eight million people, owned approximately a quarter of this land. The peasantry was no longer a peasantry in the ancient sense of the term, and instead a system of tenant farming and wage-labour had been instituted as part of what Williams describes as an agrarian form of capitalism whose production was structured by an organized market (Williams 1973: 60).

An account of the manifold ways in which agrarian capitalism came to be instituted in England and elsewhere in Europe is beyond the scope of this chapter. However, as I began to note earlier, a key aspect of this process involved the emergence of a modern economy. It is sometimes argued that the eighteenth century was a time when the economy came to be classified as a separate sphere, with a logic of its own: a logic that, in Adam Smith's (1970) famous terms, was driven by the 'invisible hand' of the balance of supply and demand. While it is true that there was a certain classification of this sphere *as* a 'sphere', even a brief analysis of the logic of exchange value, and especially of the role of the Bank of England, reveals the extent to which the new economy was at one and the same time a form of nation-building, and vice versa. The modern was always, and remains, a *political* economy.

This point can be developed by explaining the logic of the commodity, a logic that was once understood critically but which today seems either forgotten or taken for granted. Before the emergence of agrarian capitalism, a very significant portion of economic transactions were premised on a logic of 'use-value': what Karl Marx (1974) famously defined as *the utility of the thing* as actualized in its consumption. The value of any given good was, perforce, its value for a certain task to a certain person or group as it related to the social structuring of the context in which the exchange took place. By the eighteenth century, economic practices premised on use-value had largely been displaced by those premised on exchange-value.

Now exchange-value is often described as the 'quantitative' aspect of the commodity, where 'quantitative' is a reference to the price of the commodity, the 'actualization' of exchange-value. If we accept the conventional account of the nature of the commodity, exchange-value, as represented by the price of something, is in Peirce's terms apparently no more than a rhematic indexical legisign: the price is in a 'real' if conventional relation to its object. But exchange-value was always part of a more complex process inasmuch as it involved (and of course still involves) the accumulation of capital. According to Marx, capital is not just money itself, but money that is used to buy something in order to sell it again. In the new economy, 'capitalism' meant not just giving a price to things and selling them on a market, but doing so in order to accumulate capital. One of Marx's critical contributions to the study of political economy was the insight that the key to the accumulation of capital – the 'end-game' of the new economy – was to capitalize on surplus value. Surplus value could be achieved by selling something at a price that was higher than what was paid for its production, where crucially the difference in price was the result of the exploitation of labour. A capitalist made – and still makes – a profit by turning labour into another commodity, and by paying less for the labour than what it actually 'costs' the labourer. The fetishism of commodities was, in this sense, the process that eventually rendered commodities 'magical' by obscuring this process: the end user ignored the process by which a commodity was both the beginning and the end of a chain of human exploitation.

At the beginning of the eighteenth century, the principles of exchange-value were far from being 'occult' to those that stood to lose the most from them. The blatant injustice of the new economy was made more evident by the fact that, until the end of the seventeenth century, there was still little in the way of a 'universally objective' mechanism for articulating the abstract principles of exchange-value with the requirements of capitalist practice on anything other than a local scale. On the contrary, one of the reasons why Newton intervened in the way that he did was that the existing system of coinage had reached such a crisis as to almost force a return to a bartering system. It was in this context that it became vital to engage in the 'great recoinage' and to establish the supremacy of a *single* coin, one that might provide a 'sound' basis for the new economy even as it raised money for war.

The reference to war brings us to another political dimension of the new economies: their incipient nationalization. With David Held we may provisionally define modern states as *nation-states*: that is, as 'political apparatuses, distinct from the ruler and ruled, with supreme jurisdiction over a demarcated territorial area, backed by a claim to a monopoly of coercive power, and enjoying a minimum level of support or loyalty from their citizens' (Held 1992: 87). This definition, which Held derives from the work of Skinner (1978) and Giddens (1985) (see also Poggi 1978 and 1990), allows us to begin to analyse a number of aspects of the emergence of modern states that were to have direct or indirect consequences for both modern imaginary nature and the material natures of European states and their colonies.

The first of these aspects involves the claim to a monopoly on coercive power as part of a more general context of European war and militarism. Statistics cited by Held suggest a causal relation between waging war and the growth of national European economies. Fighting and funding wars, a practice that was once an everyday matter for European rulers, had a number of consequences for the development of the state. The most pressing and immediate need was to pay for armament and to procure growing numbers of soldiers. This meant in turn that states had to be controlled more effectively as the conflicts grew in intensity and size and as subjects rebelled against the escalating costs of armed conflict between nation states. As Held notes, 'the development and maintenance of a coercive capability was central to the development of the state: if states wished to survive they had to fund this capability and ensure its effectiveness (Held 1992: 93).

If this process had political consequences, it also had an impact on material nature. This could be observed most dramatically in the decimation of forests used to build the navies that the nation-states required to wage war against each other. Richard Grove (1995) notes that as overseas trade grew in importance and volume, and as competition between maritime states grew, so did the number and intensity of naval conflicts. This dynamic led to campaigns to build more and larger ships of the line. By the seventeenth century, the building of a single ship of the line could require a thousand oak trees or more. When the English and other maritime powers depleted their national woodlands, they turned to those of their colonies, frequently with devastating effects on their ecologies.

I shall return to the contexts of European colonies later in this chapter. Here it might be noted that one of the paradoxical effects of the decimation of woodlands in the recently United Kingdom and other European states involved the emergence of the first modern forms of conservationism. In England, the Royal Society, founded in 1662 to promote the new 'science', became a *de facto* 'conservationist' institution in so far as its members lobbied for policies that would better manage the woodlands that were so vital for ship-building. As noted by Grove (1995), these policies were largely ignored by the government, which came under pressure from private interests. A rather different policy was enacted in France, where alarm at the unprecedented levels of deforestation in the early 1660s led to an eight-year moratorium on the felling of trees. It also led to a massive practical and legal survey which culminated in the French Forest Ordinance of 1669. The ordinance, which remained in place until 1827, proclaimed the state's right to regulate the exploitation of forests by private persons (Grove 1995: 59–60).

My account has thus far privileged what can be described as a relatively instrumental account of the emergence of the modern state: the state as an institution that arose, however complexly, in the interests of rulers who needed to control so-called human and natural 'resources' to make war. This account, however, says nothing about the means by which the consent of the newly nationalized subjects was secured, or how it was that such means – such 'mediations' – began to engage in the process of 'massification' that nation-building both required and produced. The research of Robert Muchembled (1985) and of Jesús Martín-Barbero (1993) provides a useful account of the manner in which this process developed in France. Although there were significant differences in the character and timing of this process across different European nations, we may take the events in France as an example of a process that was eventually to take place, with significant local variations, throughout all of Western Europe.

In Chapter 3, I suggested with Martín-Barbero (1993) that the suppression of witchcraft was part of a much broader process of modernization that occurred not only in France but in much of Western Europe. In his *Popular Culture and Elite Culture in France*, Robert Muchembled (1985) further suggests that mass culture – in effect, what I describe as 'massification' and eventually as 'mass mediation' – was born as part of the process whereby the oral and popular cultural traditions associated with witchcraft were systematically suppressed and mostly destroyed. It was in this context that an 'intermediary language' emerged in the form of popular imagery and especially the peddler's literature, which, at the beginning of the seventeenth century, became something of a surrogate for popular culture. It was, in this sense, a good example of the *hegemonic* imposition of a modern culture.

As described by Martín-Barbero (1993), the *Bibliothèque bleue* from Troyes was a kind of pamphlet printed on cheap and grainy paper, which took its name from its blue cover. Its subjects ranged from religious stories to recipes, from scientific texts to love stories, arithmetic tables, almanacs and songs. The Oudot family who owned *La Bibliotèque* used this genre to engage in a process of mass mediation in the sense that they used an army of peddlers and travelling salesmen to scour the country fairs and small villages for stories that might be adapted to the literature even as the same peddlers sold the existing pamphlets. This circuit allowed the family to adapt what was primarily an oral culture to a written culture, and so engaged in what Muchembled (1985) describes as a process of 'acculturation' and what I specify as a non-formal pedagogy: the mass mediation, produced as it was 'from above', nonetheless incorporated elements of the popular cultures whose folklore it represented, and began to teach without teaching the values of a certain modernity – not least, those of what I described with Elizabeth Eisenstein as a culture 'with print'.

This hegemonic process played a role in achieving the vertical and horizontal integration (Muchembled 1985; Martín-Barbero 1993) required by the process of national centralization associated with the new economy and the emergent nation-states. Horizontal integration was imposed as the dominant groups and the institutions with the greatest investment in nation-statism became intolerant of societies made up of regional and popular cultures and of the forms of internal solidarity associated with them, and sought to replace them with forms of solidarity premised on nationalism. The peddler's literature (*colportage*) contributed to this process in so far as it both circulated and produced 'national' stories. But, if horizontal integration involved the imposition of the authority of the nation-state and its economic rules, *vertical* integration involved 'disconnecting' the subjects from the hold of the old patterns of solidarity and 'reconnecting' them to the central authority by way of a variety of mediations. If replacing the old bartering system with a national currency was such one mechanism, the *colportage* constituted another in so far as its stories extolled the virtues of a patriarchal nationalism.

This concept of a patriarchal nationalism requires some elucidation. As noted in Chapter 3, the patriarchal family played a significant role in the institution of new forms of social control. This process acquired a powerful if symbolic echo in so far as the older 'organic' solidarities came to be replaced with forms of solidarity premised on a national image of the state as a 'fatherland' that, ostensibly in the manner of a wise patriarch, ensured the predominance of the public good over private interests and privileges. As noted by Martín-Barbero, state sovereignty thereby came to be a qualisign of 'the "general will" of the people incarnate in the power of the state' (1993: 87).

The symbolism of this process was ambiguous, and was contradicted by the new social formations which it held together. The replacement of the monarchical privileges with a fatherland driven by ostensibly impersonal 'market' forces instituted a new hierarchy of privileges constructed along economic and class lines. But the general will of the *people* was at one and the same time the general will of no *one*. These far-reaching transformations may thus be regarded as forms of symbolic violence, that is, what with the sociologist Pierre Bourdieu (1991) we

83

might describe as a violence with no explicit act of intimidation, a violence that depended on a kind of 'active acceptance' or involvement in the own disempowerment.

This process had wide-ranging, if uneven, implications for imaginary and material nature. Nationalism in France (and indeed elsewhere in Europe) arguably made the way for what would become a kind of explosion of 'local' relations to environments. It nonetheless generated some contradictory responses in the form of conservationist discourses such as those of the Royal Society and the French Forest Ordinance in the second half of the seventeenth century, which I mentioned earlier. But nationalism had at least two additional implications, one of which is perhaps most deeply embedded in the imaginary, and another whose consequences would not be fully understood until the late twentieth century. Since ancient times cultural groups in Europe had, like most other groups throughout the world, articulated their imaginary relations to the environment with reference to maternal images of nature. The modern discourses of nation-statism and capitalism now encouraged an affiliation and identification with the family in the local and 'horizontal' dimension, and with the 'fatherland' in the national and 'vertical' dimension. To use the terms of the social theorist Benedict Anderson (1991), nationalism required its subjects to imagine a national community; but, at least in France, Germany and other nation-states that described themselves as 'fatherlands', this happened in a manner that involved an inversion of the gendering of the 'fundamental category'. The displacement of a maternal imaginary of nature by a paternal imaginary (as expressed in the notion of a 'fatherland') occurred even as European societies reorganized their everyday lives along the lines of modern, familial patriarchy. It does not seem a coincidence that, even as imaginary nature remained gendered as female, the forms of society that would make possible the most concentrated exploitation of material nature were now gendered as 'male'. This inversion replaced, over a period of centuries, a maternal and 'natural' 'first principle', with an 'unnatural' and paternal one; a 'universal mother' was replaced by 'national fathers' even as nature the mother, nature the woman, began to be exploited on a scale hitherto unknown to any civilization.

It is of course possible to overstate the significance of this inversion, and certainly this is not to argue that it was the product of anything like a conspiratorial or instrumental process, or one that was universally effective. It is also true that, in the case of the Romance languages, an ambiguity remained in so far as the notion of fatherland continued to be gendered as female on the level of grammar: *la France*, *la patria*. The scale of the new social structures, and the new classification of public and private interests, ensured that the rulers of nation-states at times failed to entirely impose their control over the most marginalized social groups, but also over the interests of powerful individuals and the emerging corporations that, as early as the eighteenth century, began to compete with the state for power and influence.

Moreover, it would certainly be a mistake to interpret this change alone as having direct, material consequences for the exploitation of material nature. Instead, it seems clear that what was at stake was a complex and multi-layered cultural imaginary, and thereby an equally complex and multi-layered imaginary nature mediated by numerous institutions. The overall dynamic would nonetheless make conceivable relations to nature (and to the own society) that, in another context and at another time, would have been unthinkable.

As I began to note above, the second general implication would have consequences that would not be fully understood until the second half of the twentieth century. Nationalism entailed drawing up geographical boundaries across material natures in such a way as to cause a disjunction between the continuities of natural space (and material nature), and the legisignal discontinuity of national boundaries. One of the effects of this process was that cross-border phenomena of material nature would eventually both 'nationalize' nature – making thinkable the anthropomorphically nationalist, if not racist, notions of 'alien' species or 'foreign invaders' such as are used today to describe weeds and other 'imported' 'pests' – even as it made difficult the development of environmental policies based on the continuity of a habitat or biome. In the name of the sovereignty of the state, forms of exploitation could and would occur in one nation-state that would have consequences for the material natures of other states, but which would elude environmentalist action *thanks to the principle of state sovereignty*.

The new natural histories

I have thus far focussed on what might be described as a culturally and indeed geographically European history. But, if the nature 'at home' was constructed with reference to the discourses, techniques and technologies that I have analysed thus far, it was also constructed with reference to the 'exotic' natures found 'elsewhere', in particular in the European colonies in the Americas, Africa and Asia. By the time that Newton began to reorganize the Bank of England, such a nature had long been a part of a European imaginary nature. It is well documented, for example, that, when Christopher Columbus failed to find the gold that he promised Queen Isabella, his narratives extolled instead the virtues of the geography of the 'New World': 'The land is very remarkable, and in it there are innumerable great rivers and great mountain ranges and lofty mountains. I imagine that the foliage is green all year round' (Columbus 1988: 42). To be sure, it was not just narratives: in order to 'illustrate' his written representations, Columbus and other explorers brought back some of the animals themselves. These might well be described with Peirce as both a dicent sinsign – 'any object of direct experience in so far as it is a sign, and, as such, affords information concerning its Object. This is can only do by being really affected by its Object; so that it is necessarily an Index. The only information it can afford is of actual fact' (CP 2.257) – and a dicent symbol of the exoticism of the 'New World': a sign 'connected with its Object by an association of general ideas, and acting like a Rhematic Symbol, except that its intended interpretant represents the Dicent Symbol as being, in respect to what it signifies, really affected by its Object, so that the existence or law which it calls to mind must be actually connected with the indicated Object' (CP 2.262).

Columbus and other explorers kept largely to the coasts of the land masses they explored. In *Imperial Eyes*, Pratt (1992) suggests that during the first half of the eighteenth century there was a shift from exploration by sea and of shores to the exploration of continental interiors. Pratt notes that during this period natural history maps ceased to be 'the thin track of a route taken, [or] the lines where land and water meet'; instead they became 'the internal "contents" of those land and water masses whose spread made up the surface of the planet. These vast contents would be known not through slender lines on blank paper, so many icons of dubious accuracy, but through verbal representations, in Peirce's terms arguments which were in turn summed up in nomenclatures, or through labelled grids into which entities would be placed (Pratt 1992: 30).

I shall return to the semeiotics of this change below. Here I should note with Pratt that this shift brought about, among other consequences, the emergence of new forms of 'planetary consciousness' – what in the terms used in this book might be described as a new planetary imaginary. Beyond setting precedents for the kind of globalism that many environmentalists would eventually take for granted, the new forms of planetary consciousness began to construct an early sense of what twentieth-century scientists would describe as 'biodiversity'. Each successive voyage brought back 'exotic' specimens that enlarged the increasingly vast if still largely private collections of plants, minerals and, in some cases, animals.

As I noted earlier, voyages of exploration had already brought back iconic sinsigns of nature (and not just of 'nature') as evidence of conquest and the marvellous character of the 'new' lands. But, from the eighteenth century, a modern understanding of the global diversity of flora and fauna began to be framed by the representational contexts generated by the genre of the scientific expedition. Pratt suggests that the first major expedition was headed by the Frenchman Louis Godin in 1735.

The Godin expedition was one of several that set out to find answers to questions posed in the context of what were frequently polemical and more often than not fiercely *nationalistic* debates amongst the newly constituted proto-scientific elites. In the case of the Godin expedition, the question was whether the planet was in fact a perfect sphere (as proposed by Descartes) or a spheroid that was flat at the poles (as proposed by Newton). Two teams were dispatched to measure the longitudinal degree – one went to the northern reaches of Scandinavia, and another to equatorial South America – in order to investigate whether the separation of longitudinal degrees varied in the two parts of the globe.

Like many expeditions that would follow, the Godin expedition was beset by all manner of difficulties, many of which were the result of the lack of familiarity with the visited contexts, but some of which were also to do with squabbling among the explorers themselves. The Godin expedition, for example, was co-opted by the geographer-cum-public-relationist Charles de la Condamine, who eventually managed to have the expedition named after himself. It is thus perhaps unsurprising that, like earlier accounts produced by circumnavigators and coastal explorers, many of the narratives generated by the later voyages continued to be framed from the perspective of the popular genre of 'survival' literature: they told stories of hardship and danger, even as they provided descriptions of the marvels and curiosities of the new worlds (Pratt 1992: 20). As noted by Pratt, the Godin–La Condamine expedition also produced a remarkable assortment of additional literatures: '[o]ral texts, written texts, lost texts, secret texts, texts appropriated, abridged, translated, anthologized, and plagiarized; letters, reports . . . civic description, navigational narrative, monsters and marvels, medicinal treatises, academic polemics, old myths replayed and reversed' (Pratt 1992: 23). These stand as a lively testament to the hybrid nature of scientific expeditions, and reveal the extent to which the hegemony of *mathesis* was far from consolidated.

But, even as the genres of travel literature proliferated, changes began to take place in the context of scientific inquiry that were to establish radically new forms of classifying and framing nature and, with them, new technologies of observation. These require some explanation, as they were to constitute the discursive basis for natural historical description for centuries to come.

In the second half of the eighteenth century, students of the Swedish botanist Carl von Linné (in Latin, Linnaeus) joined several of the scientific expeditions. They set out to provide a new kind of map of the natural world, one that had as its model the Linnaean classificatory principles. These principles initially gave each species a generic name in Latin which it shared with related species, as well as a phrase that briefly described or 'specified' it. Linnaeus later replaced the phrase with a name. This change was apparently prompted by a search for a kind of mnemonic device or memory aid that might enable gentlemen of science (*sic*) to remember the names of plants more easily. Linnaeus' abandonment of the use of phrases in favour of the dyadic system of classification appeared to separate the process of classification from description. In Peirce's terms, Linnaeus replaced explicit arguments with what became rhematic symbols: 'a sign connected with its Object by an association of general ideas in such a way that its Replica calls up an image in the mind which image, owing to certain habits or dispositions of that mind, tends to produce a general concept, and the Replica is interpreted as a Sign of an Object that is an instance of that concept' (CP 2.261). Linnaeus employed this system in 1745 for certain plant species, generalized it to the whole of the plant kingdom in 1753, and finally applied it to the animal kingdom in the tenth edition of his *Systema Naturae* in 1758 (Drouin 1995: 410–11).

At this point it is relevant to return to the analysis offered by Michel Foucault in *The Order of Things* (1970). Foucault suggests that, after the middle of the seventeenth century, the Renaissance *epistéme* was replaced by what he describes as a 'Classical' *epistéme*. It was at this historical moment that natural history emerged as a knowledge, that is, a separate knowledge with its own rules of formation.[2] Foucault expresses the shift in this *epistéme* neatly when he suggests that it was not during this *epistéme* that histories of non-human beings started to be written – Bacon and others had by this time long since written such histories. Rather, it was at this historical juncture that, for the first time, 'History became Natural': a new classification was introduced that distinguished between a history that followed the order of the mark – a history of a plant or animal that included, amongst other aspects, the resemblances that might be found in it, the legends written about it and, of course, its place in heraldry and travellers' tales – and a history of the living being 'itself'.

For example, Jonston's *Natural History of Quadrupeds* omitted all of the aspects concerning marks, and wrote instead about the horse 'itself', that is to say its anatomy, form, habits, birth and death, and this in such a fashion that the horse appeared to have been 'stripped naked' (Foucault 1970: 129). Put differently, the horse now became, or rather appeared to become, a 'rhematic' horse. As I noted earlier, a similar shift may be noted in Linnaeus's system of classification in so far as he dropped even the 'specifying' phrase in favour of the species name, and in favour of a system of tables of classification. The new natural history, Foucault suggests, 'finds its locus in the gap that is now opened up between things and words – a silent gap, pure of all verbal sedimentation, and yet articulated according to the elements of representation, those same elements that can now without let or hindrance be named' (Foucault 1970: 129–30).

It is at this point that signs became representations, in Foucault's specialized sense of 'double representations', a concept that describes one aspect of what I myself refer to as transmediation: double representations are 'representations whose role is to designate representations, to analyse them, to compose and decompose them in order to bring into being within them, together with the system of their identities and differences, the general principles of an order' (Foucault 1970: 221). From a Peircian perspective, it is possible to begin to describe double representations as *double* rhematic symbols, or, were this possible, 'rhematic arguments', arguments that do not seem to be arguments at all.

According to Foucault, natural history was precisely the space opened up by this kind of representation, which implied a form of analysis that was 'anticipating the possibility of naming; it is the possibility of *seeing* what one will be able to *say*, but what one could not say subsequently, or see at a distance, if things and words, distinct from one another, did not, from the very first, communicate in a representation. The descriptive order proposed by Linnaeus, long after Jonston, is very characteristic. According to this order, every chapter dealing with a given animal should follow the following plan: name, theory, kind, species, attributes, use, and, to conclude, *Litteraria*' (Foucault 1970: 130).

Whereas, for the subjects of the previous *epistéme*, the documents produced about the living beings were texts, words or records, in the new they were 'unencumbered spaces in which things are juxtaposed: herbariums, collections, gardens' (Foucault 1970: 131). In such spaces, the different species were presented with no more than individual names, names that were nonetheless the sign of a *de facto* analysis in so far as the names classified each species in accordance with the new discursive regime. Where Columbus and other explorers had produced representations by virtue of simply bringing the plants and animals 'back' to Europe, the new system of classification now had the effect of silently governing, or at any rate attempting to govern, the production of interpretants of plants, animals and other objects by establishing a technology of observation that took a step further in the direction of the double illusion: it was not just that the objects were conceived as being 'in' a 'transparent' space, but that the space might now be transparently, that is, rhematically, 'gridded'.

And indeed Foucault argues that, far from expressing a *new* curiosity about exotic plants and animals, the botanic gardens and zoological collections of the late eighteenth century were a space in which the species acquired a new kind of *visibility*. Whereas up to the Renaissance, the 'strangeness of animals was a spectacle', the Classical period replaced 'the circular procession of the "show" with the arrangement of things in a "table"' (Foucault 1970: 131). Such 'tables' – the analytical tables of the various schemes of classification but, in another paradoxically metaphorical sense, perhaps also the actual displays of the natural history museums that appeared much later, in the mid-nineteenth century – appeared to do little more than make obvious what was already visible:

> Thus arranged and understood, natural history has as a condition of its possibility the common affinity of things and language with representation; but it exists as a task only in so far as things and language happen to be separate. Natural history must therefore reduce this distance between them so as to bring language as close as possible to the observing gaze, and the things observed as close as possible to words. Natural history is nothing more than the nomination of the visible. Hence its apparent simplicity, and that air of naïveté it has from a distance, so simple does it appear and so obviously imposed by things themselves . . . In fact . . . a new field of visibility [was] being constituted in all its density.
>
> (Foucault 1970: 132)

Foucault notes that this field could not be accounted for in terms of a simple notion of scientific progress, that is in terms of some closer, more valid observation of the natural world: 'Natural history did not become possible because men looked harder and more closely'; on the contrary, 'One might say . . . that the Classical age used its ingenuity, if not to see as little as possible, at least to restrict deliberately the area of its experience' (Foucault 1970: 132). All but the visible senses were excluded – a reduction of multisensuality which I began to discuss in Chapter 3 with reference to Galileo – and even the visual was restricted: colours, for example, were left out, leaving a seventeenth-century philosopher-observer with no more than lines, surfaces, reliefs, and other forms in black and white that Foucault describes as 'screened objects' (Foucault 1970: 133).

Now, it would be a mistake to think that the new forms of inquiry put an end to the older circuits of anthropomorphism and the relations of ideology associated with them. While it is true that the new theories interrupted *aspects* of the older relations, the new forms were arguably even more conducive to the ideological naturalization of social divides. The circuit began with narratives that represented the relation between the scientific enterprise and the natural world in terms of a binary of order and disorder, order and chaos. As Pratt explains, 'One by one the

planet's life forms were to be drawn out of the tangled threads of their life surroundings and rewoven into European-based patterns of global unity and order'
(Pratt 1992: 31). Linnaeus, for example, suggested that 'The Ariadne thread in
botany is classification, without which there is chaos' (Linnaeus in Pratt 1992:
25). Putting scientific order in the midst of natural chaos was described not as an
inherently interested activity but rather in terms of a universal, and indeed universalizing, quest for knowledge, one that was strongly classified as being separate
from any material interest. The new science was for the benefit of *mankind* (*sic*).
At the same time, the very idea of exploration was itself premised from the start
on a kind of tabula rasa conception of 'other' geographies. The peoples and lands
of territories across the world remained 'blank' and colonizable so long as no
other imperial or colonial power had studied and/or claimed them. To explore
was, from this perspective, to automatically assume not just the possibility but the
need for 'exploration', a need that bracketed *a priori* the aboriginal groups' right
to self determination.

The voyages of exploration had far-reaching implications not just for the construction of discourses about exoticized 'others', but for the construction of the
European 'selves'. The forms of humanism that emerged during the Renaissance
were contested again and again by the practices of Europeans who deduced from
the 'otherness' of the explored land the otherness of its *people* even as this same
classification was employed to construct the racial superiority of the self, and to
legitimize ongoing conquest.

This dialectic process can be illustrated with reference to the features that Linnaeus ascribed to the six 'varieties' of *Homo sapiens*: where the 'European' was described as being 'Fair, sanguine, brawny; hair yellow, brown, flowing; eyes blue;
gentle, acute, inventive. Covered with close vestments' and 'Governed by laws',
the following was the account of the rest of humanity:

- *Wild Man*. Four-footed, mute, hairy.
- *American*. Copper-colored, choleric, erect. Hair black, straight, thick; nostrils
  wide; face harsh; beard scanty; obstinate, content, free. Paints himself with
  fine red lines. Regulated by customs.
- *Asiatic*. Sooty, melancholy, rigid. Hair black; eyes dark; severe, haughty,
  covetous. Covered with loose garments. Governed by opinions.
- *African*. Black, phlegmatic, relaxed. Hair black, frizzled; skin silky; nose flat,
  lips tumid; crafty, indolent, negligent. Anoints himself with grease. Governed
  by caprice.

(Linnaeus in Pratt 1992: 32)

As Pratt notes, a final category of 'monster' completed this remarkable categorization.

The consequences of such representations were not merely 'discursive': the discourse both produced and combined with practices that had bodily implications

for those subjected by the explorers. From La Condamine to Darwin and beyond, each scientific voyage employed slave labour or, eventually, guides and porters who were forced to work for a pittance and in conditions that frequently led to death by illness or exhaustion, or execution on the grounds of insubordination.

It is possible to agree then with Pratt (1992) that, far from being an 'innocent' and 'universal' quest, the institution of a new imaginary of nature by the explorer-scientists was part of a process of modernization that complexly promoted the interests of white, European, bourgeois men. Then as now, the explorer-scientists promoted an image of the relation between science and nature that radically de-politicized it by suggesting that the exploration of nature had no other aim than to widen the knowledge of 'mankind', a patriarchal term that was conceived as a generous abstract singular in some contexts, but in others – particularly those that involved the material procedures of exploration – continued to establish a very clear classification between those thought to be worthy and unworthy of a 'humanist' disposition.

The Edenic Isles

My account has thus far emphasized what might be described as an 'extractive' logic: a European nature constructed both by 'exporting' European discourses about nature, and by 'importing' the material nature from European colonies. However, a rather different logic existed with some of the colonies, one that argu-ably constituted the beginning, if not of an 'environmentalist' sensibility, then cer-tainly of a 'proto-environmentalist' disposition. Here as elsewhere in this book, I shall use the expression 'proto-environmentalist' to distinguish the practices from environmentalism, *sensu stricto*.[3]

As I noted earlier with Grove (1995), during the seventeenth century, efforts were made in Great Britain, France and elsewhere to conserve the forests that were being destroyed by the ship-building industry. Especially in Great Britain, these efforts were undermined by private interests, but also by the possibility of *exporting* environmental destruction: as noted by Grove (1995), the British colonies, most notably the region of New England, were used to procure the timber required for the warships. It might be inferred from this process that the environmental economy of empire was entirely unidirectional from the point of view of the depletion of natural resources, with the 'centre' destroying the natural resources of the 'periphery'. Certainly this is true of some contexts. But, as noted by Grove, the history of 'green imperialism' is more complex than this account suggests, especially where the tropical island colonies are concerned.

According to Grove, such colonies constituted a particularly significant ge-ography from the perspective of what I have described as imaginary nature. On the one hand, the tropical islands constituted a utopian geography for European colonizers; European philosophers, playwrights, poets, but also persecuted reli-gious groups such as the Huguenots, projected Arcadian and Edenic arguments onto the islands, and thereby classified them as sacred spaces, qualisigns of positive alterity. Grove suggests that, by the seventeenth and eighteenth centuries, such images had become so widely accepted that paradise had become 'a recognizable geographical reality' (Grove 1995: 51) for European travellers.

But the islands also had a more obviously practical significance to oceanic explorers, one that contradicted, or rendered ambivalent, their status as qualisigns of Eden. Tropical islands were frequently the sites where water and provisions were obtained after lengthy voyages. But, as Grove notes, they could pose some of the same problems found on the ships themselves: for example, a scarcity of edible materials and drinking water, and squabbles about leadership. Moreover, the geographically circumscribed character of islands, and thereby their more easily surveyable nature, made the impact of human activities more evident. An idealizing discourse about tropical islands as Edenic havens was thus frequently contradicted by direct evidence that Eden was at risk.

One example of this phenomenon could be found on the island of Mauritius, which came under French rule from 1722 to 1790. During this period, it became the scene for what Grove describes as 'the flowering of a complex and unprecedented environmental policy' (Grove 1995: 168). If in early travellers' accounts the island was commended for being full of wild trees, birds so tame they might be taken in the hand, and verdant mountains that were 'extremely delightful to the eye' (Grove 1995: 44), by the 1760s, administrators on the island (and indeed in other colonial outposts) noted that there was a relationship between deforestation and climatic change. In 1766, for example, the Duke of Praslin, a French minister, wrote a letter with instructions for Daniel Dumas and Pierre Poivre, who were about to take up posts as governor and 'intendant' respectively. In his letter, the Duke said that the new colonial administrators faced, among other challenges, the problems generated by climate change:

> If the forests do not regenerate in the island rain will be less frequent and the overexposed soil will be burnt by the sun . . . timber should be given particular attention. Complaints have been made that suggest that this very important matter has not been given all the care and attention which it deserves. Mssrs. Dumas and Poivre should hasten to control it with a good policy; they will examine existing regulations on this subject, study the exact condition of the forests, exploit them and utilise them in the most economical way possible and only allow people to cut them if they ensure their conservation.
>
> (quoted in Grove 1995: 184–5)

The Duke's letter provides evidence that at least a local relation between deforestation and climate change was already understood by the second half of the eighteenth century. But it also provides evidence that the environmentalist 'gentlemen of science' – most notably botanists and surgeons – had been successful in lobbying the French government and in persuading some of its members of the significance of this relation. Similar dynamics took place elsewhere in the French empire, and indeed Grove suggests that, during this period, scientists were able to manipulate governments with fears of local environmental disaster.

Grove argues that the interventions of such proto-scientists undermine the arguments put forward by feminist historians like Carolyn Merchant. He suggests that, while such arguments are 'superficially attractive', they contain a 'major flaw': 'In particular, the growing interest in mechanistic analysis and comparison actually enabled rational and measured observations of environmental change, as well as encouraging an organised conservationist response' (Grove 1995: 51).

By raising this question, Grove rightly directs us to the possibility of a certain continuity between mechanistic notions of science and nature, and the kinds of practices that would eventually come to be known as forms of environmentalism. But such a critique must not lead to the opposite conclusion: that there was no *discontinuity* between the different discursive formations and their associated practices. On the one hand, the notion that the emerging scientific disciplines encouraged an organized conservationist response almost certainly requires qualification; had this been universally the case, then we might well expect all scientists, then as now, to encourage such a response, but history shows otherwise. On the other hand, as exemplified in Newton, it seems clear that two or more conflicting coding orientations might well coexist within one subject, or indeed one individual. Grove's own account suggests the possibility that the subjects of what I have described as a proto-environmentalist discourse themselves experienced such a 'split' identity. We might further explain this dynamic, in Newton's case and in all those where there was a limited incorporation of competing interests, as a form of *hegemonic* practice. In keeping with this view, it is possible to argue that older or competing conceptions of nature were not simply replaced or displaced by the dominant modern institutions and their subjects; some aspects were incorporated as part of the predominant imaginary even as others were suppressed. Grove himself makes the case that, however much some European proto-environmentalists adhered to mechanistic scientific traditions that allowed them to engage in precise and detailed observations of environmental changes, some also had learned from the models of environmental management that they had come across during travels in India, China and elsewhere. This was particularly true for Poivre, who travelled to China, where he acquired a working knowledge of Chinese and probably learned about Chinese texts on the relationship between denudation, erosion and flooding (Grove 1995: 186–7). Grove also notes the influence of physiocracy, a mid-seventeenth century discourse whose subjects advocated the pre-eminence of agriculture (as it was just starting to be called) over commerce and trade. He also suggests that there is some evidence that Poivre's environmentalism was mediated by his belief in the precepts of Zoroastrianism (Grove 1995: 193), a religion that was dominant in the Persian empires from the fifth century BC to the seventh century AD. Last but not least, Grove also notes that, had Poivre not rejected the predominant 'degeneracy' theories that constructed non-European cultures as being 'degenerate' versions of the white, Northern European societies – a theory that, as noted earlier, had Linnaeus as one of its advocates – it is doubtful that his practice could have appropriated the discourses of 'other' cultures. We find then, in Grove's own work, the elements with which to explain both a degree of continuity and difference in the discourses of proto-environmentalists like Poivre with respect to the mechanistic imaginary.

Picturesque enclosure

If proto-environmentalists struggled to preserve the 'Edenic Isles', those who benefited most from the 'new economy' sought to create their own *pastoral* ideals 'back home'. In England in particular, the growing differences in the distribution of wealth enabled the landed gentry to invest fabulous sums in the creation of idealized landscapes in their estates. During the eighteenth and early nineteenth centuries, the gardens in such estates, and the paintings commissioned by their owners, were to play a major role in defining what counted as nature. At the same time, the creation of massive landscaped estates was to play a part in helping to make available the 'disposable labour' that would be required by industrial capitalism.

In her classic *Landscape and Ideology*, a study of the social construction of the English landscape, Anne Bermingham (1986) suggests that the 'disposable' labour required by the new economy in England was made available by the invention of the very landscape that many still regard as the epitome of a gentle or pastoral nature: the 'picturesque' nature of the English countryside, Blake's 'green and pleasant land'. The production of such a landscape was itself a matter of a political economy. A key aspect of this economy involved the enclosure of common lands. As noted by Raymond Williams, enclosure had been taking place in the British Isles since at least the thirteenth century, and had reached a first peak in the fifteenth and sixteenth centuries (Williams 1973: 96). It is a myth that enclosure only took place shortly before the industrial revolution. Williams nonetheless recognises what he describes as the 'critical importance' of the period of parliamentary enclosures, which took place from the second quarter of the eighteenth century to the first quarter of the nineteenth, and which allowed landowners to appropriate more than six million acres of land by means of some 4000 acts (Williams 1973: 96).

What changed during the period of parliamentary enclosures was that, as the term suggests, they were backed by the authority of the state. According to Bermingham, until the middle of the seventeenth century English monarchs opposed the enclosure of common land as a strategy to curb the power of feudal landowners. However, the late seventeenth century and especially the eighteenth saw a growing demand for food and other agricultural goods in the market towns. At the same time, landowners became more ambitious and put pressure on the monarchy to allow them to enclose lands. The crown and the parliament responded by passing the now infamous 'acts of enclosure' that gave the gentry the right to claim as their own commonly owned, or at least communally shared, lands known as 'the commons'.

As part of this process, landowners employed fences and fast-growing shrubs such as the hawthorn to enclose the commons by dividing them into fields. Bermingham notes that, if by the first half of the eighteenth century some 70,000 or so acres had been enclosed by act of parliament, by the second half that figure had increased tenfold, to some 750,000 acres. Enclosure allowed the landed gentry to institute the rudiments of a rural economy of scale. These changes, as linked to improved agricultural techniques, greatly increased agricultural yield of the still primarily local economies even as the search for larger and larger markets tied them to increasingly distant markets. This meant that a rural production cycle that was still strongly shaped by the vicissitudes of the weather and other natural or at least relatively local cycles became increasingly dependent on the 'boom and bust' cycles of capitalism. Over-production, or collapsing demand for products in lands never visited or even imagined by the labourers and tenant farmers, increasingly came to drive their agricultural fortunes, not just throughout England and Britain, but throughout Europe and the colonized world.

Bermingham notes, for example, that between 1790 and 1815 two million acres of land were enclosed for cultivation as part of an agricultural boom brought about by the latest English war with France. This war initially had the effect of producing an economic boom in Britain. However, after Waterloo, agricultural commodity prices that had been inflated by the war collapsed, leading to mass unemployment and a dramatic depopulation of rural areas as the new agricultural proletariat – what would be described by the middle classes as the 'great unwashed', 'the mob' (a shortened version of the Latin *mobile vulgus*) (Williams 1983) and later 'the masses' – left for the cities in search of employment.

It might be expected that representations produced during this period would have been devoted to portraying this 'upheaval' in the countryside, and indeed some media and some genres, such as journals devoted to farming practices, did just that. However, two genres that were to play a very significant role in the institution of imaginary nature for centuries to come were remarkable in that they constructed an imaginary nature that virtually ignored the social transformations I have just outlined: landscape gardens and landscape paintings. Indeed, at a time of extraordinary upheaval, they promoted a predominantly 'gentle' – in the sense of a 'gentlemanly' – image of a 'picturesque' nature apparently undisturbed by human activity and strife. I shall now consider each of the genres in turn.

The history of grand English gardens pre-dates the period considered in this chapter, namely the end of the seventeenth century to the beginning of the nineteenth. It is possible, for example, to find a small treatise on gardening written by Francis Bacon. Bacon's essay, published in 1625, suggested that 'God Almighty planted a garden. And indeed it is the purest of human pleasures. It is the greatest refreshment to the spirits of man; without which, buildings and palaces are but gross handiworks.' During the early seventeenth century, the landed gentry in the British Isles seized enthusiastically on the idea of conveying wealth and power by means of formal gardens modelled along the lines of French and Dutch rationalism. Such gardens were very clearly distinguished from surrounding landscape, and emphasized lines and geometry – a kind of garden *mathesis* based on a rationalist imaginary of nature. The gardens were themselves, in this sense, iconic legisigns of the virtues of *mathesis*.

Their overall structure was premised on what Bermingham describes as a single 'axial' view from the house (Bermingham 1986: 12), and their design posited a relatively immobile and central observer. In this sense, if the classification of the garden as a 'space apart' was very strong, the perceptual and conceptual space, if not the lived space of the garden, was based on an equally strongly framed mode of observation: the garden was meant to be viewed as an entirety, but this entirety could only be viewed from one place: a window or balcony in the house itself.

A certain parallel can be drawn between the immobile observer in linear perspective and the observer in the formal garden. In both technologies of observation, the production of a certain spatiality must have presumed Lefebvre's 'double illusion': the gardens were, conceptually at least, an 'empty' space in which objects might be rearranged according to the whims of designers inspired by the illusion of transparency and the realist illusion: a space was designed to illustrate, 'without words', the natural complexity – that is to say the complex 'naturality' – of geometrical forms. As in Brunelleschi's scenographic experiments, the observation would have presupposed not an absence, as suggested by Damisch's analysis, but a *presence*, the co-presence of the observer and the observed.

Of course, no natural space is ever a 'tabula rasa' in so far as the materiality of the topography enables some transformations even as it prohibits, or makes difficult, others. To be sure, in the case of forms of representation that involve organic objects such as flora or other dynamic aspects of natural space, the design process is never completely controlled, or indeed 'complete'. One of the reasons typically – and somewhat misleadingly – invoked to explain the shift from the 'mathematical' garden to the landscape garden is that formal gardens required an extraordinary amount of labour in order to be kept 'geometrical'.

In fact, this was just one of the several motivations for a change in semeiotic that took place towards the end of the seventeenth century and determined the shape of most stately gardens until the early nineteenth century. During this period, the English landscape garden became, as its name suggests, an apparently boundless 'landscape'. W.J.T. Mitchell (1994) suggests that a landscape is 'a natural scene mediated by culture. It is both a represented space and a presented space, both a signifier and a signified, both a frame and what a frame contains, both a real place and its simulacrum, both a package and the commodity inside the package' (Mitchell 1994: 5). I suggest that Peirce actually offers a more useful vocabulary with which to conceptualize landscape. It is possible to describe a landscape in the first instance as a dicent sinsign and indeed as a rheme, a sign that 'is said to represent its object in its characters merely' (CP 2.252), one that 'leaves its Object, and *a fortiori* its Intepretant, to be what it may' (CP 2.95). But perhaps the more interesting feature of landscapes is their character as instances of what Peirce described in terms of 'entelechy': 'perfect signs', or signs for which the physical materiality of the object constitutes at once its own representamen and, to some extent at least, its interpretant. This last qualification is important because of course, landscapes come to be associated with certain qualisigns, and as such may become rhematic or even dicent *symbols*. It is more accurate in this sense to say that a landscape – or indeed any other material nature that is an instance of 're/presentation' – constitutes an entelechy until that moment when its rhematic interpretants begin to be questioned, and when the silent symbolism that 'goes' with a certain interpretation of landscape begins to become explicit. Even then, there is arguably a sense in which entelechy remains: the landscape, however it is interpreted, in to some extent still *that* landscape, just as an animal in a zoo (see Chapter 5) is still *that* animal.

From the late seventeenth century onwards, landscape gardens maintained their rhematic character as 'perfect landscapes' by way of a series of conventions. A succession of famous landscape gardeners such as William Kent, Lancelot 'Capability' Brown and Humphry Repton – themselves a sign of an increasingly specializing class structure – replaced the ornate, 'artificial' and intimate spaces of the formal gardens with 'naturalistic' gardens. The new modality of framing was produced by a variety of means. There was a new emphasis on large sweeping lawns framed by the occasional tree, or 'wood', and the outer boundaries of the perimeter were dissimulated with ha-has. Ha-has were sunken ditches that established a perimeter even as they promoted the illusion of an unbounded garden. In the largest gardens, ha-has were not really necessary. Whereas the theories of French formal gardens dictated that the garden should be no more than 30 or 40 acres in size, Bermingham suggests that by mid-century this size was the norm for the English landscape garden, and indeed by the 1760s some gardens had lakes this size. This meant that, beyond being qualisigns of wealth and prestige, such gardens had the capacity to produce simulations of an idealized countryside on a scale unknown to earlier generations. The landscaped garden thereby became something akin to a total space in which one could be *immersed*.

As begins to become evident in this description, the changing forms of landscape both assumed and produced qualitatively new ways of observing and experiencing the landscape. Where the Dutch and French formal gardens almost prohibited their own use – except as mainly *visual* experiences, and this from a height and from afar – the English landscape garden was 'a series of multiple oblique views that were meant to be experienced as one walked through it' (Bermingham 1986: 12). Though every bit as contrived as the formal garden – as I suggested earlier, here too there was a legisignical dimension – the English landscape garden was far more weakly classified *as* a garden in so far it gave the rhematic *impression* of unconstrained freedom, a freedom to wander through its meandering clearings and to 'discover' new windings. Although it would be a conceptual error to conflate what I described with Lefebvre as perceived, conceived and lived space, the design of the different gardens actually suggests a deliberate conflation of these different 'levels'. Bermingham argues that, echoing perhaps the predominant philosophical vogues amongst the English elites, the relatively rationalist aesthetic of the Dutch and the French designers gave way to a more empiricist and even 'Newtonian' aesthetic, one that Bermingham notes had to be experienced not just with the eye but metaphorically by 'trial and error' and indeed by physically moving through the whole space.

The naturalism of the gardens was thus one that attempted to link the realist criteria for a certain conception of space with naturalistic criteria for its actual organization and experience. As suggested by Gunther Kress and Theo Van Leeuwen, every realism has its naturalism: 'realism is a definition of what counts as real, a set of criteria for the real, and it will find its expression in the "right", the best, the (most) "natural" form of representing that kind of reality, be it a photograph or a diagram' (1996: 163). With Peirce's triadic model of the sign, I suggest that the naturalism of any given representation may be articulated as a matter of an ascribed correspondence between the representamen or representation itself, the object of representation, and its interpretant. Naturalism, from this perspective, involves social judgement and prescription in so far as an observer must frame the relation between the three aspects of a sign of nature as being more or less continuous. Put differently, naturalism entails a judgement in regard to the degree of continuity or discontinuity between the 'natural' object of representation, the representamen and the interpretant. When an observer judges that a representation is 'naturalistic', then s/he assumes that it preserves a strong degree of correspondence between these three elements.

Two points should be clarified with respect to this account of naturalism. First, the account preserves *both* the possibility of correspondence as a matter of social ascription *and* the possibility of an indexical relation between the object and the representamen that cannot be reduced to social or cultural 'ascription'. Second, while the doctrine of naturalism is associated with a tradition of painting that dates back to the seventeenth and eighteenth centuries, it is possible to employ the term more generally to describe the sense of naturalism produced by any medium of representation, including the landscape garden.

There are few better documented examples of the transformations involved in landscape gardens than the one found in the gardens at Stowe, an estate located halfway between Oxford and present-day Milton Keynes. Images of Stowe reveal the transformation of the country home of Sir Richard Temple (1675–1749), an English general during the war with France, and the first of three generations of extraordinarily wealthy gentry who benefited from a combination of strategic marriages and the benevolent disposition of the crown.

Initially, Sir Richard Temple's garden was a 'continental' garden dominated by axial designs, with several lakes as well as over fifty buildings or 'temples' that he added to it (the expression 'temple' neatly echoed the family name and motto, 'Templa Quam Dilecta' – Clarke 1992: 502).[4] But in 1712, Joseph Addison, an English poet, essayist and politician – and indeed a kind of self-styled garden critic – famously issued what became in effect a fashion edict in the magazine *The Spectator* against the more formal style of gardens: 'For my own part, I would rather look upon a Tree in all its Luxuriancy and Diffusion of boughs and Branches, than when it is thus cut and trimmed into a Mathematical Figure' (in Clarke 1992: 504). Addison was expressing what must have been a broader change in the imaginary of nature, one that in some ways heralded a romantic imaginary of nature.

The effects of this change on Stowe were dramatic. In response to the change in fashion – a change in the interpretants used to judge gardening – the Temples ordered their gardeners to dig up walkways and replant trees, to dismantle or remove entire buildings (Clarke 1992: 504). Indeed, in the period of some 100 or so years that followed, the grounds went through a process of nearly constant adjustment and revision to match the changing interpretants. By the end of the first decade of the nineteenth century, the gardens were almost unrecognizable. The axial designs were replaced by a set of rolling lawns bordered by curving lakes and 'woods', and the 'artificial' garden had been replaced by a 'natural' landscape. Marx famously suggested that one of the hallmarks of modern culture was that 'all that is solid melts in the air', and indeed an early version of this maxim may be witnessed in what might be described as the 'conspicuous consumption' at Stowe.

This process had an unexpected effect on the less mediated forms of landscape that surrounded the estates: Bermingham notes that 'as the real landscape began to look increasingly artificial, like a garden, the garden began to look increasingly natural, like the pre-enclosed landscape. Thus a natural landscape became the prerogative of the estate, allowing for a conveniently ambiguous signification, so that nature was the sign of property and property the sign of nature' (1986: 14). Here again, it is possible to witness a circuit of anthropomorphism: even as nature was culturalized into the forms preferred by the landed gentry, it arguably served to cosmomorphize and thereby naturalize the social transformations which the design of the gardens dissimulated.

Landscape gardening was paralleled in the practice of painting by the great English 'picturesque' tradition of landscape painting that extended from the early 1700s to the mid-1800s, and included such famous painters as Gainsborough, Constable and Turner. Like the landscape gardens, virtually all landscape paintings in this tradition suppressed references to the agricultural revolution that was taking place in the English countryside during the eighteenth and early to mid-nineteenth centuries. At a time when the agricultural press described the changes in great detail – enclosure, new techniques for planting and harvesting, employment of a new rural proletariat – the landscape paintings failed to represent the changes (Prince 1988: 98).

Instead, the paintings represented themes that not only bracketed changes in the productive forces but made the landscape seem 'timeless', in Peirce's terms, a matter of endless pastoral firstness. Hugh Prince's (1988) selection of paintings in his essay 'Art and Agrarian Change, 1710–1815' provides a useful survey of the tendencies of the period. An outdoor 'conversation piece' such as the famous

Mr and Mrs Andrews by Thomas Gainsborough (1748)[5] depicted the gentry taking their leisure on their land.[6] In Prince's interpretation, 'the picture extols the present and prospective satisfactions of landownership and attendant possessions, offering a life of contented ease, a comely wife, fine clothes, broad acres, a bounteous harvest, an obedient hound at heel and the promise of good shooting ahead' (Prince 1988: 103). Some fourteen years later, Richard Wilson's Arcadian *The Thames at Twickenham* (1762)[7] depicted pastoral scenes of rivers and landscaped fields and woods. According to Prince, this painting made use of principles of composition associated with the landscape painter Claude Lorrain: 'contemplative figures in the foreground, the stream leading the eye sinuously towards a sylvan skyline, a villa half hidden by trees'. In this case the effect was intended to transport the viewer not to the Roman Campagna (a subject favoured by Claude) but to a 'timeless' English landscaped garden (1988: 105). In the first decade of the following century, Turner's *Ploughing up Turnips near Slough* (1809)[8] offered an image of labourers in fields, but represented labour in ways that associated the gruelling work with the construction of nationhood and 'intimations of Claude's golden age' (Prince 1988: 108). Whereas Turner's painting hinted at a problematic link between work and country, work and nobility, John Constable's *Landscape, Ploughing Scene in Suffolk* (1814)[9] concealed all explicit signs of landownership: 'no boundary of private property can be detected, no Palladian villa or royal castle emerges above the trees, no sign of a landlord's improvement is to be seen, no gentleman rides across his fields' (Prince 1988: 111). Prince offers a similar critique of George Robert Lewis' *Hereford from Haywood Lodge* (1815)[10]: aside from seven rectilinear intakes visible on the distant hills to the right of the picture, there was little evidence in the painting of modern farming methods. On the contrary, Prince argues that 'Lewis perceptively recognised that he had found nearly the right place at almost the right time to mirror a comforting early eighteenth-century ideal of a Georgical landscape, a landscape in which the fertility of the soil and the efforts of the cultivator united to yield a good harvest and a measure of satisfaction to the harvesters' (Prince 1988: 113).

Why was agricultural change excluded from the paintings (and indeed from the gardens) themselves? Prince argues that the answer can be found in the tastes and social position of large landowners, who he suggests were the principal patrons of landscape paintings. 'Landowners,' Prince suggests, 'did not want pictures of new enclosures or new machines or new farmsteads and they certainly did not think of themselves as transforming the countryside. They were not in the business of revolutionising rural society. On the contrary, they saw their role as pillars of stable communities and their efforts were devoted to securing and perpetuating their position at the top of the social hierarchy' (Prince 1988: 115).

Valid as these observations may be on the level of the immediate or dynamic object of the paintings, it is necessary to return to Bermingham (1986) in order to better understand a social semeiotic dimension of this naturalism. According to Bermingham, the late eighteenth-century taste for nature and the natural culminated in the 1790s during what became known as the 'picturesque decade'. The notion of the picturesque applied both to landscape and to paintings, and was indeed defined in circular reference to the two practices: 'Applied to landscape, the term *picturesque* referred to its fitness to make a picture; applied to pictures, the term referred to the fidelity with which they copied the picturesque landscape' (Bermingham 1986: 57). This account of the picturesque may be understood not simply as a 'tautological' or circular logic – the picturesque garden is one worthy of being painted, and the picturesque painting is one that is a faithful reproduction of the picturesque landscape – but as a relatively explicit process of 'adjustment' to what was itself a relatively explicit qualisign: the ideal of super-valued stability, a sense of timelessness and the lack of change in a land in the midst of enormous social transformations.

But it may also be regarded as another form of 'double representation'. Of course, all representations must necessarily be referred to other representations – other interpretants – in order to be meaningful. What is striking about the notion of the painterly was the extent to which it explicitly established the parameters of reference between two genres which, in Lefebvre's terms, worked equally hard to dissimulate the link between the double illusion of transparency and realism, on the one hand, and the relations established in social space, on the other. From this perspective, the 'picturesque' tradition was a late eighteenth-century form of transmediation. As such, it was also an early instance of one of the characteristic motivations for transmediation within a capitalist society: the dissimulation of material social relations by way of an apparently rhematic reference to an apparently unmediated world, but in fact a world legisigned by many of the same codes governing the first or 'original' context.

Rousseau's technology of the self

Today, landscape gardens are frequently referred to as 'romantic' gardens. In the mid-eighteenth century, Jean-Jacques Rousseau began publishing essays that constituted something of a watershed in European conceptions of nature, and of society more generally. Rousseau's *Discourse on the Sciences and Arts* (1750) argued that, even if an elite of learned men was necessary to provide advice to rulers, the more widespread dissemination of knowledge led to the corruption of people. In the *Discourse on the Origins and Foundation of Inequality* (1755) he put forward his now famous argument in favour of what became known as the 'noble savage': the notion of the human that, prior to civilization, might be 'stupid', but would be content with self-preservation and would show compassion to her/his fellow humans. In effect, Rousseau attacked aspects of the Enlightenment for advocating the dissemination of scientific knowledge for its own sake. In *Émile*, Rousseau suggested that humans are born sensitive and with a disposition – the disposition of the habit of nature – before this disposition is corrupted by society. The educational process should thereby be conducive to ensuring a harmony between these natural tendencies. According to Rousseau, existing forms of education failed to do so; 'forced to combat either nature or the social institutions', society was in turn forced to choose between making 'a man or a citizen' (Rousseau 1979a: 39).

While Rousseau's account of society was in some respects as pessimistic as Hobbes', he contested Hobbes' suggestion that ferocious competition and greed were natural traits. From Rousseau's perspective, they were *social* traits, and indeed in his later writing Rousseau became the advocate of what was to become one of the hallmarks of the romantic sensibility for nature, one that was premised on an individualized enjoyment of nature, a kind of 'return' to nature that might enable individuals to escape the corruption of civilization and arrive at a more authentic experience of the self.

This disposition is particularly evident in the Fifth Walk of *Reveries of a Solitary Walker* (1979b), in which Rousseau remembers an idyllic stay on the island of Saint-Pierre in Lake Bienne, Switzerland. Having recently had his house stoned by a group of residents in Motiers near Neuchatel – Rousseau's revolutionary views had caused great controversy and led to his persecution – Rousseau decided to leave the life of books and to devote himself to botany and reverie in what he described as a place 'fascinating for those solitary dreamers who love to drink deeply of the beauty of nature and to meditate in a silence which is unbroken but for the cry of eagles, the occasional song of birds and the roar of streams cascading down from the mountains' (Rousseau 1979b: 81). Armed with a copy of Linnaeus's *Systema Naturae*, Rousseau spent a period devoted to the observation of the 'sexual parts' of plants, and also to a kind of absolute day-dreaming: one of his favourite ways of doing so was to row out into the lake when the water was calm and to let himself 'float and drift wherever the water took me, often for several hours on end, plunged in a host of vague yet delightful reveries' (Rousseau 1979b: 85).

Another place for such reveries was on the shore:

> As evening approached, I came down from the heights of the island, and I liked then to go and sit on the shingle in some secluded spot by the edge of the lake; there the noise of the waves and the movement of the water, taking hold of my senses and driving all other agitation from my soul, would plunge it into a delicious reverie . . . The ebb and flow of the water, its continuous yet undulating noise . . . taking the place of all the inward movements which my reverie had calmed within me, and it was enough to make me pleasurably aware of my existence, without troubling myself with thought.
>
> (Rousseau 1979b: 86–87)

Several aspects of Rousseau's experiences and narrative are significant to the institution of imaginary nature. On the one hand, they are an exemplar of the kind of idealization of nature that was to become one of the hallmarks of modern discourses of nature, and of romantic discourses in particular. We can suggest, in this sense, that Rousseau was a precursor of the Romantic movement. Of course, as Raymond Williams (1983) has noted, the very notion of a Romantic *movement* did not come to be used as a general classification until the 1880s, and indeed over the last decades a number of scholars have taken turns to caution that the terms 'romantic' and 'romanticism' have changing meanings across national boundaries, media of expression and historical periods. It nonetheless seems quite clear that already in Rousseau we find the characteristic rejection of enlightenment values, in the form of a paradoxical rejection of books (Rousseau makes much of leaving his own books in boxes, even as he walks the island with *Systema Naturae* and then *writes* about the reverie). There is also a rejection, despite the study of the 'sexual parts' and structures of the plants, of the spaces and times of observation associated with mechanism. In this sense, Rousseau could not be more different from Newton; where the latter devotes his time to the study of minting and the persecution of forgers, the former makes a deliberate effort to forgo the intense attention associated with modern, or at any rate modernizing, forms of observation. Nature might be studied, but it was also a place for *reverie*. In Rousseau's work, reverie is close to the times and spaces, or rather the apparent *absence* of time and space, associated with firstness, i-mediacy.

In the Second Walk, Rousseau makes a telling comment: immediately after having suffered a serious accident with a horse-drawn carriage and the massive Great Dane that is running with it, he regains consciousness and says that he saw

> the night coming on. I saw the sky, some stars, and a few leaves. This first sensation was a moment of delight. I was conscious of nothing else . . . Entirely taken up by the present, I could remember nothing; I had no distinct notion of myself as a person, nor had I the least idea of what had just happened to me.
>
> (Rousseau 1979b: 39)

This is matched by the passage quoted earlier that the ebb and flow of the water 'was enough to make me pleasurably aware of my existence, without troubling myself with thought', and indeed by another comment about the temporality of happiness: 'But if there is a state where the soul can find a resting-place secure enough to establish itself and concentrate its entire being there, with no need to remember the past or reach into the future, where the present goes on indefinitely but no duration is noticed', then such a state is one in which there is 'no sign of the passing time', 'no other feeling . . . than the simple feeling of existence' (Rousseau 1979b: 88). If the mechanists had privileged the nature of secondness, the romantics would now privilege a nature of firstness, and indeed firstness more generally. This is, at any rate, one way of characterizing a romantic *structure of feeling*, a concept that Raymond Williams employs to speak of a lived present, the 'characteristic elements of impulse, restraint, and tone; specifically affective elements of consciousness and relationships: not feeling against thought, but thought as felt and feeling as thought: practical consciousness of a present kind' (Williams 1977: 132). In this context, the structure in question was itself characterized by a 'meta-feeling', by what might be described with Peirce as the pursuit of natural qualisigns of feeling itself.

Now this structure of feeling, to which I shall return in the following chapters, can be said to mark a significant challenge to the mechanism that was to underpin industrialization. The structure of feeling nevertheless shared what I described in the introductory chapter as a 'nocturnal' connection to capitalism in so far as it was also characterized by an individualized and individualizing account of the relation to nature. Rousseau's use of nature – and it really *was* a 'use' – was also romantic in the sense that it treated nature as a space in which to develop what can be described with Michel Foucault as a 'technology of the self': a way of permitting individuals 'to effect by their own means or with the help of others a certain number of operations on their own bodies and souls, thoughts, conduct, and way of being, so as to transform themselves in order to attain a certain state of happiness, purity, wisdom, perfection, or immortality' (Foucault 1988: 18). This turn of imaginary nature towards the construction of the self was eventually to constitute one of the most characteristic aspects of the modern imaginary of nature, the one that perhaps most clearly prepared the social semeiotic terrain for the advent of a fully modern environmentalist imaginary. And yet, at the same time, and paradoxically, the same technology of the self arguably situated this imaginary in the bounds of the forms of subjectivity associated with the most advanced forms of capitalism. If it is true, as Huck Gutman (1988) suggests, that Rousseau's 'psyche' played a central role in the development of a modern subject *as subject* (Gutman 1988: 105), then it is possible to suggest that imaginary nature, as experienced by Rousseau and all those who shared in a similar circuit of anthropomorphism, became another site in which capitalism was reproduced even as it was contested. Rousseau and his followers at once individualized nature (anthropomorphism) and found an echo of individualization 'in' nature (cosmomorphism). This form of romanticism, or proto-romanticism, was thus to lay the semeiotic ground for a profoundly ambivalent relation to nature, one that was at once intensely critical of mechanism but also part and parcel of the most advanced forms of capitalist culture.

5

THE NATURE OF INDUSTRIALIZATION

A working landscape is hardly ever a landscape.

Raymond Williams

Urbanity

Rousseau sought refuge in the nature of the island of Saint-Pierre. Even when he was in Paris, he sought to walk in the surrounding countryside. His predilection for a rural nature constituted another precedent for the Romantic movement: in the work of many of the romantic authors that continued Rousseau's reveries, nature came to be ineluctably associated with the countryside.

If the Romantics played a key role in instituting this classification, so did the broader social reception of the industrial revolution in Great Britain, and the rapid process of urbanization that was an integral part of this process. Britain was, of course, the first country to industrialize, and as such it set an important precedent for many countries the world over, not least in the institution of a new imaginary nature. In this chapter I shall thus consider some of its scenes.

By the late eighteenth century, the predominant imaginary nature constructed by the landed gentry in Britain began to be displaced by representations of space (in Lefebvre's sense of the term of 'conceived' space) that were predominantly produced by the bourgeoisie of the fast-growing cities. For the English landed gentry the *rural* nature of nature was not in question – what was in question was the nature of rurality, that is to say one's landed place in the rural spaces, as expressed in and dissimulated by the splendid landscape gardens and paintings. By the end of the eighteenth century the classificatory fault-lines of this nature had changed decisively, and in a manner that reflected a new discursive polarity between city and country.

In some respects this was fundamentally a *discursive* polarity: a number of social theorists have suggested that nature was no more absent from the cities than it was from the countryside, and indeed it cannot be said that there was (or is to this day) a natural, 'instinctive' yearning in people to live 'closer to nature', where nature is identified with the countryside. But this culturalist critique of the classification of city and country must be treated with some caution; there can be no doubt that certain forms of wildlife, for example, simply cannot exist in a city.[1] The boundary therefore cannot be simply treated as a legisign. I shall also suggest later that, at least in the early nineteenth century, there was an empirical basis for the claim that at least some aspects of the countryside made for a healthier lifestyle.

It is nonetheless true that the period associated with the industrialization involved a legisignical classification of the countryside as something quite separate from the city. Even as this happened, a number of technologies of observation and displacement paradoxically worked to ensure that the two sets of spatialiaties – regarded from the perspective of perceived, conceived and lived space – came to overlap more than they ever had before.

This dynamic was intimately related to the process of mass mediation. Even as the classification of city and country was more strongly instituted, indeed precisely *because* this happened, the bourgeoisie held up the countryside as a mirror, one that had the magical virtue of wiping the newly found blemishes of industrialization from the bourgeoisie's preferred urban façade. To the English bourgeoisie (and indeed not just to the bourgeoisie), one of these 'blemishes' was 'the mob': as I noted earlier, the shortened version of the Latin expression, *mobile vulgus*, an excitable crowd.

The notion of the 'mob' had its origins in the changes instituted by agrarian capitalism; as I explained in Chapter 4, the emergence of the new economic order and the growing centralization of the nation-state, as complexly related to the concentration of economic power and land in the hands of a small number of landed gentry, had produced mass migration to the cities. A class or caste system based on the ancient agricultural orders was gradually replaced by a modern class system, a historical relation that, as E.P. Thompson (1991) put it in his classic *The Making of the English Working Class*, led members of the new class to 'feel and articulate the identity of their interests as between themselves, and as against other [people] whose interests are different from (and usually opposed to) theirs' (Thompson 1991: 8–9).

As Thompson (1997) notes, in many Western European regions the distance between landowners and peasants was so great as to allow the dominant classes to fantasize with an idealized image of the peasant. This was not the case, or at any rate as much the case, in Great Britain, where one of the consequences of urbanization was that, even as the social classification strengthened, the distance in physical space between the classes in the great cities *decreased*. The juxtaposition in relatively close quarters of the rich and the poor meant that the bourgeoisie found themselves in distastefully close proximity to the 'great unwashed', that is, to the new working class whose grim living conditions were a result of the economic conditions which the gentry and the bourgeoisie themselves had imposed. Centuries of enclosure, but now also rapid urbanization and industrial capitalism, meant that commodity occultism lost some of its magic.

Indeed, the period from 1780 to the mid-nineteenth century and beyond saw repeated riots, insurrections and strikes. For many members of the bourgeoisie, the metropolis became an ambiguous and even distressing space, where one obtained access to urbanity (to be urban was in this sense to be *urbane*), but also where one was exposed daily to the 'base' or 'lowly' excesses of the 'mob', the antithesis of urbanity. An analogous disgust was felt by members of the landed aristocracy, who saw the classification of their public and private spaces encroached upon by the bourgeoisie. For both classes, this 'exposure' was an important motivation for the idealization of the countryside.

There was, however, another phenomenon that also offended bourgeois sensibility even as it affected the health of both poor and rich alike. By the early nineteenth century, English cities were becoming extraordinarily polluted places. The extensive use of coal to keep homes warm and to provide fuel for the new steam engines of industrialization meant that the urban atmosphere came to be pervaded by heavily polluted air. Until the cities were reconceived, redesigned and gentrified by a new breed of urban planners such as Paris's Haussmann and London's Nash – and this process was remarkably less successful in London than it was in Paris and many other European cities – experiencing the new urbanism meant blurring at least the *corporeal* boundaries of class. This in so far as all lungs shared the same smoke and all nostrils smelled the same excrement of domestic animals and humans. The numerous allusions of the period to the cleanliness of the country air were based at once on empirical fact and on discursive logic: the countryside air suspended fewer particles, but also *different* particles, and this made it at once a qualisign and a dicent of health to the bourgeoisie and the aristocracy alike.

To be sure, the space now classified as 'the countryside' was not without its own problems and dilemmas. The real and perceived pollution that one risked in the city had to be weighed up against the boorishness that the cosmopolitan bourgeoisie increasingly associated with the countryside. Rural areas, idealized for more than a century by landscape paintings as a place of stability and essential un-change, gradually came to be regarded by the bourgeoisie as a backward space where the unwary might well lose their cosmopolitan ways (Bermingham 1986).

The growing reliance on steam-driven technologies of production and displacement also had consequences for the countryside, and by the mid-1800s the environmental consequences of this shift had become clear. Whereas once many regarded the industrial landscape as one worthy of seeing in its own right – for example, the first iron bridge, completed in 1779 in Shropshire, was one of several sites that were treated as a spectacle and visited by large numbers of people – by the mid-nineteenth century the effects of the heavy industry on cities and the surrounding landscapes had become all too clear. As one commentator put it, many were horrified by 'the unpaved, undrained morass of the east end of Leeds . . . the sulphur-laden surroundings of the copper smelters in the Swansea Valley, the ill-built cottages scattered among the furnaces on the Black Country heaths'

(Binder 1982: 2). In this context, a new classification emerged that added to the increasingly legisignical opposition between town and country, a distinction between the 'untouched' and the 'ravaged' countryside.

Again, this classification was as much a matter of the imaginary as it was a change in natural space, in material nature; while virtually all the natural space in the British Isles had been affected in one way or another by millennia of cultivation, industrialization involved a new order of magnitude in physical intervention in the landscape. A number of observers noted this change, reacted with dismay and, as I shall note below, mobilized to prevent further transformations.

Faced with this contradiction, the bourgeoisie began to look for spaces that afforded the virtues of city while preserving the perceived benevolence of countryside. And indeed they found, or rather *produced,* at least two such spaces, each of which allowed them to engage in a certain 'rusticity' even as they remained a part of the cosmopolitan urbanism.

The first of these was the city park. Until well into the nineteenth century, the British aristocracy kept a strict control over their parks. Indeed parks were not actually regarded as *public* parks in today's sense of the term. Parks in London such as St. James's Park and Kensington Gardens were used as walled paddocks in which kings and queens kept deer and other animals for hunting, and later where the upper classes could promenade. While the bourgeoisie had been allowed some access to some of the parks since at least the second half of the seventeenth century, the parks were usually strictly off limits to the poor unless they entered as servants.

By the early nineteenth century greater access to some of London's parks was allowed to the middle classes and their servants during strictly limited days and times. Even then, only those who were judged by park guardians to be fit to enter could get in (Lasdun 1991). Even today, aspects of this tradition continue in so far as a number of gardens throughout London require a key for access.

But this highly restricted use of the parks came repeatedly under threat, both from 'below' and from 'above': on the one hand, those that were excluded entirely from the parks found ways of subverting the order by climbing the walls, by obtaining copies of keys and, in the earlier times, by poaching the game. On the other hand, members of the aristocracy fought running battles to re-establish their privileges in parks that had been opened up to the middle classes. Under Queen Anne it was proposed that access to St. James's Park might be limited by charging a halfpenny tax on all who entered, except foreign ministers, the nobility, members of Parliament and the Queen's household. This was clearly a device designed to exclude the 'meanest' people. Queen Caroline, the wife of King George II, tried to reclaim first St. James's Park and then Hyde Park for her own private use during the first half of the eighteenth century (Lasdun 1991: 126–7).

Eventually, the aristocracy decided that London's parks had become a qualisign of a middle-class disposition, and sought refuge in even more exclusive spaces such as Regent's Park, which was designed by Nash and rusticated for the 'highest of the land' (Lasdun 1991: 129). At the beginning of the twenty-first century, this park, by now a (royal) public park, still contained privately owned villas in its grounds.

In marked contrast to British practice, the figure of a truly *public* park in the city had begun to be developed in many Western European capitals by the early nineteenth century. German and French visitors to Britain were shocked at the exclusivity of British city parks, which in the words of one German royal gardener 'were kept for the nourishment of game instead of human beings' (Lasdun 1991: 142). C.J. Loudon and other British reformers who visited European capitals during the first half of the nineteenth century were, conversely, surprised and impressed by the extent to which the European cities had not just parks, but a variety of landscaped spaces that were open to one and all. As noted by Lasdun (1991), the Champs Elysées, the Bois Royal and the Jardin des Plantes in Paris, as well as the gardens at Magdeburg and Prince Pückler-Muskau's park at Bad Muskau in Prussia were some of examples of a practice that contrasted sharply with the British tradition.

One of the consequences of this process was that British reformers discovered, comparatively late in the nineteenth century, a practice that the European elite had long since planned: that such spaces could be employed to play a role in 'civilizing' the 'mob'. Put more accurately, such spaces could be employed as a tacit disciplinary means with which to frame, that is control, the popular 'excesses' – drinking, and a variety of 'grotesque' practices such as the popular blood sport of bull-baiting. All these, the Victorian reformers decided, could be curbed even as they improved the health of the working class if parks were either opened up or expressly created for the poor. Doing so would have not only 'civilizing' effects, i.e. the sustenance of a *proper* morality, but effects on the national economy; popular practices associated with drinking, themselves partly a response to the new working conditions, were leading to high levels of absenteeism in some industries. Such instrumental objectives notwithstanding, royalty, the landed classes and many in the House of Commons resisted this hegemonic discourse so strongly that it was not until the 1840s that London's Victoria Park, the first park designed for the 'masses', was laid out and then began to be used.

A second way in which the bourgeoisie 'greened' their urban spaces was by the construction of suburbs. According to H.J. Dyos (1966), the term 'suburb' is likely to have been adopted from the Old French *suburbe*, which was itself an adaptation from the Latin *suburbium*.[2] As noted by Chris Miele (1999), by the beginning of the seventeenth century Hackney had four titled residents and 100 who were classified as 'citizens of London' (Miele 1999: 32).

Even if the history of suburbs goes back centuries, it is clear that the spatialities changed dramatically over time. Indeed, in the late eighteenth and early nineteenth century, suburbs came to be premised on a new spatial practice, as well as a new representation of space. According to Anne Bermingham (1986), prior to the nineteenth century, dominant conceptions of the landscape reflected a desire both to exploit the land and its people and to dissimulate the transformation brought about by this exploitation. This occurred in paintings and gardens for which the landscape was idealized as 'scenery to be appreciated', as an 'archaic quaintness'. In contrast, after the nineteenth century the suburban areas were 'both capital *and* scenery – scenic capital and capital scenery' (Bermingham 1986: 166):

> Suburban development joined the exploitation of the land with an appreciation of its natural rustic beauties, for it was precisely these beauties that enhanced the economic opportunities of exploitation. The more rustic-looking a suburb, in fact, the more prestigious it was to live there. The suburbs most coveted in the London of the 1820s, such as Hampstead, Denmark Hill, Camberwell and Dulwich, all made a fetish of rusticity in their detached and semidetached 'villas,' each screened from both its identical neighbours and the main thoroughfares by a tiny decorative garden or 'jungle'.
>
> (Bermingham 1986: 167).

Bermingham notes that this fetish for rusticity represented a new modality of social planning which incorporated elements of the picturesque sensibility. One of its most important sources of inspiration came from an eighteenth-century ideal of the 'picturesque village' which was fashioned by Capability Brown. Brown conceived such villages with the ostensible objective of restoring the lives of the dispossessed agricultural and industrial labourers.

Extraordinarily, these very designs were now employed to 'mitigate the anomie of the middle-class and upper middle-class commuter' (Bermingham 1986: 168). Historically, many of these 'commuters' were as likely to be coming from the city as they were from the countryside (Bermingham 1986: 168); in either discursively distinct – albeit not just *discursively* distinct – space, there was dissatisfaction to be found.

The coming of steam

If Rousseau had reason to be dismayed with the mechanistic excesses of the Enlightenment, a rather more physical form of mechanism would give the romantic authors that followed Rousseau even more reason for discontent – but this even as the technology involved allowed them to travel to the places where they might both express and alleviate that discontent. In 1712 Thomas Newcomen deployed the first 'atmospheric' steam engine that used cold water to condense steam in a cylinder. This created a vacuum that drove a piston which was used to pump water out of a mine shaft. This system was itself replaced by the more efficient engine developed by James Watt, who in 1769 patented a new design which employed a separate condenser attached to the cylinder by way of a valve. This principle became the new standard and went on to be used in all manner of manufacturing systems, many of which stopped being exclusively about '*manu*-facture' – in the sense of making things with the hands.

The growing reliance on steam-driven technologies of displacement resulted in a greater extraction and burning of coal. As noted earlier, the environmental consequences of this shift started to become clear during the first half of the nineteenth century. The advent of steam *railways* played a remarkably ambiguous process where the perceived, conceived and lived space of the countryside was concerned. In Britain the first steam railway with regular services for goods and passengers began in 1825. Whereas less than 100 miles (approximately 160 km) of track had been laid by 1830, by the middle of the century there were over 6000 miles (9600 km) (Freeman 1999: 1).

The consequences for the British economy – and indeed for other countries that would follow a similar pattern of development – are difficult to overestimate. The new steam railways were more often than not the last nail in the coffin of strongly bounded regionalism in economies. Indeed, as the cultural historian Wolfgang Schivelbusch notes in his classic *The Railway Journey* (1977), it may be argued with Marx that commodities became truly that – commodities – when the advent of modern means of transportation produced a spatial gap between the location of production and location of consumption of goods. In so far as steam-driven railways made a quantum contribution to this process, they played a key role in the shift from agrarian to industrial forms of capitalism. One way of defining the new form of capitalism was precisely in terms of the articulation of the new technologies of displacement in the workplace *and* the use of related technologies of displacement on the level of transportation to produce the new markets demanded – and made possible – by the increased productivity of the workplaces.

As part of this process, the railways in Great Britain had a decisive impact on both material and imaginary nature. One oft-noted effect involved their physical impact on the landscape. In fact, as argued by James Winter (1999), this impact was actually quite sharply circumscribed when compared to the impact that road building for automobiles would have during the twentieth century. In this sense, perhaps a more significant immediate effect involved the *speed* of displacement and the relation to animals. Schivelbusch quotes Nicholas Wood, a nineteenth-century authority on railways, as saying that 'The greatest exertions have been used to accelerate the speed of the mails (which have hitherto been the quickest species of conveyance), without being able to exceed ten miles an hour; and that only with the exercise of such *destruction of animal power*, as no one can contemplate without feelings' (Nicholas Wood in Schivelbusch 1977: 8). Even if the first steam-driven railways only averaged a speed of some fifteen miles per hour, Wood notes in the same passage that this speed was kept up 'with the greatest of ease'. By contrast, the increasing pressure for greater speed in horse-driven carriages resulted in so much whipping of the horses that, as noted by Margaret Kean (1998), it helped to give rise to the first animal welfare movement in the late eighteenth and early nineteenth centuries.

Schivelbusch argues that this apparently small change in speed was part of an extraordinary shift in the relation to physical space:

As long as the conquest of space was tied to animal power, it had to proceed within the limits of the animals' physical capabilities. One way of gaining an immediate perception of the distance travelled was to observe the exhaustion of the draught animals. . . . Steam power, inexhaustible and capable of infinite acceleration, reversed the relationship between recalcitrant nature (i.e. spatial distance) and locomotive engine. Nature (i.e., spatial distance) . . . now succumbed to the new mechanical locomotive engine of the railroad that, in a frequently used metaphor, 'shoots right through like a bullet'. 'Annihilation of time and space' was the *topos* which the early nineteenth century used to describe the new situation. . . . Motion was no longer dependent on the conditions of natural space, but on a mechanical power that created its own new spatiality.

(Schivelbusch 1977: 10)

According to Schivelbusch, the cuttings, embankments, tunnels and viaducts that made their marks on the European landscapes from the 1850s onwards became a sign of an alienation from immediate, living nature. 'The abandonment of animal power in favor of steam was experienced as the loss of sensorially perceptible animal power/exhaustion, i.e., as the loss of the sense of space and motion that was based on it' (Schivelbusch 1977: 23).

But with this sense of loss there also came new experiences of the landscape. What Schivelbusch describes as the new machine 'ensemble' – the train itself and its windows, but also the rail and the infrastructure required to support it – began to mediate between the traveller and the landscape. Where the older technologies of travel had been based on natural and only 'loosely connected' elements, the new technology of displacement became a qualisign of what Schivelbusch describes as 'tremendous technical discipline'; the new machine ensemble suggested a greater artificiality, 'the end of the free play between the individual elements of machines in general' (Schivelbusch 1977: 24).

Even as the railway drastically reduced the time it took to reach previously inaccessible places, it destroyed the older experiences of travelling, and the spaces between the points of departure and arrival. As expressed by Schivelbusch:

What was experienced as being annihilated was the traditional space–time continuum which characterized the old transport technology. Organically embedded in nature as it was, that technology, in its mimetic relationship to the space traversed, permitted the traveller to perceive that space as a living entity.

(Schivelbusch 1977: 36)

This meant that the regions, now both connected to and making a space 'in between' the larger cities, lost what Walter Benjamin (1999) has described as their 'aura': their inherited place, their characteristic forms of presence (Schivelbusch

1977: 41). I shall return to the concept of the aura in another chapter; here it may be noted that, in some respects, the railways constituted a way of dramatically extending the double illusion of space described by Lefebvre. The making of railways presupposed the possibility of – indeed produced – what was something akin to an 'empty' space that might be 'gridded' for the purposes of travel.

Wordsworth's sublimity

By the second half of the nineteenth century, the railways in Britain transported large numbers of those with enough money to pay for train tickets to beautiful and, as I explain below, sublime natures: in particular, to what had hitherto been relatively remote beaches, moorlands and mountains.

Of course, tourism as a form of mass mediation pre-dated the development of the railway. Some of the forms of what we might describe today as 'day trips' existed decades before the mass travel made possible by steam railways: as noted by Winter (1999), so many textile workers in Lancashire walked or travelled by the cartload to Blackpool and other coastal resorts on Sundays that they 'darkened' the beaches, and steam packets reportedly took 650,000 clerks and artisan families to Gravesend in 1835 (Winter 1999: 210). Such excursions were regarded with benevolence by reformist leaders of the Victorian bourgeoisie, who as noted earlier thought of the countryside as having both morally redeeming and physically therapeutic qualities. Indeed, Victorian reformers organised trips to the countryside for members of the working class because they believed that recreation in 'natural' surroundings was 'the best antidote to city-induced moral and physical malaise' (Winter 1999: 210), or what became known as 'urbomorbis' (Winter 1999: 25). This is what made this practice a form of mass mediation in its own right; nature effectively came to be anthropomorphized as a reforming spatiality, one that would maintain both the physical and moral health of the working class.

This discourse was deeply paradoxical in so far as it entailed encouraging the working classes to go 'back', however temporarily, to the very countryside from which many had been displaced by enclosure a generation – or less – earlier. But this 'return' was made doubly paradoxical by the fact that, as it gathered pace, sectors of the bourgeoisie became alarmed at what they perceived as the excesses of mass tourism. As I explain below, they began to protest against it in what was in effect an early form of Nimbyism ('not in my back yard'). Historically speaking, the masses were thus caught in a process of to-ing and fro-ing, from the country to the city and back, and then back again, as the contradictions of the mass mediation of nature were played out in the English countryside.

Aspects of this process may be illustrated by considering William Wordsworth's *Guide to the Lakes,* which he first produced in 1810 and which informed British tourists about the natural wonders of the Lake District in northern England. The very existence of the guide, which Wordsworth developed and republished in several editions over a period spanning decades (I shall consider the fifth and final edition of the guide, published in 1835) attests to the development not just of a nineteenth century version, a prototype, as it were, of 'green tourism', but indeed of mass tourism more generally.

Travel to other lands, in the form of pilgrimages and grand tours, had of course long existed. In the mid-eighteenth century, Rousseau chose the island of Saint-Pierre in part because it was *not* frequented by travellers. Aspects of the romanticism of Rousseau's experiences were enacted by later travellers who, in the nineteenth century, engaged in what John Towner (1985) describes as romantic grand tours, whose preferred geographies included the Jura Mountains close to the island of Saint-Pierre. As described by Judith Adler (1989), writings about such tours involved the production of 'authoritative judgements about aesthetic merit, as travel itself became an occasion for the cultivation and display of "taste"'(Adler 1989: 22). Travellers who wrote about their experiences were expected to communicate not simply personal predilection or the subjectivity of their experiences but a form of objectivity involving the discernment of discoverable rules of harmony and proportion (Adler 1989: 22).

To be sure, as noted by John Towner (1985), the 1820s and 1830s, the time when Wordsworth produced the final version of his guide, marked a transitional period towards a more formalized tourist industry. With John Urry (2002), we can define such an industry, then at an early stage *as industry*, in terms of a leisure activity that involved, among other aspects, an alternation with and distinction from regulated and organized work; significant numbers of people moving to, and staying in, various destinations which were regarded as being outside everyday life, and where the stay was regarded as being transitory; and the emergence of mediators whose role it was to classify, frame and indeed engage in what I have described as formal, informal and especially non-formal pedagogies (Urry 2002: 2–3).

Wordsworth's *Guide* played such a role. It began with some preliminaries regarding the best way to reach various points in the Lake District. Significantly, Wordsworth implied that such preliminaries were a matter of the 'body' of the visitor in so far as he began by saying that 'it was the Author's principal wish to furnish a Guide or Companion for the *Minds* of Persons of taste, and feeling for Landscape'; however, 'for the more sure attainment . . . of this primary object, he will begin by undertaking the humble and tedious task of supplying the Tourist with directions how to approach the several scenes in their best' (Wordsworth 1977: 1, italics original).

The aspects for the 'mind', the actual guide, as it were, began by describing not the Lake District, but Switzerland – or rather an indoor model of the 'alpine country', in Peirce's terms, an iconic legisign, 'a type, in so far as it requires each instance of it to embody a definite quality which renders it fit to call up in the mind the idea of a like object' (CP 2.258). As described by Wordsworth, the observer of this model ascended a small platform and saw 'mountains, lakes, glaciers, rivers, woods, waterfalls, and valleys, and their cottages, and every other object

114

is sublime in comparison with which everything else is small'(Kant 1987: 105). But Kant parted with earlier conceptions of the sublime by suggesting that this was not a matter of the natural object itself, or even of the senses, but of the imagination of the observer. As Kant put it,

> nothing that can be an object of the senses is to be called sublime. [What happens is that] our imagination strives to progress toward infinity, while our reason demands absolute totality as a real idea, and [the imagination,] our power of estimating the magnitude of things in the world of sense, is inadequate to that idea. Yet this inadequacy itself is the arousal in us of the feeling that we have within us of a supersensible power; and what is absolutely large is not an object of sense, but is the use that judgement makes naturally of certain objects so as to [arouse] this (feeling), and in contrast with that use any other use is small. Hence what is to be called sublime is not the object, but the attunement that the intellect [gets] through a certain presentation that occupies reflective judgement.
>
> (Kant 1987: 106)

The sublime for Kant thereby was not so much material nature itself – though he continued to speak of a 'substrate' that underlay *both* nature and 'our ability to think' – but in the faculty of the imagination. In the context of something sublime, this faculty struggled both to project anthropomorphically and to identify cosmomorphically with the infinity of a nature that was nonetheless constructed anthropomorphically, and identified with cosmomorphically, *as* sublime. Sublimity, by this account, was a matter of a dialectic of firstness and thirdness, a tension and a pleasure to be found in *both* the possibility *and* the impossibility of representing an incomprehensible magnitude.

A more detailed development of this argument is beyond the scope of this book. Here I wish to return to Wordsworth's *Guide,* in which the categories of the beautiful and the sublime provided a mode of framing intended to produce a 'proper' appreciation of nature. In some respects, Wordsworth's *Guide* echoed an attenuated Burkian distinction between the beautiful and the sublime: Wordsworth found the Lake District superior as a landscape to the landscapes found in Scotland and Wales in so far as it allowed the tourist to view, merely by turning his (*sic*) head, either a beautiful or a sublime landscape. If, Wordsworth said, 'the spectator [in the Vale of Winandermere] looks for gentle and lovely scenes, his eye is turned towards the south; if for the grand, towards the north'; one view will allow the spectator to see the surface of the lake at sunset reflecting 'before the eye correspondent colours through every variety of beauty, and through all degrees of splendour'; the other will allow the spectator to see the sun 'sending forth . . . broad streams of rosy, crimson, purple, or golden light, towards the grand mountains', 'which, thus illuminated, with all their projections and cavities, and with an inter-mixture of solemn shadows' (Wordsworth 1977: 25–6). Sublimity, he said, 'is the result of Nature's first great dealings with the superficies of the earth'

117

(Wordsworth 1977: 35). Throughout the *Guide*, Wordsworth nonetheless made it clear that its perception was a more complex matter than a simple opposition of the 'awful' and the beautiful, what struck terror in the heart and what produced love. Part of it involved a certain temporality or sequencing, that is to say a certain modality of framing; he suggested, for example, that mountain lakes should be approached from their outlets, 'for, by this way of approach, the traveller faces the grander features of the scene, and is gradually conducted into its most sublime recesses' (Wordsworth 1977: 97).

As begins to be clear from this account, Wordsworth used these and other aesthetic categories in an effort to produce a total technology of observation, one that governed everything from one's approach to different aspects of the land-scape, to what species of trees should be planted and what types of houses built and painted with colours that did not adversely affect the qualities of the 'original' landscape. In this sense, the *Guide* was quite explicitly conceived in the terms of a relatively formal instance of pedagogic discourse: the *Guide*, Wordsworth hoped, would 'become generally serviceable, by leading to habits of more exact and considerate observation than, as far as the writer knows, have hitherto been applied to local scenery' (Wordsworth 1977: 22). As part of this, and as noted by Judith Adler (1989) and John Urry (2002) with respect to broader tourist practices of the time, the emphasis was very much on a *visual* form of observa-tion. Wordsworth was concerned with what might be described as a pedagogy of landscape spectatorship.

But there was an additional aspect of the Guide that makes it particularly significant to a history of the present nature of mass mediation. In the *Guide*, Wordsworth denounced the deleterious effects of poor taste and mass tourism on the Lake District. He did so in terms of a logic of narrativization that described a kind of 'fall from grace', a loss, as it were, of Eden. With Gerard Prince (1991), I define narrative as the recounting of two or more real or fictitious events by one or more narrators to one or more narratees. By this account, *narrativization* is a process that transforms events and actors that work according to a logic that is not itself narrative, into one that obeys the conventions of a story: that is to say, a narrative which emphasizes chronology, causality and, as part of this, a more or less tacit moralization of the sequence of events. In Peircian terms, narrativization involves the production of arguments that are characterized by what we might well describe as a quasi-indexical quality on the level of temporality: the time of the telling and the time of the told seem to establish a real relation between the narrative representamen and its narrative object.

Wordsworth's narrative exhibited the characteristics of what was to become something like a 'paradigmatic' narrative progression in environmentalist accounts of environmental degradation: first there was a 'land before the fall' *and then* humans (in this case human *tourists*) entered and destroyed beautiful and sublime nature. As a narrator-guide, Wordsworth invited the reader to 'look down upon this scene', but now did so with reference to a time 'before the country had been penetrated by any inhabitants'. He asked the reader to 'form to himself an image of the tides visiting and revisiting the firths . . . the rivers pursuing their course to be lost in the mighty mass of waters . . . may think of the primaeval woods shedding and renewing their leaves with no human eye to notice, or human heart to regret or welcome the change' (Wordsworth 1977: 52). He then moved on to a nature that was 'affected' by inhabitants, initially not adversely thanks to what Wordsworth described as a 'perfect Republic of Shepherds and Agriculturalists, among whom the plough of each man was confined to the maintenance of his own family, or to the occasional accommodation of his neighbour' (Wordsworth 1977: 67). This ideal and idealized 'republic' – one, we might note, that continued to institute the *family* – then gave way to the modern 'bad effects' caused by the poor taste of more recent residents, and indeed, by mass tourism. According to Wordsworth, the 'introduction of discordant objects' had destroyed the landscape (Wordsworth 1977: 73); 'the lakes [have] now become celebrated; visitors [flock] hitherto from all parts of England; the fancies of some were smitten so deeply that they became settlers; and the Islands of Derwent-Water and Winandermere . . . were instantly defaced by the intrusion' (Wordsworth 1977: 70). If, as I suggested earlier, narrative has its own temporal indexical (or quasi-indexical) qualities, pushing the reader forward by inviting her/him to establish real relations between events, Wordsworth played a significant role in establishing a genre that employed this form of indexicality to critique what he regarded as the devastation of beautiful and sublime landscapes. This proto-environmental narrative was to become the hallmark of environmentalist narratives in the twentieth century.

As I noted earlier, the emerging tourist industry eventually came to constitute a form of mass mediation in its own right. Where tourism had once been limited to the aristocracy and then to the sons of the middle classes, eventually the 'ordinary people', the old 'mob' whose mobility was so feared, were now themselves mobilized as part of the reformist project mentioned above. However, when the masses were encouraged to find leisure and health in the areas from which many had been historically displaced by enclosure, many of the middle-class residents of the same areas began to worry that 'their' nature might be destroyed by mass tourism. As quoted by Winter (1999), one resident in Wordsworth's Lake District suggested that '[A] great monster ploughs up our lake and disgorges multitudes upon the pier . . . our hills are darkened by swarms of tourists; our lawns are picnicked upon twenty at a time; our trees are branded with initial letters' (Winter 1999: 211). In Derbyshire, what Winter describes as an upper-class woman remarked that excursion trains used to 'vomit at Easter and in Whitsun week, throngs of mill hands of the period, cads and their flames, tawdry, blowsy, noisy, drunken . . . tearing through the fields like swarms of devastating locusts' (Winter 1999: 211). If Wordsworth's guide decried the destruction, so did his poems, which famously protested at the efforts to extend the rail line from Kendal to his beloved Windermere: 'Is then no nook of English ground secure/From rash assault?' (Wordsworth in Winter 1999: 2). The poem might equally have said 'From *mass* assault,' for Wordsworth was particularly concerned with the effects that the burgeoning leisure industry was having on the Lake District.

Wordsworth became known as one of the most famous advocates of *preservationism*, one of two mid-century movements that attempted to persuade the British government that, in the words of George John Shaw-Lefevre, 'open spaces in their natural state, adding so much to the beauty of their districts and to the general enjoyment of the public, had a value' and so must be preserved (Shaw-Lefevre in Winter 1999: 25). John Ruskin, another famous preservationist and one of the founders of the British National Trust, called as early as the mid-nineteenth century for a society to protect the landscape from the ravages of industrialization. In fact, as noted by Winter, it was not until the 1860s and 1870s that such societies were actually formed in Great Britain.

A second group, which Winter (1999) describes as 'conservationists' and which had precedents at least as old as the critiques offered by the Royal Society in the 1660s, produced what might be described at the beginning of the twenty-first century as a precedent for the discourse of 'sustainable development'. Conservationists were not concerned with an intrinsic value of nature but rather with the need to manage it for economic and other purposes. According to Winter, conservationists were those who would 'control exploitation, limit waste, and increase productivity in sustainable ways' but would not 'stand at the barricades or supply the rhetoric' (Winter 1999: 5). The conservationist discourse offended romantic preservationists like Wordsworth, who saw in conservationism the kind of mechanism and progressivism that threatened ancient woodlands. Where conservationists were the advocates of a 'pragmatic' stance, preservationists lived by way of a romantic conception of a beautiful or sublime nature that privileged the experience of nature for its own sake.

These differences to one side, it is possible to suggest that both sets of movements conceived a nature that now required systematic intervention in order to prevent it from being destroyed by the encroachment of industrialization and, with it, mass tourism. In so doing, both groups paradoxically assumed what was in some respects the most *modern* discourse vis-à-vis nature, one that took for granted not just the necessity but the very *possibility* of working to pre- or conserve nature. While aspects of this discourse had arguably already been developed at least a century earlier in the context of the 'Edenic islands', its advocacy in the context of the much larger physical geographies of Europe constituted a remarkable shift, one that presupposed a form of totalization that would later constitute the basis for the discourses which took for granted the possibility of managing entire *environments*.

Humboldt's adventures

Until the mid-nineteenth century, most people assumed that nature was God-given. The work of the great natural philosophers such as Galileo, Bacon, Newton and Descartes can be interpreted, with the benefit of hindsight, as the beginning of a reclassification of the relation between God and nature. However, even at the beginning of the nineteenth century, few amongst the intellectual elite in Europe doubted that the 'laws of nature' discovered by the natural philosophers were the explicit and detailed work of God. Even the most naturalistic notions of the sublime were strongly influenced by religious discourse in so far as many regarded sublime landscapes as privileged places in which to witness the work of God.

A significant step in the direction of a more secular understanding of nature was taken by the explorer and travel writer Baron Alexander von Humboldt. A Prussian aristocrat born in 1769, Humboldt has been variously described as a natural scientist, geographer, painter, geologist, miner, liberal, diplomat, archaeologist and, as part of the romantic tradition, the 'last universal man'. Although he was criticized by some romantics for being too much of an empirical scientist, it is possible to assign Humboldt a pre-eminent place in the elite circle of natural philosophers, 'gentlemen of science' and critics associated with *Naturphilosophie*.

As noted by Pratt (1992), Humboldt wished to reveal at once the 'occult' forces of nature – a point I shall return to below – *and* its natural harmonies, its natural 'luxuriance' for the 'enjoyment' of the 'sensitive mind' (Humboldt in Pratt 1992: 124). But Pratt suggests that, in contrast to earlier, more sentimental narratives of exploration, Humboldt 'sought to pry affect away from autobiography and narcissism and fuse it with science' (Pratt 1992: 124). This had the aim, in Humboldt's own words, of reproducing in the reader 'Nature's ancient communion with the spiritual life of man' (Humboldt in Pratt 1992: 124). This was, in some respects, a return to an organic imaginary and circuit of anthropomorphism of the kind described by Merchant (1980).

Humboldt sought to study this communion by travelling to South America. He could do so thanks to his great personal wealth, but also to his cultural and symbolic capital, in particular his familiarity with the ways of the European nobility, which he used to persuade the King and Queen of Spain to allow him to travel to their jealously guarded colonies in South and Central America. Humboldt left in 1799 with the botanist Aimé Bonpland on a five-year expedition that included travel in present-day Cuba, Venezuela, Colombia, Ecuador, Peru, Mexico and the eastern United States. At the time, one of Humboldt's most famous feats was his ascent to the summit (or near summit) of Mount Chimborazo in present-day Ecuador. Chimborazo was then thought to be the highest mountain in the world, and it is possible to begin to imagine the sensation that Humboldt's endeavour caused by considering that he climbed the mountain at a time when climbing high mountains in 'remote' locations was almost unthinkable. Why place one's own body at such risk? If today this same question is still asked of those who climb Everest or Annapurna or Kanchenjunga, in the early nineteenth century such a practice would doubtless have caused stupefaction.

Humboldt and Bonpland also collected tens of thousands of plant specimens that were unknown to European gentlemen of science, and conducted a series of proto-scientific experiments which moved beyond visual classification to the investigation of the 'internal workings' or the organic structure of the specimens. This stance, which I described with Pratt earlier as an interest in the 'occult' forces of nature, may be linked to Foucault's third *epistéme*, which replaced the Classical *epistéme* by the end of the eighteenth century.

In marked contrast to the Classical *epistéme*, scientific texts produced in the context of the modern *epistéme* mistrusted 'representation'. In the words of Foucault, 'The order of words and the order of beings no longer intersect except along an artificially divided line. Their old affinity, which had been the foundation of natural history in the Classical age, and which had led structure to character, representation to denomination, and the visible individual to the abstract genus, all with one and the same movement, is beginning to dissolve. There is talk of things that take *place* in another space than that of words' (Foucault 1970: 230).

Naturalists, says Foucault, no longer trusted the purely *visible* principles of taxonomy which were the hallmark of the Classical age. Instead, beings were understood from the perspective of a concept of *organic structure* which was determined by linking the 'visible' to the 'invisible'. The new method of characterisation 'subordinates characters one to another; it links them to functions; it arranges them in accordance with an architecture that is internal as well as external, and no less invisible than visible; it distributes them throughout a space that is other than that of names, discourse, and language' (Foucault 1970: 231). We can say in Peircian terms that this *epistéme* constituted a remarkable semeiotic paradox. On the one hand, it might well be regarded as the culmination of the kind of anti-semeioticism that I suggested had been inaugurated by, amongst other practices, the work of Galileo. Nature – at least amongst such gentlemen of science – was manifestly *not* about *signs* of nature. But, whereas the Linnaean 'Classical' *epistéme* sought to mediate between the two extremes by way of a few words – what I described as rhematic symbols – the subjects of what Foucault describes as the modern *epistéme* established a radical disjunction: nature was not about signs, and indeed it could not be simply *represented* by rhematic symbols; but nor was its 'space' a matter of dicent indexical legisigns of the kind found in herbariums and botanic gardens. Rather, it was a matter of rhematic indexical sinsigns – the 'signs-that-were-not-signs' found in the pulsing organs of a vivisection – 'not-signs' which, paradoxically, could only be explained in essays and other scientific media, by way of an abject return to symbols, to arguments and, of course, to narrative.

The following account, which appeared in *Personal Narrative*, a part of an encyclopaedic work completed in 1834 which was titled *Relation Historique du Voyage aux Régions Equinoxiales du Noveau Continent*, gives a sense of this tension as well as of Humboldt's stylistics, which some credit with inventing the modern travelogue. It describes Humboldt's experiments with electric eels, which in this case involved driving a herd of wild horses and mules into a muddy pond in the *llanos* or savannah found in eastern Colombia and western Venezuela:

> The extraordinary noise made by the stamping of the horses made the fish jump out of the mud and attack. These livid, yellow eels, like great water

snakes, swim on the water's surface and squeeze under the bellies of the horses and mules. A fight between such different animals is a picturesque scene. With harpoons and long pointed reeds the Indians [Humboldt's guides and porters] tightly circled the pond; some climbed trees whose branches hung over the water's surface. Screaming and prodding with their reeds they stopped the horses leaving the pond. The eels, dazed by the noise, defended themselves with their electrical charges. For a while it seemed they might win. Several horses collapsed from the shocks received on their most vital organs, and drowned under the water.

(Humboldt 1995: 170)

After this opening narrative, Humboldt reported a series of empirical observations such as '[eels] attack the heart, intestines and the *plexus coeliacus* of the abdominal nerves' (Humboldt 1995: 170), 'the water temperature where these animals live is 26 °C to 27 °C' and '[t]he skin is constantly covered with a mucus, which, as Volta has shown, conducts electricity twenty to thirty times more efficiently than pure water' (Humboldt 1995: 171).

While the first description of the 'experiment' suggests an older adventure literature, the fact of the experiment itself and the comments that follow it point to the profound shift in *epistéme* and, we might add, the concomitant shift in techniques of observation. Humboldt's descriptions of the eel, like his experiments with curare and numerous other aspects of the physical and human geography of South America, all attest to the extent to which, in Humboldt's own words, his eyes were 'always directed to the combination of forces, to the influence of the inanimate creation on the animate world of animals and plants, to this harmony' (Humboldt quoted in Pratt 1992: 123–4).

But, despite the revolutionary character of his work, Humboldt continued to adhere to a notion of nature that interpreted its 'occult' workings as an expression of divine intervention in the world. In this sense, it was not before the work of George Perkins Marsh, and of course Charles Darwin and Alfred Russel Wallace, that a truly secular account of the nature of nature was produced.

Nature as secular abstraction

By the mid-nineteenth century, one of the foremost advocates of conservationism was George Perkins Marsh, a geographer, one-time US minister to the Ottoman Empire and man of letters, who grew up in New England but then moved to Europe where he wrote, among other texts, *Man and Nature*. Marsh published *Man and Nature* in 1864. However, years before this, Marsh gave addresses and delivered reports which may be read today as establishing important precedents for a fully modern *environmentalist* discourse, and indeed an environmentalist imaginary.

I noted earlier that aspects of this discourse had been centuries in the making in the context of island colonies. However, in Marsh's nineteenth-century work

123

we find one of the first analyses of ecological relations in the United States and Europe. It is possible to illustrate this discourse by considering one of Marsh's more famous addresses, given to the Agricultural Society of Rutland County in 1847. In it Marsh noted that:

> Men now begin to realize what, as wandering shepherds, they had before dimly suspected, that man has a right to the use, not the abuse, of the products of nature; that consumption should everywhere compensate by increased production; and that it is a false economy to encroach upon a capital, the interest of which is sufficient for our lawful use.
>
> (Marsh 1847: 8)

Even as Marsh defended the use of the 'mechanical arts' – technologies that he viewed as being inherently democratic – and even as he made the case for a more scientific form of agricultural management – the very 'arts' that would themselves be used eventually to devastating effect by agribusiness – he critiqued the destruction of forests in New England. This critique was arguably one of the first instances of what today might be described as an ecosystemic critique of environmental exploitation:

> The functions of the forest, besides supplying timber and fuel, are very various. The conducting powers of trees render them highly useful in restoring the disturbed equilibrium of the electric fluid; they are of great value in sheltering and protecting more tender vegetables against the destructive effects of bleak or parching winds, and the annual deposit of the foliage of deciduous trees, and the decomposition of their decaying trunks, form an accumulation of vegetable mould, which gives the greatest fertility to the often originally barren soils on which they grow, and enriches lower grounds by the wash from rains and the melting snows. The inconveniences resulting from a want of foresight in the economy of the forest are already severely felt in many parts of New England, and even in some of the older towns in Vermont. Steep hill-sides and rocky ledges are well suited to the permanent growth of wood, but when in the rage for improvement they are improvidently stripped of this protection, the action of sun and wind and rain soon deprives them of their thin coating of vegetable mould, and this, when exhausted, cannot be restored by ordinary husbandry. They remain therefore barren and unsightly blots, producing neither grain nor grass, and yielding no crop but a harvest of noxious weeds, to infest with their scattered seeds the richer arable grounds below.
>
> (Marsh 1847: 17–18)

Winter (1999) notes that, by the time that Marsh published *Man and Nature*, 'nature' was already a modern secular abstraction: for Marsh, nature's governing principle was 'a mechanical equilibrium; humankind stood outside nature and inflicted damage that could be irreparable without further human intervention. The forces of his natural world were certain to strike back, but blindly, without malevolent or benevolent intent' (Winter 1999: 32). The purpose of conservationist intervention was therefore to manage woods in a rational manner and with the intent of improving the resource base required for material progress (Winter 1999: 32–33).

As Winter notes, the word 'environment' would have been used rarely in the nineteenth century – and then in relation to a kind of social Darwinist discourse (see below). It is nonetheless possible to suggest that Marsh established an important discursive precedent for twentieth-century environmentalism in so far as he not only privileged a secularized notion of nature, but did so from a discursive perspective that recognized the significance of the interrelationship between organic and non-organic dynamics in specific habitats.

Important as Marsh's contribution was, it was to be eclipsed by what was perhaps the single most decisive contribution towards the notion of a uniform, regular and above all *secular* discourse of nature that would underpin much modern environmentalism: the publication of the theory of evolution proposed jointly by Charles Darwin and Alfred Russel Wallace.

Like many gentlemen of science before him, Darwin constructed his theory of the nature of nature partly by means of travel – not least by way of his famous voyage to the Galapagos. However, his work was at least as dependent on his research on domestic breeding. As noted by Robert Young (1985), it was also contingent on the work of earlier scientists: Young suggests that historians of science have tended to isolate Darwin from his predecessors and contemporaries. Darwin's work was indebted to the discourse of many authors, including Alexander Humboldt himself (whom Darwin once described as his 'personal hero'), Jean Baptiste Lamarck, Robert Malthus and Nicholas Lyell.

A detailed account of the work of each of these is beyond the scope of this chapter. Lamarck, one of the great but 'forgotten' naturalists and zoologists of his time, proposed in 1801 what Darwin later described as the first theory of natural selection, which suggested that changes in the organic and inorganic world were the result of natural law, and not of divine intervention. Despite this, Lamarck's theory was, like Humboldt's, still 'teleological' in that it assumed that evolution was driven by processes that tended in a particular direction. Lamarck was, in some respects, an early nineteenth-century equivalent of today's advocates of 'intelligent design' in the United States.

The geologist Nicholas Lyell's *Principles of Geology*, published in the 1830s, revolutionized geological theory by giving renewed credence to a 'uniformitarian' theory of geology, according to which it was possible to read ancient geological processes from the structure of *current* formations. His 'uniformitarianism' put forward the notion that the geological processes were far older than suggested by biblical narratives, and that, far from being static, they were undergoing what was at once a dynamic and an unimaginably ancient process of transformation.

Robert Malthus, the son of a wealthy country gentleman, was the curate of Alby, a town south of London. In 1798 he published his *Essay on Population*, which argued that, left to its own devices, population growth would always exceed the growth of the means of subsistence. Malthus' theory was presented in the context of the so-called 'perfectability of society' debates, in which British intellectuals sought to find ways of improving social life and, in particular, the fate of the poor. In his essay, Malthus argued that such proposals were doomed because the working classes would have more children and the increased population would cancel the effects of the improvements. In a second edition of the *Essay*, Malthus added 'empirical evidence' for this claim and made proposals consistent with a laissez-faire politics: he suggested that universal suffrage, an unregulated national labour market and the elimination of the 'Poor Laws' as well as of state-run education would teach the working classes the 'moral restraints' necessary to reduce birth rates. In the style that is typical of what is known today as neoliberalism, Malthus was an advocate of deregulation, but saw no contradiction in the principle that the state should intervene to discipline the workforce. As part of this discourse, and perhaps most significantly for Darwin's future theory of natural selection, Malthus conceived of a social world which was driven by a Hobbesian law of struggle. It is thus remarkable that today so many advocates of conservationism still invoke what is an essentially Malthusian logic when they argue that the main problem faced by the planet is human overpopulation.

Despite these 'proto-evolutionary' discourses, Darwin did not make public his own theory until some twenty years after he began work on it. His decision to do so was prompted by the news that Alfred Russel Wallace had arrived independently at virtually identical conclusions after working for a much shorter time and under less favourable economic conditions. An agreement was brokered that allowed both men to have their work jointly presented to the Linnaean Society in July 1858, with Darwin represented as the contributor with research priority.

As summarized by Stephen Jay Gould (1980), the new theory of evolution (or of *natural selection*, as Darwin called it) suggested first, that organisms varied, and that the variations in question were inherited, at least in part, by their offspring; second, that organisms produced more offspring than could survive; and third, that on average those offspring that varied most strongly in the directions favoured by the environment would go on to survive and propagate. This process would lead to the accumulation of favourable variations by way of the process of natural selection. However, if evolution was to be, as Gould puts it, a *creative* process (and not just one that eliminated the 'unfit'), then it was necessary to recognize that chance or random variation played an important role. The variations were, moreover, likely to be a matter of small mutations, rather than dramatic changes (Gould 1980: 11–12).

As this account begins to suggest, Darwin and Wallace developed a theory that explained the *mechanism* whereby organisms varied over time thanks to the action of environmental forces. Their conception of mechanism was, however, quite different from Newton's. Wallace and Darwin found a way of introducing a certain logic of *mathesis* – a principle of variation based on the statistical principle of chance – to the process of evolution. But this same principle was, in some respects at least, a clear refutation of mechanistic epistemologies: where Newton and other scientists had favoured the metaphor of a (paradoxically) timeless clock, Darwin and Wallace at once returned time 'to' nature and organicism 'to' time by conceiving of mechanism as a *process* that involved organic, and to some extent indeterminate, *variation*.

It is, in this sense, perhaps unsurprising that Peirce himself embraced evolutionary theory. Evolutionary theory reconciled, or seemed to reconcile, the nature of thirdness, secondness and firstness by respectively formulating a *law*, showing how this law might *determine* relations and yet preserving the element of chance, that is to say of indetermination.

This last aspect – the recognition of the significance of firstness or indetermination – is one that makes it possible to read Darwin as being a 'romantic' himself. But there was, and still is another dimension of evolutionary theory that made the space – and indeed the time – for a return, if not to mechanism, then certainly to determinism. Darwin paved the way for a natural *history* in the sense that his work made it possible to conceptualize a chain of material changes for any given species, a chain that was, as a chain, wholly independent of divine intervention. In the context of a society that remained convinced that each individual being was God's final determination, this theory was nothing less than revolutionary. At a stroke, Darwin at once undermined existing circuits of (theological) anthropomorphism. But even as he did so, his choice of metaphors laid the groundwork for a new and in some respects far more insidious circuit of anthropomorphism: the one associated with what is now known as social Darwinism.

To understand social Darwinism, it is necessary to return to the concept of natural selection. Darwin later came to regret the use of this term because it suggested a degree of voluntarism – the notion that evolution was a matter of voluntary processes or procedures. As noted by Robert Young (1985), certainly the choice of metaphor contributed to the voluntaristic reading of his theory. The notion of selection, natural or other, went against Darwin's own dialectic account of evolution as a matter of determination *and* indetermination, secondness *and* firstness.

As I began to suggest in Chapter 2, anthropomorphism is an unavoidable 'by-product' of representation. What is of interest is thus not Darwin's anthropomorphism per se, but the *form* of his anthropomorphism, and indeed the history of this form. It now seems clear that Darwin's metaphor – in Peirce's terms, his icon and his argument – was strongly influenced by a Malthusian and ultimately a Hobbesian discourse: his discourse was informed by an imaginary that conceived society in terms of a battle for survival amongst selfish individuals. In so far as this was the case, it reproduced a pessimistic and reactionary discourse about the nature of nature, a nature of unmitigated and indeed warring secondness.

As noted by Williams (1980), Darwin himself abhorred crude efforts to apply his theory to human social situations. Moreover, he later suggested that the notion of 'natural selection' should perhaps be changed to 'natural preservation' in order to ameliorate the voluntaristic aspects of his theory. The damage of voluntaristic secondness was nonetheless done in so far Darwin's choice of metaphor allowed the subjects of a *capitalist* materialism to appropriate his theory by way of a circuit of anthropomorphism and cosmomorphism that returned it to a kind of Lamarckianism and applied it to people. Socially and historically contingent aspects of society such as class, the unequal distribution of wealth and the marginalization of social groups came to be read as the work of an evolutionary process conceived along Lamarckian or Lamarckian–Malthusian lines. The notion of *natural selection* was thereby interpreted as a kind of natural index that identified and isolated the 'unfit'. More generally, the relations of ideology promoted by industrial capitalism came to be conceived as the result of natural selection, even as capitalism itself became the ultimate 'natural' *selector*.

Indeed, as reconceived by a number of nineteenth-century scientists, politicians and lay observers, Darwin's model was arguably made more fiercely teleological than earlier theories had been. In his classic *Ever Since Darwin*, Gould notes the extraordinary variety of ways and contexts in which Darwin's version of evolution was transformed to suit the discourses of the time. For example, Gould notes that anthropologists specializing in criminality described the inmates of jails as being genetically retarded and thereby closer to the children of 'Africans' or 'Indians'. One of these, the Italian physician Cesare Lambroso, claimed that the shape of the skulls of the male inmates (whose form he meticulously quantified and analysed) revealed that the inmates were throwbacks to a previous evolutionary state – that they were, in effect, apes living in modern society (Gould 1980: 222). An evolutionary process that had somehow been stunted could now be blamed for causing criminal activity. By contrast, law-abiding citizens could tacitly be described as conforming to the 'right' evolutionary process, though presumably Lambroso did not carry out extensive measurements of their skulls to confirm or disprove his theory.

Another example discussed by Gould is particularly relevant to the subject of this book. Ernest Haeckel, a scientist widely credited with coining the term and model for the study of ecology, used evolutionary theory in the late nineteenth century to attack discourses of religious determinism even as he employed the now discredited theory of recapitulation to promote racial determinism. Recapitulationists believed that individuals repeated the adult stages of their ancestors in their own embryonic and juvenile growth (Gould 1980: 216). Haeckel and others promoted this account as a scientific theory that explained the alleged inferiority of 'Negroes'. In its many guises, social Darwinism thereby served to normalize a social order that might now be described as being the work of an 'objective' nature, and thus beyond change.

Heterotopias of nature

Charles Darwin was made a Fellow of the Zoological Society of London in 1831. The Society, founded in 1826, was the parent institution of the new zoological gardens which opened in London in 1828. The gardens were situated in the newly formed Regent's Park, which was to be an exclusive suburb, a refuge from the contamination of the middle classes in other once aristocratic parts of London. The zoo was one of a group of modern institutions that appeared in the late eighteenth to mid-nineteenth centuries and were devoted to the scientific study and the representation of natural specimens: botanic gardens, zoological gardens and natural history museums. Each genre classified its own nature or its own 'subset' of nature. In this section I consider only the modern forms of these genres (i.e. those that appeared between the end of the eighteenth century and the middle of the nineteenth) and focus on just one of their features: what may be described as their *heterotopic* nature.

Zoos, botanic gardens and natural history museums were 'heterotopic' institutions in at least three fundamental respects: first, and perhaps most importantly, all were devoted to assembling something like a representative sample of all species, and this in one place. In zoos, this 'universal' sample was devoted mainly to the animal kingdom. In the botanic gardens, this sample included the plant kingdom. For their part, natural history museums shifted from a synchronic sample to a diachronic or 'historical' sample and included as part of this the inorganic aspects of nature.

If I suggest that each of these nevertheless produced *something like* a universal sample, it is because the sample was an arbitrary one, even within the arbitrary bounds established by the generic classification of each institution. Then as now, for example, zoos were as unlikely to display blue whales as they were to display amoebas and indeed 99 per cent or more of the rest of the planet's named species. However, the arbitrary nature of the ensemble did not contradict the fact that, unlike the older menageries, many modern zoos were organized on the basis of a disposition that nonetheless *aspired* to assemble a kind of universal, global 'sample' on the basis of a planetary consciousness such as I described earlier with Pratt (1992).

The same was true of the natural history museums and the botanic gardens. The current Natural History Museum in London, which opened to the public in 1881 but whose collection was built up by Sir Hans Sloane beginning in the late seventeenth century, eventually amassed some 68 million animals, plants, fossils and minerals. Many of these became 'types', that is, the specimens used to produce the first classifications and published descriptions of their kind (Rice 2000). For its part, the Royal Botanic Gardens at Kew, transformed into one of the world's great botanic centres by Sir Joseph Banks in the late eighteenth century, used the voyages of Captain Cook to the South Pacific, and then travels expressly planned to collect further plant specimens, in order to build up a global collection of plants that might compete with those found in Vienna or Paris (Desmond 1995:

91). Whereas the old tradition of physic gardens attached to medical schools had emerged in sixteenth-century Europe to provide a space for the study of the medicinal properties of plants, the premier botanic gardens now became heterotopic centres where nation-states might flaunt the global reach of their empires.

To be sure, the botanic gardens were not simply centres for collection and accumulation; they also served as centres for the distribution and redistribution of plants. Amsterdam's renowned Hortus Botanicus managed to grow an arabica coffee tree which reportedly provided the basis for arabica plantations in Central and South America. Potted oil palm plants taken from Mauritius to the same botanic garden allowed the highly profitable propagation of the species in the Dutch East Indies. As noted by the historian Richard Drayton (2001), Kew Gardens served similar purposes by importing, amongst others, breadfruit, cocoa, quinine and rubber. Scientists at Kew studied the plants' structure and possible benefits, and then exported them to the British colonies where they were exploited.

While such samples were to have, and to this day continue to have, spectacular functions, officially they were assembled for the purposes of scientific investigation. As the prospectus of the London Zoological Society put it, the Society's zoological gardens, the first in the UK and a model for many other zoos in the world, should provide 'A collection of living animals such as never existed in ancient or modern times . . . animals to be brought from every part of the globe to be applied either to some useful purpose, or as objects of scientific research, not of vulgar admiration' (quoted in Mullan and Marvin 1999: 96).

This prospectus was written in the first half of the nineteenth century, during the heyday of British imperialism. As noted by Harriet Ritvo (1987), no doubt Sir Stamford Raffles and other founding members of the London Zoo wished to produce a space which might be used to display 'wild' animals (and not just *wild* animals; domestic animals were also included) in a manner that reflected the global reach of the British empire.

But the London Zoo was also a response to the perceived need to move away from what the prospectus describes as 'vulgar' forms of observation, perhaps a none too veiled reference to popular cultural forms of displaying animals such as those found in travelling circuses and commercial zoos, but also to the 'common' way of *looking* at animals. Aside from the tacit class reference, this statement signalled an aspiration to replace older techniques of observation of animals with forms that were deemed to be more modern.

It is indeed possible to regard the prospectus as the expression of a discourse that sought to produce a space that might enable the study of specimens from the discursive perspective of Foucault's modern *epistéme*. As noted earlier, a mistrust of representation meant that it was no longer enough to classify specimens along the discursive lines established by the Classical *epistéme*'s forms of visibility; scientists now wished to explain specimens with reference to their *anatomy*, and zoos, natural history museums and botanic gardens provided precisely the space required. Ritvo (1996) notes, for example, that anatomists had standing orders for, amongst other organs, the hearts and diseased joints of animals at the London Zoological Gardens.

It is a matter of some interest that, nonetheless, in the actual display areas the spaces associated with the older Classical and even Renaissance *epistémes* continued to prevail. Natural history museums, for example, used cabinets and actual tables to represent the relations between species long after the Classical *epistéme* had been replaced in the scientific field. The architecture of the London Zoo's first buildings, their layout and some of the places within the overall space suggested a rustic and romantic disposition; they were gardens where visitors could promenade, and be seen to promenade, at their leisure. This was a practice that would be found in most zoological gardens throughout Europe: the zoo was as much a *garden* as it was a zoo. Indeed, the idea of a public *garden* in the growing *cities* of Europe perhaps holds one of the keys to the modern zoo: the zoological garden was at once a sinsign and a legisign of 'nature', a sign of global nature perhaps, but nonetheless a sign of nature *coming into* an urban environment.

In Chapter 2, I suggested that heterotopias simultaneously represented, contested and inverted the relations normally found in the sites they included. This was certainly true of zoos, natural history museums and botanic gardens: in all the different kinds of displays, the specimens' biological or indeed bio-social relations were at once represented and inverted by removing the specimens from their original or 'natural' contexts and recontextualizing them, dead or alive, in a cage, greenhouse or cabinet. While it might be argued that the illustrations of plants produced by Linnaean botanists performed a similar representational operation, in fact zoos, botanic gardens and natural history museums engaged in what was in some respects a radically different practice. In all three kinds of institutions, the representation could not be neatly separated from the empirical object of representation: the living lion in the zoo, the stuffed lion in the natural history museum and of course the living plant in the botanic garden were all instances at once of a nature *represented* (as species, as object of spectacle/observation) and of a nature *presenting itself* by way of its corporeal presence in the very space of representation. In zoos, botanic gardens and natural history museums as in landscape gardens, it was thus possible to speak of peculiarly rhematic indexical sinsigns, i.e. of specimens that were at once their own occurrence (and so sinsigns); their own, or at any rate part of their own, designative indexes in so far as they 'pointed' (or were *made* to point) to themselves; and yet at the same time their own interpretant, that is, a rheme, or apparently no interpretant whatsoever. Put differently, the specimens in the different institutions were instances of what I described in Chapter 4 in terms of entelechy.

The display of such 'perfect signs' was made possible in part by the institutionalization of the new social mobilities mentioned earlier in this chapter. The speedier forms of travel made possible by steam engines and boats meant that specimens could be more easily moved and removed, displaced, placed and then *replaced* to satisfy the requirements not just of scientists but also of larger and larger number of visitors who acquired access to new geographies of natural history.

From an early stage, such representations were accorded a didactic function. The masses were given access to the displays for educational reasons. It would, however, be a mistake to regard this access in naïvely educational terms. The

London Zoo, for example, remained closed to all but the Fellows of the Zoological Society of London and their friends and relations for its first twenty years or so. One of the reasons for this may be that the good Fellows feared that the masses would bring their real or imagined preference for 'grotesque' naturalism, and its concomitant pleasures, to the carefully manicured gardens. However, a mixture of economic considerations and reformist voices in favour of the kind of civilizing role that was accorded to city parks eventually persuaded the Society that the Zoo should be allowed to become a mass medium, that is, a site dedicated to mass mediation in the senses described in earlier chapters.

In the context produced by such reformist discourses, zoos became conceived as spaces that could play a role in teaching the masses not just about the nature of 'exotic' nature but also about the nature of modern ways of *observing* nature: where bull-baiting and other popular blood sports involved the 'grotesque pleasures', the zoo was to exemplify a quiet and 'composed' form of observation, one which, though clearly 'embodied', privileged more controlled forms of *visual* forms of observation. A central aspect of this was the institution of technique of observation *from a distance*.

This could only happen by interrelating two apparently simple, but in fact rather complexly embedded, sets of social boundaries. First, and in keeping with Foucault's theory of heterotopia, the new institutions were clearly bounded off from their surrounding physical space by walls or fences, a practice which signalled the production of a special social space. While the rules of admission to such a space varied from country to country – whereas most British zoos charged for entry once they allowed the 'commoner' access to the grounds, France's Muséum National in Paris offered free entrance (Mullan and Marvin 1999) – the different institutions shared a heterotopic rule in so far as they placed nature 'behind closed doors'. Of course, it might well be argued that, in one sense, the nature of the world was now 'opened up' to the masses – it was moved to public displays. But this paradoxically presupposed placing natural objects *in* buildings, *in* the grounds of menageries or *in* botanic gardens. As a result, even in those cases where visitors were not charged, a very strong empirical and symbolic classification was created that placed nature quite literally within the physical and social boundaries of the new institutions.

Such a classification, and the modality of framing that maintained it, both required and presupposed a second, 'internal' form of classification. The outer perimeter of the new institutions of nature was corresponded by a series of internal display boundaries: the bars separating visitors from wild animals, the glass cabinets and tables of natural history museums, and the less strongly classified borders of flower beds or greenhouses in botanic gardens. Even as such barriers kept the *specimens in* and the *visitors out* of the displays, a principle of observation was taught, explicitly and implicitly, that replaced a kind of working, or at least lived, everyday relation 'to' nature as an integral part of the self. It is paradoxical in the sense that even as nature was in one respect 'interiorized' – that is taken quite literally to the 'interior' of modern institutions – it was 'exteriorized' in so far as it was objectified for the purposes of contemplation.

I would like to suggest a caveat with respect to this argument. Even if the new institutions presupposed a more strongly *visual* form of observation, their characteristic forms of design and display cannot be described as a simple continuation of the forms of *askesis* associated with the camera obscura discussed with Crary (1990) in Chapter 3. Especially in the new zoos and botanic gardens, the new technologies of observation constituted spaces where a certain negotiation took place between the demands of a bourgeois, individuated form of visual practice, premised on the apparent decorporealization of observation, and the demands of popular practices embedded in traditions of grotesque naturalism. For the latter, touching, prodding, 'gaping' and above all engaging in *collective* forms of observation were of the utmost importance: the very practices of *vulgar admiration* explicitly repudiated by the London Zoo's prospectus continued to exist, both in the practices of visitors and in the practices of the institutions themselves. The latter continued to accommodate, at times grudgingly, at least some of the tastes of their audiences by incorporating, in the hegemonic sense of this term, forms of display that echoed some of the popular preferences. So it was, for example, that people were allowed to ride on elephants, that zookeepers 'kissed' sea lions (as in the celebrated case of Lecomte, the French sailor at the London Zoo) or that families could take pictures of themselves holding monkeys dressed up as humans, a practice which continued as late as the 1960s in some zoos.

The modalities of observation in these new heterotopias of nature reflected these contradictory demands in so far as they produced a space for a hybrid form of observation: one that, as Kean (1998) and others have rightly noted, *did* privilege the visual spectacle, *did* attempt to institute a general 'look but don't touch' form of spectacle, but also one that still generated the spaces for, and eventually actively encouraged, 'mass' observation. This such that a certain 'contact zone,' which was by no means purely *visual*, remained between plants, animals or natural objects and the corporeality of the institutions' visitors. This contact zone allowed visitors to *reach out* (and *in*) with their limbs, but also to hear, smell, touch and on occasion feel the vibrations of the animals. But the very act of 'reaching out', through bars and eventually across moats, symbolized the very exteriorization of nature that was and remains a hallmark of the modern imaginary of nature.

6

THE NATURE OF SUBLIMATION

I had a passion for maps. . . . At that time there were many blank
spaces on the earth, and when I saw one that looked particularly
inviting on the map (but they all look like that) I would put my
finger on it and say, When I grow up I will go there.

Marlow in *Heart of Darkness*

The nationalization of parks

Even as Wordsworth suggested ways in which the Lake District in England might
be saved from 'rash assault', across the Atlantic similar concerns would result in
the emergence of a figure that was to become emblematic of modern environmentalism: the institution, beginning in 1864, of national parks.

Nominally the first such park was the Yellowstone, which was formally established in 1872 by an act of the US Congress. However, the practice of setting
aside a vast swathe of land as an 'inalienable public trust' had first been tested at
least eight years earlier in what is now the Yosemite National Park.[1] Although the
Yosemite was accorded national park status much later (in 1890), it was arguably
the first instance in which a national government classified, as Abraham Lincoln's
did in 1864, a large area for public 'enjoyment'.

It is clear from the discourse in the act that created Yellowstone that the members of the US Congress did not quite know what they were helping to invent:
the description of the new Yellowstone Park, for example, spoke of setting apart
the land 'as a public park or pleasuring-ground for the benefit and enjoyment of
the people'. Today this description seems better suited for an urban park than it
does a 'national park'.[2]

Beyond its significance from the point of view of a conventional history of
modern conservationism, the formation of these and eventually of several other
US parks marked an extraordinarily paradoxical moment in the history of the
modern institution of imaginary nature. On the one hand, the material prerequi-
site for the 'enjoyment of the people' was, as I will explain below, a form of ethnic
cleansing, if not genocide. But also, at the very moment when modern cultural

134

practices arguably began to fatally undermine the possibility of maintaining an unambiguous classification of nature and culture – at the historical juncture when the last 'untouched' natures were colonized and photographed, and when air pollution produced by the industrial North began to make its way around the entire globe, inaugurating by its circulation a new kind of globalism – steps were taken to classify by juridico-geographical means a land that might now be classified *as* 'nature': in effect, as a *sublime* nature.

Henceforth, 'nature' was framed as a massive enclosure, a form of entelechy that might be exploited as so many gargantuan dicent sinsigns of nature by all except those who had originally inhabited its natural space. But at the same time the parks were, and today remain, dicent symbols of a fast vanishing natural space.

The invention of national parks is usually credited to one of a handful of pioneering individuals that proposed the idea. For example, the National Park Service and a number of historians credit George Catlin with having come up with the idea of setting aside large areas of land as national parks. Catlin, described as 'a noted painter of the American Indian', is reported to have become concerned with the effect of migration by white settlers on aboriginal groups and the wildlife of the 'American West' during a trip to the Dakotas in 1831. By one account, '[h]e wrote of his dream that there might be "by some great protecting policy of the government preserved . . . in a magnificent park . . . a nation's park, containing man and beast, in all wildness and freshness of their nature's beauty!"' (History of the National Park Service, http://www.nps.gov/wrst/npshistory.htm, accessed 2 August 2005).

Aside from establishing a certain equivalence between the preservation of wildlife and 'the American Indian', such references overlook the broader historical significance of a dynamic that might well be compared to Newton's interest in alchemy, or Nisard's interest in the *colportage* literature. Echoing Jesús Martín-Barbero (1993), we can say in this sense that painters, and later photographers and anthropologists, became interested in the aboriginal groups in the US precisely when the groups in question were no longer allowed to speak for themselves.

The verity of this dynamic seems particularly evident in the events that led up to the 'discovery' of the Yosemite. In January of 1848, some workers building a sawmill near Sacramento found some tiny gold nuggets. The discovery was the beginning of the infamous California Gold Rush, a migration of an estimated half million fortune-seekers who travelled from all over the world to work in the mines. In their rush to find the precious metal, the gold-diggers invaded the ancestral lands of several aboriginal groups. California had been colonized by the Spanish for centuries, but Spanish colonial outposts, in the form of *pueblos*, *presidios* and Franciscan *misiones* tended to be located close to the coastal regions. While the Spaniards forced aboriginal groups to work for them in these regions, the land east and north continued to be controlled by groups such as the Miwok and the Yokut. The independence of Mexico in 1821 led to a shift towards large *rancherías*, but it was not until the Mexican–American War of Annexation of 1846, and especially the beginning of the Gold Rush, that growing encroachment and then state-sponsored displacement (if not genocide) began to modify drastically the conditions that had prevailed for most of the aboriginal groups since the arrival of the Spanish. Wherever the groups resisted with some success, they were killed or forcibly resettled by the US government or by mercenary expeditions organized by gold-diggers. At this juncture in the history of the US, as in others that would follow, the expansion and consolidation of the nation-state was driven by a particularly brutal political economy.

One of the mercenary expeditions organized by the US government and the gold-diggers had among its members a medic called Lafayette Houghton Bunnell. Whilst pursuing one of the aboriginal groups into a mountain valley, Bunnell and the rag-tag battalion that he joined came upon what would be known eventually as the Yosemite Valley. By his own account, Bunnell saw the Yosemite for the first time on 21 March, 1851. His description in *The Discovery of the Yosemite* is evocative: 'we suddenly came in full view of the valley. . . . The immensity of the rock I had seen in my vision on the Old Bear Valley trail . . . was here presented to my astonished gaze. The mystery of that scene was here disclosed. My awe was increased by this nearer view'(Bunnell 1990: 56).

In the next paragraph he added a passage that exemplifies the discourse on the sublime which I considered in Chapter 5: 'It has been said that "it is not easy to describe in words the precise impression which great objects make upon us." I cannot describe how completely I realized this truth' (Bunnell 1990: 56). This passage evokes the Kantian sublime particularly clearly: here was, in Kant's words, a landscape that was 'absolutely large', 'beyond comparison', one which forced Bunnell to become both aware, and aware of the limitations, of his 'mental attunement' with it.

Now Bunnell decided that the valley should be given the name of the people he was pursuing. In his words,

> I remarked [during a discussion about the naming of the valley] that 'an American name would be the most appropriate;' that 'I could not see any necessity for going to a foreign country for a name for American scenery – the grandest that had ever yet been looked upon. That it would be better to give it an Indian name than to import a strange and inexpressive one; that the name of the tribe who had occupied it would be more appropriate than any I had ever suggested.' I then proposed 'that we give the valley the name of Yo-sem-i-ty, as it was suggestive, euphonious, and certainly American; that by so doing, the name of the tribe of Indians which we met leaving their homes in this valley, perhaps never to return, would be perpetuated'.
>
> (Bunnell 1990: 62)

Today it is suggested that the groups that inhabited this region of the Sierra were in fact of Southern Miwok ancestry. In Bunnell's naming of the landscape we nonetheless find at once the logic of a remarkable anthropologist-cum-etymologist intent on recognizing the names and traditions of the 'savages' – the term used at the time by most whites in the US – but also the logic of an ideologue of a paradoxical process that can be metaphorically compared to palimpsest. In literary studies the concept of palimpsest refers to the process of writing over existing 'text'; in this context, it can be employed to describe a dynamic by means of which white gold-diggers in effect overcoded one culture with their own. Even if Bunnell was intent on memorializing the Yosemites, it is clear that his proposed name blurred the boundary between the classification 'American' and what he described as 'Yo-sem-i-ty'. Moreover, his framing of this passage dissimulated the fact that the 'Yosemites' were not just 'leaving' their ancestral lands: they were being brutally displaced by a combination of mercenary gold-diggers and US government forces intent on disabling any resistance to rapacious, state-sponsored capitalism in the so-called 'American West' – or as one traveller put it, 'our new west' (Bowles 1869).

As this episode begins to make evident, however much the notion of sublime used to describe the US western frontier owed to modern European romanticism, it came to constitute an explicitly nationalist circuit of anthropomorphism. While many observers in the US travelled to Europe and learned from European technologies of observation, eventually the sheer scale and apparent infinity of natural resources in the United States came to be regarded as a complex qualisign of all that Europe was *not* and all that the new nation *could be*. Whereas the European nation-states had decimated their own material natures thanks in no small part to centuries of warmongering, one of the distinguishing features of the new 'America' was that its natural resources were not just sublime but bountiful, indeed apparently boundless. This nationalism is evident in Bunnell's discourse about an appropriate name for Yosemite (it should be an '*American*' name).

Although Bunnell's account was not published until some thirty years after the event, his account of the sublimity of the land echoed the discourse of several other representations in paintings and photographs that helped to establish the Yosemite Valley as the world's first large-scale natural park, and eventually as one of the most visited tourist sites in the United States.

An analogous process would later take place in Yellowstone: there too the US government displaced aboriginal groups, and the publication in 1876 of Hayden's *The Yellowstone National Park* with a written account of the land and 15 chromolithographs – lithographic replicas in full colour of the watercolour sketches produced by the landscape painter Thomas Moran, which were deemed to be more naturalistic than photographs as they included colour – were to play an important role in establishing the Yellowstone as the world's first actual national park.

The nature essayists

It might be thought that the perceived sublimity of the landscape was a sufficient cause for the formation of natural parks. But park-making was a function of a complex matrix of discourses, interests and new technologies of observation.

One such discourse was produced by nature essayists such as Ralph Waldo Emerson, Henry David Thoreau and other members of the so-called 'Concord Circle'. Emerson and Thoreau worked to produce a philosophy which in many respects continued and developed the romantic tradition considered in Chapter 4. They did so primarily by way of the genre of the essay, whose length and publication in nineteenth-century journals made it an ideal medium with which to reach 'learned' readers.

Emerson was an advocate of 'transcendentalism,' a literary and philosophical movement that developed in New England in the mid-1800s and reacted against eighteenth-century rationalism. The movement also reacted against the puritanical Calvinism that prevailed in the northeast of the US at the time. Perhaps the most influential of the nature essayists, in his collection *Nature* (1836) and in later essays Emerson evoked the movement's characteristic belief in the unity of God and nature. But his discourse also privileged a nature of appearances, a 'phenomenal nature' that was in effect a kind of icon or spectacle whose diversity might be read in order to divine the underlying and unifying presence of God. Indeed, the diversity of nature was a dicentical symbol of 'the currents of the Universal Being' (Emerson 1906: 374).

But Emerson's discourse also incorporates nature in a circuit of anthropomorphism that suggests an almost narcissistic technology of the self. As Emerson puts it in *Nature*, 'The greatest delight which the fields and woods minister, is the suggestion of an occult relation between man and the vegetable. I am not alone and unacknowledged. They nod to me, and I to them' (1906: 375). In this discourse, we can say that being 'at one with nature' is at the same time 'being one in nature' but also 'being nature's one'.

Henry David Thoreau's work produced what was in some respects a more radical discourse about the nature of nature. In one famous essay on walking published in 1863, Thoreau spoke in 'an extreme statement' 'a word for Nature, for absolute freedom and wildness, as contrasted with a freedom and culture merely civil' (Thoreau 1863: 161). In the essay Thoreau made the case not just for walking in the woods but for doing so in ways that confounded the times of capitalism: 'I confess that I am astonished at the power of endurance, to say nothing of the moral insensibility, of my neighbours who confine themselves to shops and offices the whole day for weeks and months, ay, and years almost together' (Thoreau 1863: 165). Thoreau applied the same critique to himself, noting not only that at times he found himself taking the village with him into the woods – 'I am alarmed when it happens that I have walked a mile into the woods bodily, without getting there in spirit' (Thoreau 1863: 168) – but also the extent to which this transgression went hand in hand with the decorporealization and desensualization that he associated with the town: 'The thought of some work will run in my head, and I am not where my body is, – I am out of my senses' (Thoreau 1863: 168).

An analysis of the differences in these two authors' philosophies is beyond the scope of this chapter.[3] Here I simply wish to note that their work made available a discourse that established important precedents for the environmentalist movement and the green imaginary that would emerge in the United States in the mid-twentieth century. The essays gave new life to a pastoralist version of the romantic discourse that suggested that the observer might find a kind of sensual solace in a 'nature' that was strongly classified and framed in opposition to the town or the city. While the transcendentalism of Emerson still made this a means to an end – the divination of God's diverse and unifying presence – in the writings of Thoreau this solace was increasingly an end in itself. The experience of nature must not be contaminated by any form of modernity whatsoever; not even by the times or 'thoughts' of modernity – 'what business have I in the woods, if I am thinking of something out of the wood?' (Thoreau 1863: 169).

Paradoxically, the terms of Thoreau's discourse could not be more modern in so far as they so strongly opposed nature and culture, nature and work. His discourse, like that of Emerson, reflected an urban, and no doubt a bourgeois, disposition which Thoreau rejected in favour of a sublime and indeed *sublimated* encounter with nature. In Freudian theory sublimation refers to the transformation of a natural impulse or instinct into one that is socially acceptable. We may fuse this notion with older alchemical meanings of the term[4] and with the meanings of the sublime discussed in Chapter 4 to describe a process whereby a certain natural space – or material nature more generally – is transformed into a dicent symbol charged, if not with a certain sexuality, then with a certain sensuality.

Sublimation, thus defined, seems to be particularly evident in the writings of an author that many regard as the 'father' of modern environmentalism: John Muir. Muir contributed directly to the establishment of several of the most prestigious natural parks and wrote prolifically about their natural wonders. While he reproduced elements of the transcendentalism and of the romantic sublime described earlier in this book, he combined his writing skills with those of a naturalist. More than a 'philosopher', he wrote popular essays that were invocations, even incantations of the wonders of an intensely lived and indeed sensualized nature, which he sought and found especially in the Yosemite. Where Emerson's and Thoreau's discourse was still strongly an appeal to the 'mind', Muir's discourse suggests a corporeality and a practical quality that was to inform environmentalist 'direct action' in the century to come. Muir's work was, in this sense, his life, and there can be little doubt that part of the success of his writings lay in his capacity to engage in dramatic and no doubt self-dramatizing accounts of encounters with a much 'wilder' nature than that experienced in the still predominantly urban or exurban experiences of Emerson and Thoreau.

One such famous encounter involved the experience of a mountain storm whilst Muir was up in a tree:

> After cautiously casting about, I made choice of the tallest of a group of Douglas Spruces that were growing close together like a tuft of grass, no one of which seemed likely to fall unless all the rest fell with it. Though comparatively young, they were about 100 feet high, and their lithe, brushy tops were rocking and swirling in wild ecstasy. Being accustomed

to climb trees in making botanical studies, I experienced no difficulty in reaching the top of this one, and never before did I enjoy so noble an exhilaration of motion. The slender tops fairly flapped and swished in the passionate torrent, bending and swirling backward and forward, round and round, tracing indescribable combinations of vertical and horizontal curves, while I clung with muscles firm braced, like a bobo-link on a reed.

(Muir 1997: 176)

The strikingly erotic character of this account and Muir's own gendering of nature as female in other passages of his work are examples of what I described earlier as the sublimation of nature.

If Muir's sublimation of nature involved a more radically corporeal experience of nature than was found in the work of Emerson and Thoreau, his *A Thousand-Mile Walk to the Gulf* (1996), an account of a botanical expedition that Muir commenced in Indianapolis in 1867, also suggests a more radical classification of the city and the country. By Muir's own account, he 'steered' through Louisville 'by compass without speaking a word to any one', and his plan was to 'simply push on in a general southward direction by the wildest, leafiest, and least trodden way [he] could find, promising the greatest extent of virgin forest' (1996: 1).

Finding such a forest was a matter of finding God's creation, a creation that was by no means made *for* 'man'. Indeed, a central aspect of Muir's discourse was a critique of the anthropocentric character of capitalism. As he put it in the sixth chapter of *A Thousand-Mile Walk*:

The world, we are told, was made especially for man. . . . In the same pleasant plan, whales are storehouses of oil for us. . . . Among plants, hemp, to say nothing of cereals, is a case of evident destination for ships' rigging . . . all was intended for us.

(Muir 1996: 65–6)

In fact, Muir argued, numerous natural phenomena were irreconcilable with this view:

How about those man-eating animals – lions, tigers, alligators – which smack their lips over raw man? Or about those myriads of noxious insects that destroy labor and drink his blood? Doubtless man was intended for food and drink for all these? Oh, no! Not at all! These are unresolvable difficulties connected with Eden's apple and the Devil.

(Muir 1996: 66)

In a passage that suggests the kind of ecocentrism attributed more than half a century later to environmentalists such as James Lovelock (1979), Muir argued that:

Nature's object in making animals and plants might possibly be first of all the happiness of each one of them, not the creation of all for the happiness of one. Why should man value himself as more than a small part of the one great unit of creation? And what creature of all that the Lord has taken the pains to make is not essential to the completeness of that unit – the cosmos? The universe would be incomplete without man; but it would also be incomplete without the smallest transmicroscopic creature that dwells beyond our conceitful eyes and knowledge.

(Muir 1996: 66)

These and numerous other writings provided the basis for what was perhaps Muir's most significant contribution not just to the environmentalist imaginary but to the institution of a *field* dedicated to what are now environmentalist *causes célèbres:* his role in campaigning to protect areas of outstanding natural beauty such as the Yosemite, and in founding the Sierra Club. It was thanks in no small part to Muir's publications[5] that the Yosemite was transformed into an actual national park in 1890. To be sure, Muir participated in numerous other campaigns and made the more general case for what was described at the time as the need to keep the parks 'forever inviolate'. This was a patriarchal reference to the fact that, long after many of the national parks were established, they continued to be used for hunting and other commercial purposes. Though Muir himself worked at a sawmill in the Yosemite and had once been a shepherd in the region, he campaigned successfully to eliminate many forms of exploitation from natural parks, not least shepherding, which he compared in the frontispiece of *The Mountains of California* to the spreading of locusts.

As part of this process, and as I began to suggest earlier, he was one of the founding members of the Sierra Club, which, by the beginning of the twenty-first century, had approximately 700,000 members. Established in 1892, the Sierra Club was to allow its members 'to explore, enjoy, and rendure [*sic*] accessible the mountain regions of the Pacific Coast; to publish authentic information concerning them,' and 'to enlist the support and cooperation of the people and government in preserving the forests and other natural features of the Sierra Nevada' (Sierra Club, http://www.sierraclub.org/history/origins/chapter3.asp, accessed 19 September 2004). The Sierra Club was to become one of the first environmentalist or proto-environmentalist non-government organisations.

The great whites

Another discourse played a significant role in the formation of the national parks. It was the one produced by an elite group that offered a rather different form of intellectual leadership in the United States: the so-called 'great white hunters,' wealthy men for whom hunting was at once the ultimate space 'with' nature – in fact the *contest* of nature – and thereby the ultimate test of masculinity.

Perhaps the most famous and powerful of the great whites was Teddy Roosevelt.

Roosevelt played an active role in fostering a movement that continues to this day: an early form of environmentalism which effectively blurred the boundary between conservationism and preservationism in so far as its subjects advocated the setting aside of wilderness areas, albeit for the purpose of hunting. Indeed, whereas the preservationist romantics used a sublimated nature space to develop a technology of the self based on the kind of experience of firstness described by Rousseau, the hunter-conservationist technology of the self was premised on an explicitly masculinist discourse of secondness in so far as the relation to nature was constructed very much as an individual contest of strength, stamina, astuteness and determination.

The businessman-cum-hunter, Samuel Hammond, offers a good example of the technology of the self in question. Hammond published his influential *Wild Northern Scene; or Sporting Adventures with the Rifle and the Rod* in 1857. In it, he developed what was arguably a more sexualized description of a pastoral idyll set in the Adirondacks: 'What I wanted was, to get outside of the city . . . to lay around loose in a promiscuous way among the hills, where beautiful lakes lay sleeping in their quiet loveliness' (Hammond 1857: 22–3). He combined this with what seem today examples of extraordinary cruelty to animals: in one instance, Hammond and his friends trapped a deer on a small island and harassed it for some time 'by way of experimenting upon his fears, or rather as Martin said, "to see what he would do."' (Hammond 1857: 228).

Hammond regarded such expeditions as a much needed respite from work and modernity. Indeed, like Emerson and Thoreau, he complained at the encroachment of 'civilization' in the Eastern United States: 'who ever thought that Vermont would be traversed by railroads, or that the echoes that dwell among her precipices and mountain fastnesses, would ever wake to the snort of the iron horse?' (Hammond 1857: 21). He contrasted these and other scenes of the encounter between an explicitly gendered nature and economic development with the apparently untouched qualities of places like the Rackett River:

> The woodman's axe has not marred the loveliness of its surroundings, and no human hand has for all that distance been laid upon its mane, or harnessed it to the great wheel, making it a slave, compelling it to be utilitarian, to grind corn or throw the shuttle and spin. It moves on towards the mighty St. Lawrence as wild, and halterless, and free, as when the Great Spirit sent it toward on its everlasting flow.
>
> (Hammond 1857: 82–3)

This idyll, Hammond noted, could not last for long if the present rates of encroachment were to prevail, and radical steps were needed to be taken to prevent further loss:

> Civilization is pushing its way even towards this wild and, for all agricultural purposes, sterile region, and before many years even the Rackett

will be within its ever-extending circle. When that time shall have arrived, where shall we go to find woods, the wild things, the old forests, and hear the sounds which belong to nature in its primeval state? Whither shall we flee from civilization, to take off the harness and be free, for a season, from the restraints, the conventionalities of society, and rest from the hard struggles, the cares and toils, the strifes and competitions of life? Had I my way, I would mark out a circle of a hundred miles in diameter, and throw around it the protecting ægis of the constitution. I would make it a forest forever. It should be a misdemeanour to chop down a tree, and a felony to clear an acre within its boundaries. The old woods should stand here always as God made them.

(Hammond 1857: 83)

We find here another early and explicit recommendation for setting aside land which, protected by the constitution, would presumably be available to the public. We also find, however, an allusion to a consideration that would prove to be crucial for the formation of parks: only those lands that were thought to be 'sterile' or useless from the point of view of capitalist exploitation survived the litmus test applied by the all-powerful developers of the time.

The last point reminds us of a key early difference vis-à-vis the contemporary notion of national parks. Even after the Yosemite and Yellowstone parks had been formed, there was no question but that the exploitation of natural resources should continue in both parks. As the legislation for the Yosemite park made clear, it was expected that the parks should be 'improved' – that is to say developed – in order to pay for their own management as parks. This is one of the reasons why Muir campaigned to have the Yosemite transformed into a new kind of park.

An example of such 'improvement' may be found in the activities of Frederic Olmsted, a noted landscape architect who established Central Park in New York City, and who was named chair of the commission charged with running the new Yosemite Park. Olmsted allowed hotels and other tourist venues to be established on the park grounds, and asked, among others, the photographer Carleton Watkins (discussed below) to take pictures of the park in order to promote it (Nickel 1999).

As noted by Joseph L. Sax (1980), Olmsted was the first to make the case for the setting aside of the parks as parks in a manner that did not simply take for granted the significance of the sublimity of the landscape. Olmsted clearly thought that the geography *was* sublime: as he put it in the *Saturday Evening Post* of 18 June 1868, 'The union of the deepest sublimity with the deepest beauty of nature . . . constitutes the Yo Semite the greatest glory of nature. No photograph or series of photographs, no paintings ever prepare a visitor so that he is not taken by surprise.' However, in his report on the management of Yosemite, he suggested that the primary motive for preserving the park lay in what he described as the 'contemplative faculties':

143

It is unquestionably true that excessive and persistent devotion to sordid interests cramps and distorts the power of appreciating natural beauty and destroys the love of it which the Almighty has implanted in every human being, and which is so intimately and mysteriously associated with the moral perceptions and intuition, but it is not true that exemption from toil, much leisure, much study, much wealth, are necessary to the exercise of the esthetic and contemplative faculties. It is the folly of laws which have permitted and favored the monopoly by privileged classes of many of the means supplied in nature for the gratification, exercise and education of the esthetic faculties that has caused the appearance of dullness and weakness and disease of these faculties in the mass of the subjects of kings. And it is against the limitation of the means of such education to the rich that the wise legislation of free governments must be directed.

> (Olmsted 1865 in http://www.cr.nps.gov/history/online_books/
> anps/anps_1b.htm, accessed 5 July 2005)

The conservation and restoration of such 'contemplative faculties' was, Olmsted argued, the moral and philosophical basis for the parks. On one level, this discourse is strongly reminiscent especially of the transcendentalists whom I referred to earlier. It is nonetheless clear that, in Olmsted's discourse, and indeed in the US more generally, an appreciation for the wonders of the nature of the 'American West' went hand in hand with a keen awareness of its economic potential. Contemporary references to California's giant sequoias, for example, noted the astonishing nature of the trees even as they made precise calculations as to the number of boards that each tree might yield (N. Anderson 1991: 273). Perhaps for this reason, Olmsted emphasized the therapeutic potential that nature contemplation would have for everyday productivity, and indeed, on the faculty of attention itself:

there is a special reason why the reinvigoration of those parts which are stirred into conscious activity by natural scenery is more effective upon the general development and health than that of any other, which is this: The severe and excessive exercise of the mind which leads to the greatest fatigue and is the most wearing upon the whole constitution is almost entirely caused by application to the removal of something to be apprehended in the future, or to interests beyond those of the moment, or of the individual; to the laying up of wealth, to the preparation of something, to accomplishing something in the mind of another, and especially to small and petty details which are uninteresting in themselves and which engage the attention at all only because of the bearing they have on some general end of more importance which is seen ahead.

In the interest which natural scenery inspires there is the strongest contrast to this. It is for itself and at the moment it is enjoyed. The attention is aroused and the mind occupied without purpose, without a continuation of the common process of relating the present action, thought or perception to some future end.

(Olmsted 1865 in http://www.cr.nps.gov/history/online_books/
anps/anps_1b.htm, accessed 5 July 2005)

Setting aside the land of the parks was thereby a form of mass mediation in so far as the restoration of the attentive faculties contributed to the general well-being of the nation, and in so far as this in turn contributed to nation-building.

The pencil of nature

It is time to return to the United Kingdom in order to consider a remarkable development that was mentioned by Olmsted in his article of the *Saturday Review* and was to play a significant role in the mass mediation of both the Yosemite and Yellowstone parks: the invention of photography.

The invention of analogue photography is commonly credited to Henry Fox Talbot, a nineteenth century 'gentleman of science' with interests in botany, astronomy, philosophy, art and philology (Weaver 1992: 1). Talbot developed what he described as 'the new art of photogenic drawing' (Weaver 1992: 75), one of two competing photographic media.[6]

In some respects, Talbot's 'new art', like Gutenberg's printing press and Alberti's perspective technique, was actually based on an assemblage of 'old' techniques and technologies. Talbot made the first photographic cameras with box-like camera obscuras – hence the name, still used to this day, of camera. Moreover, natural philosophers had known since at least the end of the Renaissance that silver chloride, the substance used by Talbot to coat the first photographic papers, was darkened by sunlight. But the actual photographic medium had still not been invented well into the nineteenth century, and it would be a form of inverse technological determinism to suggest that this technology was simply 'waiting to be invented'. It is more accurate to suggest that a complex set of social motivations, as articulated in and by Talbot, produced the circumstances for its development.

One such motivation was the romantic appetite for landscape tourism, a practice which, as explained in the last chapter, became increasingly popular in the UK during the first half of the nineteenth century. Talbot's wealth allowed him to travel overseas in search of painterly landscapes, and he was, by his own account, 'a wanderer in classic Italy' (Talbot 1992: 78). Even if as a philologist Talbot quarrelled with those who defined the sublime as a matter of a threshold (Weaver 1992: 12), there can be little doubt that he reproduced aspects of the romantic sensibility for beautiful and sublime landscapes.

But Talbot's interest in Italian landscapes is only one in a matrix of other equally significant motivations. As Talbot explained in *The Pencil of Nature* – an early history of the invention of photography, as well as the first book to be illustrated with photographs – in October of 1833 he was amusing [himself] on the lovely shores of the Lake of Como, in Italy, taking sketches with Wollaston's Camera Lucida, or rather I should say, attempting to take them: but with the smallest possible amount of success. For when the eye was removed from the prism – in which all looked beautiful – I found that the faithless pencil had only left traces on the paper melancholy to behold.

(Talbot 1992: 76)

The *camera lucida* was a device used by painters to produce the outline of a scene on canvas. It employed a prism to reflect an image of a landscape onto a canvas, so that the outlines of the scenery might be traced and used as the basis for the actual painting. Talbot's immediate ostensive interest was, by his own account, his dissatisfaction with this technology, which failed to produce the 'perfect' representation he wished to produce: a representation which, in effect, was not meant to be a representation at all, an absolutely rhematic representation involving what Peirce described as entelechy.

In fact, photography and the photographic media to follow photography *sensu stricto* were not instances of entelechy in so far as they presupposed a clear discontinuity between sign object, representamen and interpretant. It might therefore be more accurate to describe such media as 'quasi-entelechies'. It is possible to explain Talbot's *desire* for this entelechy with reference to two discursive shifts which took place between the second half of the eighteenth century and the first quarter of the nineteenth. First, as I noted in Chapter 5, this period saw a change to new forms of naturalism; one way of interpreting Talbot's invention is as a continuation, in the field of the visual arts, of the discursive shift described by Foucault in *The Order of Things* from 'double representation' to, allegedly, 'no representation at all'. We may, in this sense, interpret the photographic technology as perhaps the most radical expression of this shift in *epistémes*: the problem was no longer to find a better way of painting nature but, rather, to engage in its naturalistic reproduction. In effect, Talbot invented a medium that, barring the dimensions of colour, extra-visual senses and movement, suggested a very high correspondence between the immediate object of representation, the representation and its immediate (visual) interpretant – what might be described as a high degree of naturalism.

However, what made it seem even more naturalistic was the fact that photographic representations were, at one and the same time, utterly indexical: on one level at least, it was the action of light on a surface that caused Talbot's coated paper to darken in direct correspondence to its natural qualities, and this in such a way that it produced at once an icon and an index of the photographed object. As Talbot himself noted, 'Now Light, where it exists, can exert an action, and, in certain circumstances, does exert one sufficient to cause changes in material bodies' (Talbot 1992: 77).

This is not to suggest that his photographs lacked a legisignical or symbolic dimension. Clearly, the art of photography continued to be ineluctably selective, and remained structured by social dynamics of classification and framing. Talbot himself spoke of photography as a new *art*, and indeed many of his images appeared to be structured by relatively explicit and carefully planned cultural references. For example, Weaver (1992) makes the case that one of Talbot's most famous images, 'The Open Door',[7] which depicts what appears at first glance to be a rustic scene, in fact makes legisignical references to the Enlightenment – the lantern of Diogenes, one of Rousseau's intellectual 'heroes' – as well as to Stoicism – the 'bridle of passion' and 'the broom that sweeps the threshold of the dark chamber clean' (Weaver 1992: 2).

It is nonetheless the case that the photographic art was radically different from the painted art in so far as a 'mechanical' form of indexicality played a far more significant role in the production of the images. This constitutes the second general discursive context for the emergence of photography. As noted by Paul Valéry and quoted by the philosopher Walter Benjamin, 'Just as water, gas, and electricity are brought into our houses from far off to satisfy our needs in response to a minimal effort, so we shall be supplied with visual or auditory images, which will appear and disappear at a simple movement of the hand, hardly more than a sign' (Valéry in Benjamin 1999: 213). Whereas Brunelleschi's invention signalled an early version of this kind of indexicality, and previous media such as lithography had made significant inroads in the actual process, photography introduced qualitative changes by virtue of what Benjamin describes as the mechanical reproduction of art: 'for the first time in the process of pictorial reproduction, photography freed the hand of the most important artistic functions which henceforth devolved only upon the eye looking into a lens' (Benjamin 1999: 213).

This process had a number of consequences for the representation and indeed the social experience of nature. On the one hand, the medium of photography began to dramatically alter the ways of sensing the world – to photograph something was to render two-dimensional, black and white, silent and exclusively 'visual' what might otherwise be perceived multisensually. But, more significantly, any given photograph might itself be dramatically altered by way of the process of enlargement. As noted by Benjamin, 'photographic reproduction, with the aid of certain processes, such as enlargement or slow motion, can capture images which escape natural vision' (Benjamin 1999: 214). Photography, in this sense, made it possible not just for nature to ostensibly 'draw itself' but for humans to see entirely new natures: natures that had escaped observation thanks to the limitations of the human eye; but, equally importantly, natures that might be plainly seen by the human eye but would only now be observed in a new manner thanks to the peculiar framing possibilities of photography. I suggested an analogous point when I argued in Chapter 5 that railway travel, a technology of displacement that was instituted at about the same time as photography, began to alter, prosthetically, the sensorium with which both physical and social space might be perceived.

But, in so doing, photography also shattered what Benjamin describes as the aura of phenomena. If the aura of social phenomena was a matter of tradition and authenticity, in the case of nature it was 'the unique phenomenon of a distance, however close it may be' (Benjamin 1999: 216), a phenomenon which Benjamin illustrates with the act of gazing upon a mountain range or a branch: 'If, while resting on a summer afternoon, you follow with your eyes a mountain range on the horizon or a branch which casts its shadow over you, you experience the aura of those mountains, of that branch' (Benjamin 1999: 216). While Benjamin's account suggests a relation of secondness, with Peirce we might suggest that the aura is closer to, if not quintessentially a matter of, *firstness*.

So, even as photography made certain natures 'universally available', it did so at the expense of their 'auras'. A nature that once could only be experienced in a certain place, but paradoxically with the benefit of a certain distance, might now be substituted by an icon imprinted indexically on a piece of chemically treated paper. This same print might be reproduced hundreds of times, if not indefinitely. It was a qualisign of the times that the new medium brought nature 'that much closer' and yet made its experience increasingly a matter of simulation – a theme that I will return to in later chapters. In Peircian terms, we might say that the loss of the aura entailed the loss of the firstness of nature in favour of its photographic thirdness, but, paradoxically, this thirdness was itself represented as a kind of substitute firstness. Where the 'old' numerical indexes described in Chapter 3 required a relatively explicit 'adjustment' in order to achieve their indexical status, this process was now concealed behind the veil of an apparent firstness, the paradoxical immediacy suggested by the expression 'the pencil of nature' and by quasi-entelechy.

What was the motivation for this transformation? Benjamin argues that it was the result of a process of mass mediation: what he describes as the masses' desire 'to bring things "closer" spatially and humanly, which is just as ardent as their bent toward overcoming the uniqueness of every reality by accepting its reproduction' (Benjamin 1999: 217). We may, in this sense, associate the invention of photography with the 'invention' of the masses. Photography was, from this perspective, at one and the same time a medium for a new naturalism and also one possible if not necessary consequence of mass mediation: if trains had enabled industrialists to transport the masses 'to nature' in ways that destroyed the aura of *places*, photography now made the obverse dynamic possible: in the context of a new desire for 'nature', photography made it possible to take this nature to the masses. Whereas the technology of displacement of steam locomotion involved the physical displacement of the masses, now it involved the physical, or rather the quasi-physical, displacement of nature. Photography, like the railways, was thus to become a profoundly ambivalent medium: as noted by Benjamin, 'to pry an object from its shell, to destroy its aura, is the mark of a perception whose "sense of the universal equality of things" has increased to such a degree that it extracts it even from a unique object by means of reproduction' (Benjamin 1999: 217).

Carleton Watkins' views

This form of mass mediation may be illustrated with reference to the work of Carleton Watkins, who by the mid-nineteenth century had taken up and further developed Talbot's technology. Watkins is regarded as one of the foremost landscape photographers of the nineteenth century, and his 'views' of Yosemite were described by one California State Geographical Surveyor as 'the finest I've ever seen' (Palmquist 1999: 216). There can be no doubt that the representations had considerable influence on the perceived, conceived and lived spaces of prominent nature essayists, painters and politicians. Many of these had never been to the Yosemite, but now felt able to form an opinion thanks in no small measure to the photographic medium's ability to both recreate and transform 'views' and, of course, its capacity to be indefinitely reproduced and transported to a large number of publics over vast distances. The significance of the photographs, and the extraordinarily rapid dissemination and success of the medium versus older media such as painting, is illustrated by the fact that Thomas Hill and other famous landscape painters used the photographs as the basis for some of their paintings.

Watkins was born in New York but migrated in the mid-nineteenth century to San Francisco, where he is thought to have begun photography by chance as an apprentice in a studio. By 1858, Watkins' outdoor work had achieved enough of a reputation to earn him a commission providing photographs of a quicksilver mine. Three years later, Watkins designed a camera capable of handling negatives of 18 by 22 inches (the so-called 'mammoth plates') which he fitted with a Grubb Aplanatic Landscape lens for wide-angle work (Palmquist 1999: 216). Watkins made what must have been an extraordinarily laborious trip with this massive camera to the Yosemite, which he reached by travelling mostly on foot or by mule. Once there, he took the first of a series of pictures of Yosemite which made him famous.

Unlike Talbot, Watkins produced and sold photographs for a living, and did so in a variety of formats. In this section I consider three of the formats that Watkins adopted: the large format pictures produced with the mammoth plates, the panorama and the stereoscopic images.

I will begin with the large format photographs. *Yosemite Falls, River View* (1861)[8] is one of the photographs taken by Watkins before the Yosemite land grant was given to California. Another was probably taken after the grant was established, and its caption is a striking instance of the gendering of landscape: *The Bridal Veil Falls* (*c.* 1864–6).[9] Both pictures combine the framing of elements in the fore-, middle- and background, so that the viewer is given the impression of three-dimensionality and looking 'through' the landscape (see also *Yosemite Falls*, *c.* 1864–6).[10] Most if not all of Watkins' photographs produced 'privileged' viewpoints that can be likened to a transmediated version of what Mary Louise Pratt (1992) has described, with reference to another geographical and genre context, as the imperialist 'monarch-of-all-that-I-survey' trope.

I will return to this trope in the next section. Here I would note that the comparatively large size of the photographs, and the fact that they were viewed as picture frames on the wall, invites a comparison with the older perspectivalist tradition of a 'window' to nature. Douglas Nickel, for example, suggests that Victorian observers 'usually reacted to Watkins's images as if confronted with the actual landscape' (Nickel 1999: 21). He quotes one critic as suggesting that 'Each pebble on the shore of the little lake . . . may be as easily counted as on the shore of nature itself . . . . We get a nearer view of the mountains, only to make their perpendicular sides look more fearful and impossible of ascent' (Wilson quoted in Nickel 1999: 21).

This statement evokes the dynamic of nearness and distance considered by Benjamin's theory of the aura. However, it also suggests that one of the keys to the pleasures found in viewing the landscape photograph – and perhaps the photograph more generally – lay in the reception of photographs as *acknowledged* icons. On the one hand, Wilson employs a relatively explicit simile – counting the pebbles in the picture was *as easy* as counting the pebbles in nature itself. On the other hand, his observation refers to the difference between the 'actual' view and the photograph: 'we get a nearer view of the mountains', where presumably the tacit reference was to standing on the mountains themselves.

From this perspective, Nickel's most appropriate comments are those that explain that Watkins' photographs *amplified* and *manipulated* the picture experience 'to more effectively naturalize a selective, abstract investigation of the world' (1999: 21). It seems in this sense highly unlikely that most viewers thought that the photographs were the landscape, *tout court*; rather, photographs were more likely to be regarded as being astonishingly 'like' the landscape, even as they afforded a perspective which was in some respects different from – and indeed perhaps better than – what could be afforded by the 'unaided' eye. In the language of Peirce's semeiotic theory, we might say that the selective, legisignical qualities of the photographs remained and perhaps even today remain in a silent tension with their assumed, and in some respects truly, indexical qualities. It was, in this sense, not just that the photographs intensified the viewing experience of the Yosemite; they also lent themselves to, indeed demanded, a 'mental' to-and-fro comparison with the 'real'. This was a comparison whose pleasure might well have been the 'verification', real or imagined, of the contiguity between photograph and landscape, sign and nature.

Watkins strove to provide an even more realistic form of representation by joining up three to five mammoth plate negatives to suggest a 180-degree view, a 'panorama'. In so doing, he created a context of observation that was in some respects the obverse of the one that might be thought to be implicit in the conception of single photographs (or indeed traditional paintings), if not in their actual viewing process: that a view might best be taken in 'at a glance', even if a more detailed form of observation required more sustained attention to aspects of frame. As noted by Nickel (1999), panoramas actively required the observers to move their heads this way and that – in some painted panoramas one would actually have to walk around – to 'take in' the view. This constituted what might be likened to a limited re-corporealization of the procedures of observation: if with Crary (1990) I noted in Chapter 1 that camera obscuras established a very strong distinction between the inside and the outside in order to produce a relatively immobile observer in a darkened chamber, the panorama device now constituted a simulation not just of what might be seen, but also of a part of the (physical) process of how the landscape might be 'walked', or might have been (unselfconsciously) observed. Watkins himself described his work as a pursuit of 'the spot which would give the best view' (Nickel 1999: 21), and indeed it may be suggested that the panorama constituted a particular kind, in Peirce's terms, of designative index: it was not just a matter of 'see this' (a command implicit to all photography), but now 'see *all* of this', where 'all' itself pointed to increasingly totalizing efforts to represent nature.[11]

A somewhat different mode of framing and observation accrued to a third medium of photographic observation, the stereoscopic images. Stereoscopes were one of several 'visual toys' that were popular in the 1850s. Special twin-lens cameras were employed to produce a double image that was viewed through a binocular device. They were, in effect, personal (and personalizing) viewfinders that produced, in Nickel's words, a stereographic space:

> An optical illusion . . . its recession exaggerated and multilayered, lending it an oddly planar, 'cutout' effect. The intensity and peculiar artificiality of the sensation are encouraged by the stereoscope, whose eyepiece makes peripheral vision and concentrates attention in the kinaesthetic scanning and refocusing demanded of the eyes.
>
> (Nickel 1999: 28)

Nickel quotes one nineteenth-century critic, who suggested that:

> The first effect of looking at a good photograph through the stereoscope is a surprise such as no painting ever produced. The mind feels its way into the very depths of the picture. The scraggy branches of a tree in the foreground run out at us as if they would scratch our eyes out. The elbow of a figure stands forth so as to make us almost uncomfortable. Then there is such a frightful amount of detail . . . . all must be there, every stick, straw, scratch.
>
> (Oliver Wendell Holmes in Nickel 1999: 28)

This account echoes the arguments made by Benjamin: this nineteenth-century observer was amazed at the extent to which the photograph was an 'authentic' *replica* of reality. But, if the large-scale photographs intensified visual observation by way of framing, lighting and the distribution of objects in different depths of field, the stereoscope took this process one step further by eliminating, however momentarily, the 'distractions' of peripheral vision. We can say in this sense that the stereoscope almost literally focussed and framed the observer's attention. In so doing, and like some forms of single lens photography that used telephoto lenses with a shallow depth of field, it began to undermine centuries-old principles of linear perspective described in Chapter 3. The Euclidean geometry of modern perspectivalism began to be displaced in practice, if not in photographic theory, by non-Euclidean principles that, in Nickel's terms, made for a dramatic shift from 'the unifying rationalization of pictorial space' to a space that seemed 'deranged, its elements unpredictably aggressive or flat in their dimensionality, its field [perhaps we should say 'fields'] a visual patchwork of distractions and delights' (Nickel 1999: 28).

It seems no coincidence that the stereoscopes, which were the most popular, 'massified' and 'massifying' form of reproduction and dissemination of Watkins' photographs, were also the most effective in producing a sense of nearness. One might be amazed by the mammoth plate photographs and engrossed by their detail; but, when viewed by way of the stereoscope, the Yosemite would have seemed a hallucination, an incantation, of proximity: reach out, and you might almost touch the Bridal Veil or El Capitán.

To be sure, stereoscopic photography also signalled another key shift, which has been analysed by Jonathan Crary (1990). While I suggested in Chapter 2 that a certain decorporealization of vision persists to this day, Crary notes that during the first half of the nineteenth century a fundamental change occurred vis-à-vis the corporeality of vision. A combination of romantic discourses of subjectivity and increasingly detailed *empirical* studies of eyesight resulted in the formulation of new theories and technologies of observation, in particular those that made use of the phenomenon of 'persistence of vision' and presupposed, indeed actively promulgated, a practice of 'subjective vision'. This practice was the visual analogon, at once of Rousseau's intensely 'personal' technology of the self, but also of Kant's theory of sublimity: henceforth, it would be acknowledged that observation might well conform not so much to the observed things as they are in themselves as to the rules of the mode of representation.

Heart of darkness

If the persecution of US aboriginal groups was an integral aspect of the process that eventually led to the creation of the Yosemite and Yellowstone parks, it was also a kind of staging point for one Henry Morton Stanley, a Welshman christened John Rowlands who renamed and naturalized himself as an American citizen. After serving briefly with the Confederate and then the Union Army and Navy in the American Civil War, Stanley deserted and travelled to St Louis and the 'American West', where he began his career as a journalist. He spent the year of 1867 writing racist accounts of the Indian Wars for US newspapers (Hochschild 1998).

In the 1870s and 1880s Stanley wrote influential accounts about the Congo region of Africa, an area that was then becoming, and indeed remains today, one of the archetypal icons of modern nature: my first two chapters were, of course, about this nature. Stanley is perhaps most famous today for his words, 'Dr. Livingstone, I presume', which he uttered when he 'found' David Livingstone in 1871. In this section I would like to provide an account that highlights the role that Stanley played in mass mediation, and vice versa: the role that mass mediation eventually played in the invention of Stanley, and 'his' Congo.

Whatever his own skills and the daring of his expeditions, Stanley's rise to fame owed much to the emergence of modern newspapers, the first fully modern medium of *mass communication*, as defined in Chapter 2. Stanley's racist dispatches from the West attracted the attention of James Gordon Bennett Jr, the heir of a fortune amassed by his father with the *New York Herald*. Bennett saw the opportunity to revive his paper's flagging fortunes when speculation grew in America and Europe about Livingstone's whereabouts. In 1871, he commissioned Stanley to organize an expedition to search for Livingstone.

Stanley has often been idealized as a kind of daring explorer who also wrote dispatches for newspapers. The opposite order of description almost certainly provides a more accurate sense of the history involved: Stanley was one of the first and most successful 'spin doctors' of his time, and his success owes as much to his keen sense of the emergent spaces and times of mass communication as it does to his sheer determination to expose himself to, and survive in, hostile contexts; contexts, it should be reiterated, that were for the most part of his own making.

In order to understand how and why Stanley's expeditions took place, it is necessary to engage in a brief excursus about the medium that made him and that, in some important respects, he also helped to remake. The *New York Herald* was one of the most innovative of the newspapers that came to be described as the 'penny press': papers that sold for only one cent each. Prior to the advent of the penny press, the older forms of mass communication, known as journals, were bought by subscription, had a weekly circulation, and were sold for six cents, or roughly one tenth of a working man's daily wages at the time. This contributed to their exclusivity: readers had to be able to pay a sizable lump sum for a yearly subscription or make the journey to the journal's printing presses (Schudson 1978).

In the 1830s a new mode of distribution in the US – the result of a new political economy – revolutionized the trade: in addition to a sharp reduction in price – the newspapers recouped the loss in this form of earning by advertisements – the newspapers paid young boys to hawk the papers on the street. As noted by Michael Schudson (1978), this shift at once reflected and produced a more profound one: whereas previously the content of journals had reflected quite explicitly the political and commercial interests of the US elites, the modern newspaper became devoted to circulating everyday news. As part of this shift, the popular press began to circulate narratives about everyday events that might captivate the imagination of people 'on the street'. In the United States, but eventually also in Great Britain and elsewhere in the world, news values, always at least partly contingent on readers' tastes, were now made to reflect the tastes of the new middle classes (Schudson 1978).

After the printed book, newspapers were arguably the first true modern medium of mass communication in so far as they as they circulated the news as symbolic goods to audiences at one remove in space and time from the moment of production, but also, and crucially, in so far as they came to be produced by hierarchically organized bureaucracies. The reference to newspapers as symbolic goods highlights the new political economy of the news. Where the older journals were financed mainly by subscriptions, the new newspapers produced profits by delivering audiences to advertisers, who 'bought' the audiences (or their readership) by agreeing to pay a certain sum for each advertisement. As the new media began to compete with each other to deliver more and more readers to advertisers, they came under increasing pressure to find new ways of generating narratives that might captivate the imagination of readers and, with it, the desire to consume more stories.

James Gordon Bennett Jr's bid to generate interest by sending Stanley to 'find' Livingstone was one such strategy. By the time that Stanley was employed to carry out this expedition, the *New York Herald*'s sales, which were once among the highest in the industry, had declined, and it was necessary to look for new ways of generating readership. An international expedition that might also satisfy the interests of a sizable readership in European capitals constituted a useful strategy, albeit one that eventually had genocidal effects.

By the time that Stanley reached Africa, many if not most regions of the continent had had some form of contact with British, French or Portuguese empires for centuries. Central Africa was an exception; perhaps the most significant obstacle to European colonization was the widespread presence of largely incurable illnesses, in particular yellow fever. It thus remained a 'blank space' in European maps, a firstness in a continent that, by the second half of the nineteenth century, was otherwise all too well signed by European colonial powers.

The absence of geographical knowledge of much of central Africa meant that the region was considered to be available for conquest by Europeans. Its apparent firstness also had the effect of titillating the imagination of all those who dreamed that most modern dream: of being the first to explore an 'unknown' region and, thereby, an unknown nature or wilderness. In a world increasingly consumed by the modern industrial systems of knowledge and power, a space conceived as a great unknown lent itself to particularly radical circuits of anthropomorphism premised on notions of finding an absolute other, be it human, in-human or un-human.

The quest for 'blank spaces', so central to the history of the geographical imagination, is well described by Marlow in Joseph Conrad's *Heart of Darkness*: 'I had a passion for maps. . . . At that time there were many blank spaces on the earth, and when I saw one that looked particularly inviting on the map (but they all look like that) I would put my finger on it and say, When I grow up I will go there' (Conrad 1973: 11). As Stanley himself put it in one of the telegrams to the *New York Herald* 'That this remarkable river (the Lualaba) isn't the Nile and none other no one doubts, but this one little blank – this one little link – who will fill it up? How will imagination fill up the void?' (Stanley 1874: 30).

The answer was provided by Stanley himself. He organized an expedition that soon found Livingstone. First by telegrams, then in longer letters to Bennett, and finally by means of multi-media lectures and book-length accounts, he circulated self-aggrandizing accounts of his exploits that transformed him into a veritable nineteenth-century media celebrity. His success was a result of a combination of dynamics. There was, on the one hand, the fact that the *Herald* narrativized Livingstone's apparent disappearance into a kind of suspense thriller coached in the terms of a hyper-secondness: where was Livingstone? What had happened to him? And if he was in peril – as he *must* be – who would save him?

But Stanley was also very aware of the importance of mobility and speed of displacement to his business. For example, in an earlier expedition to cover the British war against the Abyssinian emperor, he reportedly bribed Suez Canal telegraphy officials so that they might send his dispatches first, and this foresight earned him a journalistic coup when the telegraph wire went down shortly after his dispatch was sent off (Hochschild 1998).

I shall return to the medium of telegraphy in Chapter 7. Here I should note that Stanley's awareness of the importance of mobility was combined with an effective use of established literary tropes, one of which Mary-Louise Pratt describes as the 'monarch-of-all-I-survey' scene, which was widely employed by Romantic and Victorian writers. This 'imperialist trope', as Pratt describes it, made extensive use of promontories to aestheticize, intensify and ultimately 'master' the African landscape. I noted that Wordsworth made use of a high elevation to describe the Lake District, and now Stanley did the same in his letters to the *New York Herald*:

> Were one to ascend by a balloon, and scan the whole of Unyamwezi, he would have a view of one great forest, broken here and there by the little clearings and the villages, especially around Unyanyembe. The forests of Southern Unyamwezi contain a large variety of game and wild beasts. In these may be found herds of elephants, buffalo, giraffe, zebra, eland, hartebeest, springbok, pallah, black buck and a score of other kinds. In the neighbourhood of the Gombe (Southern) may be seen any number of wild boar and hogs, lions, and leopards. The Gombe itself is remarkable for the number of hippopotamus and crocodile to be found in it.
>
> (Stanley 1874: 47)

Stanley, like Wordsworth and other male Victorian observers, favoured high vantage points. Pratt contrasts this style with that of Mary Kingsley, whose accounts of her passage through lowlands in *Travels Through West Africa* constitute a kind of humorous, ironic and self-effacing antithesis of the self-confident, masculinist discourse of promontories:

if you are a mere ordinary person of a retiring nature, like me, you stop in your lagoon until the tide rises again; most of your attention is directed at dealing with an 'at home' to crocodiles and mangrove flies, and with the fearful stench of the slime around you. What little time you have left over you will employ in wondering why you came to West Africa, and why, having reached this point of absurdity, you need have gone and painted the lily and adorned the rose, by being such a colossal ass as to come fooling around in the mangrove swamps.

(Kingsley 1993: 25)

With Pratt, it is possible to suggest that Stanley and others used elevated places to 'paint' a kind of scene of Africa, a form of transmediation that entailed a sublimation of the land into a 'wordscape': the forest was turned into a 'scene', a 'view' described with words. In Peirce's terms, this device was akin to the paradoxical production of iconic sinsigns by way of legisigns: the landscape gave way to a 'wordscape' and vice versa.

Stanley's reference to a vantage point afforded by a balloon nonetheless constituted an innovation in this trope, one that suggested something closer to a cinematographic imaginary than a static view. Stanley was not just standing on a promontory looking over the land; he was imagining an elevated vantage point made possible by mechanical means in what was a remarkable forerunner of widespread – and in many cases highly disruptive – tourist ballooning practices employed in African parks during the twentieth and twenty-first centuries.

Stanley also intensified the scene by populating the space with 'big game' even as he depopulated parts of the land of its human inhabitants. As Stanley puts it in another letter:

The glorious park land spreading out north and south of the Southern Gombe is a hunter's paradise; it is full of game of all kinds, herds of buffalo, giraffe, zebra, pallah, waterbuck, springbok, gemsbok, black buck, and kuder, besides several eland, warthog, or wild boar, and hundreds of smaller antelopes. We saw all these in one day, and at night heard the lion's roar and the low of the hippopotamus. I halted here three days to shoot, and there is no occasion to boast of what I shot here, considering the myriads of game I saw at every step I took. Not half the animals shot here by myself and men were made use of.

(Stanley 1874: 74–75)

The image of an Africa congested with large wild animals might well have projected readers in Europe and the eastern United States into a kind of Edenic nature that had long since vanished in most of Europe and was now also threatened in the 'American West'. This discourse would also have thrilled readers fascinated with the exploits of the big game hunters mentioned earlier. The late nineteenth century was a period when, as the historian John Mackenzie puts it, 'European world supremacy coincided with the peak of the hunting and shooting craze', a craze that had become a 'ritualized and occasionally spectacular display of white dominance' (Mackenzie 1988: 7). White hunters had begun to appear in central Africa by the 1850s, and Mackenzie notes that, by the 1870s and 1880s, they had become 'very nearly a flood' (Mackenzie 1988: 122). In addition to the work of ivory hunter-traders and other professionals supplying the markets for skins, hunting came to be widely practised in the region both for sport and as a way of paying local inhabitants for services.

As I noted in an earlier section, it is a paradox that big game hunters became some of the most ardent conservationists in the United States. A similar development took place in Africa, where local inhabitants were either removed from lands designated as 'park lands' or transformed into 'poachers' if they dared to engage in subsistence hunting in regions 'protected' by the hunters (Mackenzie 1988). The figure of the poacher, long employed in Europe by the royalty and by landowners to dispossess peasants of their own natural resources, now became the favoured figure of wealthy men in African and other colonies who invoked it to defend 'their' 'game'. The genre of the safari was itself an imperial palimpsest in so far as the great white hunters 'borrowed' the Swahili name for a trip to describe hunting expeditions.

It would nonetheless be a mistake to assume that Stanley constructed central Africa in a manner that simply echoed his imagined readers' imaginaries. Much of his skill lay in engaging in an informal pedagogy that both contradicted and magnified readers' sense of a pastoralized Africa:

> Yet you must not think of the Unyamwezi as you would of an American swamp. You must not imagine Unyamwezi to have deep morasses, slushy beds of mud infested with all abominable reptiles, or a jungle where the lion and the leopard have their dens. Nothing of the kind. Unyamwezi is a different kind of country altogether from that. . . . To know the general outline and physical features of Unyamwezi you must take a look around from one of the noble coigns of vantage offered by any of those hills of syenite in the debatable ground of the Mgunda Makali, in Uyanzi. From the summit of one of those natural fortresses, if you look west, you will see the Unyamwezi recede into the far blue mysterious distance in a succession of blue waves of noble forest, rising and subsiding like blue water of an ocean.
>
> (Stanley 1874: 45)

In a strange reversal of the logic of hunter-conservationism, Stanley further contradicted any simple sense of the exotic by suggesting the possibility of using the African landscape as a space to build a kind of suburb:

> Ah, me, what wild and ambitious projects fill a man's brain as he looks over the forgotten and unpeopled country, containing in its bosom such

stores of wealth, and with such an expanse of fertile soil capable of sustaining millions! What a settlement one could have in this valley! See, it is broad enough to support a large population. Fancy a church spire where that tree rears its dark crown of foliage, and think how well a score or so of pretty cottages would look instead of those thorn clumps and gum trees. Fancy this lovely valley teeming with herds of cattle, and fields of corn spreading to the right and left of this stream. How much better would such a state of things become this valley than the present deserted and wild aspect. But be hopeful the day will come, and a future year will see it, when happier lands have become crowded, and nations have become so overgrown that they have no room to turn about. It really wants an Abraham or a Lot, an Alaric or an Attila, to lead their hosts to this land, which, perhaps, has been wisely reserved for such a time.

(Stanley 1874: 86)

To be sure, not all was paradise: Stanley contrasted this Edenic construction of nature with a more 'insidious' nature, one that lay lurking behind the apparent beauty, and could be likened to the notion of the sublime described by Burke. Indeed, in another letter, written with reference to the same scene of apparently Edenic beauty mentioned above, Stanley suggested that:

It is only after a long halt . . . only when one has been stricken down almost to the grave by the fatal chilly winds that blow from the heights of the mountains of Usagara, that one begins to criticize the beauty which at first captivated. It is found then that though the land is fair to look upon, though we rejoiced at the sign of its grand plains, at its fertile and glowing fields, at the sign of the roving herds which promised us an abundance of milk and cream – it is one of the most deadly countries in Africa, that its fevers, remittent and intermittent, are unequalled in their severity.

(Stanley 1874: 46)

This was the other 'half' of a dualistic circuit of anthropomorphism that oscillated between identification with an Edenic nature and a recoiling in sublime horror – in Burke's sense of the sublime – at those aspects of nature that not only refused 'penetration' but were in fact readily able to penetrate if not destroy the bodies of white men – what might be described as a kind of *Natura horribilis*, a nature which, like its Edenic or pastoralist version, was at once material and semeiotic in character, but resisted the logic of assimilationism that was implicit in the Edenic/pastoralist modes of classification and framing.

This was, perhaps, its fascination: at a time when wealthy, white Europeans and Americans had reached a point where material nature was, or seemed to be, under control, reminders of the ultimate lack of control over it became the objects of a kind of fetishism, first in the anthropological sense of the term (as phenomena endowed with magical or mysterious qualities), and then in the Marxist sense, as symbolic goods that were sought out and experienced for the benefit of audiences at one remove, audiences who might then shudder delightedly at their horror.

I shall return to the question of *Natura horribilis* in subsequent chapters. I referred earlier to a logic of assimilationism, and here it is pertinent to note a parallel between Stanley's narratives and those studied by the historian and narratologist Tvetzan Todorov (1984) with reference to the Spanish conquest of the Americas. According to Todorov, Columbus's narratives were articulated by a discourse that oscillated between assimilationism, or the incorporation of the 'benevolent' natives, and the will to enslave the 'natives' when they resisted assimilation. A similar oscillation may be noted in Bunnell's narrative, and indeed in Stanley's accounts of the aboriginal cultures he encountered in central Africa. Where 'natives' were docile, they were subjected by means of a discourse that likened the culture to the 'good' nature of Africa, as the following remarkable passage exemplifies:

> Kululu [Stanley's seven-year-old waiter and 'butler'], young antelope, is frisky. I have but to express a wish, and it is gratified. He is a perfect Mercury, though a marvellously black one. Tea over, Kululu cleans the dishes and retires under the kitchen shed where, if I have the curiousity to look to know what he is doing, he may be seen with his tongue in the teacup licking up the sugar that was left in it, and looking very much like he would like to eat the cup for the sake of the divine element it has so often contained.
>
> (Stanley 1874: 50).

Stanley contrasts Kululu with Selim, 'the Arab boy', whom Kululu had 'ousted' and who 'cannot wait at table' (Stanley 1874: 50). Aside from engaging in a classically colonial form of divisionism by opposing the two imagined ethnicities, the above passage reveals a mode of classification and framing that likens Kululu to a non-human animal: it is not even that he is *like* an antelope (the trope of the simile), he *is* a 'young antelope' and, to the readers of the time, the validity of the metaphor may well have been confirmed by the suggestion that Kululu went beneath the shed and licked the cup for its sugar. The discourse is nonetheless assimilationist in that it frames the activities with a benevolent and arguably sexual gaze of approval.

Where docility was replaced by resistance, assimilationism was replaced by the ideology of enslavement: in *Through the Dark Continent*, a book about a later expedition, Stanley suggests for example that:

> Whatever deficiencies, weaknesses, and foibles the people [of East African villages] may develop must be so manipulated that . . . they may only just suspect that behind all this there lies the strong unbending force

which will eventually make men of them, wild things though they now are.

(Stanley 1878: 45)

Here again we witness the circuit of anthropomorphism: it was not just that Stanley represented nature in a way that quite explicitly anthorpomorphized it; he also identified, that is explicitly cosmomorphized, the people he encountered with images derived from the region's nature.

Despite the importance of such discursive procedures to imperialist projects, it would be a mistake to suggest that this was only a 'discursive' process. The representations at once legitimized, dissimulated and provoked the deaths of hundreds of porters, and of those people who refused to cooperate or opposed Stanley's journalistic project. It might be assumed that this was a fact of the times. But one magazine, the *Saturday Review*, suggested otherwise when it noted that 'He [Stanley] has no concern with justice, no right to administer it; he comes with no sanction, no authority, no jurisdiction – nothing but explosive bullets and a copy of the *Daily Telegraph*', an ironic reference to the role that this newspaper would later have in co-funding with the *Herald* Stanley's explorations.

To be sure, Stanley's exploits, produced initially in the name of sending good stories to the US and British press, were the beginning of something far worse, a form of genocidal imperialism that was made possible thanks in no small part to the fact that, even before Stanley wrote for the *Daily Telegraph*, his work was read by many in the European elites. As noted earlier and explained by the historian Adam Hochschild (1998), Stanley's knowledge and experiences along the Congo river eventually made him a key figure in King Leopold II's plans to establish a Belgian colony in the region. Stanley is regarded for this reason as a founding figure in what became known as the 'scramble for Africa'.

Hochschild (1998) describes the brutal nature of this project, and as part of it, the murderous character of King Leopold II's colony, which eventually led to the death, by disease, starvation, overwork and sheer murder, of an estimated half of the region's original population, that is, approximately 10 million people were killed (Hochschild 1998). *Heart of Darkness* stands today as a kind of paradigmatic fable of the loss of civilization, an imaginary tale about the excesses of 'mankind'. But, as noted by Hochschild, Conrad's novel, which was originally published in 1902, is in fact a remarkably accurate account of the imperial devastation that I have just referred to. Conrad himself suggested that '*Heart of Darkness* is experience . . . pushed a little (and only a very little) beyond the actual facts of the case' (Conrad in Hochschild 1998: 143). In this context, as Hochschild explains, it is remarkable how the novel has been treated by scholars as a kind of placeless metaphor for all of 'mankind', a purely fictional tale that might be read without any concern for its original frame of reference. A similar depoliticization may be noted in all those accounts of rainforests that, like those considered in Chapters 1 and 2, allude to *Heart of Darkness* in ways that convert colonial or neocolonial forays in Africa and elsewhere into heroic tales in which men enter into contest with a sublime, and indeed we might also say a paradoxically sublimated, nature.

Panoramic nature

Earlier, I considered at some length the racist conflation of nature and culture in the context of Henry Morton Stanley's forays in Africa. I would now like to consider an analogous conflation that took place in Europe but involved two rather different genres of mass mediation.

I explained that Watkins also produced photographs designed for the 'panorama' format. Watkins' panoramas were a transmediation of 'actual' panoramas, circular galleries with 360-degree paintings that constituted, in the words of one late nineteenth-century dictionary entry,

> faithful reproductions of what a place looks like when viewed from all angles and from as far as the eye can see. To that end the spectator is placed on a platform or circular gallery that simulates a tower and that is located at the centre of [a] rotunda; the light . . . flows in from above, through an area of frosted glass . . . a huge parasol, suspended . . . keeps the spectator in the dark and conceals the sources of light above the platform.
>
> (*Dictionary of Building Terms*, quoted in Comment 1999: 7)

Significantly, the first name given to the panorama was 'La Nature à Coup d'Oeil' and, as exemplified in the definition above, the invention was indeed described in the terms of modern forms of naturalism. As noted by Stephan Oetterman (1997), the term panorama was actually coined in the late eighteenth century by juxtaposing the Greek words *pan* (all) and *horama* (view). Oetterman suggests that the medium must be regarded as 'an apparatus for teaching and glorifying the bourgeois view of the world', and therefore the first true visual 'mass medium' (Oetterman 1997: 7). The panorama was 'both a surrogate for nature and a simulator' of this process, 'an apparatus for teaching people how to see it' (Oetterman 1997: 12). This was the case in so far as the panorama naturalized 'the reaction of artists to discovery of the horizon' (Oetterman 1997: 12).[12]

The notion and experience of the horizon is taken for granted by modern subjects in the twenty-first century. However, in the late eighteenth century it constituted at once a conceptual and experiential discovery. The discovery was the result of a coming together of the principles of linear perspective (which, as noted in Chapter 3, themselves postulated at once a mathematical or geometrical and a visual horizon), and the quest on the part of romantic travellers to find, as noted earlier with respect to Watkins, the 'best viewpoints' in mountainous and other landscapes (Oettermann 1997).

The very end of the nineteenth century and the beginning of the twentieth witnessed a significant transmediation of the principle of the panorama in the domain of zookeeping, one that acquires an ironic significance in the context of the events discussed earlier in this chapter. In the early twentieth century, Carl Hagenbeck Jr, a wild animal trader and zoo owner in Hamburg, effectively redefined the state of the zoo art by landscaping 25 acres of potato fields into mountains, gorges, lakes and islands which, in 1907, opened as two 'panoramas' that Hagenbeck called Africa and the Arctic (Reichenbach 1996).

The popularity of the panoramas had peaked at the turn of the nineteenth century, at the time when Hagenbeck developed his own version. It is thus perhaps unsurprising that he attempted to capitalize on the success of the genre by way of transmediation. As I noted in Chapter 4, in the eighteenth and early nineteenth century landscape gardens and paintings had engaged in a practice of transmediation that was motivated by a logic of 'double representation' and by an ideology that sought to dissimulate the sweeping changes taking place in the English countryside. By the end of the nineteenth century, the practice of transmediation had an even more material motivation: making a profit by transposing modalities of observation, or aspects of modalities of observation, from one medium (in this case, the actual panorama) to another (the zoo).

In this as in all practices of transmediation, the transposition was never simple or 'complete', and of course it involved complexities which cannot be reduced to the profit motive. Whereas traditional panoramas involved a process that simulated 'looking out', Hagenbeck's panorama involved a process of looking *in* or *across* at a series of enclosures, each of which was built slightly above the other, and which employed concealed or semi-concealed moats to separate animals. While the desired effect was perhaps to give zoo visitors the illusion of looking out, Hagenbeck's displays could not simulate a horizon in the way that actual panoramas did.[13] This display was, if anything, closer to a theatrical set (Rothfels 2002), one that used animals as props in a kind of *mise en scène* of the exotic.

It is nonetheless remarkable that even as parks such as the Yosemite and the Yellowstone were being created – so that 'nature' was effectively enclosed, symbolically if not in terms of actual fencing, to produce nature-like re/presentations – a form of re/presenting nature emerged that sought to create the impression of an unenclosed nature, of a nature not bounded by the classification of the observer and the observed. We may, in this sense, regard both dynamics as a development of the naturalistic coding orientation described in earlier chapters.

But, even as this set of boundaries were blurred, so was another, one that arguably undermined the very humanism upon which the nature–culture divide was premised. Hagenbeck organized so-called ethnographic exhibits in his new Tierpark in Hamburg, in which he displayed aboriginal groups from around the world. The practice began when, looking to import reindeer, Hagenbeck reportedly took advice from a friend to also bring along a 'family of Lapps'. His account of his meeting with the Lapps speaks for itself: 'Here was a truly interesting sight. On the deck three little men dressed in skins were walking among the deer, and down below we found to our great delight a mother with a tiny infant in her arms and dainty little maiden about four years old, standing shyly by her side. Our guests . . . were so totally unsophisticated and so totally unspoiled by civilization that they seemed like beings from another world. I felt sure that the little strangers would arouse great interest in Germany'(Hagenbeck quoted in Mullan and Marvin 1999: 84).

In the following years Hagenbeck brought Somalis, Native Americans, Kalmucks, Cingalese, Patagonians, Hottentots and Eskimos to his new Tierpark (Mullan and Marvin 1999: 87). Herman Reichenbach (1996) suggests that the most popular of these was a 'Wild West' show that Hagenbeck put on in 1910 with 42 Sioux Indians from the Pine Ridge Reservation in South Dakota, which a million or so visitors paid to see that summer.

Fifty or so years, then, after one aboriginal group in the US was forcibly dispossessed of its ancestral lands in a process that led eventually to the formation of a natural park, another group was displayed in a zoo that developed some of the first fully modern naturalistic displays in zoos. Whereas the park worked by enclosing landscape so that it might be protected from exploitation, zoos such as Hagenbeck's Tierpark now attempted to give the impression that the animals were protected from exploitation by being displayed in relatively unenclosed spaces. Both practices, for all their differences, were informed by a circuit of anthropomorphism that had the same politics of classification and framing: in both, an effort was made, however unselfconsciously, to create a sublime nature that appeared to be not only unbounded in itself but also fundamentally unchanged by humans. This happened at the very historical moment when human intervention began to make it far more difficult to speak of an 'untouched' nature.

7

THE NATURE OF
INCORPORATION

> The locomotive engine has not thus far been adapted to common
> roads, and notwithstanding the brilliant anticipations of some
> projectors, the day has not yet dawned, when every producer
> shall be whirled to market by the steam of his own teakettle
> George Perkins Marsh, 1847

Krakatoa

In Chapter 6 I suggested that white explorers' desire to 'fill in' 'blank spaces', and their fear of fevers and other illnesses, as complexly interwoven with a racist ideology, constructed central Africa in terms of an oscillation between Edenic images of nature and a kind of *Natura horribilis*; between what Todorov (1984) describes as assimilationism and a will to enslavement. Towards the end of the nineteenth century, an unambiguously natural *Natura horribilis* nonetheless provoked what was to become one of the most modern natural disasters of the nineteenth century. A series of volcanic eruptions took place in 1883 on Krakatoa, an island in the Sunda Straits. Although the resulting death-toll now seems low in comparison with the effects of the tsunami of 2004 – the tsunamis triggered by Krakatoa's seismic activity wiped out entire towns and killed an estimated 36,000 people in the vicinity of the region that was devastated in 2004 – the after-effects of the eruption, and aspects of its observation and mass mediation, helped to inaugurate a new era of globalism.

This book is not the place to describe in detail the sequence of catastrophic events, which have been narrated by Simon Winchester (2003) in *Krakatoa: The Day the World Exploded*. It suffices to note that the volcanic eruptions began in May 1883, but a lull of some months followed before the volcano began to erupt again on the afternoon of 26 August. Then, over a period of some twelve hours, four cataclysmic explosions produced audible reports that were heard as far away as the islands of Diego García and Rodríguez, 2375 and 3080 miles away respectively. The volcano's airwaves were recorded by barometers the world over as they travelled an estimated seven times around the globe. Krakatoa poured so much ash into the sky that the surrounding area was plunged into a daytime darkness (Winchester 2003).

Natural catastrophes of an equal or greater magnitude had occurred before. For example, in the previous decade a typhoon in the Bay of Bengal killed an estimated 200,000 people. As early as 1633, a catastrophic earthquake in Lisbon made waves of a social kind across Europe. What was remarkable about Krakatoa was that the sheer magnitude of the explosions, and the volume of ash that they produced, had not just an *observable* but an *observed* impact, and this on a *global* scale. The eruption of Krakatoa occurred at a time when a host of new or *newly assembled* technologies of observation made it possible to both communicate about, but also to *study*, the natural phenomenon as it affected physical and social spaces across the planet. Indeed, as noted by Winchester, Krakatoa was one of the first events of *Natura horribilis* that was communicated nearly instantaneously around the globe.

I shall begin by considering this aspect of the catastrophe. When the volcanic activity first began in May 1883, the Lloyd's agent in Batavia sent a telegram to head office in London, which passed on the 'intelligence' – the term then used for 'news' – to *The Times* (Winchester 2003). Close to the bottom of page 12, under the heading 'Latest Shipping Intelligence', a tiny article appeared that said:

> **Volcanic eruption**. – Lloyd's Agent in Batavia, under date of May 23rd, telegraphs:– 'Strong Volcanic Eruption, Krakatowa Island, Sunda Straits.'

According to Winchester, the article made history in that it marked not just the consolidation of a global network of telegraphic communication but the emergence of what Marshall McLuhan famously described as a 'global village' : in Winchester's words, 'It would not be stretching a point to suggest that *the Global Village . . .* was essentially born with the worldwide apprehension of, and fascination with, the events in Java that began in the summer of 1883' (Winchester 2003: 182). Whether this formulation takes this point too far or not, the article in *The Times* was undoubtedly the first of a sequence of representations that helped to institute, if not a global village, then certainly something akin to a new form of planetary consciousness in the United Kingdom, in the US, and in several other countries around the world.

The Times of the 1880s was both the most likely and, from a twenty-first-century perspective, a rather unlikely place for such a consciousness to begin to emerge. Like the *New York Herald* of the 1860s, *The Times* was quite different from newspapers today. There were, on the one hand, still no photographs. Each page was still divided into a series of columns (six in this case) of what seems, by today's standards, a remarkably densely *linguistic* text. On the other hand, in *The Times* as in the *Herald*, the first pages were devoted in their entirety to what are described today as classified advertisements. Page 1 advertised, amongst other subjects, births, marriages and deaths (in that order), but also horse shows, concerts, 'lost or stolen' and 'rational dress' exhibitions. Page 2 included numerous advertisements for 'ships sailing', but also for carriages, perambulators, dahlias and geraniums. Page 3 included advertisements for 'positions', capitalists wanted, nurses, kitchenmaids, North German ladies, coals, collieries and even an advert for 'Nuda Veritas, gray hair restored'. Page 4, the first proper 'news' page, reported on share prices, proceedings in the House of Commons and law notices. Page 5 came closest to what might be described as 'international news' in so far as it had the 'latest intelligence' organized by countries. Page 6 had, for its part, 'sporting intelligence', 'naval and military intelligence' and 'university intelligence'; the following pages included law reports, court of bankruptcy news, the mails, letters to the editor, more advertisements, leading articles or editorial pieces and a page devoted mostly to Ireland.

In the late nineteenth century, this layout revealed a logic of imperial interest. News about Krakatoa reached London as quickly as it did largely as a function of a colonial geography and its concomitant technologies of displacement. Although Java was a part of the Dutch East Indies, the Sunda Straits were of vital strategic significance to the shipping of all the imperial powers at the time. This was the passage that connected the South China Sea with the Indian Ocean, and the presence of an agent of Lloyd's, the insurance underwriters of Western shipping, was therefore no coincidence.

But the sheer speed of the news owed much to the invention of the telegraph. In my analysis of Stanley's exploits, I briefly mentioned the significance of telegraphy earlier in the nineteenth century. This medium is all too easily overlooked by histories of mass communication.[1] The Morse telegraphic system, which came to dominate others, had existed since the 1840s. But, as Winchester (2003) explains, it was not before the installation of a reliable network of submarine cables over the next twenty or so years – a remarkable technological innovation in its own right – that the telegraphic system could live up to its promise of revolutionarily fast communications across the globe.

Once such a system was in place, the technology helped to create the impression that natural events around the world were, if not co-temporaneous with their reception by Western audiences, then certainly far 'closer' – the blurring of space and time is evident – than had hitherto been the case. If older forms of communication emphasized the thirdness of geography by being manifestly at one remove from the here and now of the observer, the telegraphic system conveyed a sense of firstness in so far as it seemed to do away with the mediation of the time of communication. Of course, the telegraphic system did not mean that Krakatoa was any *closer* to European or other similarly distant observers in terms of *physical* space. But it did mean that the *time* of communication was drastically reduced, and this meant, paradoxically, that *social* or imaginary space was, to use the notion of David Harvey (1989), 'compressed'.

Coverage of Krakatoa's main eruptions in 1883 exemplifies this process. On 28 August 1883, on page 5 of *The Times*, under the heading 'latest intelligence', but once again towards the bottom of the page, the following article appeared, sandwiched between a small piece on the recent Ischia earthquake and news about the international corn and seed market.

VOLCANIC ERUPTIONS IN JAVA.
BATAVIA, AUG. 27.
Terrific detonations from the volcanic island of Krakatoa were heard last night, and were audible as far as Soerakarta, showers of ashes falling as far as Cheribon. The flashes from the volcano are plainly visible from here. Serang is now in total darkness. Stones have fallen at that place. Batavia is also nearly in darkness. All the gaslights were extinguished during the night. It is impossible to communicate with Anjer, and it is feared that some calamity has happened there. Several bridges between Anjer and Serang have been destroyed and a village near the former place has been washed away, the rivers having overflowed through the rush of the sea inland.

By the newspaper's later admission, two more days passed before further news was provided because the editors were reluctant to believe the news they received. This news, as before in the form of 'cables', was then dramatically reported as follows:

THE VOLCANIC ERUPTION IN JAVA.
BATAVIA, AUG. 28, NOON.
All quiet. Sky clear. Communication Seran restored – Telegraph Inspector reports while trying to repair line at Anjer early on morning 27th, saw high column sea approaching with roaring noise and fled inland. Knows nothing further of fate of Anjer, but believed all lost.

AUGUST 29, 10 A.M.
Sky continues clear. Temperature fell ten degrees on 27th, now normal; native huts all along beach washed away. Birds roosted during ash rain; and cocks crowed as it cleared away; fish dizzy; town covered with thin layer ashes, giving roads quaint bright look. Sad news just coming from West Coast; shall wire again.

11 A.M.
Anjer, Tjeringen, Telokbetong, destroyed.

11 20 A.M.
Lighthouses Sunda Straits have disappeared.

NOON.
Where once mound Kramatau stood, the sea now plays.

The inclusion of this sequence of cables was the late nineteenth-century equivalent of 'live' reporting, that is, reporting 'as it happened'. But in order to explain
the catastrophic events *The Times* included on that same day (albeit on page 4, the
page *before* the news) an editorial that began as follows:

VOLCANIC ERUPTIONS AND TIDAL WAVES.
Seismology is one of the youngest of sciences, but its progress is not
likely to be hindered from lack of material. Scarcely have we recovered
from the shock of the Ischia calamity when vague news of a somewhat
similar catastrophe reaches us from the other side of the world . . . . To
complicate matters, what is called a 'tidal wave' had rushed over the west
and north-west coast of the islands, choked up the rivers, overflowed the
land, and swept away the European quarter at Anjer.

The mere presence of this editorial reveals the extent to which the events in
Krakatoa caused far more commotion amongst the journalists than was suggested
by the comparatively reduced coverage – by today's standards – of the event. As
this quote begins to suggest, the paper offered what was in effect a pedagogy of
the nature of tidal waves, and the relation between tidal waves and volcanic activity, a relation which had not yet been fully understood.

Given the virtually instantaneous communication across continents enjoyed
by many people in the twenty-first century, it is easy to take this coverage for
granted. But in the late nineteenth century it constituted a revolutionary change.
Long before pictures of the planet were taken from space, we can say that the
telegraph, as mediated by the newspaper, played a key role in instituting not just a
new form of planetary consciousness but a new form of planetary temporality. It
does not seem an overstatement to say that this new firstness of a *globalized* nature
constituted a significant precedent for the global environmental consciousness
that was to emerge in the twentieth century.

The last point brings us to what is perhaps the most significant aspect – from
the point of this history of the present – of Krakatoa. Krakatoa was one of the
first natural catastrophes whose immediate global consequences were scientifically
recorded around the planet, as they took place, by the members of a number of
different scientific disciplines. Crucially, it was also one of the first instances, if not
the first, in which such recordings were then interpreted by a single globalized and
globalizing text, published by the Royal Society in 1888, which was the product
of a multidisciplinary team of researchers. After the loss of life, it can be argued
that this text was almost as momentous as the events that it represented. If some
of the century's subjects had witnessed the emergence of new and quite explicitly
'heterotopic' forms of planetary consciousness in modern zoos and other institutions, the Royal Society's report signalled the emergence of a form of planetary
consciousness whose subjects were capable of tracking the displacement of signs
of nature across the globe, as they took place. As I noted in Chapter 3, instruments such as thermometers and barometers – what I described as dicent indexical

legisigns – had existed for centuries. What changed now was the development of a technology of observation that might record the dicent sinsigns of natural events such as those produced by Krakatoa as they occurred around the planet.

Why this interest in recording Krakatoa's effects? A month or so after the main eruptions, a number of extraordinary environmental phenomena took place that were subsequently linked to the eruption. These included blue and green suns seen in various tropical countries, records of a 'peculiar haze', the 'extraordinary twilight glows' in the British Isles, and then reports of the 'great air-wave' produced by the blast (Symons 1888: iii). The relationship between these events and the eruption were not immediately apparent. As reported by *The Times* on 8 December 1883 in an article titled THE RECENT SUNRISES AND SUNSETS,

> there has been a new idea super-added, an idea suggesting a cause for them so far outside ordinary conceptions that it will be scouted by many as beyond even legitimate imagination, though it is not now suggested for the first time. We are, in fact, brought face to face with the question whether or not we are now, in the month of December, witnessing effects for the cause of which we must go back to a gigantic experiment, by far the biggest terrestrial experiment on record, made by Dame Nature during the month of last August.

As is evident in this report, the article continued to gender nature as being female, but accorded to nature that status of a hitherto 'masculine' science: 'Dame Nature' engaged in a process of *experimentation*. Nature was transformed, in an age of considerable interest in geology and chemistry, into a kind of chemist.

This being so, the members of the Royal Society in Britain decided to set up a 'Krakatoa Committee' charged with 'collecting the various accounts of the volcanic eruption . . . and subsequent phenomena, in such form as shall best provide for their preservation and promote their usefulness' (Symons 1888: iv).

The report, which was published five and a half years after the eruption, was divided into five parts. A first section by the President of the Geological Society, Professor J.W. Judd, described the volcanic phenomena and the 'nature and distribution of the ejected materials'. A second section, prepared by the Metereological Office, analysed the 'air waves and sounds caused by the eruption', which were heard thousands of miles from the eruption. A third section, written by Captain W.J.L. Wharton of the Royal Navy, who was later described as a 'hydrographer', provided an account of the seismic sea waves caused by the eruption, while a fourth section, by the Hon. F.A. Rollo Russell and Mr E. Douglas Archibald, described the 'unusual optical phenomena of the atmosphere' from 1883 to 1886. A final section, prepared by G.M. Whipple, B.Sc, Superintendent of the Kew Observatory, reported on the 'magnetical and electrical phenomena' accompanying the explosion (Symons 1888: xi–xiv).

Together, these different sections produced a report that developed new forms of planetary consciousness. On the one hand, the report obtained information about the global effects of a single environmental phenomenon from a variety of sources scattered throughout the globe. For example, the first section of the report collated information on where and when pumice or volcanic dust had been observed in Africa, Australia and Asia.

Significant as it was, this aspect paled beside the fact that the report reconstructed the atmospheric and marine displacements of the natural phenomenon *as they affected different parts of the globe*. For example, one chart recorded the barometrical registers of the successive passages of the 'air waves' as they were recorded in locations such as Sydney, Mauritius, Berlin, Armagh, Loanda, New York, Toronto and Havana. A similar form of globalization was evident in efforts to chart the movements of the sea waves that spread to distant shores, including the east coast of Hindustan, the south coast of Africa, the west coast of France and, of course, the south coast of England. A map on page 157 showed the entire globe with the movements of sea waves. The new technology of observation thereby became a technology for the recording of sinsigns of nature as part of global *sequences* and spatialities.

It might be argued that the report was the result of the invention of more recent dicent indexical legisigns such as the barometer, the hemispherical cup anemometer or other devices used to measure environmental phenomena. A better explanation is provided by the fact that, during the second half of the nineteenth century, a series of international conventions were held that standardized scientific protocols for measurement in a variety of areas. One protocol which was to be particularly significant for the Royal Society's report on Krakatoa was the First International Metereological Convention, held in Brussels in 1853. As suggested by one of its members, Lieutenant Matthew Fontaine Maury, an officer in the US Navy, 'all maritime nations should cooperate and make these meteorological observations in such a manner and with such means and implements, that the system might be uniform and observations made on board one public ship be readily referred to and compared with the observations made on board all other public ships in whatever part of the world' (Maury in http://www.austehc.unimelb.edu.au/fam/0811.html, accessed 22 July 2004).

This dynamic of standardization, like the report that it helped to make possible some 35 years later, was as much a sign of the industrialized times, as of the emergence of a form of planetary consciousness that aspired to use *mathesis* and the logic of *legein* to map not just the world, but its physical displacements in 'real time', or 'proto-real time'. As an article in *The Times* about the publication of Royal Society's report put it on 1 October 1888:

> The truth is, however, that science has had more to do with the interest excited by the Krakatoa eruption and its sequel than anything else. Such things, if we may trust the records which exist, have occurred before; but there was only an isolated observer here and there to note them. Humanity had not advanced far enough to be able to penetrate into their real significance. Now we have trained observers all over the globe.

Instruments of the most delicate construction are planted at many points of vantage, sensitive to the least disturbance of the elements; our ships plough every sea, the telegraph is ready even while the battle is waging, be it a war of the elements or a deadly fight between men and men, to flash the story red hot to all of the world. All these circumstances combined, no doubt, to intensify and widen the interest taken in this last great outburst of terrestrial energy. It was not likely that science, with the restless inquisitiveness that marks her at the present day, would neglect so splendid an opportunity of trying to unravel the mysteries of Nature's workings.

In so far as this logic used maps, graphs and especially tables to tabulate the displacements, it is possible to suggest that scientific rationality never left behind the tables that Foucault suggests are characteristic of the 'Classical' *epistéme*. On the contrary, these continued to be produced with a vengeance in the late nineteenth century, and in the case of the Royal Society's report – and indeed newspapers such as *The Times* – constituted new kinds of heterotopic and heterochronic spaces. But, as the commentary in *The Times* also reveals, they were unequivocal evidence of the institution of forms of observation that were *themselves* both heterotopic and heterochronic: the figure of the single observer of nature was now both displaced and replaced by an observer which, as in the case of newspaper articles, was premised explicitly on manifold, multiple sites whose observations would henceforth need to be 'gathered' and articulated.

(In)corporation

The report on Krakatoa was by no means the only instance of a growing process of standardization, or indeed of specialization, that is to say classification, of practices. By the turn of the twentieth century, most practices in the modern world had begun to be affected by forms of organization that derived much of their power from standardization and compartmentalization. This was particularly true of modern business enterprises, which the historian Alfred Chandler (1977) has defined as a form of business organization that is structured into distinct operating units. These units tend to be geographically dispersed, involve multiple economic functions and product lines, and are managed by a hierarchy of salaried executives. The emergence and eventual predominance of the modern business enterprise marked the beginning of a shift from industrial forms of capitalism to what I will describe henceforth as managerial capitalism. From this point onwards, it was the top managers of such enterprises that were arguably to have the most wide-ranging power over all manner of social – and indeed 'natural' – formations in a growing number of fields.

Chandler notes that, as late as 1840, no such business organization existed. The management of the larger enterprises was carried out by owner-managers who tended to specialize in one product line, operated within a given region, and did so without the aid of middle managers. Less than a century later, the modern business enterprise with multiple units and tiers of middle managers was the dominant business institution.

The emergence of this form of organization had a number of far-reaching consequences for both imaginary and material nature, and indeed for the fate of the modern observer. First, the organization of business along increasingly segmented and bureaucratic principles entailed a dramatic loss of social accountability. Aspects of this problem were not new; since colonial times, large corporations such as the East India Company had raised similar issues for European monarchs by virtue of their capacity to mobilize economic and symbolic capital to conceal corrupt practices and/or to silence resistance to their practices. But this risk was now compounded as enterprises became more compartmentalized and as ownership passed from families or individuals to hundreds if not thousands of shareholders. As the companies extended the geographical reach of their activities, the key decision-makers frequently became more and more distant from the regions they affected. Who might now be held responsible for the enterprises' actions? And how might a few relatively poor individuals – or even thousands of relatively dispersed members of the middle class – resist the power of such an accumulation of economic and, eventually, symbolic capital? It can be suggested in this sense that, long before the so-called 'new risk' society emerged – as described below with reference to the work of Ulrich Beck – a key element of its politics had begun to be instituted by the emergence of managerial capitalism.

This shift had a number of consequences for the nature of observation. First, the model of a corporate bureaucracy increasingly served to structure the nature of activities both in and beyond the economic sphere. Second, the corporations produced increasingly standardized technologies of observation and displacement, such that increasingly scientists (and all manner of observers interested in nature) became increasingly confident in the apparent universality of their measurements. Third, as had begun to be evident in the case of the increasingly corporate organization of newspapers, the production of observations was itself increasingly a matter of multiple and compartmentalized practices.

The shift towards the modern business enterprise required, among other conditions, the sanction, if not active support, of the institution which produced the conditions for its emergence, but whose sovereignty the new forms of enterprise began to undermine: the nation-state. In the United States, this sanction was provided indirectly by the Supreme Court, which before and especially after the Civil War passed down a series of rulings that arguably conflated the nature of 'artificial' and 'natural' persons, and in so doing worked to establish and consolidate a notion of 'corporate personhood' that effectively assigned corporations the same rights as the individual 'person'. A detailed analysis of this complex process, its long antecedants and the numerous rulings by means of which this process took place are beyond the scope of this section. Here, I only wish to note that it is remarkable that at the very point when modern business enterprises in the United States ceased in most respects to be a matter of individual persons – the arrival of the twentieth century witnessed a series of mergers that created veritable

industrial giants managed by mushrooming corporate bureaucracies – the Supreme Court granted the corporations the juridical rights of the 'person'. To be
sure, the very notion of a 'corporation' or of 'incorporating' ironically echoed
this point: the Latin root for 'incorporation' (*in* [into] + *corporare* [form into
a body]) is the same as that for *corporeality*. The modern business corporation
gained a certain corporeality, in the sense of individual juridical rights for itself as
a 'person', at the very historical moment when it lost its body, that is, when the
business enterprise as an organization distributed its 'corporeality' across growing
bureaucracies. The multiplication of the observer which I described in relation to
Krakatoa was, in this sense, both preceded and followed by its corporate equivalent in the economic sphere.

Few enterprises were to have more significant consequences for the modern
imaginary of nature than the Ford Motor Company. Henry Ford, the company's
larger-than-life owner-manager, incorporated the Ford Motor Company in 1903,
and went on to become the almost super-human symbol of the duality of such
enterprises as 'individuals' and vast enterprises. Ford famously proclaimed that
he would build a car for 'the great multitude', a statement that signalled a significant change in the discourse of some capitalists towards mass culture. Whereas
the British middle and upper classes had once regarded the mobility of the new
working classes as a threat – as I explained with Raymond Williams, 'mob' was
a shortened version of *mobile vulgus* – Henry Ford now anointed himself as the
purveyor of a new kind of mass mobility. In a remarkable contradiction of this
inversion, Woodrow Wilson worried that the automobile would spread 'socialistic
feeling' to the 'countryman' who would regard the first automobiles, driven by
the rich, as 'a picture of the arrogance of wealth with all its independence and
carelessness' (quoted in Gartman 1994: 15). Ford however suggested that, in
effect, the best method to keep such social 'pathologies' at bay was to encourage
the urban working classes *to drive themselves*. Any dangers resulting from it would
be more than compensated, once again, by the therapeutic effects of nature: as
Ford famously put it,

> I will build a motorcar for the great multitudes. It will be large enough
> for the family but small enough for the individual to run and care for . . .
> it will be so low in price that no man making a good salary will be unable
> to own one – and enjoy with his family the blessing of hours of pleasure
> in God's great open spaces.
>
> (Ford quoted in Wolf 1996: 70)

Here again, a new technology of displacement was employed to take the
middle and even the working classes 'to' nature. Or rather, the new technology
allowed them to *take themselves* to nature: where trains had once popularized
mass travel to the British countryside and had done so on the basis of collective principles of mobilization, Ford now devised a means whereby massification
itself might be individualized, and eventually, personalized. Cars became a mobile
principle of private property and individuation, and a kind of mobile space for the

development of new technologies of the self. Whereas Rousseau had drifted in an open rowboat on a lake, American citizens were now invited to drive themselves along scenic roads in a kind of privatized 'interior' on wheels with which and from which 'God's great open spaces' might be visited. It can be suggested in this sense that cars were to trains what television would be to film: the windshield became a mobile and personal window to the world, a kind of *perspectiva* on wheels, a panorama made mobile by the self: auto-mobile, a word derived from the Greek *'autos'* for self and the Latin *'mobilis'* for mobile. Beyond the 'privatization' that this medium presupposed when compared to train travel, a significant difference was constituted by the fact that the observer would now observe looking *forward*: where views were once sideways, and so only allowed the observer to gaze at the world as it blurred by, at least those sitting in the front seats of automobiles would be able to observe the world coming *at* them.

I shall return to this little-noticed change when I consider a technology of observation and displacement that in some respects preceded this disposition: the cinema. Here I will note that key to the new technology of displacement was a new system of production, what we might describe with Mark Rupert (1995) as 'true' mass production. The distinction implicit in this classification is important as Ford by no means invented mass production. Instead, he and his team of managers – and it was very much a collective effort – synthesized and perfected existing technologies of production even as they invented new ones. They adopted precision manufacturing methods and specialized machine tools, introduced novel production methods such as sheet metal stamping, developed a more detailed division of labour and, in 1913–14, perfected the famous moving assembly line, which meant that teams of workers could add parts to each vehicle as it moved past them, dramatically reducing the time it took to build an automobile. Whereas it took about ten worker-hours to build a Ford motor prior to the institution of this system, after its introduction this time was famously reduced to 3.75 worker-hours. These and other improvements in productivity meant that the cost per unit was dramatically reduced; the cost of a Ford Model T was reduced from $850 in 1908 to $360 by 1916 (Rupert 1995: 63).

This last point begins to explain how Ford's automobile instituted a technology of displacement even on the level of its production. The conventional economic wisdom for the introduction of such a technology was that it ultimately reduced unit costs by greatly increasing the output. While such an account is not invalid, it overlooks the political economic dimension of mass production. David Gartman (1994) notes that the late 1800s were a period in US history when medium and large enterprises responded to economic depression, lowering profit margins and increasing competition by creating a series of mergers that, as I mentioned earlier, produced corporate giants: in effect, a kind of doubling or tripling of the logic of bureaucratization already at work in the pre-merger modern business enterprise. The massive new enterprises, still structured along the lines described by Chandler, sought to maintain or increase their profits by lowering wages and intensifying labour. When the industrial workforce, initially made up in large part by craftworkers, resisted the changes, corporate leaders began to invest in technologies of production that displaced skilled labour, and effected the change to the so-called 'Fordist' systems of assembly line production.

The new form of production produced a radical new form of alienation of workers by adopting the techniques of Winslow Taylor and other 'scientific managers.' At the turn of the century, the new managers sought to increase productivity by intensifying the division of labour and the routinization of tasks, and by increasing the supervision and control of work according to detailed managerial control (Rupert 1995: 60–1). The new managerial technology was meant to reduce an individual worker's control over the process, effectively 'dumbing down' the work. In this sense, even as workers were encouraged to drive themselves, they became increasingly driven.

Far from regarding this as a problem, Ford proclaimed that 'The average worker, I'm sorry to say, wants a job in which he [*sic*] doesn't have to put forth much physical exertion – above all he wants a job in which he does not have to think' (Ford in Wolf 1996: 71). In fact, the estrangement produced by the new technology was met with a wave of strikes, and more tactical forms of resistance of the kind famously documented by Charlie Chaplin in the film *Modern Times*. Ford was thus forced to offer hegemonic concessions that included what was then a relatively high $5 hourly wage – as noted by Rupert, this was approximately twice the normal wage – and incentives to buy Ford Model Ts.[2] In this way, Ford was able to link the system of mass production with a corresponding form of mass *consumption*.

In so far as the products of mass production could be afforded by masses of people, mass production instituted mass consumption by making it possible for the masses to *afford* consumption. Doing so produced a vast market for Ford's goods even as it incorporated the working class in what became known as the Fordist system of managerial capitalism. Automobility – in the fullest hegemonic sense of the term – took the United States, and then much of the rest of the industrializing world, by storm.

As I began to note earlier, a key aspect of this involved a certain dynamic of apparent individualization. Whereas travel over long distances by train constrained the individual to the existing network of railways and rail timetables and thereby drastically constricted mobility in both spatial and temporal terms, the car appeared to 'liberate' the individual from such collective constraints by allowing the individual to travel wherever, and whenever, s/he wanted.

In fact, this was by no means simply the case: cars could only go where roads went, and even when roads went where individuals wanted to go it soon became clear that a host of mediations were required to prevent the 'accidents' that began to proliferate. What was in fact every bit a mass, and *collective*, technology of displacement and observation was made to seem, and today is still made to look, like a matter of individual will: whereas trains were obviously a matter of collectivity, cars seemed obviously 'individual'.

The automobile was, from this perspective, the analogon of what Theodor

Adorno (1941) describes as the phenomenon of pseudo-individualization in the context of popular music: a process whereby cultural mass production is endowed with a halo of free choice on the basis of standardization itself. If standardization in music kept and still keeps customers 'in line' by doing their listening for them, pseudo-individualization kept them in line by making them forget that their music had already been listened to for them.

This dissimulation of the mass-mediated nature of automobility was consolidated once Fordist principles of vehicular uniformity were replaced by Alfred Sloan's principles of part-interchangeability. Sloan, the president and then also chairman of General Motors Corporation from 1923 until 1956, led the development of a system that allowed the company to produce what seemed to be a plethora of entirely different models and brands which actually shared the same underlying mechanical parts. The individual consumer could apparently choose which model best suited her/his finances and class aspirations and, in doing so, was apparently encouraged to engage in a fashioning of the own identity.

As articulated by way of the codes of familiarity – increasingly it was suggested that each family *ought* to have their own car, a principle that was partly forced by the fact that giant automakers, led by Sloan, did their best to eliminate effective public transport – automobility encouraged new forms of suburbanization. These in turn eventually *required* automobility. Automobility, at least in its American, suburban guise, is thus one of the great and ecologically disastrous technologies of displacement, one that both allowed people to move great distances and played a significant role in forcing them to move from the inner cities.

National Geographic automobility

As noted above, Ford justified the production and consumption of the automobile in pastoralist terms. While this was of course by no means the only justification, let alone the only use, given to automobiles, its very invocation (and eventual operationalization) constituted a remarkable, indeed remarkably successful, continuation of both Victorian and Olmstedian versions of mass mediation via the ostensibly therapeutic qualities of the countryside.

The first automobile entered the Yosemite Valley in 1913, and by 1917 maps were being made that provided, amongst other information, the alternating hours when visitors could drive up or down single-track and (then) largely unsurfaced roads. As automobiles grew in popularity and became more widely used for tourism, the new National Park Service, established in 1916, the same year that John Muir's 'Thousand-Mile Walk to the Gulf' was published, embarked on a road building programme in parks like the Yosemite. The programme was shaped by landscape engineers' and architects' recommendations, such that the roads should protect landscape features, but also, and significantly, that they should 'take advantage of scenic points previously overlooked' (McClelland 1998: 175).

As noted by Paul S. Sutter (2002), more widespread car ownership and exurban tourism were part of a growing classification of work and leisure time and, with it, the rise of the figure going on vacation for both middle-class and also working-class families. The promotion by Ford and others of car travel to 'God's great open spaces' made it possible to use the national parks for the purposes that Olmsted had originally conceived. It is possible to get some idea of the role that mass mediation played in this practice by returning to the *National Geographic*, albeit to a somewhat older issue than I considered in Chapters 1 and 2: the October 1923 issue, which included an article by William Joseph Showalter titled 'The Automobile Industry: An American Art that has Revolutionized Methods in Manufacture and Transformed Transportation'.

The *National Geographic* was the magazine of the National Geographic Society, which was established in 1888 in Washington DC. As the Society's Certificate of Incorporation put it, 'The particular objects and business of the Society are: to increase and diffuse geographic knowledge; to publish the transactions of the Society; to publish a periodical magazine, and other works relating to the science of geography; to dispose of such publications by sale or otherwise; and to acquire a library' (National Geographic Society 1888a: 89). The Society's magazine's aims were articulated from the start in both heterotopic and pedagogic terms: '[The Magazine] will contain memoirs, essays, notes, correspondence, reviews, etc. relating to Geographic matters. As it is not intended to be simply the organ of the Society, its pages will be open to all persons interested in Geography'; and 'As it is hoped to diffuse as well as to increase knowledge, due prominence will be given to the educational aspect of geographic matters, and efforts will be made to stimulate an interest in original sources of information' (National Geographic Society 1888b: i).

This explicitly pedagogic discourse was accompanied and indeed articulated by a non-formal pedagogic discourse that was to constitute the Society and its magazine as one of the most influential 'nature media' in the world. As noted by Catherine Lutz and Jane Collins (1993), part of the success of the early magazine – and one of its continuing functions – was its ability to both find a niche in and capitalize on the recently expanding national magazine market; but to do so in a way that promoted the nationalist discourse that swept through the United States as it assumed an increasingly imperial role in global affairs. The nationalism of the Society was evident in all of its magazine's articles, not least in the 1923 article on automobiles, which described the automobile industry as an 'American Art' that was making 'transport history' (Showalter 1923: 337).

The magazine was nonetheless able to maintain a certain space for itself by initially refusing finance by way of advertisements, and by appealing to the authority of science. The magazine's science was nonetheless more a work of the amateur *recontextualization* of geographic discourses. As noted by Lutz and Collins, many of the Society's founding members were genteel 'amateur' geographers and *patrons* of science, and their practical inclination and interest in philanthropy, as well as the development of the magazine itself into a medium of mass circulation, meant that the Society initially remained relatively isolated from the more academic forms of scientific research that began to develop in US universities at the turn of the century. This tendency is illustrated by an anecdote concerning Gilbert Hovey Grosvenor, the managing editor at the time that the volcano Pelée erupted on Martinique and killed virtually every inhabitant in the French colonial city of St. Pierre. Grosvenor reportedly wished to send a two-man (*sic*) scientific expedition to cover the events for the magazine, but was wired by Alexander Graham Bell, the second president of the Society, and told 'Go yourself to Martinique . . . this is the opportunity of a lifetime – seize it' (Bell in McCarry 1988: 287). According to Lutz and Collins, practices such as these and the magazine's growing circulation eventually meant that the magazine came to be situated as a 'middlebrow' publication, where the notion of 'middlebrow' reflected the changing class structuring of the US, in particular the emergence of immigrant businessmen who transgressed the old classifications of culture and money. This 'middlebrow' position was to remain one of the hallmarks not just of the *National Geographic* but of what I will describe later as the more didactic forms of mass-mediating nature in the US and in the UK. The representation of nature – and in this case of physical and human geography more generally – involved a double pedagogy: teaching about the nature of the world, but also teaching tacitly or non-formally about the (proper) nature of the self.

The first issue of the magazine was unrecognizable from the point of its current style. The magazine contained no photographs and, even if it did offer articles such as one about the 'Great Storm' of 11–14 March 1888, the style was comparatively dry and still somewhat specialized. In 1905, Grosvenor took an unprecedented and expensive step in the direction of its current style when he decided to include the magazine's first photographs – of the 'prohibited' city of Lhasa, Tibet – in the January edition. Grosvenor expected to be fired for this decision, but instead the popularity of his decision reportedly led people to stop him on the street and congratulate him (McCarry 1988: 296). Encouraged by the success, Grosvenor began to publish more and more photographs in the magazine, and this ultimately inverted the image–text relation: starting from no photographs at all, the magazine went from having photographs conceived as rhematic indexical legisigns, that is to say so many 'straightforward' 'illustrations' that were placed randomly throughout the text, to having photographs that served as the co-vehicles of the narrative, that is to say the equivalent of 'arguments' in their own right.

By the time that the 1923 article on automobiles was published, the latter logic had been instituted. Of the article's 77 pages, only six were devoted exclusively to text; the rest of the pages had full-page photographs, photographs across half or two thirds of the page or, in a few cases, photographs that occupied one third or less of the page (all of the photographs continued to be in black and white). In 1907, Bell reportedly wrote that 'The features of most interest are the illustrations . . . . The disappointing feature of the magazine is that there is so little in the text about the pictures . . . . It seems to me that one notable line for improvement would be either to adapt the pictures to the text *or the text to the pictures*. Why not the latter?' (Bell in McCarthy 1988: 296). The layout of the 1923 article

nonetheless suggested an image–text relation that could not be so unambiguously classified. The written aspects of the main text were structured in a relatively
conventional manner, with a heavy emphasis not just on a nationalist but also
on a masculinist discourse about the statistics of car ownership, the production
methods and the technical improvements in automobiles. However, the progression of images in the magazine was by no means clearly adapted to illustrate the
verbal text, or vice versa. The article interspersed images of automobiles in the
countryside with images of the assembly lines in automobile factories, images of
car races and, in a few instances, images of cars, mostly parked, in urban settings.
The magazine also included some 'historical' images of the first automobiles, as
well as pictures of mechanized agricultural and military vehicles, and pictures of
women in or around cars, in some cases engaging in automobile camping. While
there was some relation between the last three subjects and the content of the
main text, and while especially the pictures of the production methods reflected
the verbal text's focus on these matters, the reader was allowed to construct a
rather different narrative by looking at the pictures. This relatively 'open' semeiotic landscape (Kress and van Leeuwen 1996) was only partly contradicted by the
captions, which tended to be organized on two levels. Beneath each photograph
there was a capitalized caption that provided what might be described as no more
than a rhematic symbol, or perhaps even a rhematic indexical legisign 'pointing to'
or, in Peirce's terms, 'establishing an association' between the sign and its object
(in this case another sign). For example, on page 338, an image was shown of ten
cars going up a hill above a city; the first level of caption read 'TEN OF A KIND
TAKING THE TWIN PEAKS' GRADE ON HIGH AT SAN FRANCISCO'.
Beneath these captions, a longer text in smaller letters provided an explanation,
that is to say an argument (in Peirce's terms) that both provided more details as
to the subject of the photograph and related the photograph to more general
qualisigns. In the cited example, this text read 'A San Francisco distributor decided
to show the world what his cars could do on heart-breaking hills. Ten owners,
one a woman, came to the scratch at the foot of the hill and not a gear was shifted
after the start. The power of the American-built motor represents an outstanding
engineering achievement' (Showalter 1923: 338). With Roland Barthes (1985a),
it might be argued that such texts were in fact 'parasitical' to the photographs,
thereby inverting the order suggested by the concept of illustration. We might
however agree with Gunther Kress and Theo van Leeuwen (1996) when they
suggest that Barthes' (1985b) notion of 'anchorage' – whereby the text 'directs
the reader among the various signifieds of the image, causes him (*sic*) to avoid
some and to accept others' (Barthes 1985b: 29) – misses a significant aspect of the
image–text relation: 'the visual component of a text is an independently organized
and structured message – connected with the verbal text, but in no way dependent
on it: and similarly the other way around' (Kress and van Leeuwen 1996: 17).

It is possible, in this sense, to imagine a reader leafing through the article who
might read none of the captions, read only the main caption or read some of the

captions. The point is not to deny the possible significance of the captions, but rather to note that by 1923 the magazine's format had established a code that allowed for any of these forms of reading/viewing. It was arguably this organization, more than the inclusion of photographs per se, that eventually came to make good one editor's suggestion in 1915 that the magazine had discovered a seemingly 'universal language which requires no deep study . . . one that is understood as well by the jungaleer as by the courtier; by the Eskimo as by the wild man [*sic*] from Borneo; by the child in the playroom as by the professor in the college; and by the woman in the household as by the hurried business man – in short, the Language of the Photograph' (Bryan in Lutz and Collins 1993: 28).

Two further aspects of the article stand out from the point of view of the mass mediation of automobility. First, the extraordinary effort put into promoting the automobile as a kind of higher stage of civilization and, as part of this process, dissimulating the ideological nature of a variety of aspects associated with the production and consumption of the automobile. On the one hand, Showalter implied a relation of causality between automobile ownership and all manner of indexes of national wealth and progress: 'the motor vehicle has assumed the role of a highly efficient factor in our transportation system, touching the lives and promoting the welfare of America as few developments in the history of any nation have done'; and 'Transportation has been the ladder upon which humanity climbed from a condition of primitive life to that of a finely wrought and complex civilization' (Showalter 1923: 341–3). On the other hand, the article attempted both to deny the implications of mass production for the workforce and to normalize the gendering of automobility built into car design itself: 'Does the reduction of the intricacy of the work a man performs deaden his initiative . . .? In one factory . . . perhaps the most monotonous task is that of a man who picks up a gear with a steel hook, shakes it in a vat of oil, and then places it in a basket . . . . He has done the same job for eight years and has refused offers of promotion' (Showalter 1923: 393). As to the gendering of automobility, 'another [company] puts on an improved type of brake-equalizer, so as to insure, in a measure at least, Milady driver against skidding. Gear shifting and clutch operation have been made easier to catch her eye. Accelerator pedals have been redesigned, so that they function equally well with high-heeled dress boots and low-heeled dress shoes. Spark and gas control levers . . . are being redesigned to obviate the danger of feminine fingers being caught' (Showalter 1923: 381).

Second, and of particular interest to the present chapter, was the article's visual representation of automobiles in a variety of scenic landscapes. The following list of captions provides an idea of their subjects:

'Drifting down the mountain side on the Pikes Peak Highway'; 'A section of the Storm King highway between Cornwall and Westpoint, New York'; 'A picturesque piece of road-building on Signal Mountain, Tennessee'; 'Motoring through the famous Wawona tunnel tree, Mariposa Grove, California'; 'At the end of the trail: Glacier Point, Yosemite Park, California'; 'Through the automobile, the American people have broken the bonds that formerly tied them to narrow localities'; 'Beside a mountain of ice cast upon the shore of Green Bay, near Escanaba, Michigan'; 'Caught in a snowstorm on the rim of Crater Lake, Oregon'; 'The Lake Crescent Road, Among the Fine Firs of the State of Washington'; 'Hanging on Behind: Through a Ford in Rock Creek Park, Washington'; 'Heavy going in the wake of a rainstorm in the Cedar Breaks Region of Southern Utah'; and 'At the Foot of Yosemite Falls, Yosemite National Park'. This list, which is not exhaustive, provided what was in effect a kind of heterotopic cross-section of scenic landscapes in which automobiles could be found. The preferred framing for such photographs usually placed the car in the foreground or middleground of a very wide shot showing the nature of 'God's great open spaces'.

Significantly, little mention was made of this use of automobiles in the main text; one exception was a reference to a car whose design had been adapted to camping: 'Press a button and the back of the front seat drops down. Reverse the cushion on the rear seat, and lo! You have a bed inside your car! Tents eliminated, your are ready to make your bed wherever night overtakes you – by a babbling brook, under a fine willow, or wherever fancy dictates' (Showalter 1923: 381). This example suggests that readers were expected to make sense of the relatively open framing of the photographs with reference to what had become, as I noted earlier, an extremely popular pastime: travelling by car to go camping in national parks and other rural locations. Some sense of the scope of this activity can be gleaned from the captions of two of the photographs, which explained that: 'Camping outfits of many kinds and degrees of comfort are on the market to-day, and the demand for them is showing a remarkable increase with each succeeding tourist season' (Showalter 1923: 395); and 'Hundreds of cities and towns have provided camps for tourists . . . . One Missouri town of 7,000 inhabitants recently made a count. Its citizens welcomed 23,520 cars, carrying 100,000 passengers, during the touring season' (Showalter 1923: 397).

The *National Geographic* article may be regarded as a precedent for many of the strategies that would be employed by car advertisers throughout the twentieth century. One of these was the suppression, or in the best of cases the minimizing, of references to the main context in which automobility would both take place and generate new forms of modern neurosis: the busy, if not jammed, city street. Moreover, and perhaps equally unsurprisingly, there was no reference to the effects that road building would have in the scenic areas. However, in much the same way that tourism by railway in Victorian Britain came to be contested by preservationists like Wordsworth, many preservationists in America eventually realised that automobility could have deleterious effects on the environments used for tourism, especially when the road building programmes were not as carefully designed as they were in Yosemite. As more and more roads were built in areas that were regarded as being of outstanding natural beauty – the *National Geographic* article extolled, for example, the virtues of road building in one photograph captioned 'A picturesque piece of road-building on Signal Mountain, Tennessee' – a wilderness movement emerged that was prompted by a concern to protect parks and other areas from the incursion of automobiles. Whereas Ford regarded the automobile as the benevolent means of reaching areas where sublime nature could be experienced, some now began to suggest that automobility might threaten that selfsame sublimity.

It was in this context that a new generation of preservationists mobilized to create institutions devoted to the protection of the areas in question. As documented by Sutter, in 1934 Bob Marshall, Benton MacKaye and other foresters decided to create the Wilderness Society. The anecdote about the circumstances under which the society was created is deeply paradoxical. Marshall, MacKaye and others were reportedly driving on the road between Knoxville and Lafolette in the Tennessee Valley discussing the idea of such a society, and decided to pull over to agree the principles of the new society (Sutter 2002).

As noted by Sutter:

> The group had come together to define a new preservationist ideal because of a common feeling that that the automobile and road building threatened what was left of wild America. Wilderness, as they defined it, would keep large portions of the landscape free of these forces. And yet, despite their flight from the Franks' car, a gesture evocative of their agenda, they could not escape the fact that, literally as well as figuratively, the automobile and improved roads had brought them together that day. . . . That paradox gave wilderness its modern meaning.
>
> (Sutter 2002: 4)

The anti-road protests in the United Kingdom in the 1990s had, in this specific sense, a remarkable precedent in the United States as early as the 1930s: long before anti-road protesters used cars to reach the protest sites, an anti-road building movement faced similar dilemmas. From the start, 'road protests' depended at least partly on roads, and on cars.

The image-movement

The invention of the gasoline-powered automobile coincided with the invention of *cinematography*. Indeed, one of the key technologies employed by some of the scientific management experts to conduct time and motion studies was time-lapse photography, the immediate precursor to film.

Time-lapse photography was perfected in the late 1800s by the photographer Eadweard Muybridge in California, and by the physician Etienne-Jules Marey in France. Marey is credited with being the first to use a single camera to produce the illusion of movement for more than a single viewer at once by producing photographs on a strip of sensitized film in real time (Braun 1992: 150). His invention in 1882 of a photographic 'machinegun' which 'shot' a series of pictures by means of a revolving drum – a dynamic that heralded what feminist critics describe as the camera/gun tradition – enabled him to record and analyse the flight of birds, and then to analyse the movement of a man running. From the mid-1890s onwards,

Marey's principles were employed to study physical labour in the context of mass production.

For his part, Muybridge made his first fame in the Yosemite Valley, where, like Watkins, he took prize-winning photographs of the landscape. But, unlike Watkins, Muybridge's fame ultimately hinged not on panoramas of El Capitán or the Bridal Veil, but on sequences of photographs which were taken by a horse when its legs pulled strings that triggered the shutters of cameras set up in parallel to its path. Just as Watkins was employed by Oneontan Collis Huntington to take pictures of his railway, Muybridge was asked by Leland Stanford, another of California's 'big four' railway-owner capitalists, to prove that, for a split second, a horse's four legs were all off the ground.

Muybridge's results, like those of Marey, were revolutionary. Hitherto, no one had managed to get sharp stills of locomotion, and it is possible to suggest with Gilles Deleuze (1986) that time-lapse photography instituted a shift from representations of movement that relied on idealized poses to representations that revealed 'any-instant-whatevers' (Deleuze 1986). This process is taken for granted in the early twenty-first century, but in the late nineteenth century it had far-reaching and revolutionarily prosthetic consequences for the process of observation. Muybridge travelled widely to make presentations of his sequences of photographs, and the following account, which appeared in the *San Francisco Chronicle*, provides an indication of the extent of the changes, and the manner in which some audiences responded to the new way of representing movement:

> The stride of Abe Edgington, and of the still more celebrated trotter Occident, was depicted in a clear manner in ten photographs . . . the strange attitudes assumed by each animal excited much comment and surprise, so different were they from those pictures representing our famous trotters at their full stride. But that which still more aroused astonishment and mirth, was the action of the racer at full gallop, some of the delineations being seemingly utterly devoid of all naturalness, so complex and ungraceful were many of the positions.
>
> (9 July 1878, p. 3, quoted in Musser 1990: 49)

Such responses suggest that one of pleasures of these lectures was the denaturalization of everyday perceptions and understandings of motion and, with it, a kind of deconstruction of perceived space. It is thus paradoxical that, when the Lumière brothers first projected an actual *film* for a public in late 1895, their *cinematographe* apparently worked to *reverse* this analytic dynamic. The technology of displacement apparently operated by 'setting in motion' the any-instant-whatevers. Deleuze (1986) nonetheless argues that, far from simply 'adding motion' to photographic stills, cinema revolutionized the representation and social experience of movement by interrelating two different forms of movement: the movement between the elements contained within any given shot, but also the movement produced by the relation between those elements, and everything that lay beyond the shot, beyond the montage and indeed beyond the film: the 'out-of-field', which Deleuze defines as 'what is neither seen nor understood, but is nevertheless perfectly present in any given framing' (Deleuze 1986: 16). Cinema thereby made it possible to relate dynamically what might be described as a logic of mobile sets, or what Deleuze describes as systems of information – the elements contained within any given shot, themselves in movement – with a relational logic that constantly referred the spectator to the dynamic universe *beyond* any given shot. This could be achieved thanks to the fact that cinema produced shots that were not just images *of* movement, but what Deleuze describes as the 'image-movement' (1986: 22). With Peirce, we might suggest that cinematography instituted a form of visualization that effectively collapsed firstness and secondness into image-movements where all was kinesis, and where all such iconic kinesis appeared to be a matter of i-mediate experience.

I shall return to this point below. Here I should note that this analysis is far removed from the discourse of most late nineteenth-century observers, for whom the cinematic images were apparently simply 'life-like'. Even so, it is possible to find clues to significant transformations in modern imaginary nature in this discourse. The reference to 'life-like' images may be interpreted as a popular way of saying that the images were 'animated' in the sense that they had movement. But, with Edgar Morin (2001), it is also possible to suggest that the *anthropological* experience of animation, as produced by way of cinematographic images, entailed an extraordinarily complex dynamic that must itself be explained in order to understand how cinematic images enabled new forms of anthropomorphism and cosmomorphism.

In its everyday sense, animation refers to the sense of 'giving life' to something that is otherwise inert – I have noted that the film technology made dynamic the nature that its pre-cinematographic forms analysed and froze, even if such forms arguably began to emphasize a relational quality by revealing 'any-instant-whatevers'. However, the notion of animation may also be linked to 'animism'. Indeed, at the very point when modern discourses of nature seemed closest to dispelling animist and vitalist conceptions of nature – witness, for example, Marey's efforts to conceive and study what he regarded literally as being the 'animal machine' or the 'animate motor', which undermined the fundamental principles of vitalism (Rabinbach 1990) – the cinematic technology arguably produced a new means of instituting the double that allegedly only haunted primitives.

In Morin's *The Cinema or the Imaginary Institution of Man*, the notion of the double refers to an *alter ego* but, as he puts it, also to an *ego alter*, a oneself-another which is the projection of a human individuality in an image that is externalized in myths and shadows, in mirrors and in dreams, and, as Morin also suggests, in the wind and nature more generally (Morin 2001: 32). Part of the power of this process in the cinema relied, and still relies, on what may be described as the 'phantasmagoric' qualities of film. The actual phantasmagoria or 'phantasmagorie' was a spectacle developed by users of the *Linterna Magica* or magic lantern in Europe and the US in the early 1800s. This chapter will not consider this mass medium; it suffices to note, however, that the magic lantern was as much a fore-runner of cinema as was the photography of Muybridge or Marey. It involved the projection of images which seemed to appear 'as if by magic' in a darkened hall full of people. The cinema continued this tradition in so far as it too, involved the projection of an image – this time an image-movement – which appeared, again as if by magic, in a darkened hall. As Morin notes, where photography still involved a material object, cinematic images were, like the phantasmagoria, ethereal, a kind of transubstantiation that would appear (or disappear) at the pull of a lever.

It is tempting to compare the forms of viewing associated with this obser-vational technology with the *askesis* associated with the camera obscura. But, as suggested by Morin, cinema was from the start emphatically *public*. When the Lumière brothers' cinematograph ceased being a scientific curiosity for the elite and began to be used for mass entertainment, viewing films – or rather viewing 'views' as they were appropriately called at first – entailed going to halls, many of which had been, and in some cases continued to double up as, vaudeville theatres (Chanan 1980). From the start, then, the views were viewed in spaces of mass entertainment for the middle and working classes. Such spaces could not be more different from the form of silent decorporealization that was presupposed by the camera obscura. The theatres were animated not just by the sound of musical accompaniment or the deafening roar of sound effects, but at times by raucous audience participation: shouting, cheering, fainting, singing, crying and other forms of 'excessive' corporeality were commonplace in the misnamed era of the 'silent' cinema.[3] It is possible to suggest, then, that, whereas the camera obscura classified the relationship between the interior and the exterior as a function of a strong classification of an individualized observing subject and the observed object, cinema preserved the distinction between interior and exterior, but now 'massified' the technology of displacement in much the way that trains had done throughout the nineteenth century; in both contexts, people sat together and took in the views-in-movement.

As is evident in the work of Carey and Muybridge, some of the earliest forms of what might be described as proto-cinematography involved the representation of animals. Once the actual technology of cinema was invented, nature continued to be a subject of interest to the first film-makers. A detailed history of this aspect of the earliest films remains to be written; here it might be noted that, amongst other subjects, early cinema included the representation of the Niagara Falls in *Niagara* (1897), one of the most popular tourist spots in North America, which had a long and significant tradition of transmediation in its own right;[4] but also of a *Natura horribilis* such as was portrayed by *Rough Sea at Dover* (1895). As noted by the British Film Institute's *Early Cinema: Primitives and Pioneers* documentary, to audiences unaccustomed to the image-movement, the secondness of images of flowing rivers or approaching waves must have seemed truly remarkable; specta-tors were as amazed, for example, by the movements of people in the scenes of documentaries as they were by the movements of the leaves of trees in the background.

During the first twenty years of the twentieth century, a natural history film-making industry began to emerge in the United States and elsewhere in the world. From an early stage, many nature films, if such a term may be used, were organized around the figure of the hunt for big game in 'exotic' places. This is perhaps unsurprising given the history considered in Chapter 6. However, as documented by Gregg Mitman (1999), during this period the cinematographic representation of nature became contested in a manner that was to have far-reaching consequences for wildlife films in the century to come. The earliest popular films about hunting big game became the subject of a controversy. An elite group, led by Teddy Roosevelt and representing the tradition described in Chapter 6 as 'hunter-conservationism', suggested that films about natural history should be used as part of a civilizing process. Roosevelt, other 'great white hunters' and their reformist allies recommended a cinematographic form of mass mediation that might entice the masses away from film genres that, like the blood sports of the English late eighteenth and early nineteenth centuries, were deemed to corrupt the morals of the working and middle classes. According to this discourse, films about natural history should be based on scientific fact, and should be educational, *even if entertaining*. This formula would soon be reversed, and the justification for this can be found in a film showing Teddy Roosevelt on a safari in Africa, *Roosevelt in Africa* (presented in 1910). The film was supposed to show the way for a form of representation that was both educational and tasteful: it showed the courtship dance of the Jackson dancing bird, hippopotami at play, and Roosevelt planting a ceremonial tree in Nairobi. Thanks to the slow film technology, it did not show any of the actual hunting scenes, or any motion pictures of lions in the wild (Mitman 1999: 6–7).

Unsurprisingly, the film was not very popular, and the emergent genre was overtaken by another, that of the fictional and 'dramatic' nature film, a genre whose producers' greatest concern was to produce 'crowd pleasers' that were able to compete for audiences with other popular film genres. The most obvious way of doing this was to tip the balance of fact and fiction in the direction of relatively explicit conventions of fiction. For example, Selig Polyscope Company's *Hunting Big Game in Africa* (1909) faked a scene of a lion being shot by a great white hunter, and its success led Selig to establish a game farm in Los Angeles where the company shot jungle adventures whose narrative innovation involved using popular actresses as heroines in the stories (Mitman 1999: 10).

Between 1910 and the early 1930s, this tradition became the site of a number of remarkably complex developments in the cinematic technology of observation. It was the period when synchronous sound was invented, and films became 'talkies'. This shift paradoxically made cinemas increasingly silent, in the sense that spectatorship now took place in theatres where vocal audience participation was still possible but increasingly discouraged and eventually disciplined by theatres and audiences alike.

But it was also the period that witnessed the emergence of what Noël Burch (1990) has described as an 'Institutional Mode of Representation' (IMR). The

IMR was a characteristic method of montage that instituted, amongst other conventions, temporal linearity, a narrative logic of cause and effect, and the modality of framing (in the restricted cinematographic sense, but also in the broader 'code' sense) associated with Hollywood's predominant forms of naturalism. The advent of this mode of representation was to have such far-reaching implications for modern imaginary nature that it is necessary to engage in a brief excursus about the mode in order to contextualize subsequent analyses.

According to Burch, the IMR was developed and taught over a period that went from 1895 to 1929. By cutting together shots according to this mode, filmmakers were able to teach audiences to follow what Burch has described as a *voyage* and what film theorist Francesco Casetti (1989) has described as a visual 'trayectory' or *itinerary*, a term that is particularly felicitous in so far as it reminds us of the ability of films to make spectators travel and, thereby, of the medium's status as a technology of displacement related, however distantly and indirectly, to railways, to telegraphy and then to automobiles. As noted earlier with Schivelbusch, railways instituted an order in which motion 'was no longer dependent on the conditions of natural space, but on a mechanical power that created its own new spatiality' (Schivelbusch 1977: 10); much the same could be said about the cinema as compared to photography.

Indeed, in one sense at least cinema was to seeing what telegraphy was to communication: it constituted at once a technology of observation and a technology of displacement that instituted a new way of compressing space and time. In the new medium, it was possible to juxtapose image-movements of different spaces and times in a single film. In effect, the cinematic apparatus combined the spatialities and temporalities of the railroad and of the telegraph to produce a technology of observation and displacement that could, quite literally in the blink of an eye, *visually* and eventually *acoustically* leap from one place to another. There was, nonetheless, a difference in the observational process vis-à-vis the railway window or *perspectiva*: the view afforded by the film camera, a kind of rheme-in-movement, was more directly analogous to that found in cars in so far as the observer was made, or at any rate could be made, to 'face forward' as s/he looked. In the terms of Herbert Zettl (1990), movement along the 'z' axis of the frame – its depth – as mediated by the codes of the IMR – now instituted an observer that might move mechanically *at* objects, and not just *past* them. This arguably established a fundamentally different form of secondness and indexicality, one that, as anecdotal accounts of the surprise of spectators confirm, was capable of producing energetic interpretants in a manner that photography could not.

And indeed Burch (1990) argues that, where until the second decade of the twentieth century films emphasized the spatial continuity of the shot over the linearity of time, by 1929 the consolidation of the IMR had inverted this order of priority. Shots were now edited using a variety of devices that seemed to show events according to a logic of temporal narrative progression, and in a way that transformed the film spectator from a relatively external observer that looked *at* a film, and thereby *at* 'nature', to one who was made a 'ubiquitous' observer 'within' the film, eventually 'within' represented *nature*. In Peircian terms, we can say that cinema instituted in this way a paradoxically disembodied analogon of the human body as the firstness of observation: if the body is not normally questioned 'in' or during observation, the cinematic 'body' itself came to constitute a kind of unquestioned prosthesis for observation.

As Burch and other film theorists have noted, key to this shift was the emergence of a code which transformed the observer/spectator from an explicitly male *voyeur* to a more implicit voyeur (in the sense of voyeurism, but also the French voyage: 'voyageur'); one who more than just 'watched', was made to feel that s/he *experienced* the world with her/his ('his') gaze – a gaze that had in fact already been gazed *for* him/her. Here again, an analogy can be established with the dynamic of pseudo-individualization (Adorno 1941) described in the context of mass production.

The technology thereby instituted a silently organizing device, a simulation of a viewing/hearing/*knowing* subject – what some film theorists have described as a subject of enunciation (Bettetini 1984; Casetti 1989) – that appeared to unify rhematically the various audio-visual processes: image-movement and different channels of sound, apparently for the benefit of *each* observer. With Peirce, we can say that film would eventually work by producing a string of rhematic indexical legisigns, in effect the audio-visual equivalent of 'demonstrative pronouns'. Returning to the work of Morin, it can be suggested that the film spectator's double was *itself doubled* in the sense that the cinematographic observer not only gazed at ghosts on the silver screen but was compelled to become one of the ghosts her/himself by way of this technology, and indeed by way of techniques of narrative identification.

This articulation was to be crucial to the workings of the circuit of anthropomorphism in film; if anthropomorphism had always involved a projection 'onto' the non-human, and if cosmomorphism had always involved an identification 'with' that more or less humanized non-human, the IMR helped to double the terms of this circuit: even as the film projected the cosmomorphic double, the spectator identified with the anthropomorphic projection.

I will now consider a film that at once signalled the 'maturation' of, and made significant contributions to, the IMR: *King Kong, Eighth Wonder of the World*, which was first produced by RKO and released in 1933.

King Kong arguably played a key role in establishing a new genre of film which had a far-reaching role in modern imaginary nature, but which remains under-researched to this day: the genre of the animal attack, which may be regarded as a subgenre within the social genre of *Natura horribilis*. While film theorists have traditionally classified films like *King Kong* as belonging to the horror, monster, or science fiction genres (see for example Grant 1996 and Tudor 1989), a different approach might well classify the animal attack films in relation to the discourse of '*Natura horribilis*'. That is to say, in relation to an (almost) uncontrollable nature represented, in this particular case, by 'man-eaters' (*sic*) – the very nature which, by the early 1930s, was least likely to pose a threat to the vast majority of such films' audiences.

King Kong was directed by Merian C. Cooper and Ernest B. Schoedsack, who had hitherto specialized in animal and travel adventure films. The film, produced under the aegis of the 'studio mode of production' described by David Bordwell *et al.* (1985), was structured as a kind of meta-critique of the excesses and dilemmas of what I described earlier as the 'dramatic' tradition of nature films. Indeed the point of departure of *King Kong* was precisely the problematic of the competing traditions of 'didactic' and 'dramatic' films: Carl Denham (Robert Armstrong) was introduced as a natural history film-maker who complained, shortly before embarking on a new filming adventure, that the critics thought his films should have a 'love interest'. Forced to meet the requirements of the market, he set out to find such an 'interest' in the streets of New York, and found Ann Darrow, a woman with 'bad luck', whom he saw trying to steal from a fruit stand, but whom he saved from prosecution by bribing the owner of the stand. Denham took advantage of this logic of juncture to persuade Darrow to join him on an expedition which, as noted by the film analyst Cynthia Erb (1998), was structured partly in the terms of the camera-as-gun ('camera/gun') trope described by Donna Haraway (1989) and Susan Sontag (1977).

Denham, Darrow and the ship's crew travelled to an uncharted island 'somewhere close to Sumatra' where a massive creature was reportedly idolatrized by the 'natives'. In the tradition of the camera/gun trope, the expedition was to go not to *hunt* this creature but to 'shoot' it with a camera, and eventually to capture it. This was a practice that was pioneered, amongst others, by the US taxidermist/hunter Carl Akeley. Haraway and Sontag suggest that this phenomenon is a continuation of the masculinist logic of the hunt, albeit in a form that entails a shift from a fearful disposition to an expression of nostalgia for a nature of the past: the nature of hunting.

This trope can be characterized as being patriarchal in so far as it produces a relatively passive characterization of the role of women within the story-world or diegesis; and in so far as it adopts a masculinist perspective on the level of the pragmatics, that is to say the structuring of enunciation: in particular, what Gerard Genette (1980, 1988) describes as 'focalization', the manner and extent to which the narrative is framed from the narrational perspective of a specific character or narrator; and what Francois Jost describes as 'ocularization', the manner and extent to which the framing adopts the *visual* perspective of different characters (Jost in Stam 1992: 93).

In *King Kong* we find evidence for the 'diegetic' form of patriarchy in the relative disempowerment of the apologetic Ann Darrow who must be repeatedly rescued. But it is also evident on the level of enunciation: Darrow is made the object of an explicitly sexualized and sexualizing gaze both by Denham and by Kong. Indeed, the film transforms Darrow into the object of a conflation of human and non-human 'gazes': those of the rhematic camera-narrator which ocularizes the scene; those of the camera *within* the diegesis, as handled by Denham and by means of which audiences appear to observe Darrow as Denham sees her through *his* camera; those of the sailors and other male characters within the story, whom the camera-narrator also ocularizes; and those of Kong 'himself'. The film's subject of enunciation – what I described in Chapter 2 as the semeiotic 'puppeteer' of complex signs such as this – circulates among all these figures in a manner that objectifies Darrow's femininity. To be sure, the most recent perspectives in film theory might well suggest that the relatively explicit qualisignal attributes of this gendered ocularization may well have enabled at least some spectators to objectify this process. Moreover, it might well also be argued that Darrow's own expressions of desire constitute her as rather more than the passive figure suggested by an older form of feminist analysis.

It might further be suggested that the film promoted not just patriarchal but racist relations. As Erb notes, this was one of the most overtly racist periods in US history, and Kong can be read anthropomorphically as a 'monstrous' black man who reaches, 'transgressively', for a white woman. Whether such a racist interpretant is reproduced by audiences or not, Erb rightly establishes a link between *King Kong* and what Haraway (1989) describes as the 'drama of the touch', a trope that occurs again and again in the period's jungle films, in which the white explorer is shown touching or being touched by a 'native'.

Many of the scenes in *King Kong* can be analysed from this perspective; indeed, one of the mechanical devices expressly made for the film is a large 'arm' that allows the film-makers to show the massive Kong holding the tiny Darrow in his hand. At one point what Erb describes as the 'electricity' of this form of contact is expressed in a scene in which Kong is shown daintily 'peeling off' pieces of Darrow's dress and smelling them. Among other available interpretants, we may suggest that here the drama of the touch 'confirms' Darrow as a fruit or flower that might be picked or plucked. The transgression is not so much that this happens, but that it is *Kong's* hand that does it. From this perspective, the film may be said to establish a matrix of interlocking dualisms: male/female is to culture/nature is to active/passive and to white/black. The transgression – and indeed ambiguity – of Kong is that he is at once 'active' (as agent) *and* 'black' *and* 'nature'.

The new risks

By the end of the 1930s, a rather more terrible – and this time quite literally 'man-made' – *Natura horribilis* was in the making, one that made Kong's rampage in New York City seem rather tame by comparison. Its precedent on the level of conceived space – in fact, in *re-conceived* space–time – may be found in the epoch-making work of Albert Einstein, who in the 'miracle year' of 1905 published his famous papers, one of which introduced his special theory of relativity.

As developed in these papers and in his later general theory of relativity, Einstein's work at once showed a way of confirming the existence of atoms – and in this restricted sense consolidated the long hold of mechanistic cosmologies

– but fundamentally undermined Newtonian mechanics by eliminating gravity as a force. Instead, gravity came to be regarded as a consequence of the curvature of space–time.

Einstein's famous equation, $E = mc^2$, was in effect the beginning of a theory of radioactivity. It is thus both consistent and deeply paradoxical that six years after Nazi foes in Germany forced Einstein to migrate to the US – Einstein left Germany in 1933, the same year that *King Kong* was first shown – he was persuaded by fellow scientists to write his famous letter to President Franklin Roosevelt. The letter, which warned of the Nazis' intention to manufacture an atomic bomb, is credited with having set in motion the Manhattan Project, the code name for the US military organization that produced the first atomic bombs. On 6 August 1945, the United States became the first, and thus far the only, nation to use such weapons of mass destruction against another. Hundreds of thousands of people were killed outright or seriously wounded by the blasts first in Hiroshima and then in Nagasaki; untold numbers died subsequently from the long-term effects of nuclear fallout. The science and technology used to make the bomb went on to be used in a number of civilian applications, the most notable of which was the construction of nuclear power stations.

These and other applications of nuclear energy ushered in an era that the sociologist Ulrich Beck (1992) describes as one of a 'reflexive' modernity. According to Beck, older forms of modernity generated dynamics and conflicts structured by the unequal distribution of relatively scarce resources – so-called 'societies of scarcity' where the principal problem and the main generator of conflict was the struggle to earn 'one's daily bread', to 'make nature useful' or to 'release mankind [*sic*] from technical constraints' (Beck 1992: 19). Beck argues that in the twentieth century this logic began to give way, at least in the industrialized countries, to a new logic: one that was increasingly driven by the need to manage the distribution of, and the conflicts arising from, the hazards and risks produced by techno-scientific institutions. The notion of a 'reflexive' modernization refers not so much to a 'critical' modernization as to one whose subjects were increasingly concerned with this modernization's 'own theme'; that is, with managing its own 'fallout'. While Beck notes categorically that 'we do not yet live in a Risk Society' (Beck 1992: 20) – where the 'we' presumably refers to readers in fully industrialized nations – he suggests that by the late twentieth century a transition was under way from the older form of modernity, based on scarcity and associated with the process of industrialization, to the newer 'Risk Society'.

Central to Beck's account is what might be described as a phenomenology of risk. While risks and risk-taking have always posed problems for humans, Beck suggests that risks in reflexive forms of modernization are of a qualitatively different nature. One difference involves their 'sensibility': where older forms of hazard 'assaulted the senses', this is no longer the case with the newer risks. Beck argues that 'the risks of civilization today typically escape perception and are localized in the sphere of physical and chemical formulas (e.g. toxins in foodstuffs or the nuclear threat)' (Beck 1992: 21). With Peirce, we can say that the new threats are something akin to invisible indexes, or indexes that only become indexes, that is actual *signs*, when they emerge as dicent sinsigns of catastrophe on a human's body, or in some aspect of material nature.

The relation between risk and geography also changed in so far as the afflictions that the new risks produced were no longer tied, as Beck puts it, to their industrial place of origin (Beck 1992: 22). As was dramatically illustrated by Chernobyl in 1986, the risks of nuclear fallout and other analogous hazards were no longer confined by the boundaries of nation-states, let alone the actual physical space of their production. Nor were they confined to human lifetimes; on the contrary, the new risks might well have to be managed over a period of hundreds if not thousands of years. The scandal of Bhopal, which to this day continues to have effects on the health of new generations of residents, suggests that a similar politics, as tied to the practices which I mentioned earlier in the context of incorporation, might well accrue to non-nuclear forms of pollution.

What Beck describes as 'Risk Society' was thus characterized by qualitatively new ways of both representing and dealing with risk. Far from being so many empirically verifiable 'threats', risk now became conceived as 'a systematic way of dealing with hazards and insecurities induced and introduced by modernization itself' (Beck 1992: 21). Returning to the semeiotic formulation of Peirce, we can say that, if threat and risk had thus far remained relatively indistinct, threats now became the objects of different forms of representation. These did not work to produce what I described in Chapter 3 as an 'absolute' link between knowledge, regarded as legisign, and the world, regarded as dicent, by way of measured, and indeed measuring, indexes. Instead, they worked to produce representations of the *degree* of firstness – in the sense of the indeterminacy – of the new threats.

It is possible to question whether the distinction made by Beck between industrial and reflexive forms of modernization and his characterization of the 'new' risks is overly dualistic.[5] It is nonetheless possible to agree that the environmentalist movement that emerged in the late 1950s was motivated at least in part by a consciousness of the new risks associated with this 'reflexive' modernization. In the United States, two sets of 'new risks' played particularly significant roles in triggering what might now be described as properly, or at any rate the later twentieth-century forms of, 'environmentalist' activism: nuclear energy and the indiscriminate use of persistent pesticides such as DDT. I will consider both threats and the movements they inspired in Chapter 8; in this chapter, I will focus on aspects of a process that arguably played a key role in the emergence of something like a 'risk society', and which I describe in terms of the process of the hygienization of the US, and eventually of other modern cultures.

While a naturalistic conception of hygiene may define it as an 'absolute' pursuit of cleanliness, a more critical approach conceives it as a combination of secondness and thirdness, a matter of natural indexes and the production of energetic interpretants. This point requires some elaboration. There can, on the one hand, be no doubt that hygiene, and the related category of dirt, are a matter of the representation of nature. Indeed, with the anthropologist Mary Douglas (1983), we may conceptualise hygiene with reference to the symbolic construction of categories of dirt. A similar argument can be made with respect to the category of pollution. On the other hand, to suggest that all dirt, and especially all pollution, is no more than a matter of thirdness is too drastic a step in the direction of culturalism. A more critical intepretation suggests that frequently only part of what counts as dirt, or as the dirty, and by extension only part of what counts as pollution is a matter of classification in a culturalist sense of this last term. The point is not to deny that there is a representational dimension in the ascription of dirt and pollution. Indeed with Douglas we might question whether the dynamic described by Beck is not in fact an ongoing cultural process of identification and resymbolization – 're-semeiotization' – of environmental threats. But it seems more productive to conceive pollution in terms of 're/presentation' and the logic of dedoubling described in earlier chapters. It may be suggested in this sense that even if 'dirt' and 'pollution' are *classified* as such in certain contexts, the classification may well be based on a relation of indexicality. Many of the elements classified as pollution *are* in a 'real' relation to human (and not just human) bodies in so far as they have the capacity to make the bodies ill and ultimately to destroy them. It is also the case that the technologies of observation, and indeed of displacement, produced to detect and remove such elements themselves may have 'real' effects in the sense that they are designed to destroy the threats.

This caveat to one side, it is true that in the United States, and indeed elsewhere in the world, Douglas' analysis provides an accurate insight in so far as hygienization entailed a matrix of qualisigns, an imaginary, that has worked to establish a certain morality in the 'war' against 'dirt' and then 'bugs'. The research of historian Suellen Hoy (1995) suggests that hygienization began in the mid-1800s, when American philanthropists, sanitation officials, schools and business enterprises engaged in a collective pedagogy that sought to institute a coding orientation that made new notions of cleanliness central aspects of a religious, then a class-bound, and finally an increasingly nationalistic imaginary. In the early 1800s, being 'clean' was a value and prerogative of the upper classes who could afford relatively expensive cleaning goods used to construct a sense of cleanliness. However, here too, middle- and especially upper-class reformers in the United States took it upon themselves to 'improve' the lot of the poor by instituting a host of technologies of hygienization. The immediate motivation was initially found in the religious asepsis of statements such as John Wesley's 'cleanliness is a virtue next to Godliness' and in the morality of Benjamin Franklin's 'if you teach a poor young Man to shave himself and to keep his Razor in order, you may contribute more to the happiness of his live than in giving him 1000 Guineas' (quoted in Hoy 1995: 4).

However, the process was also driven by racist and xenophobic ideologies. During and after World War I, cleanliness came to be represented as an 'American' virtue, and 'dirtiness' as an 'ethnic' characteristic of the southern Europeans who were migrating to the US at the time. One of the aims of schooling was thus to teach immigrants how to be 'American' by being 'clean'. Eventually, the pursuit of cleanliness came to afford the space for another technology of the self, especially but not only for women: if spending time in pristine nature was, in Hammond's terms, a man's way to 'take off the harness and be free', then staying home and cleaning the domestic space until it was 'pristine clean' came to be promoted as a woman's way of putting *on* the harness and making sure that the home, and by implication, the self, were *dirt* free.

The moral and racist discourses were incorporated by businesses, which used them to discipline the labour force and to promote new forms of commodification. According to Hoy, corporations in the United States became involved in the quest for cleanliness in two ways. First, their owners helped to consolidate the emergent imaginary by establishing employment criteria that embraced the importance of cleanliness. Here, as in other social spheres, Henry Ford led the way: he suggested that 'the most advanced people are the cleanest' and had company inspectors visit the homes of workers to ascertain that the $5 wages were being spent to maintain 'clean, and well conducted homes' with 'plenty of soap and water' (quoted in Hoy 1995: 137). This was one of several ways in which Fordism went far beyond the shop floor and affected everyday life. As Gramsci himself noted:

> The enquiries conducted by the industrialists into the workers' private lives and the inspection services created by some firms to control the 'morality' of their workers are necessities of the new methods of work. People who laugh at these initiatives . . . and see in them only a hypocritical manifestation of 'Puritanism' thereby deny themselves any possibility of understanding the importance, significance and objective import of the American phenomenon, which is *also* the biggest collective effort to date to create, with unprecedented speed, and with a consciousness of purpose unmatched in history, a new type of worker and of man.
>
> (Gramsci 1971: 302)

A new type of worker, and a new kind of business, which brings us to the second way in which business became involved with cleanliness: corporations in the United States also sought to capitalize on hygiene and the obsession with eliminating dirt. Indeed, during the last decades of the nineteenth century, an industry emerged which was devoted to selling household goods for this purpose. With it came the development of a new perceived, conceived and lived domestic space in the form of separate spaces *within* the home dedicated to cleansing and bodily 'functions' – most homes did not have separate 'bathrooms' until after the first decades of the twentieth century. By the 1950s, the movement had led to the production of a variety of mechanized products for home cleaning, and the sale of numerous and highly toxic substances devoted to making homes 'whiter than white'.

As suggested by the media historian Julian Sivulka (2001), advertising played a key role in this process. Until the late 1800s, soap and many other goods for

194

the masses were not branded or individualized in any manner. If someone could afford them, they were bought in a store that kept them as generic 'cakes' that were cut into smaller pieces and wrapped by the store owner in plain paper.

With the emergence of mass consumption, Sivulka suggests that manufacturers began to employ branding, trademarks, the use of more elaborate packaging, promotions and finally advertisement, especially in women's magazines, to differentiate products, to cultivate consumer loyalty and finally to promote identification with the products. As is implied by the choice of *women's* magazines, it was the women in households that were the primary target of campaigns which, as I noted earlier, worked to establish an equivalence between 'good hygiene' and being a 'good housewife'. Until the advent of the germ theory of illness – and indeed long after – it was assumed that domestic asepsis was tantamount to good health.

The manner in which advertising attempted to stimulate demand for the goods – and thereby for cleanliness – is itself significant. It is possible to distinguish between those forms of advertisement which alert potential users to the existence of a product; those which extol the virtues of the product mainly in terms of the product's use-value, in more or less instrumental terms; those which provide the potential user with a pedagogy as to what the product can do for *her/him* in terms of a social 'exchange-value'; and those which imply, without any explicit verbal or other ostensive pedagogic discourse, a product's association with a 'whole' *lifestyle*. I describe these as 'product existence', 'use-value', 'symbolic exchange-value' and finally 'lifestyle acquisition' respectively.

Although these categories are not mutually exclusive, we may nonetheless say that, from the late 1800s to the mid-1900s in the United States, and later in much of the rest of the world, the emergence of consumer culture both was made possible by, and entailed a shift from, 'product existence' to 'lifestyle acquisition' forms of marketing and advertisement. The development of more sophisticated forms of advertisement, made possible in part thanks to the appearance of more specialized magazines and other forms of mass communication, instituted an informal and non-formal pedagogy of consumerism in general, and of cleanliness or hygiene in particular, and, by these means, new pretexts (indeed pre-texts) for massification.

By the 1950s, the pursuit of cleanliness had extended from the interior of homes to include suburban gardens and lawns. This strategy coincided with a dramatic increase in the suburbanization of the US. Higher wages, a wider availability of automobiles, a marked increase in the proportion of people occupying white-collar jobs, and the continuing if increasingly paradoxical quest for 'God's great open spaces' led more and more city dwellers to buy houses with a miniature version of such spaces: the suburban back garden.

In middle-class homes, this space was used to arrange a selection of bushes, trees, lawn tables, garden toys or indeed swimming pools in ways that were more often than not premised on a kind of popular horticultural *mathesis*. A key element in this space was the immaculately cultivated lawn. As noted by the historian

Virginia Scott Jenkins (1994), this was a concept that was imported from European landscape gardens. It became an integral aspect of suburban gardening in the postwar period, when the US Department of Agriculture (USDA), the US Golfing Association and the Garden Club of America worked to establish an equivalence between class, moral propriety, aesthetic value and the quality of the own lawn.

Whatever other motivations played a part in the process, there can be little doubt that the shift to lawns generated a mass demand for products sold by the agrochemical industry. The lawns, domestic versions of monoculture, required herbicides, pesticides and fertilizers, as well as untold quantities of water. Managed as it was by men, this space became a visible symbol of a kind of *masculine* 'cleanliness' and, thereby, of good morals. In this context, so-called 'lawn and turf pests' – and arthropods more generally – became a kind of invertebrate army that must be defeated at all costs. This last metaphor is not casually chosen; many of the men that managed the lawns might well have noticed the logic of equivalences established immediately after World War II in popular magazines such as *Time*, *Popular Mechanics* and the *Science News Letter* (Lear 1997: 119–120). For example, in an article in the issue of 27 August 1945, *Time* suggested that:

> It looked as if one of the early blessings of peace would be deliverance from the fly and mosquito. With the Army & Navy releasing some of its new insecticides for civilian use, the war against winged pests was under way. [. . .] besides DDT, three other highly effective weapons have been developed for the Army & Navy: 1) an insect 'bomb,' consisting of a small can which, when opened, releases an 'aerosol' gas loaded with an insecticide (such as DDT or quick-killing pyrethrum) that instantly fills a room; 2) a new mosquito repellent, 'Formula 6–12,' . . . and 3) N.M.R.I. 201, a still more effective repellent just developed by the Navy, said to last eleven hours.

As suggested earlier, the US agrochemical industry stood to gain the most from such ways of framing the relation to invertebrates. Along with the USDA, it is thus unsurprising that they spent millions on advertisements and leaflets designed to persuade consumers to buy high maintenance varieties of grass and the chemicals which were ostensibly required to keep them green.

In addition to providing fertilizers, pesticides and herbicides for domestic use, the agrochemical industry found that it could also rely on the USDA for support in campaigns to use pesticides such as dieldrin, aldrin and DDT, first throughout crops and forests in the South and Southwest to eradicate the fire ant (Lear 1997: 305), and then in Pennsylvania, New York and New England to eradicate mosquitoes, tent caterpillars and gypsy moths (Lear 1997: 313). From early stages, aerial spraying of DDT was employed to test a number of hypotheses, including the possibility that the eradication of flies with DDT in wide areas might eliminate polio. This use was to have momentous consequences for the history of modern environmentalism: a number of scientists expressed concern over the possible effects of widespread domestic use of DDT, and in the late 1950s concern coalesced in a grass-roots movement against the aerial spraying of the pesticides. The first truly *environmentalist* field began to emerge as constituted by such movements and by the trajectories of a new generation of activists such as Rachel Carson, who employed a combination of scientific research and mass communication to make 'visible' the risks posed by uses of pesticides and other toxic substances. It is to this process that I now turn.

THE NATURE OF
ENVIRONMENTALISM

In a letter written in January 1958, Olga Owens Huckins told
me of her own bitter experience of a small world made lifeless,
and so brought my attention sharply back to a problem which
I had long been concerned. I then realized I must write this
book.

Rachel Carson in *Silent Spring*

Rachel Carson

In 1962 Rachel Carson published *Silent Spring,* a book that is widely regarded as
the inaugural event of modern environmentalism and of the 'ecological revolution' that took place in the 1960s. *Silent Spring* documented meticulously and
rigorously, but in an accessible style, the far-reaching effects that a number of
industrially produced pesticides, most notably DDT, were having on the health
of people and the broader environment. The book sent shockwaves throughout
the academic community, the agrochemical industry, the government (which employed Carson) and the media of mass communication.

Carson spent a number of years preparing the book. In the context of hygienization described earlier, it is unsurprising that much of her effort was invested in
preparing a case that could not be easily attacked by the agrochemical industry and
its allies in the USDA. As she noted in a letter to a friend, 'They are such powerful
adversaries: the U.S. Department of Agriculture and the business empires and the
ever-increasing practice of monoculture' (Carson in Lear 1997: 388).

The adversaries did not disappoint: according to Linda Lear (1997), the pesticide trade industry group, the National Agricultural Chemicals Association, spent
in excess of $250,000 to persuade publics that Carson was wrong. It mounted an
extraordinary campaign that portrayed Carson as an emotional 'female alarmist'.
One former Secretary of Agriculture, Ezra Taft Benson, reportedly asked 'why a
spinster with no children was so concerned about genetics', a question which he

himself answered by suggesting that Carson was 'probably a Communist' (Lear 1997: 428–9).

Such attacks reveal the extent to which a gender politics played an important role in the controversy that followed the publication of the book. On the one hand, Carson's gender went very much against the grain of a scientific establishment which, by the standards of similar institutions in the early twenty-first century, was overtly sexist. But Carson was, in Lear's words, an 'attractive middle-aged woman' who dressed fashionably (Lear 1997:4), and was clearly in possession of irrefutable facts, making for a rather more complex gender politics than Benson seemed to be aware of. Indeed, it might well be argued that Carson's gender enabled her to speak and be heard on a register that complexly acknowledged the subjectivity of hygienization mentioned in Chapter 7. Although Carson's own language continued to reflect a patriarchal discourse that established an equivalence between 'man' and humanity, 'mankind' and humankind, this same discourse arguably placed Carson outside the dynamics critiqued in her book. If it was the case, as one quote by the philosopher Albert Schweitzer suggested, that 'Man can hardly even recognize the devils of his own creation' (in Carson 1962: 24), then Carson (the woman) was certainly able to recognize them for what they were.

To be sure, Carson's ability to engage with publics also resided in her ability to bring together the worlds of science and mass mediation by way of narrativization. *Silent Spring* began with a fable: 'There was once a town in the heart of America where all life seemed to live in harmony with its surroundings' (Carson 1962: 21). All was well in this rural idyll until 'a strange blight crept over the area and everything began to change. Some evil spell had settled on the community: mysterious maladies swept the flocks of chickens; the cattle and the sheep sickened and died' and there were 'several sudden and unexplained deaths, not only amongst adults but even amongst children' (Carson 1962: 21). The cause? 'In the gutters under the eaves and between the shingles of the roofs, a white granular powder still showed a few patches; some weeks before it had fallen like snow . . . . The people had done it themselves' (Carson 1962: 22).

In this context, as in the one analysed with respect to Wordsworth's *Guide to the Lakes*, narrativization worked in a manner that established a seemingly *causal* chain of events; as described by the semiologist Roland Barthes, *post hoc ergo propter hoc*. In the context of a risk politics increasingly driven by the dissolution of manifest responsibility, narrativization invited audiences to transmediate the genre of the *whodunnit*: in whodunnits, unlike 'real world' risk politics, there is always a 'good' and a 'bad' character, or at any rate somebody who can be *blamed*. Carson's choice of the genre of the fable thereby had the relatively explicit effect of establishing not just a strongly indexical frame but also a strongly moral one.

This device, and indeed the devastating indictment found in the rest of her book, generated considerable media interest, and on 3 April 1963 Rachel Carson was interviewed by the *CBS Reports* television programme. Carson explained that it was now necessary to redress the balance of information regarding pesticides: 'we have heard a great deal about their safety, but very little about their hazards'

(Carson in Lear 1997: 449). The dignified and quietly competent nature of her presentation contrasted sharply with that of the chemical industry's representative, Dr Robert White-Stevens, who, dressed in a white lab coat, suggested that 'If man were to faithfully follow the teachings of Miss Carson, we would return to the Dark Ages, and the insects and diseases and vermin would once again inherit the earth' (White-Stevens in Lear 1997: 449).

According to Lear (1997), CBS estimated an audience of between 10 and 15 million viewers for its *Report*. The vast majority would not have read *Silent Spring*, were not familiar with the science at stake, and so were unlikely to be critical with respect to the claims being made about the book in the media by Carson's friends and foes alike. Remarkably, in a news context dominated by the funding and ideology of agrobusiness – some of the corporations sponsored television and radio programmes – the programme not only favoured Carson's perspective but in effect 'set the agenda' for forthcoming debates. As suggested by Lear, 'in a single evening . . . [the] broadcast added the *environment* to the public agenda' (Lear 1997: 450, emphasis added).

I shall consider the role of television in this process below. It is however first necessary to explain a broader risk politics that Carson helped to develop. Carson responded to the problematic that Schweitzer hinted at when he suggested that the 'devils' of 'man's creation' could hardly even be *recognized*: the politics of knowledge in the time of the 'new' risks. From the perspective of such a politics, Carson's work consisted not so much in denouncing environmental destruction – in the way that Hammond, or indeed Thoreau or Muir had – but rather in making public the new risks or, as Carson herself put it, the 'unknown harm' (Carson 1962: 23) posed by DDT and the host of other pesticides which began to be used extensively after World War II. But where the older traditions of conservationism could denounce the 'visible' destruction of areas of outstanding natural beauty, the role of environmentalists such as Carson was now to denounce the relatively 'invisible' threats posed by the new generation of chemicals to both sublime and *everyday* environments.

The new category of the environment presupposed a fundamental reclassification of the human/non-human nature divide: even if the writings of Aldo Leopold and other conservationists continued to privilege the nature of wilderness, the emerging science of ecology contributed a vocabulary in which and for which this distinction became less important. The notion of an ecosystem, proposed by Arthur Tansley in the 1930s and developed by Eugene Odum in the 1950s, provided a legisign that was far less explicitly premised on the qualisigns of sublimity.

While Carson was by no means the first person to warn about the possible risks of DDT, and a number of people had already begun to mobilize against the indiscriminate use of such chemicals, Carson was amongst the first 'true' environmentalists – environmentalists in the present sense of the term – in so far as she perfected an environmental risk politics that entailed a complex and multi-level form of mass mediation. The first aspect of this mediation involved discovering hitherto unknown threats to, or indeed from, an environment. Doing so required using scientific research to classify risks and non-risks. This in turn frequently required environmentalists to transgress, and effectively reclassify, public/private divides – in both the economic and social senses of the term – in order to find out what corporations or governments 'were up to'. This was made more difficult by the fact that, as I noted earlier, corporations were accorded a quasi-private status by the judiciary in the US, and this status, aided as it frequently was by the bureaucratization and geographical dispersal of the modern business enterprises and of the state apparatus itself, meant that a kind of sleuth work was required. This work frequently entailed searching state or corporate records – experimental, veterinary, medical or other – for evidence of risks which, until the 1950s and 1960s, were not usually associated with the use of pesticides. Carson was uniquely qualified for this thanks to her scientific credentials and knowledge, but also thanks to her ability to make use of an extensive network of scientists both within and beyond the government who were willing to supply her with first-hand information.

Once the initial 'sleuth work' established the nature of the risk, perhaps the most significant work of twentieth-century environmentalism began: one of the main functions, if not the main function, of environmental activists was and remains to engage in a pedagogy of risk. Doing so required environmentalists to attempt to transgress another public/private divide, one that now involved not the state or corporate practice but everyday life within the domestic sphere.

It is here that the media of mass communication, and especially television, played a fundamental, indeed constitutive, role in the emergence of modern environmentalism. If the *CBS Reports* programme could put the environment 'on the agenda', it was thanks to its prestige, but also to the fact that, by the time that Carson appeared on television, the medium had become the most popular form of mass communication in the United States, and was fast doing the same in the rest of the world.

Although Philo T. Farnsworth is widely credited with having invented the medium in the late 1920s, a combination of disputes over patents and the onset of World War II meant that television remained a relatively marginal medium until the 1950s. During this period, television sets became more affordable and broadcasting institutions began to develop better schedules. By the early 1960s, public opinion surveys suggested that television news had begun to displace newspapers and radio programmes as the main sources of news for both British and US audiences (Allan 1999: 47).

It is often assumed that the success of television was a result of its visual character. In fact, in the context of the predominantly naturalistic discourses about the visual, TV was a relatively poor medium when compared to film. To begin with, it was black and white. Moreover, where cinema worked by 'fixing' any-instant-whatevers photographically, TV translated light into electronic signals – 'any-*field*-whatevers' – with a comparatively low resolution.[1] Finally, even if the medium presupposed elements of the kind of firstness of observation that I described for cinema, its sense of immediacy was of a fundamentally different nature: the earliest history of television broadcasting was, until the invention of videotaping technologies in the mid-1950s, largely one of live broadcasting. Television was, in this sense, even more of a 'sinsignical' medium than the cinema was. As developed in the context of mass consumption in the US, this had the paradoxical effect of generating icons that were at one and the same time more evanescent and more indexical than their cinematic equivalents. Put differently, television was watched, and indeed occurred, not in reel, but in real time.

Television was, from this perspective, more indebted to radio, a medium from which TV producers borrowed programming styles and, in the genre of news, the convention of an authoritative news presenter (Allan 1999: 44). The adoption of radio's characteristic programming style meant not only that any given 'show' was immersed in programming 'flows' but also that many shows were part of *series* that were structured by an aesthetics of seriality (Calabrese 1992). This in turn meant that, from the start, television was less about the production of qualisigns of modern literary or otherwise 'artistic' innovation, and more about the reiteration of habit, that is to say the repetition of relatively tried and tested and initially slow-changing formulas with minor variations on a theme. This aesthetic coding orientation arguably facilitated the incorporation of the medium in the everyday routines of households.

In turn, the diurnal or quasi-diurnal character of the space (most TV viewing rooms were not darkened as in cinema) suggested a rather different relation to the question of the double. If, as Morin notes, we can say that the double was located in those 'natural and impalpable forms that constitute shadows' (Morin 2001: 34) and if cinema created viewing conditions that echoed the nocturnal space of dreams, a space in which 'humans lose their shadow and the shadow possesses them' (Morin 2001: 34), then watching television involved a rather different experience. The luminous images,[2] emitted so materially if still so mysteriously by a box in a well-lit household might well have contributed to the modern 'decadence of the double' discussed by Morin.

Whether they did or not, the everyday life quality of the medium worked to consolidate a new form of observation and a new spatiality with respect to all manner of broadcast (or indeed broadcastable) events. Henceforth the observer, immersed in the buzz of everyday domesticity, could be, and indeed was required to be, at once fundamentally *distracted* but, for the same reason, increasingly *attentive*: TV viewers would need to be able to watch television thanks to, but also despite, the domestic setting.

This same domesticity would enable a spatiality that Claude Lefort (1986) describes in terms of the phenomenon of '*entre-nous*'. According to Lefort, media representations produced what he describes as an 'incantation of *familiarity*', a 'hallucination of *nearness* which abolishes a sense of distance, strangeness, imperceptibility, the signs of the outside, of adversity, of otherness' (Lefort 1986: 228, emphases in the original). It would be a mistake to attribute this phenomenon to any single television show, and indeed to any single medium of mass communication. However, the overall ensemble of media, which had by now become utterly immersed in everyday domestic life and in the transmediation of its own characteristic qualisigns and narratives, acquired the capability of making 'familiar' even the most distant or adverse phenomena (see for example Alfonso and Lindahl Elliot 2002).

In the case of television, these characteristics arguably had two apparently contradictory implications for the environmentalist field. First, if and when interlocutors such as Rachel Carson managed to 'join' this sense of '*entre-nous*', they might well become 'household names'. Given the advertising dynamics that made *goods* and *brands* household names, getting a 'toe' under this screened 'table' of consumption would have been as important as, if not more important than, negotiating the complex codes for news-making.

The second implication was a direct consequence of the first, but at the same time its contradiction. This self-same 'everyday lifeness' of the medium, as related to an increasingly congested news 'agenda' – a congestion prompted in part by the growing institutional realization of the importance of a televised 'public opinion' – led many institutions to manufacture extraordinary events: so-called 'media events'. The object of this was, first, to secure the media institutions' *attention*, but, second, to do the same again vis-à-vis the viewers, *within their households*. In both levels, the risk was that any one message might well be lost.

Bearing witness

Perhaps the environmentalist group that perfected the most effective technology of displacement and observation for this context was Greenpeace.

At around the same time as Rachel Carson began to write *Silent Spring,* a group of Quakers attempted to stop the atmospheric testing of hydrogen bombs near the Bikini Atoll by sailing a ship towards the test site. The group was unsuccessful, but their example was taken up, some ten years later, by Jim and Marie Bohlen. At the behest of Marie, the Bohlens, members of the Vancouver chapter of the Sierra Club, decided to emulate Quaker practices in order to try to stop the US testing its nuclear weapons off the Aleutian island of Amtchitka.

The group, which began by calling itself the 'Don't Make a Wave Committee', a reference to fears that the testing might produce an earthquake followed by a tsunami, chartered a small fishing vessel and were accompanied by three journalists, including one who radioed back reports on progress and one who took pictures. Eventually they succeeded in stopping the US by generating massive media interest, and Greenpeace was born.

While Carson was arguably transformed into a victim by the USDA and the chemical corporations, we can say that Greenpeace set out to 'victimize itself' by entering the area where the nuclear testing was to take place. This paradoxical form of victimization – in fact a way of acquiring new agency in a mass communicated world via simulacra of battles – can be explained initially with reference to the politics of 'bearing witness'.

Jim Bohlen's account of Greenpeace's actions emphasized the importance of 'bearing witness', a Quaker principle that suggested that, whatever an individual's disempowerment, s/he always had the option to express public but peaceful disapproval of bellicose action by making her/himself present at the scene of the action. Yet Greenpeace's campaign actually suggested a more complex dialectic, which probably underpinned the Quaker politics itself but acquired a new significance in the context of mass communication. The efficacy of 'bearing witness' in the globalized world of mass communication hinged not so much on 'bearing witness' as on 'being witnessed bearing witness'. In effect, Greenpeace constructed itself at once as icon and dicent of dissent via the media of mass communication, to and for *distant* publics. Conversely, by way of a logic of mediated quasi-interaction, Greenpeace transformed itself into an icon and dicent of absent publics at the scenes of imminent environmental destruction and/or risk.

As defined by John B. Thompson (1995), mediated quasi-interaction refers to a form of communication characteristic of the media of mass communication. It is one in which communication tends to be monological as opposed to dialogical, and is produced, potentially at least, for an indefinite range of recipients, or 'distant others' (Thompson 1995: 82–7). While we can agree with Thompson that a deep asymmetry does indeed pervade mass communication (with the producers having much more say over what gets communicated than the audiences), we may nonetheless agree with Bettetini (1984) that this process may involve a simulated 'dialogue' by way of what I described earlier as a subject of enunciation, that is to say an apparently unifying and unified 'puppeteer' or better yet subject of communication that interpellates addressees by way of the polysemeiotic combination of channels used in and by the medium at hand (e.g. the combination of images, sounds and modes of address used by television). 'Being witnessed bearing witness' was a instance of this phenomenon in so far as Greenpeace used the *mise en scène* of its campaigns on television in a manner that suggested that it was no more than an 'activist group' 'acting on our behalf' or, as one Greenpeace sympathizer put it, 'acting for us all' (Brown and May 1991: 5).

While such actions and the simulation of dialogue with distant audiences might be regarded as a form of radical democracy, the Greenpeace actions were actually premised on a form of mass mediation that was arguably driven by a form of symbolic violence. During the twentieth century, Greenpeace was governed by a board of managers without a democratic mandate, within or beyond the organization. Unlike Friends of the Earth, its managers were not elected by members of the organization. Its implicit or explicit claims to political representation were thus largely based on sympathetic coverage by the media of mass communication, whose institutions themselves operated on the basis of this same logic. In Greenpeace's case, this fundamental lack of accountability was nonetheless dissimulated by the invocation of a sense of the sacred, that is to say, the defence more often than not of a sublime nature: the sublime nature found, at least until the late twentieth century, in the oceans, Edenic isles and whales. As one of Greenpeace's promotional books put it, '*[b]y placing itself between the natural world and the forces that seek to destroy it*, Greenpeace is acting for us all' (Brown and May 1991: 5, emphasis added).

In so far as this was the case, Greenpeace arguably adopted the form and practice of the modern multinational media corporation, albeit to defend certain green interests. In later years, the organization engaged in the merchandizing of its name as a brand; this meant that aspects of its actions were funded by the very forms of consumption that were at the heart of the modern environmental crisis. More generally, as Greenpeace's funding depended on membership, and its membership hinged on the success of its campaigns, its campaigns arguably acquired a dual purpose which mirrored that of news production itself.

The news media initially thrived on Greenpeace stories. As I have suggested, the news media were themselves caught in a similar contradiction in that they had to produce 'objective' news that nonetheless attracted audiences to the advertisements that paid for their operations, or, in the case of public broadcasters, the increasingly contested public service taxes. The narrativized and narrativizing images of Greenpeace activists in inflatable dinghies trying to stop nuclear or other forms of waste from being dumped into the North Sea had all the drama required to make 'good television' in a news format that increasingly relied on 'visual bites' for its characteristic forms of montage or segmentation. The choice of the oceanic encounters was a particularly good one as it anthropomorphicized the environment along the lines of a masculinist 'drama at high sea' at a time when the documentaries of Jacques Cousteau and other natural history film-makers were at the apogee of their popularity. It is no coincidence that women were excluded from Greenpeace's first expedition: as noted by the journalist and Greenpeace founder Robert Hunter (2004), the first expedition – and we might add many of those that followed – was 'destined to be every bit as machismo-oriented as the military system it was opposing' (Hunter 2004: 18).

The nature of television

I have just mentioned nature documentaries, and I now wish to turn to this, perhaps the single most important form of mass mediating nature in the twentieth century.

During the first decade or so after World War II, most nature TV programmes were broadcast live in studios, or in locations that had long provided the chief venues for informal pedagogies of nature: zoos. The 1940s and 1950s were a time when zoos still constituted the most popular site for observing a geography of a 'wild' animality in most industrialized cities.

Despite some notable exceptions, by the late 1950s the original zoo TV format began to lose some of its popularity. This fact, along with developments in the technologies of film-making – most notably the invention of new, more portable and quieter 16mm film cameras – led to experiments with programmes 'shot in the wild'. The earliest forerunner of this genre was the tradition of 'didactic' films mentioned in Chapter 7. A more recent antecedent could be found in the work of husband and wife safari films such as those produced by Martin and Osha Johnson and Armand and Michaela Denis. But perhaps the most immediate precursor could be found in the films produced by the Disney Studios, which Alexander Wilson (1992) credits with having popularized some of the new forms of the genre. Disney's films employed what Bill Nichols (1991) has described as an expository mode of representation, that is, one that used the 'voice of god' narrator to frame a sequence of images that told a story of 'nature itself', a seemingly rhematic nature that, in the pastoralist or Edenic tradition, was devoid of humans. The films, which were originally shown in film theatres and had titles like *The Vanishing Prairie* (1954), *The African Lion* (1955) and *White Wilderness* (1958), all told stories that 'began at the beginning – the spring, the dawn, the birth of a bear cub or otter' and all 'ended in the beginning too with words like new life, rebirth, hope' (Wilson 1992: 118). As Wilson also notes, this form of narrativization was in some respects no different from the lore of stories told in US summer camps, or by the Bible. To many viewers, such narratives would have offered a reassuringly pastoral antidote to the spaces and times of hectic city life. In this sense, the genre was to wildlife what the suburban back garden once was to 'God's great open spaces'.

In the United States, an early version of the 'blue-chip' genre appeared in 1963, when Marlon Perkins, hitherto known for presenting *Zoo Parade*, began to produce the long-running (and recently resurrected) *Mutual of Omaha's Magic Kingdom* series. The blue-chip natural history documentary was to become the paradigmatic version of the genre. The expression 'blue-chip' was and remains the one used by members of the documentary film-making industry to describe hour-long[3] documentaries with high production values that show animals ostensibly in their natural geographies, i.e. in their 'first nature', the nature preferred then and still today by the documentary film-makers for their representations.

In Britain a version of the blue chip documentary appeared before it did in the US, on what was to become known as Anglia Television's *Survival* series. In particular, Anglia's *SOS Rhino* (1961) established the precedent for what was to be a long association between the natural history genre on television and game reserves and wildlife parks. This association not only suggested a return to the 'old' classification of nature and culture, but generated a narrative context in which such parks were normalized as the sites for 'nature itself'. This classification may well have also helped to normalize the discourse, reproduced at least until the 1990s by organizations like the WWF, that local populations should be excluded from their own lands in order to secure the well-being of endangered species.

Despite the film-makers' preference for 'first natures', and despite the apparent discontinuity in terms of the represented space vis-à-vis the older zoo-based shows, it is remarkable that many of the animals represented continued to be many of the animals found in *zoos*. The 'nocturnal' connection lay in the continuing popularity of the camera/gun trope, and the film-makers' lingering legacy from hunting and their concomitant predilection for the 'big game' found in the African and Indian continents. Lions, tigers, cheetahs and leopards were shown preying again and again on wildebeest, zebra, antelope and other ruminants in what became a 'natural' aesthetic of repetition.

But not all the animals represented by the new genre conformed to this mascu-linist logic of the hunt: for example, elephants, giraffes, chimpanzees and gorillas were valued by the genre as qualisigns of the exotic, extraordinary size, height, or indeed proximity to humans. Eventually, whales and dolphins were represented in a manner that both produced and reproduced the idealizing conservationist discourse that was eventually taken up by some of the Greenpeace campaigns. By the end of the twentieth century, and following the success of *Jaws,* sharks came to constitute a sub-genre. With the advent of cable TV channels devoted to nature documentaries, some channels such as *Discovery* scheduled 'shark weekends', 'shark months' and other special programming events which transformed sharks into a dicent symbol of *Natura horribilis.* By contrast, the wildlife of some areas such as much of Latin America[4] or northern Africa tended to be under-represented. So was the plant kingdom, which served largely as a backdrop for documentaries about animals. Even a BBC series ostensibly devoted to plants – *The Private Life of Plants* – arguably worked to make the plants more animal-like to meet the genre's thirst for kinesis and predation. The techniques used to achieve this involved not just time-lapse photography but complex, studio-based set-ups which combined time-lapse techniques with computers that synchronized the opening and closing of camera shutters with camera movements, with the turning on and off of lamps, and with plant growth (Lindahl Elliot 2001).

These and a variety of other techniques instituted what was, from the start, a deeply paradoxical logic in the genre. On the one hand, the shift from zoos and explicitly studio-based formats appeared to establish the rhematic credentials of the genre: natural history documentaries were promoted, and still are promoted, as being no more than indexes of first nature. Indeed it can be argued that, just as photography itself involved an indexical dimension, the documentaries, them-selves made with actual film, were, within any given shot, rhematic indexical legi-signs of and for the nature being represented.

To focus only on this dimension would nonetheless be to overlook the fact that the films involved montage and that, from the start, filming was conducted in studios and/or involved the staging of events, many of which led to the death of specimens in order to create a sense of drama. Perhaps the most famous instance of the latter was Disney's *White Wilderness,* which in the late 1950s represented lemmings as engaging in mass suicide. Aside from contradicting biological fact, this construction required the lemmings to be transported to a cliff's edge from which they were reportedly forced off. Disney was by no means the only film-maker to engage in such practices, which mostly escaped the critiques of animal rights activists. For example, in 1973, Anglia's *Survival* series imprinted snow goslings to fly behind a truck with a camera to give the impression that the cam-era was flying with them. *The Flight of the Snow Geese* went on to receive Emmy awards, and was highlighted in Colin Willock's autobiographical account of his role in the series. A full twenty years later, Mike Linley, a wildlife cameraman who worked on Willock's pioneering *Survival* series and then for the *National Geographic*, was found guilty by a court in Western Australia of attempting to smuggle out hundreds of specimens – marbled geckos, squelching froglets, cockroaches, snakes and western bearded dragons – from Australia. The judge reportedly suggested that he found it 'hard to understand' why Linley would have done 'such an incredibly stupid thing' (BBC News, http://news.bbc.co.uk/2/hi/uk_news/3313385.stm, accessed 12 December 2003).This was presumably a reference to the fact that Linley's filming had won prizes for conservationism, and that the judge regarded his documentary work as being devoted to this cause. Even though Linley reportedly suggested that he collected the animals to save them from death on Australia's outback roads, his own solicitor also suggested that Linley wished to film the animals in Britain under 'controlled conditions' (http://news.bbc.co.uk/2/hi/uk_news/3313385.stm).[5]

As I noted in relation to *The Private Life of Plants*, the genre was, from the start, hooked on kinesis. This was expressed in the choice of subjects and the genre's characteristic forms of montage, but it was also expressed in the logic of trans-continental displacement perfected in the BBC's *Life* trilogy. These three series (*Life on Earth* with *The Living Planet* and *The Trials of Life*) were characterized by a remarkable exploitation of the space–time compression techniques afforded by the movement-image: as Attenborough himself put it, 'Sometimes I came back having been filmed speaking the first half of a sentence that fitted neatly on to a second half that we had filmed another continent two years earlier' (Attenborough 2002: 294). These programmes were, in some respects, the late twentieth-century equivalent of the Royal Society's report on Krakatoa; they juxtaposed signs of a living, dynamic nature with samples drawn from all around the world 'even as they took place': heterotopic dicent sinsigns of a certain nature. But, whereas the Royal Society's report used tables and the zoos used enclosures which established a clear boundary between the observer and the observed, many if not all of the scenes in the Attenborough series gave the impression that *viewers* might be, could be, 'there' despite being 'here'. It is a monument, a problematic monument perhaps, to the genre and to television culture more generally that animals far more distant in the sheer physical space, and equally if not more bounded by the rectangle of a TV screen, could nonetheless seem to be far more natural than they did in zoos.

Whereas the narrators in the older forms of documentary, particularly those found in the genre of zoo shows, literally 'spoke' for the animals, the blue-chip documentaries mostly rejected this kind of commentary, either by presenters on camera or by way of voice-over narrations. Instead, the new genre employed what Bill Nichols describes as *observational* modes of representation (Nichols 1991) on the visual level, with an *expository* 'voice of god' narration (Nichols 1991) to promote 'scientific' forms of naturalism in which, and for which, the represented animals apparently remained silent.[6]

Even a cursory analysis of the new genre revealed that the animals were still made to 'speak', that the genre continued to be anthropomorphic, and that its programmes were at least as reliant on the codes of fictional dramatization as they were on the discourses of science. On the one hand, the blue-chip programmes, and indeed the macro-genre as a whole (made up of the half-hour shows, the specials and so forth) narrativized nature by incorporating some of the codes and techniques from fictional cinema. As I began to suggest earlier, the apparently rhematic and indexical nature of the genre was at one and the same time a nature of narratives in which scenes of predation became the staple montage to audiences by now long habituated to the IMR.

It is nonetheless remarkable that their 'drama' came to be interpreted rhematically as the drama of 'nature itself'. Again, the point is not to deny a natural secondness in the scenes of predation that were and still are endlessly depicted; what is at issue is the extent to which the polysemeiotic ensemble was itself more than a rheme, and clearly it was. During the 1960s, a characteristic style emerged based on relatively loosely knit montages or 'segments' (Ellis 1992). These typically involved simple narratives or fragments of narratives based on one or more of the following: close-ups of the animals, suggesting an enunciative first nature; 'action' shots or *arguments* involving scenes of predation, territorial disputes, reproduction or some other behaviour deemed to be extraordinary, emphasizing the secondness of nature; and descriptive or establishing shots for the geographical location, suggesting the thirdness of nature as 'set' or context for the first two kinds of shots.

Superimposed over such segments, the oral narration provided an argumentative overcoding which itself acted as a narrative frame structured predominantly along sociobiological lines (a discourse to which I return below). Over time, variations were introduced both in terms of the actual mode of address and in the manner in which the presenter was embedded in the narration. Attenborough, for example, usually acted as an extra-diegetic narrator (a narrator located outside the narrative of nature), or as a 'hybrid' presenter who appeared as 'our man in nature' but in so doing usually refrained from intervening 'in' nature and, in this sense, emphasized the classification of culture and nature. For his part, Cousteau was an *intra*-diegetic narrator whose preparation for filming and then actual filming was made a central aspect of the narrative. While Cousteau himself arguably reproduced the classification of nature and culture, his discourse and narrative structuring was far closer to the *environmentalist* imaginary in so far as aspects of its *mise en scène* and his own idealizing narration provided an almost formal pedagogy about the unity of humanity and nature.

The genre was, from the beginning, strongly structured by much the same patriarchal discourse as was reproduced by the pastoralist discourse of hunter-conservationists such as Hammond. Barbara Crowther (1995) has noted that much of the genre was narrativized in terms of masculinist quests and adventures. In this context, voice-over narrations either reproduced predominant gender classifications even in situations where nature seemed to contradict these (e.g. 'pregnant' male sea horses), or used grammatical modalities that assigned males the active roles and females the passive. For example, in the 'Continuing the Line' episode of the BBC's *Queen of the Beasts*, David Attenborough offered the following narration:

> This is a male Heleconius butterfly and he's settled on a pupa which he knows contains a female. He's waiting for that moment when the female will emerge, a virgin, and then in the first few seconds of her adult life he'll mate with her. [When another male is brushed with a female that has just mated the male butterfly flies away.] The reason he left is because this female, when she was mated, was given a particular smell, which even I can detect.
>
> (Attenborough quoted in Crowther 1995: 129)

According to Crowther, the inclusion of the appositional phrase, 'a virgin,' the use of the passive voice in the phrase 'when she was mated' and then the active agency in 'he mates with her' suggested a patriarchal disposition towards the sexual act (Crowther 1995: 129–30).

This disposition was usually embedded within a popular sociobiological form of anthropomorphism. Sociobiology can be regarded as a late twentieth-century version of the social Darwinism that I considered in Chapters 1 and 5. As noted in Chapter 1, one of the pioneering and most successful exponents of this discourse was Edward O. Wilson, whose classic book on the zoology of ants, *Sociobiology: The New Synthesis*, concluded by presenting an argument in favour of the biological determination of human behaviour. In later books he was an advocate of epistemologies of research that reproduced the naturalistic fallacy (see for example E.O. Wilson 1992) and attacked the principle of methodological pluralism (see Wilson 1998).

Many natural history documentary film-makers followed in the footsteps of Wilson and other sociobiologists such as Dawkins (1974) and Pinker (1994), and reproduced circuits of anthropomorphism which directly or indirectly promoted a variety of social stereotypes. The modes of this circuit ranged from explicitly cosmomorphic forms of animalization in which zoologists such as Desmond Morris offered a zoological 'analysis' of the behaviour of humans (as in *The Human Animal* [1994]) to more tacit forms of cosmomorphism such as those found in the enormously popular *Meerkats United* (1987). Programmes such as this one, which was voted the most popular nature documentary ever by BBC viewers, left the viewer to establish the relation of cosmomorphic identity between the gently 'socialist' meerkats and the plight of audiences in an increasingly neoliberal Britain.

It must be emphasized again and again that the circuit of anthropomorphism was instituted by both oral and visual semeiosis. An example of the extent of the sociobiological transformations produced by this process was particularly evident in a BBC series titled *The Velvet Claw* (1992). This series recycled footage used in other series with pioneering, if by later standards quite crude, digital techniques to offer a natural history of carnivores. This history – for once, the genre actually attempted to be '*historical*' – suggested that the evolution of carnivores was a matter of a voluntaristic evolutionary process involving 'hired assassins'. For example, the second episode in the series, on the evolution of cats, began by explaining that 'one supreme dynasty of skilled assassins was to claw its way to the top: the cats. This is their story' even as a cheetah was filmed running along the 'z' or depth axis at the camera. In this series, as in many others, the use of this axis, and the use of close-ups of the animals' heads, was designed to involve viewers by making it seem that the animals were 'coming at them' – thereby contradicting any simply 'environmentalist' argument – but by encouraging, at the same time, an identification with the animals as quasi-humans.

I have already discussed aspects of the nature of identification in film in the context of my analysis of the emergence of the IMR. The process may be further explained with reference to Gilles Deleuze, who, reflecting on the relation between affect and the close-up, suggests that the close-up 'facefies' ('*visagéifiée*') even those things that do not resemble a face (Deleuze 1986: 88). It is possible to suggest, in this sense, that on the visual level one fundamental strategy for the production of circuits of anthropomorphism in the genre was precisely to 'facefy' and thereby humanize the heads of animals by means of close-ups. With some species, this phenomenon arguably extended to the whole body in what might be described as the anthropomorphic practice of humanizing or animalizing 'bodyfication'.[7]

Returning to *The Velvet Claw*, what was remarkable about the series was the manner in which analogue facefication gave way to a digital facefication. For example, in one segment the voice-over narration (read by Derek Jacobi, one of many actors/celebrities used by producers in the genre) suggested that

> already hidden in the mouths of these cats lay the secret weapons of the confirmed killer. The teeth of these creatures reflected one of the most significant turning points in their evolution: the sharpening of the tooth. Quite literally, they lost their ancestral chewing teeth at the back and replaced them with a set of knives: daggers at the front to kill, and carnassial scissors at the back to slice up meat. Armed with a battery of blades, and dextrous agile limbs, the cats were to become the skilled assassins of the trees.
>
> (*The Velvet Claw*, Episode 2)

As this voice-over was heard, images of an animation of a computer-aided design of the jaws of a fossa were superimposed onto an image of the jaws of an actual fossa. In Peirce's terms, an icon of the fossa was displaced by an iconic legisign. This had the effect of transforming the evolutionary process into a matter of *mathesis* by way of a digital 'topographical' rendering of the jaws. The rotation of the computer generated image on the 'y' or vertical axis, the blue lines and black background all suggested, quite literally, that the evolution of these 'assassins' was a matter of natural 'engineering'. The contrast between the two images could not be more striking; if the icon of the actual fossa was premised on a close-up of the animal's head, with aspects of the environment visible – a reduction of the field of view which nevertheless left the viewer to 'fill in' the out-of-field – the digital animation was a kind of paradigmatic instance of the double spatial illusion mentioned with reference to the work of Lefebvre in Chapter 2.

Producers of programmes such as these might well argue that references to 'hired assassins' and other similarly voluntaristic metaphors made it apparent that the programmes were constructing metaphors. They might further argue that viewers/listeners of such narrations were likely to be aware that the programmes were charged with irony, and even a humour which was not meant to be interpreted rhematically. While this might be true for some audiences, it seems unlikely that all viewers would bring to bear such interpretants, or indeed would be critically aware of the social Darwinist imaginary instituted by the programme's narration. In so far as such a discourse was widely used throughout the genre and was widely reproduced *beyond* it, the risk remained that the programmes might well act as sites for the legitimization of social Darwinism.

To cite just one of the innumerable examples by means of which such relations were reproduced *beyond* the programmes, in the UK one issue of FHM included a two-page spread that showed a large image of a male gelada baboon apparently attacking what it described as a (smaller) female. While many viewers might simply glance at the image, the verbal text that accompanied it acted as a framing device that could serve to normalize patriarchy amongst FHM's readers, albeit by way of a paradoxical and largely silent circuit of anthropomorphism. Underneath a large title that said 'MANIMAL!', a red arrow contained white text in bold lettering that said, 'Forget the fact that his cock's hanging out. This gelada baboon has another problem: a world run by females.' The text of the article echoed the complex inversion, suggesting, 'It's true. Found only in the mountains of Ethiopia, the grass-eating gelada endures a life dominated by women' (*FHM* 2004: 18). The article concluded by inviting viewers to 'tune to the National Geographic's *Wild Thursday*', which the article was presumably advertising, 'to see more of these amazing moments'. Such articles illustrated the way in which individual programmes in the natural history genre were both mediated and transmediated across media, and the way in which the life of the discourses tacitly promoted by the film-makers went far beyond the programmes themselves.[8]

As I began to suggest earlier, the documentary film-makers' claims to fostering a conservationist ethos amongst their publics could also be questioned. To begin with, it could be argued that the genre's emphasis on a primordial or pristine nature reproduced the coding orientation associated not so much with the environmentalist imaginary but with an older modern imaginary of nature. Indeed, until the end of the twentieth century, explicit references to environmental destruction tended to be excluded in most of the programmes. One significant though problematic exception was the 'drug and tag' sub-genre, which later became what might be described as the 'cam and follow' genre, which entailed harpooning sharks or netting birds and other animals in order to place a miniature video camera on them. This technique then allegedly provided, quite literally, a 'bird's eye view' (or a shark, eagle or other animal's eye view) of a certain geography, i.e. a kind of visual firstness, as transmediated from the animal. But, in addition to the fact that the 'crittercams' offered no more such a view than they might of similarly equipped humans, such practices constituted a flagrant reproduction of the discourse of the domination of nature. In effect, animals were humanized by the very techniques of observation (Lindahl Elliot 2001). If Brunelleschi had once included indexes of clouds by using reflective paint, and if Wordsworth had used words to conceive a 'cloud's eye view' with which to survey the Lake District's landscape, natural history film-makers now used the animals themselves to physically mount cameras in order to harness material nature visually.

The predominant ethos amongst film-makers nonetheless suggested the opposite, that the genre 'showed what there is to be saved'. However, as I have begun to suggest, the genre arguably went, almost literally, to the ends of the earth in order to silently position viewers to partake in the kind of spectacular consumption that linked the genre to the very practices of environmental destruction that were endangering many of the species in the first place.

During the 1990s, this contradiction deepened in so far as the documentaries came to be viewed in a multichannel context in which competition for audiences sharpened. Increasingly, the editing of the programmes had to be geared to secure a 'watch' from the very moment the programme began. To this end, one strategy was to structure each programme as a succession of what some producers referred to as 'hey May's': segments in which the Bills or Johns or Tims of the all-important American market reportedly call the Mays or Jills or Mollys to the TV set: *hey May, come and see this!* From this perspective, it might be argued that the documentaries showed what there was to be saved, but also what there was to be *consumed*. And indeed, one of the forms of consumption that was arguably stoked by the genre was 'ecotourism' or visits to the areas represented on television. At the time, for example, when the BBC's award-winning *Life in the Freezer* was shown, the corporation's own TV listings magazine, *Radio Times*, offered a BBC promotion with a private tour operator for a 17-day voyage of adventure to Antarctica and the Falkland Islands, 'the last true wilderness on Earth', with prices beginning at £4767 (*Radio Times* 1993: 68).

It might be argued that such experiences might transform visitors into environmental activists. But some studies suggested that even a minimal presence of tourists in some of the habitats disrupted the natural patterns of behaviour of certain species. For example, one researcher, Rochelle Constantine at the University of Auckland, found that dolphins on New Zealand's north-eastern coast rested as little as 0.5 per cent of the time when there were two or more tourist boats in the vicinity, as compared to 68 per cent of the time when in the presence of a single research boat. For their part, Markus Dyck and Richard Baydack at the University of Manitoba found that signs of vigilance among male bears increased nearly sevenfold when vehicles were around (Ananthaswamy 2004).

I will return to the question of so-called 'green consumerism' later in this chapter. By the end of the twentieth century, there were some signs that some producers were reassessing this stance and moving towards a more unequivocally conservationist stance. While many of the contradictions remained in the genre, it would be a mistake to underestimate the capacity that the 'blue-chip' and associated documentaries had to generate at least something akin to conservationist structure of feeling amongst at least some of the audience groups. It would also be a mistake to overlook the extent to which the public service broadcasting discourse, personified especially by David Attenborough and instituted by the BBC since the times of its first chairman, Lord Reith, maintained what Thompson (1995) describes as a 'mixed' institutional space from the point of view of the private/public economic divide. In a context increasingly structured by the private, and at times even personal, interests of the owners of large media conglomerates, intermediate positions such as those of the BBC could by no means be dismissed as neatly serving the purposes of managerial capitalism. Indeed, the heterogeneity of interests within such large institutions rendered problematic any simplistic account of 'media domination' or 'media alliance with big business' as was suggested by some environmentalist critics (see for example Edwards 1998).

But this shift amongst some sectors of natural history film-makers nevertheless appeared to be more than offset by two trends in the genre. The first of these involved the rise in popularity of 'extreme' or 'dangerous' nature shows, of which two sub-genres could be distinguished: documentaries that described a catastrophic nature, in the form of erupting volcanoes, earthquakes or atmospheric disturbances such as tornadoes and hurricanes; and those concerned with dangerous animals. I will consider an example of the former in the epilogue. Here I wish to concern myself with a variant of the latter sub-genre – the extreme nature of dangerous animals – which marked a turn to a more 'violent nature', and to a more explicitly interactive mode of representation (Nichols 1991). As presented by figures such as Steve Irwin and Steve Leonard, this sub-genre specialized in bodily encounters involving animals capable of killing humans, in particular reptiles such as crocodiles and snakes.

In these programmes, it was possible to discern the conjunction of the old modern quest for an absolute *ego alter* with the times of a naturalism that was in some respects the twentieth-century *fin de siècle* equivalent of the grotesque naturalism that animal welfare activists had tried to suppress in Britain and the US some two centuries earlier. This tradition, represented since the nineteenth century by circuses, popular bloodsports, animal tamers and the early cinematic 'dramatic' films, returned with a vengeance to television, perhaps in part as a result of the increasingly competitive context alluded to earlier.[9]

The extreme nature/dangerous animal show involved a new body politics, one that might well be described in terms of a new version of the 'drama of the touch'.

214

If in *King Kong* the scenes involving the hands were 'electric and transformative moment[s] of contact' (Erb 1998: 92), in the new sub-genre this trope came to involve contact between the animals and the whole (human) body. For example, in *Crocodile Hunter* (1996), Steve Irwin's 'struggles' to capture crocodiles produced the sublime bravado of 'one-to-one' combat that culminated in three-way encounters between three 'faces': the triumphant face of the presenter, frequently shown in close up addressing the camera/viewer whilst holding a struggling second 'face' of the dangerous animal for the benefit of the amazed third 'face' of the viewer-spectator – a viewer that, by way of the firstness and secondness of direct address, was positioned to identify, both narratively and cosmomorphically, with such one-to-one, body-to-body encounters. As suggested by Francesco Casetti (1995) in the context of film, such a mode of address *interpellated* the observer by inviting her/him indexically to participate in the action, but also by encouraging her/him to feel *recognized* by the presenter. At the same time, the mode 'insist[ed] that [the viewer] recognize himself [*sic*] as its immediate interlocutor' (Casetti 1995: 119).

Irwin's and other presenters' ways of interpellating viewers instituted at once a new proximity to, and an old distance from, nature. If Irwin was 'face to face' with the animals, he was also 'in your [the viewer's] face', speaking at once *at* and *with* 'you' in a manner that replicated with animals the pragmatics of his 'matey' encounters with humans, and vice versa. But the same weakening of the human/ non-human classification on the level of the pragmatics of the mode of address marked the strengthening of the boundary of human/non-human nature on the level of the overall narrative: 'you and I' are going to 'catch some nasty crocs'.

I noted earlier that one of the motivations for this sub-genre may have been the increasingly competitive nature documentary market – the extreme nature shows tended to be cheaper to make than the blue-chip programmes, and so could more easily address the requirements generated by 'wall to wall' nature programming in channels like *Animal Planet*. But the popularity of the 'body-to-body' sub-genre was arguably also linked, however nocturnally, to the emergence of what some referred to as the 'new laddism', a form of masculinism most obviously expressed in a proliferation of magazines devoted to soft porn, and to the cult of what might be described as the hyper-bloke: a masculinity metonymically constructed around a sexual gaze, a prosthetic identification with new technologies of communication, but also a cosmomorphic identification with the most dangerous natures.[10]

In 2005, a phenomenon emerged which forced analysts to reconsider the critique of sociobiology in natural history documentaries. If the documentaries called for a critique of social Darwinism, the remarkable appropriation of a documentary about penguins suggested that henceforth it might be necessary to engage in the critique of Christian fundamentalist circuits of anthropomorphism. *The March of the Penguins*, a feature-length documentary produced by the filmmaker Luc Jaquet and shown in cinemas, was co-opted as evidence of the thesis of 'Intelligent Design' among Christian fundamentalists in the US. The thesis of 'Intelligent Design' masqueraded as a scientific critique of evolutionary theory.

Its advocates nonetheless posed a significant challenge to the mechanistic forms of determinism that continued to dominate Western science by insisting on the divine firstness of a natural *complexity*, which was taken as evidence of God's role as the ultimate 'designer' of all things in the universe.

The fundamentalists' promotion of the film as a site for Christian pedagogy, and the controversy that this practice generated in the press, are likely to have helped the documentary to become what was then the second most popular documentary in American film history, and the highest-grossing natural history documentary. The reception proposed by the advocates of Intelligent Design was as arbitrary as that of *FHM*'s gloss on the gelada baboons. However, in the *March of the Penguins* as in the *National Geographic* documentary, several aspects of the film arguably lent themselves to an ideological form of appropriation. First, and in marked contrast to the French-language version, the English-language version encouraged an identification with a sublime, indeed sublimated landscape. This aspect was arguably underscored by the pragmatics of a cinematic viewing, which involved the 'double' of cinema's darkened chamber as opposed to television's more diurnal character. It was also strengthened by the film's highly conventional use of the qualisigns of 'timeless' seasonality: in the manner of the 1950s Disney films, the documentary began in the summer and ended at the start of a new season. Second, the film represented the penguins as natural dicents of a nuclear familiarity, i.e. as hard-working, self-sacrificing parents intent on raising children 'despite all odds'. Here were 'two-parent families' that not only went to the ends of the earth to look after their children but even took turns doing so, and returned faithfully to their partners and their 'duties'. (In fact, as noted subsequently by biologists, the penguins changed mate every season.) Third, despite producer Luc Jacquet's protestations about his own faith in the theory of evolution, the documentary made no verbal reference to evolutionary theory, and this arguably paved the way for the interpretants of Intelligent Design.

Last but certainly not least, the film was able to capitalize on the extraordinary popularity of the 'funny' penguins. This aspect meant that the documentary achieved something of a 'balance' between its sublimating discourse and an anthropomorphic circuit that capitalized on the humour, not least the apparently rhematic humour of the juvenile penguins. No doubt much of the film's box office success was a result of this factor alone: the popular semeiotics of penguins has a long history that might well be the subject of a book-length analysis in its own right. Here I will simply note that, during the London Film Festival premieres of the film in 2005, organizers of the festival gave out penguin cuddly toys, and the French version of Amazon.com offered to sell a French-language version which included 'un peluche' – the same as was given out to children at the London Film Festival. This aspect of the merchandising, like the film's attention to juvenile penguins, invited viewers to establish a relation of transmediation between the 'real' penguins and the fluffy, cuddly toys – a strategy long exploited by zoos and numerous other institutions devoted to the representation of animals.

The newest zoos

As I noted earlier, there was a relationship of transmediation between zoos and television in the 1950s and, before that, between the Hagenbeck principle of design and panoramas in the early twentieth century. Another form of transmediation emerged most clearly during the last quarter of the twentieth century, when a new generation of zoos – the so-called 'new zoos' – appeared, first in the United States, and then in various parts of the world. Zoos such as San Diego's Wild Animal Park, Seattle's Woodland Park and New York's Bronx Zoo engaged in what amounted to a process of reinvention of the zoo genre.

This reinvention involved changes on at least two levels. First, many of the most prestigious zoos began to reposition their institutional *raison d'être* along the lines of conservationism. Aspects of this practice dated at least as far back as the nineteenth century, when the founding members of New York Zoological Society, which was set up to create the Bronx Zoo, suggested that 'No civilized nation should allow its wild animals to be exterminated without at least making an attempt to preserve living representatives of all species that can be kept alive in confinement' (quoted in Goddard 1995: 43). The New York Zoological Society was perhaps exceptional in that it was founded partly at the behest of Teddy Roosevelt in the heyday of white hunter-conservationism. Crucially, its policies were influenced by William Hornaday, a taxidermist who introduced naturalistic display principles to the National and Bronx Zoos (Hanson 2002). To be sure, the statement quoted above makes it evident that the emphasis was on conserving *some specimens*, rather than participating actively in the conservation of viable *species*. By contrast, the institutional shift that emerged in the 1970s and 1980s involved the incorporation of conservationism as a central *organizational* goal, and as a, if not *the*, fundamental aspect of zoos' *identity* in the public sphere. It also involved a change in the geography of conservation: new zoos should intervene actively beyond their own boundaries to help to save species from extinction.

These changes can be illustrated with reference to a pronouncement made by the director of the world famous San Diego Zoo in its *Zoonoos* newsletter in 1963. In an article titled 'Conservation is our business', Charles Schroeder stated that 'Conservation broadly embodies all natural resources. At a zoo, however, where we are concerned primarily with animals and plants, our immediate interest is with the fast-disappearing exotic birds, reptiles and mammals around the world. . . . Animals [from vanishing species] will be secured only with the full knowledge of those in charge of conservation in the countries of origin on the recommendation of the International Union for the Conservation of Nature and Natural Resources' (Schroeder quoted in Myers 1999: 161).

The San Diego Zoological Society also went on to institute changes on a second level: the level of the actual displays, which, from the 1970s onwards, began to be described in terms of the *immersion* of visitors in zoogeographically organized displays. It is possible to gain a sense of the shift in the following description of the 'vision' that Schroeder had for a new zoo – in fact, a new kind of safari park – in the San Pasqual Valley north of San Diego. According to his biographer, Schroeder envisaged the 'zoo of the future' while standing in the hills around the valley: 'Over there, he'd point, will be the East African valley. Over here will be Asian plains. And right there, a watering hole designed exactly like one in the South African wild. The animals will roam free – rhinos, antelopes, giraffes. People will see them all from a train winding through the preserve, having an experience they could never have anywhere this side of a transcontinental adventure in the wide-open world' (Myers 1999: 171).

The plan was to have the animals 'roam free over hundreds of acres', and '[p]eople – rather than animals – would be enclosed. Visitors would view them from a small train winding through the preserve, and Charlie [Schroeder] believed they would willingly drive to this remote spot and pay to view it all' (Myers 1999: 172).

The new San Diego Wild Animal Park opened in 1972 and became one of the first of the so-called 'new zoos': zoos which, in the words of one account written by the same *National Geographic* photographer whose work I considered in Chapter 1 – Mike Nichols – went from being 'places of depression, bastions of captivity, filled with bored, lifeless animals that might just as well have been stuffed' to 'ecosystem-style exhibits that point out the intricacies of nature, bringing special attention to the interconnectedness of all the world's most threatened and precious resources, and highlighting the message that they could well be destroyed before we understand what we have lost' (Nichols 1996: 10–11).

While the shifts are likely to have saved zoos from institutional decline – during this period, 'old' zoos began to lose visitors and, in some cases, to close – the institutional reinvention and the shift in display philosophy were not without criticism, at times by members of the field constituted by the zoos themselves. The new forms of naturalism, like the older forms, took architectural license to introduce forms of landscaping that were not found in the region that the displays supposedly represented. As noted by David Hancocks, a zoo director and himself a pioneer in the 'new zoos' movement, the mountain habitat in the Arizona-Sonora Desert Museum, which claimed to represent the desert site it was located in, was formed with artificial rockwork that 'has no texture that can be found in nature' (2001: 72–3). This observation was particularly significant in so far as the Arizona-Sonora Desert Museum was at the (relatively) self-effacing end of a continuum of architectural intervention. Most new zoos could be located at the opposite end, and did not hesitate to engage in the production of monumental displays. For example, the 'Desert Dome' in Omaha's Henry Doorly Zoo, completed in the early twenty-first century, could be seen for miles. Zoos like the Henry Doorly practised a particularly paradoxical form of naturalism: the lofty domes and expanding glass surfaces in a variety of zoo designs celebrated their architects' capacity to engage in extraordinary flights of design imagination, even as the interiors of the displays invited visitors to 'make believe' that they were underwater, or in a rainforest, or in a desert. As technologies of observation, the newest zoo displays encouraged the production of naturalistic, that is, rhematic, forms of observation, i.e. 'being there'. But this selfsame aspect revealed how the displays were at one and the same time technologies of displacement: 'being there' was premised in part on *not* being '*here*' (the zoo's actual location) and, of course, on the non-human animals not being '*there*', in their original habitats.

The conventional wisdom suggests that the change to the 'new zoos' was a response to sharpening animal rights activism. There can be little doubt that a resurgent animal welfare movement did play a significant role during and after the 1970s. First in a book on animal welfare edited by Stanley and Roslind Godlovitch with John Harris (1972), and then in what became Peter Singer's (1976) famous *Animal Liberation*, an increasingly radical critique was offered of 'speciesism', the ideology that justified the domination of non-human animals with reference to the alleged superiority of the human over all other species.

This conceptual effort to fundamentally undermine the human/non-human boundary – at least as constructed by centuries of modern cultural discourse – played a significant role in the movement and in the popular dissemination of its discourse. However, it is possible to suggest that equally if not more significant were the lived spaces and structures of feeling mobilized in popular books and films such as Joy Adamson's and James Hill's *Born Free* (1966) and the television series that followed.[11]

Born Free offered a romantic account of the manner in which a naturalist living with a British game park warden in Kenya managed to reintroduce to the wild a lioness that they had 'adopted' when the warden shot dead a pride of lions suspected of being 'man-eaters'. The film produced what was arguably a neocolonial version of the rural idyll set in Kenya, and engaged in a form of anthropomorphism with lion cubs that echoed the forms of domestication which characterized zoo shows in the 1950s. In effect, Joy Adamson transformed Elsa and the two other lion cubs into child-like pets or pet-like children, albeit in a context that suggested an Edenic 'nature'.

A crucial aspect from the point of view of the history of forms of observation in new zoos was Joy Adamson's struggle to 'save' Elsa from being sent to the zoo in Rotterdam (by George Adamson's account in the diegesis, a 'good zoo'). This struggle culminated in the remarkable scene of the Adamsons having a heated discussion after having failed in their most recent effort to reintroduce Elsa to the wild. The following exchange took place in a scene in which George spoke while pacing angrily behind Joy. Wide shots of the scene were interspersed with cuts to close-ups of an emotive Joy making a passionate case for Elsa, even as Elsa was herself shown in a series of facefying close-ups lying on the floor, apparently looking up at her rowing 'parents':

George: What's wrong with a zoo anyway!?
Joy: Nothing! Except that she won't be *free*!
George: And is freedom so important?!

Joy: Yes! *Yes!* She was *born* free and she has a right to *live* free! . . . We
            chose to live out here because it represents *freedom* for us, because
            we can *breathe* here . . .
George: She'll be *safe* in a zoo!
Joy: Yes, safe, and sad and lazy and dull and *stupid* . . . [If she were
            reintroduced] at least she would be *free*, at least she wouldn't be in
            a *cage* for the rest of her life.

The scene, viewed as it was in a social context already strongly structured by pacifist debates about the Vietnam War and opposition to the nuclear arms race, was likely to have led many to identify with the romanticism of Joy's discourse, and to disregard the pragmatic arguments that were so forcefully put by George: the Adamsons, he suggested, were in effect torturing an animal that had been too thoroughly domesticated to be reintroduced to the wild.

But in the end Joy was 'proven' right. Elsa was finally reintroduced, and the success of the mission was 'confirmed' when Elsa returned to 'show' her cubs to the Adamsons. This constituted a tacit condemnation even of 'good zoos'. After all, here was living 'proof' – the film ended with a title that explained that it was based on a 'true story' – that freedom could be achieved for humans and non-human animals alike by those determined enough to struggle for their ideals. The movie's theme song, played by an orchestra throughout the film but sung at the end with lyrics by Don Black, became a popular hit in the late 1960s and won the film an Oscar. The lyrics carried and repeated the circuit of anthropomorphism proposed by the film's narrative, for which the plight of Elsa became the plight of Joy, and of 'caring' humans more generally:

> Born free, as free as the wind blows
> As free as the grass grows
> Born free to follow your heart
> Live free, and beauty surrounds you
> The world still astounds you
> Each time you look at a star
> Stay free, where no walls divide you
> You're free as the roaring tide
> So there's no need to hide.

Both Joy and George Adamson were eventually killed by local inhabitants described as 'poachers'. In his memoirs, Attenborough noted that, during a trip as part of *Zoo Quest,* he'd expected to find an idyll but instead found that 'violence lay beneath the surface [of the Adamson's camp] wherever we looked' (Attenborough 2002: 152). During the filming of *Born Free* itself, lions trained by George to play the part of Elsa at different stages of her life became dangerous. One reportedly attacked and killed one of George's assistants. Attenborough, who described Joy Adamson as 'tall and slim with a forehead that was slightly too broad and a chin that was slightly too prominent for her to be described as beautiful, but she was nonetheless strikingly handsome' (Attenborough 2002: 149), claimed that the 'brusqueness' with which Joy told George of her wishes 'was exceeded only by the imperious way with which she dealt with her African staff' (Attenborough 2002: 152).

The romantic sublime legacy of *Born Free* nonetheless lived on in the form of a television series, and a charity of the same name, which, as its website explained, devoted itself to 'campaigns for the protection and conservation of animals in their natural habitat and against the keeping of animals in zoos and circuses and as exotic pets' (www.bornfree.co.uk/index.shtml, accessed 1 July 2004).

The structure of feeling reproduced by the film arguably also lived on, paradoxically, by way of displays that gave not just *animals* the opportunity to 'roam free over hundreds of acres', but visitors as well. Contrary to what was suggested in an earlier quote by Myers (1999), that one of the principles of the new displays was to enclose the visitors, the success of the new zoos arguably hinged giving the *visitors* this anthropomorphic and cosmomorphic 'freedom to roam', a freedom to 'immerse' themselves in Edenic or Arcadian idylls such as were represented in films like *Born Free*.

From this perspective, the new forms of display engaged in a complex dynamic of transmediation that attempted to produce, in Peircian terms, *replicas* of the signs that inspired the structure of feeling in the first place. Whereas the earlier generations of zoos made no effort to hide the boundaries of enclosures, in the new zoos the emphasis was on transposing the 'points of view' constructed by films and natural history documentaries. Viewing areas were 'composed' visually to create a sense of depth, to highlight and indeed intensify some aspects of the display and not others, and to vary the 'point of view' by means of platforms, tunnels and raised vantage points. However, whereas a spectator in a cinema or at home watching television might sit and be offered changing forms of ocularization, the new zoos required the visitor to *walk* – or at times *ride* – in order to take in new 'views'.

The above all suggests the pre-eminence of visual iconicity. But multisensuality played a key role and allowed zoos to suggest that, in zoos, one might not just 'see' nature but also 'sense' it (Lindahl Elliot 2006). Beyond the smells of the animals themselves – indexes of a corporeality absent from other forms of mass mediation – some exhibits incorporated sound effects akin to those found in documentaries. These included the sounds of piped 'nature' or 'new age' music of the kind sold in nature stores. Others used fine mist sprays to make the exhibits look and *feel* like tropical rainforests. And of course many zoos included 'petting zoos' or, as one zoo called it, an 'affection section' where some of the animals themselves –or their lifeless skins – could be touched.

Perhaps the most complex example of transmediation was found in the acrylic tunnels and other underwater viewing areas found in aquaria and zoo displays that showed species underwater. These literally suggested an immersion 'in' nature, but did so in a manner that tacitly invited visitors to transmediate the forms of underwater photography found in natural history documentaries. Of course, neither the acrylic tunnels themselves nor the vantage points afforded by them could be described as being 'natural'. While the promotional discourses framed such displays in naturalistic terms, such devices were more likely to involve the pleasure of a *tension* between naturalism and technological intervention, between rhematic forms of iconicity and a manifest indexicality, between the secondness of the experience and the thirdness of the display as convention. Put differently, even as the displays invited the visitors to rejoice in the wonder of the nature on display, they invited them to partake in what was an architectural celebration of the power of humans to intervene in nature by technological means. This constituted the paradox of many new zoo displays: they achieved a (transmediated) sense of naturalism by engaging in extraordinarily interventionist forms of engineering and architecture.

The animal attack film

It might be assumed from the above accounts that the last three decades of the twentieth century were dominated by forms of mass mediation premised on a collective desire to be closer to nature and to engage in environmental activism. But this period also saw the production of a number of films which centred on *Natura horribilis,* i.e. films about natural disasters, mutant or 'long lost' animals, and animal attacks. The genre of the natural catastrophe film included *The Poseidon Adventure* (1972), *Earthquake* (1974), *Twister* (1996), *The Perfect Storm* (2000) and *The Day After Tomorrow* (2004); and the science fiction film with mutant or otherwise threatening natures included *The Andromeda Strain* (1971), *The Abyss* (1989) and *Godzilla* (1998), to name just three.

In this chapter I focus on what I describe as the 'animal attack' film. In particular, I shall consider the cinematic context that emerged in 1975, when Steven Spielberg directed *Jaws,* the first of the 'summer blockbusters'. *Jaws* was to be followed not just by a long line of sequels – *Jaws 2, Jaws 3* and *Jaws: The Revenge* – but also by a host of imitations which sought to repeat the formula's success with different species. These included *Piranha* (1978), *The Swarm* (1978), *Arachnophobia* (1990), *The Beast* (1996), *Anaconda* (1997) and *Deep Blue Sea* (2001).

While it may well be argued from a culturalist perspective that no 'empirical fact' (e.g. the actual existence of the named species) automatically justifies a certain genre-classification, it seems clear that films like *Jaws, Arachnophobia* and *Piranha* derived their specificity from a tension between the indexical 'fact' or secondness of a nature that *did exist* in the form of an actual species; and the legisignical 'fiction' or thirdness of a form which the species acquired within the film. The key feature of this form was an excessive corporeality, that is to say a corporeality that defied either expectations or an everyday sense of plausibility, and which was capable of producing extreme energetic interpretants in the audiences.

In this context, the power (and pleasure) of the genre could be said to be derived from the *exceptional* appearance of a *plausible* or quasi-plausible nature: a nature that might be classified in some shape or form as being 'real', but which now disrupted everyday life, and for which either there was no warning, or a warning was issued but disregarded by individuals or communities whose risk assessment was 'biased' by profit motives, the pursuit of pleasure or some other form of personal gain. In *Jaws*, for example, Chief Brody pleaded with the town's mayor to close the beaches of Amity. However, his request was refused on the grounds that tourism, and thereby business, was more important. Animal attack films seemed in this sense to be morality tales about the risks of (human) greed, itself a moralized account of individualism and a capitalist logic of accumulation.

And indeed, in virtually all of the films in this genre, *Natura horribilis* was fought and ultimately conquered (or at any rate, 'survived') by *persons*. *Natura horribilis*, at least in its animal attack variant, did not randomly attack nameless, 'faceless' individuals; or, if it did, the attack usually provided a 'pre-text' for the identification, in narrative terms, of the existence of the person and subsequent biographical explanation of the individual that was attacked. In *Jaws*, the attack on Alex Kintner, initially an 'unknown' child, subsequently led to a remarkable condemnation of Brody by Mrs Kintner, who made public Brody's failure to act on his own risk assessment.

As was particularly evident in *Arachnophobia*, a film in which spiders engaged in a veritable assault on familial domesticity, this personalizing principle was frequently articulated in relation to *families*. The *Jaws* sequels even projected familiality anthropomorphically onto the sharks themselves. Despite having different actors (Roy Scheider only acted in the first and second films) and indeed different generations of the Brody family, the series culminated with a film in which, as the trailer put it, 'This time it's personal'. This presumably meant that the shark – itself some unexplained relative of the first shark – was now definitely after Brody's family, because it was *Brody's* family, a theme that was analogous to the one developed in *Orca* (1977). In this as in so many other Hollywood films, the family, that most modern of institutions, thereby became both the victim of, and the last bastion against, 'the elements'.

Where gender and sexuality were concerned, the films suggested at once a confirmation and a remarkable transformation of the circuits of anthropomorphism described throughout this book. Especially in the 1970s, the reproduction of modern patriarchy took the form of particularly savage attacks on young women. In the *Jaws* films and in *Piranha*, the attacks took place in ways that suggested a policing especially of sexual encounters initiated by young women. In this context, the expression of 'man-eater' was a misnomer; in one sense at least, the animals appeared to be 'woman-eaters'.

In this non-formal pedagogic practice we find a remarkable transformation of the circuit of anthropomorphism. On the one hand, it was nature – long anthropomorphized as being female – that was policing this 'wild' 'female' 'nature'. But this observation must be followed up with another on the level of the pragmatics of enunciation: in the first *Jaws* film, and then again in *Piranha*, *Anaconda* and others, it was only the women who were shown naked or scantily clad both by and to an ambiguous audio-visual narrator: a narrator that was at once an extra-diegetic camera-narrator but also the intra-diegetic 'narrator' constituted by an ocularization of the 'animal-eye' view. *Jaws* famously began with the attack on Chrissie, which included ocularizations – from the shark's underwater 'point of view' – of her swimming naked as a silhouette framed against the moonlight. In the case of *Piranha*, a frame-by-frame analysis of one attack on a female swimmer reveals an extraordinary scene in which the fish were filmed attacking one of her nipples. In *Arachnophobia*, one of the most striking attacks or near-attacks occurred when a spider was shown sliding down the body of an unsuspecting teenager as she was taking a shower. An initial shot, taken from above the woman, showed the spider sliding down between her breasts. The next shot, shown immediately before a cut to the woman's face shown screaming, was a close-up of the spider about to reach her crotch.[12]

At least in these films, it was difficult to avoid the conclusion that the generic expression of 'man-eater' was, from this new perspective, appropriate, albeit in an unexpected way. In terms of the gendering of the ocularization, but also in terms of the dynamic of cosmomorphic identification, the films appeared to be driven by forms of enunciation in which misogynist and male subjects of enunciation relied on prosthetic animals to do the sexual 'eating'. The animals, in this sense, could be taken to be literally 'man-eaters', that is to say men eating women by way of a 'natural' technology of observation. They were, to return to the title of the *FHM* magazine considered earlier, *manimals*.[13]

The films were nevertheless premised on a more complexly gendered articulation of the relation between animality, technology and the human body than this first account might suggest. On the one hand, numerous 'extra-textual' or para-cinematic descriptions of the making of the films (in newspapers, magazine articles, TV documentaries and later DVDs) tended to emphasize the *technological prowess* of the 'animals', which were paraded as superb machines capable of performing many of the forms of kinesis associated with the animals themselves. But, at the same time, from *Anaconda* to *Arachnophobia* nature had to be conquered by technological means, which only or mainly men used in hunting for *Natura horribilis*. However, again and again, the natures in question seemed capable of eluding technological control. In some cases, technologies that had always worked before, as in the case of the 'normal' insecticide used by the scientist and then by the exterminator in *Arachnophobia*, were incapable of stopping the naturally superior animals. In other cases, the natures had themselves acquired a 'technological edge', as in the case of the fish in *Piranha*, which had been endowed with the capacity to breed in fresh or salt water; or indeed again with the sharks in *Deep Blue Sea*, which had a superior intelligence. Again and again, characters described the animals in terms of 'killing machines' or other mechanistic metaphors. But, surprisingly, more often than not such techno-beasts could only be killed by recourse to comparatively primitive and 'human' means, with a favourite being fire or other comparatively simple forms of combustion. It might thereby be suggested that, even if the animals acted as a kind of cyborg-like prostheses of masculinist forms of observation and desire, it was frequently only possible to control them with the most 'natural' – if not most 'naturally male' – of forces.

By the 1990s, a number of aspects of the gendering of the films had changed. For example, in *Anaconda* (1997), the gender politics mentioned above seemed to be both contradicted and confirmed in so far as there was a return to a *female* nature: Danny Rich exclaimed 'Bitch!' when he apparently succeeded in killing the anaconda which only killed (that is to say 'coiled') *male* protagonists. In the same film, greater scope was given to the female lead – played by Jennifer López – no doubt thanks in part to her celebrity value within the star system, and a calculus of her 'sex appeal' to masculinist voyeurs.

These and other transformations aside, it can be suggested that the animal attack films played a relatively complex role with respect to the institution of modern imaginary nature, and the environmentalist imaginary in particular. With respect to the former, it would appear that the films reproduced that most modern of boundaries by creating an absolutely 'other' nature capable of destroying humans. But this aspect was made more complex, and perhaps became a form of articulating the more recent anxieties associated with 'risk society' in so far as the animals could be read, at the same time, as cyborgs out of control. This was paradoxical in so far as the films tended to overcode the depersonalized, 'random' and seemingly unattributable risks associated with what Beck (1992) describes as a 'reflexive' modernization with their mirror opposite: a risk, a *natural* risk, that could (eventually) be clearly identified, embodied, personalized and, even if it was 'hard to kill', destroyed by the heroism of 'a few good men'.

I have now explained one of the ways in which the expression 'man-eater' both was and was not an appropriate one in the context of animal attack films. I would however like to conclude this section by noting one additional way in which it remained grossly inappropriate. Especially in the case of sharks, it was actually 'man' (*sic*) that did most of the eating of the non-human animals. Beyond the overfishing with long lines and other even more destructive industrial fishing systems, *Jaws* is widely credited with having unleashed first a hatred and then a fascination for white sharks, and sharks more generally. While the outright killing that reportedly followed the release of the film may have been replaced with a greener discourse about the need to 'understand' sharks, it seems clear that in this, as in so many other contexts, the mass mediation of nature went hand in hand with the development of tourist industries dedicated to the exploitation of the geographies, floras and faunas that it brought to the attention of publics.

Sustainable developmentalism

Even as animal attack films like *Jaws* were shown on screens throughout the world, the 1970s saw the establishment of the Environmental Protection Agency in the US and, with it, legislation that regulated air and water quality and banned or controlled the levels of many toxic substances – not least, pesticides such as DDT, Heptachlor and Chlordane. In one sense, the EPA could be regarded as a regulator of hygienization; where the emphasis was once on eradicating 'dirt', the by-products of this process and indeed of industrialization more generally now became reclassified as pollution. In Europe, similar agencies developed, and in 1983 members of the Green Party (*Die Grünen*) were elected to West Germany's Bundestag.

By the early 1990s, many assumed that environmentalism was on the cusp of a major breakthrough. In 1992 the first Earth Summit took place in Rio de Janeiro, and significant agreements were hammered out that began to address the new threat of climate change (see Epilogue). In 1995, Greenpeace launched another campaign that managed to sway public opinion against France when Jacques Chirac broke the moratorium on nuclear testing and exploded nuclear devices under the Moruroa Atoll.

By the beginning of the twenty-first century, it had become apparent that such optimism was premature and that, if anything, the environmentalist movement ran the risk of either being incorporated hegemonically as part of mainstream politics and economics or, worse, having its achievements undone by a new wave of neoconservative governments in the United States, the United Kingdom and other industrialized nations.

In order to understand how and why this was the case, it is necessary to consider the emergence of new forms of mass mediation, of what some have described as a 'post-Fordist' political economy and, with it, a neoliberal ideology. Where Fordism was marked by a hegemonic 'social contract' between employers and labourers in the United States (and indeed other parts of the world), post-Fordism involved a shift towards a greater 'flexibility' in this relation. The concept of flexibility or of a 'flexible labour force' dissimulated what was actually a decisive shift in the balance of power towards employers, and particularly towards multinational corporations and the sectors of the political establishment that identified most closely with their interests. One of the aspects that made this shift possible was the threat of the multinationals to relocate production facilities to other countries or regions if the local workforce resisted the imposition of low wages or other unfavourable working conditions. For the multinationals, and indeed for the industrialized nation-states in which they were predominantly based, the advantage of this system was that it enabled them to institute a new way of 'exporting' environmental destruction in a way that minimized or eliminated the risk both to the exporting nation-states and to the managers.

The Bhopal disaster in India stands as a catastrophic example of this dynamic. The world's worst chemical disaster took place in India in 1984 when a pesticide plant owned by the US chemical giant Union Carbide released a gas laced with a cocktail of toxic substances into the neighbouring town. While the employees of the factory were given enough warning to leave the plant, no warning was given to the surrounding community; on the contrary, the corporation stands accused of having systematically dissimulated the extent of the risk. Some 20,000 people are thought to have died since the toxic leak, with another 500,000 injured. The president of the US corporation, Warren Anderson, was never brought to trial, and the corporation abandoned the site without properly decontaminating it after paying out the equivalent of approximately US$500 each to some of the victims that survived the catastrophe.

Post-Fordism also entailed a shift in emphasis, from the rationalization of production to the rationalization of consumption. Whereas Fordism was still premised on a relatively simple model of social stratification and marketing – Henry Ford himself reportedly said that a customer could have a Model T of any colour so long as it was black – post-Fordism was associated with increasingly sophisticated forms of 'niche' marketing and increasingly abstract and seemingly all-pervasive forms of advertisement to increase demand for goods.

It is in the context of this dynamic that the rise in the mid- to late 1980s of so-called 'green consumerism' must be understood. Of course, strictly speaking there is no such thing as 'green' consum*erism*: the two terms stand in contradiction. Moreover, it may be argued that 'green consumerism' was actually at least as old as the commodification of symbolic goods promoted on the basis of an appeal to the sublime qualities of represented nature. What changed in the 1980s was that an industry emerged which both recognized and began to promote what the social critic Kevin Hetherington has described as 'expressive identities': identities which were characterized by, amongst other aspects, a quest for 'authentic experiences' and personal growth; an effort to 'recognize' the body and treat it as a focus for well-being and communication with others; a rejection of the instrumental knowledge associated with the predominant forms of science and technology; and, as part of this, the embracing of 'ethnic' traditions or 'alternative' forms of knowledge (Hetherington 1998: 5).

Green consumerism took part in this process by means of a variety of social genres. These included the viewing of natural history documentaries and visiting new zoos, but also travelling to the national parks of countries in Africa and Asia as part of a new wave of 'green' tourism, and engaging in a variety of extreme sports that involved sublime tests of endurance and daring: climbing the most difficult mountains or cliff-sides, surfing the world's biggest waves and so forth. It also involved engaging in 'adventures' that expressed a desire to be 'close' to nature by whale-watching or by swimming with dolphins.

But green consumerism was by no means purely a matter of the consumption of services, or the consumption of symbolic goods. It also involved an element of 'actual' consumption of material objects such as those found in nature stores,[14] or in the numerous outlets that specialized in the sale of organic, fair trade or other ostensibly 'green' goods. These and the practices mentioned earlier suggested a remarkable inversion: the environmentalist imaginary now became the target of a process of capitalist incorporation which, in the practices of high street traders, reified its 'green values' not just by way of the sale of 'green' commodities, but by way of forms of advertising which interpellated media users' green structures of feeling and technologies of the self.[15]

Perhaps the best example of this process could be found in the Body Shop. Established by Anita Roddick and her partner Rod in 1976, the chain promoted the sale of cosmetics and other toiletries on the basis of a naturalistic discourse that sought to identify the retailer with apparently 'ethical' business principles, the use of 'herbal' or organic substances and, in many cases, the products' sourcing in the knowledge and/or geographies of indigenous communities throughout the world.

It is possible to attribute the Body Shop's success simply to its capacity to sell environmentally friendly toiletries. But even if the toiletries *were* 'green' or at any rate *more green* than the usual – a point that was hotly contested by many critics – the Body Shop's success was arguably the result of a rather more complex and paradoxical dynamic. As constructed not only by its actual shop space but, crucially, by its advertisements, leaflets and 'non-traditional' advertisements in the form of numerous media interviews by Anita Roddick, the company articulated a remarkably sophisticated relation between three aspects: a green structure of feeling; a feminized relation to globalization (and indeed to business); and a personalized relation to a new form of hygienization.

A personalized relation to hygienization had long been promoted by the cosmetics industry in advertisements that encouraged a relation of personal intimacy and identification between beauty products and women. What changed was that Roddick was able to link this relation to her own version of 'feminine' globalization: her at once wholesome, 'hippy' and 'caring' feminity, as represented in numerous interviews and advertisements, worked to construct a seemingly essential link between herself and the indigenous groups she claimed to be both assisting and learning from. In turn, this dynamic involved a more or less explicit invocation of a feminized nature, one that apparently gave Roddick the authority to act as a translator between the modern world and an indigenous world that was tacitly constructed as being closer to nature.

The choice of the colours of the brand (dark green and a white font), and the numerous in-store allusions to the ostensibly organic qualities of the products enabled the chain to both produce and reproduce a green structure of feeling, one that attempted to replace the petrochemical qualities of an older form of hygienization with the 'non-artificial' qualities of 'herbal'. Even the one aspect that most clearly signalled the fiction of such an association – the use initially of non-recyclable plastic containers – was dissimulated by an invitation to clients to bring back the containers to have them refilled.

The Body Shop symbolized the ethos of what became known as 'sustainable development'. But even as corporations such as the Body Shop promoted green consumerism in some nations and among the middle classes, the post-Fordist logic that drove the new forms of consumption produced a growing gap between the rich and the poor within industrialized nations, within industrializing nations and, in many cases, between the two sets of countries. In 1987 the World Commission on Environment and Development (WCED) published a report that offered what seemed like a damning critique of this dynamic. The report, known as the Brundtland Report after its widely respected chairwoman, argued in favour of policies that promoted what it described as 'sustainable development', a concept that it defined as development which met the present needs without compromising the ability of future generations to fulfil their own needs (WCED 1987).

From the point of view of its propagation as the dominant discourse in environmental policy circles, the success of this discourse was remarkable. Throughout the 1990s, the Brundtland and some seventy other definitions of sustainable development (Holmberg and Sandbrook 1992) provided the basis not just for numerous conferences, publications and developmentalist action plans, but also for the growth of bureaucracies of environmental planners on the international, national, regional and corporate levels. The work of these planners – and of the academic institutes and programmes that sprang up around them – was to ascertain the 'sustainability' of all manner of socio-economic endeavours. The European Union, for example, called its fifth environmental action plan, which was to be operationalized between 1994 and 2000, 'Towards Sustainability'.

Some of the older environmentalist NGOs incorporated, and were themselves incorporated by, the subjectivities associated with this discourse. Perhaps unsurprisingly, the so-called 'green fundamentalism' of these NGOs gave way to more pragmatic policies. For example, organizations such as the World Wide Fund for Nature and the World Conservation Union (IUCN), two of the most prominent members of the 'Top Ten' group of environmentalist NGOs – conducted what they described as 'sustainability assessments' of environmental objectives. These objectives were shown to be, in the words of one journalist, 'wanting, both morally and practically' (Pearce 2003: 42). The NGOs found that they had failed to take into account the needs of the social groups closest to the nature parks and reserves that became the focus of their efforts during the 1950s and 1960s, if not earlier.

In some respects, this critique was welcome and long overdue: as I have already noted, from the nineteenth century onwards, the imaginary nature promoted by colonial and then neocolonial discourses had transformed local inhabitants into 'poachers' in their own ancestral lands. As late as 1985, Dian Fossey, the renowned naturalist, had waged war on 'poaching' and had steadfastly opposed any tourism whatsoever in Rwanda; it was only after her murder that new policies were introduced and the population of the mountain gorillas that she sought to protect began to recover. In Kenya, a country where over one tenth of the land was transformed into parks and reserves, a former park director argued that that the majority of animals still spent most of their time outside the parks because human activities promoted conditions that enabled a higher density of wildlife (Pearce 2003: 42).

However welcome the shift to policies consistent with the aims of 'social' environmentalism – aims that had been advocated unsuccessfully for decades by green groups on the left (for an overview, see Merchant 1992) – the risk now was that 'green fundamentalism' might be replaced by an even more conservative 'neoliberal fundamentalism'. Indeed, many environmental activists expressed concern that the 'sustainable development' discourse had been co-opted by the dominant systems of production and that, as such, it was little more than a license for economic growth (Holmberg and Sandbrook 1992). Events over the following decades were to prove this assessment to be more than justified.

Epilogue

CLIMACTIC CHANGE

> We are about taking back public space from the enclosed private arena. At its simplest this is an attack on cars as a principal agent of enclosure.
>
> Reclaim the Streets

Global warnings

Shortly after the Brundtland Report was published in 1987, another report was published whose implications were to have far-reaching consequences for the mass mediation of nature.

In response to many climatologists' growing concerns over the possibility of climate change, in 1988 the United Nations set up the Intergovernmental Panel on Climate Change (IPCC). The function of the IPCC was to assemble a team of experts to investigate the extent of the threat posed by climate change. The panel reported in May 1990 that its members were certain that human activities were substantially increasing atmospheric concentrations of greenhouse gases, leading to an average increase of global surface temperatures of 1°C by 2030, and 3°C by the year 2100.

In fact, as a Greenpeace counter-report (Leggett 1990) and the IPCC's own later reports were to reveal, this was a conservative estimate; the third report, published in 2001, suggested that the figures were more likely to be of 1.4°C to 5.8°C (http://www.ipcc.ch/pub/syreng.htm, accessed 25 July 2004). Depending on the intensity of the phenomenon, the report suggested that climate change would produce an uneven distribution of threats; it was, however, clear that 'Overall, climate change [was] projected to increase threats to human health, particularly in lower income populations, predominantly within tropical/subtropical countries' (http://www.ipcc.ch/pub/syreng.htm: 9). But in the following years it became increasingly clear that a change of 4°C or more was likely, and this would lead to adverse effects for *all* regions, contradicting the politically convenient notion that only the poorest and most marginalized groups would suffer the effects.

The initial errors notwithstanding, the findings of the Intergovernmental Panel on Climate Change, along with those of the Brundtland Report, created a context for the first Earth Summit (the UN Conference on Environment and Development) which took place in Rio de Janeiro in 1992 and involved 153 countries. This was a historic event in any number of ways, not least because it inaugurated a new – or seemed to inaugurate a new – planetary consciousness, one which was premised on the possibility of, and indeed called for, *global* action based on the observation of multiple dicent indexical legisigns of climate change. The conference agreed on a new convention on biodiversity, and also on an action plan, Agenda 21, which had at its core the recommendation that all nations should produce their own sustainable development strategies. Aside from highlighting the need for a 'healthy and productive life in harmony with nature' as a basic right for all humans, the Rio Summit identified environmental protection and the eradication of poverty as integral aspects of any economic development process (www.un.org/esa/sustdev/agreed.htm, accessed 10 June 2004).

Even as the declaration weakened the classification of the economic and environmental spheres, its rhetoric, and that of much of the media coverage of it, weakened the classification, in principle at least, of nation states as sovereign entities by way of an appeal to 'One World' globalism. This discourse was symbolized by an image of a tree with four clusters of foliage upon which could be discerned outlines of the Americas, Europe/Asia/Africa, the Arctic and Antarctica. This image was a development of what started out as an iconic sinsign of the planet, but which itself became an iconic legisign: the 'Blue Marble'[1] photograph taken of the Earth by the Apollo 17 crew in 1972. Throughout the last three decades of the twentieth century, this image was used extensively by environmentalist groups as a dicent symbol of the planet's environmental unity.

But this latest form of planetary consciousness came after some four centuries of nation-building, and the leaders of many nations now employed the classifications of nation-statism to resist the imposition of global agreements. Indeed, while it might have been assumed that the crescendo of a green planetary consciousness and the seemingly incontestable indexes of a looming environmental catastrophe would give new life to the most utopian of green agendas, subsequent events proved otherwise. During the decade that followed the Rio Summit, it became apparent that the 'One World' utopianism was premature, if not misguided. Although a treaty, the Kyoto Agreement, was negotiated in 1997 that compelled participating countries to reduce their greenhouse gas emissions by 5.2 per cent vis-à-vis their levels in 1990, not all countries subscribed to the pact. Indeed, the agreement only came into force in early 2005 after Russia finally signed up to it. According to the International Institute for Sustainable Development, in the ten years that followed the Rio Summit the consumerism analysed in Chapter 8 came more fully into its own; the world's richest nations failed to deliver on the commitments made at the summit, the gap between the rich and the poor increased, as did levels of consumption in the richest nations. For example, in the decade ending in 1999, the number of miles travelled per vehicle in the US and in the European Union had risen by 80 per cent, and air traffic had doubled (http://www.iisd.org/briefcase/ten+ten_failures3.asp, accessed 25 July 2004).

The Johannesburg Summit in 2002 failed to address these problems and confirmed, if anything, the power of governments and institutions with neoliberal agendas to dominate environmental policymaking. In this context, many environmentalists accepted the theory of a 'green backlash' (Rowell 1996). This 'backlash' may have begun as a conspiracy led by governments and institutions interested in maintaining global dependence on an oil-based economy, and preventing the *economic* fallout of treating climate change as a significant risk. But by the end of the century it had become an overt coalition that was led by right-wing administrations in the US. In 1992, George Bush Sr threatened not to attend the Rio Summit, famously arguing that US national interests were 'non-negotiable', and in 2001 George W. Bush enacted this dictat when he announced that his own government would not ratify the Kyoto Agreement.

This news was accompanied by reports that some media corporations in the US were actively censoring information that might affect public opinion regarding climate change. For example, it was reported that weathercasters on *The Weather Channel* and at least one other US commercial channel were forbidden by their corporate owners from using the term 'global warming' in newscasts; it was alleged that this might put the broadcasters in 'a very difficult political situation' (Seabrook in Wilson 2002: 251). The front page of the 29 January 2006 edition of the *New York Times* apparently provided evidence of the ongoing nature of such censorship when it reported that NASA 'top climate scientist' James E. Henson had been pressured by the Bush administration to refrain from giving speeches that called for a prompt reduction in greenhouse gases linked to global warming.[2]

However valid, accounts of conspiracy and censorship could not explain on their own why the apparently 'clear and present danger' posed by climate change did not lead to the emergence of a coalition capable of stopping the 'green backlash'. Some accounts suggested that the prevalent forms of mass mediation, in the form of news reporting, either provoked confusion or obeyed a logic of cycles of reporting that failed to sustain attention with respect to what was an ongoing and worsening crisis.[3] It is, however, also possible to argue that climate change posed a textbook case of what I described in earlier chapters as the new risk politics: here was a risk that, initially at least, could only be 'modelled', that is to say articulated, by way of arguments whose explicitly legisignal status were at odds with the kind of icons produced in the context of the prevalent representations of *Natura horribilis*. To be sure, as I noted earlier, the IPCC itself suggested that climate change entailed an unequal distribution of risks, with some countries or regions of countries more likely to be affected than others; if temperatures did not rise beyond 3°C or so, climate change might have 'beneficial' effects in some regions.

But the argument of such a risk politics overlooked the broader *cultural* economy of post-Fordism: climate change required lifestyle change, and in a world driven by consumerism – a consumerism that made even the sinsigns of a disastrous nature a matter of economic exploitation – such a change required, or if imposed could provoke, nothing less than a revolution. In this context, the widespread expectation amongst many social observers that disaster films such as *The Day After Tomorrow* (2004) might radically alter environmental politics in the US initially seemed naïve. While the verdict had to remain open in the absence of audience research on the matter (and even audience research would not necessarily prove anything), the film arguably *undermined* its capacity to mobilize viewers to engage with the phenomenon of climate change thanks to a number of its narrative innovations. On one level, the film continued a long established tradition, both in cinema and television, of transforming *Natura horribilis,* in this case disastrous meteorolgical conditions, into a spectacle. But the film took this 'disastrous spectatorship' to new heights in combining nearly all of the extreme forms of celestial and earthly disturbance in one film: the film included hurricanes and hailstones, tsunamis and twisters, blizzards and even zoo wolves on the rampage. Moreover, instead of going from a 'normal' everyday life to terrible scenes of devastation and the struggle to survive the aftermath of the disaster – the hallmark of disaster movies such as *Twister* or *The Perfect Storm* – it plunged viewers straight into what became a relentless saga of 'bad weather'. This rendering of *Natura horribilis* arguably fitted well with a form of mass mediation that involved the production of – and the production of a demand for – the hyperkinetic, energetic interpretants of the kind that climate change itself might well provide. In short, the film arguably worked to exaggerate the risks involved as part of a cinematic strategy of exploitation of climate change. At least on the level of audio-visual mass mediation, the film was evidence, if any were needed, that capitalist institutions were more than capable of incorporating climate change as part of a money-making venture.

This logic took a significant turn from late 2004 onwards, when a series of catastrophic sinsigns of nature – most notably the tsunami in the Indian Ocean, and especially a devastating series of hurricanes in the Caribbean in 2005 – provided at once paradigmatic dicents of the possible effects of climate change, and pretexts for increasingly spectacular forms of 'storm-chasing'. Even as the risk politics of climate change continued to be fought ferociously and culminated in the extraordinarily weak statement made by the parties that participated in Montreal's 2005 United Nation Climate Change Conference,[4] the representation of the firstness of such natural catastrophes suggested for the first time that the materiality of such a nature might supersede the logic of spectacle described by Guy Debord (1995) and others, i.e. a nature premised on the logic of an 'immense accumulation of spectacles' for which and in which 'all that once was directly lived has [now] become representation' (Debord 1995: 12). Of course, the disasters continued to be *represented*. But the fact that they occurred in industrialized nations (as in the case of New Orleans), or in sites frequented by the tourists of industrialized nations (as in the case of the 2004 tsunami), apparently drove home to many audiences the possibility that in future they might experience such a nature first-hand, that is to say, by way of the firstness of directly experienced and lived environmental disaster.

In the interim, environmental scientists provided plenty of information to feed this concern. In January 2005, the UK's *Horizon* series described the paradoxical threats posed by the eventual *elimination* of 'global dimming', the recently discovered phenomenon of a reduction of sunlight caused by pollution, and whose reversal thanks to better pollution control might itself increase global warming. Almost a year later, it was reported that scientists measuring the flow of the Gulf Stream detected what appeared to be a 30 per cent decrease in the circulation when compared to measurements taken 12 years earlier (http://www.guardian.co.uk/climatechange/story/0,,1654804,00.html, accessed 1 December 2005). In early 2006, the British government published a rather misleadingly titled report, *Avoiding Dangerous Climate Change*, which suggested that both the Antarctic and Greenland ice sheets were likely to melt as part of the process of global warming. In the report's foreword, Tony Blair said that 'It is now plain that the emission of greenhouse gases, associated with industrialization and economic growth from a world population that has increased six-fold in 200 years, is causing global warming at a rate that is unsustainable' (Blair quoted in www.guardian.co.uk/climatechange/story/0,,1698217,00.html, accessed 30 January 2006). Whereas the statement delicately dissimulated the UK's own responsibility in the process by invoking a Malthusian discourse, this and numerous other reports quite suddenly transformed what initially seemed like little more than the fictional excess of *The Day After Tomorrow* into veritable dicent symbols of catastrophe.

But despite some signs of mobilization – represented for example, by the US Mayor's Climate Protection Agreement,[5] and most promisingly by a variety of anti-consumerist movements[6] – there was little evidence of a sea change in the politics of everyday life, let alone the everyday life of politics. The IPCC's insistence that some areas might benefit from global warming, the blurring of the boundary between the signs of spectacle and the signs of nature, and, above all, the formidable strength of the everyday non-formal pedagogies of consumerism suggested that it was unlikely that anything like a concerted response would emerge any time soon within most countries, let alone on a global basis.

Biotechnology

Even as the challenges of climate change became apparent, so did those posed by more unambiguously 'man-made' natures. By the beginning of the twenty-first century, environmentalists were forced to compete for the attention of the media of mass communication in a rather different arena of mass mediation: the field constituted by developments in biotechnology and, as part of this, the practice of genetic engineering – the transformation of the genetic make-up of a cell by transferring parts from one cell to another, or by changing the cell outright.

As in the case of climate change, the stakes in this process were extraordinarily high. From the point of view of environmental activists, biotechnology, and in particular genetically modified (GM) foods, suddenly seemed to make real the possibility, long resisted by environmentalists and humanists alike, that at least some aspects of nature might ultimately become impossible to classify (insulate) from culture. By contrast, for the corporations with the greatest investment in biotechnology, the technology was almost literally a goose modified genetically to lay golden eggs.

It is thus perhaps not surprising that, whereas environmentalists emphasized the dramatic changes instituted by the new technologies, corporations like Monsanto attempted to frame the technology in a manner that minimized or even concealed the classification of the new techniques vis-à-vis older forms of genetic manipulation. Perhaps the most brutal form of this new occultism could be found in the biotech industry's efforts to flood the market with genetically modified (GM) foods without label, so that the classification between GM and non-GM foods might be blurred by virtue of a *fait accompli*; this both on the level of the consumption of GM foods and in the production of foods by contaminating so-called 'organic' foods. In the US this strategy initially appeared to be successful; as late as 2004, a search for a definition of biotechnology on Google, the most widely used search engine on the Internet, produced definitions originating in US websites that almost always began by emphasizing the continuity between biotechnology and existing forms of biological modification.

By contrast, in the UK environmentalists and journalists alike engaged in what seemed at first like a successful pedagogy, one that made very visible the risks associated with GM foods. Greenpeace, for example, staged campaigns in which its members were photographed destroying trial GM crops wearing white protective suits. The use of the suits was intended to conjure qualisigns of the dark side of hygienization: GM foods were made to seem 'toxic' in the way that Heptachlor and Chlordane had once been shown to be. Some of the press further represented GM foods as 'Frankenstein Foods', a headline coined by the UK's *Daily Telegraph* in 1997, mobilizing a remarkably anachronistic but effective icon of monstrosity (Turney 1998 and Allan 2002). No doubt the ground was prepared by the fact that, only a few years earlier, the UK had witnessed the extraordinary BSE (Bovine Spongiform Encephalopathy) or 'mad cow' debacle, which became a dicent symbol of both the nature of industrial food production and the nature of the 'new' environmental risks in the age of 'invisible' threats. Even the so-called 'transparent' and independent BSE Inquiry[7] in the UK into the disaster failed to critically establish the responsibility that was shared by the UK government's former Ministry of Agriculture, Fisheries and Food (MAFF), the industrial farming community and eventually all those members of government who sought to conceal, or dissimulate the significance of the risks involved. Unwittingly the government of Margaret Thatcher sowed the seed of an extraordinarily deep-seated hermeneutics of suspicion amongst consumers in the UK: not just one – the original Conservative – but two governments – Labour too – came to be suspected for aiding and abetting the kind of economic laissez-fairism that had been repeatedly shown to be responsible for environmental catastrophes.[8]

In the case of biotechnology, an additional element fuelled such suspicions. However anachronistic, the 'Frankstein' image conveyed something of the potential of the technology, which could now use recombinant DNA to transform organisms on the level of genes. Recombinant DNA entailed a dramatically new technique that was developed by biologists in universities in California in 1973 – the 'same' California of Yosemite, of Muybridge's photographic experiments, and of the 'landmark' decision by the Marshall court. The technology involved the recombination of the genes of two unrelated organisms in a manner that transcended not only the 'species barrier' but indeed any 'real world' possibility of forming a new organism by way of a breeding process based on 'real time'. If it was always true that the classification of species was susceptible to challenge in so far as it involved a legisignical dimension, biotechnology had the paradoxical effect of reminding us of the extent to which species categorization were, and remain, a matter of dicent indexical *legisigns*.

Henceforth, the existing categorization, and indeed the very category of the species, would no longer be classifiable as an unproblematic, that is rhematic, indexical legisign. In principle, scientists would now be able to 'mix and match' genes from any combination of species in order to create any organism, so long as it 'worked'. The transcendence of natural reproductive boundaries *and* the ability to entrely bypass the usual space–time limitations of the older genetic technologies meant that, by the beginning of the twenty-first century, biotechnologists could clone a sheep from an adult cell; successfully fuse human skin cells and rabbit eggs to create the first human chimeric embryos; or bypass the need for a male-imprinted set of chromosomes in order to produce an offspring from two female mice. In 2005 it was further reported that the experiments with lengthening lifespan were also achieving some success. The ultimate technology of biological displacement was apparently in the process of being invented.

If, as I suggested in the introductory chapter, it was still possible and indeed necessary to speak of a material nature, biotechnology marked the culmination of a process for which the discourse of 'hybrid' nature not only provided meaningful categories, but forced a radical reconceptualization of everyday use of the notion of nature in a growing number of contexts.

Reclaiming the streets

How to respond to the threats of climate change and biotechnology, and who might lead the responses in the wake of the hegemonic success of the institutions pushing the discourse of sustainable developmentalism?

By the middle of the first decade of the twenty-first century, it seemed unlikely that the 'traditional' environmentalist non-government organizations would do so. As I began to suggest earlier, Greenpeace changed the focus of some of its campaigns to meet the new challenges. But after its successes in the 1970s and 1980s, the organization began to find it more and more difficult to gain access to the media of mass communication. As noted by John Gummer, the former minister for the environment during the last Conservative government in the UK, and the man who assured the UK public that eating beef burgers was perfectly safe at the height of the BSE food crisis, 'Greenpeace's stunts have to be ever more audacious if they are to catch the headlines. The media is much more cynical about these things than they were' (http://society.guardian.co.uk/aid/comment/0,,1127206,00.html, accessed 1 October 2003).

A significant motivation for this cynicism may have been the disastrous *Brent Spar* campaign in the mid-1990s, and indeed the increased awareness amongst politicians and publics alike that Greenpeace was now engaging in an explicit dynamic of mass mediation which entailed a form of 'vertical' integration: Greenpeace employed the latest technologies – including the Internet – to feed the media with its own signs.

An article published in 1995 by the journal *Business Video* (Curtis 1995) revealed how far Greenpeace had come since Amchitka. The article described in some detail the function and facilities of the Greenpeace Communications centre in London. The centre provided press, stills, video and Internet services to Greenpeace International. As the author put it, 'All the local Greenpeace offices have their own press departments, but when the group's actions have implications that reach beyond national boundaries, then Comms steps in' (Curtis 1995: 18). During Greenpeace's second Moruroa campaign, the centre provided JPEG stills of French commandos storming the SV Rainbow Warrior for the front pages of the *Sydney Morning Herald*, the *New York Times* and the *Washington Post* (Curtis 1995: 19). The pictures were also uploaded to a Greenpeace website as a QuickTime movie. There was such demand for the clip that the site was overloaded, and 'the BBC, which has an advanced web site, saw how frantic the demand [was] for the material . . . and offered to take the QuickTime clip and hold it on their own system to be accessed' (Curtis 1995: 20). This helpfulness was to cost the BBC dearly when the UK government accused it of putting forward Greenpeace's views during the *Brent Spar* campaign.

At about the same time that Greenpeace began to lose some of its power to engage with the media of mass communication, a new form of environmentalist direct action began to emerge in the UK, and then in the rest of the world. In the 1990s, a new generation of environmental activists engaged in protests that eventually instituted what was in some respects a radical departure from the modern imaginary of nature. The protests started out as road protests when an alliance of groups attempted to stop the Conservative government in the United Kingdom from transforming physical spaces of outstanding natural beauty into motorways.

These protests, which at an early stage continued to reproduce the modern nature–culture classification, received what was, on the whole, sympathetic coverage
from the UK's media (Wykes 2000).

But during the mid- to late 1990s a remarkable transformation took place.
The earlier forms of protest, centred largely around the protection of rural parts
of the UK that were under threat by road building programmes, began to give
way to a rather more radical form of subversion, one that transferred the location
and justification of protest to the city, and indeed to the spheres of *everyday* urban
life. One of the groups involved, Reclaim the Streets, combined anarchist forms
of organization (or as its members put it, 'dis-organization'), with situationist
aesthetics, and extensive use of the Internet and mobile phones to plan protests
that in some respects turned the environmentalist imaginary on its head. As one
Reclaim the Streets website put it:

> Ultimately it is in the streets that power must be dissolved: for the streets
> where daily life is endured, suffered and eroded, and where power is
> confronted and fought, must be turned into the domain where daily life
> is enjoyed, created and nourished. The street is an extremely important
> symbol because your whole enculturation experience is geared around
> keeping you out of the street. . . . The idea is to keep everyone indoors.
> So, when you come to challenge the powers that be, inevitably you find
> yourself on the curbstone of indifference, wondering 'should I play it
> safe and stay on the sidewalks, or should I go into the street?' And it
> is the ones who are taking the most risks that will ultimately effect the
> change in society.
> (http://www.reclaimthestreets.net/, accessed 12 July 2004)

On the same website, the group explained that:

> We are about taking back public space from the enclosed private arena.
> At its simplest this is an attack on cars as a principal agent of enclosure.
> It's about reclaiming the streets as public inclusive space from the private
> exclusive use of the car. But we believe in this as a broader principle,
> taking back those things which have been enclosed within capitalist cir-
> culation and returning them to collective use as a commons.
> (http://www.reclaimthestreets.net/, accessed 12 July 2004)

The reference to the commons was a critique of the capitalist tenets of neoliberalism, but also a reference to the history that this book began by considering.
The implication was that the loss of the commons had happened not once but
repeatedly in the history of modern culture, and indeed it continued to take place.
RTS was now suggesting not that 'nature ought to be saved', in the manner of
Greenpeace and an earlier generation of environmentalist mediation, but that the
continuing loss of a collective *social* space ought now to be redressed, and *could* be

redressed. This process ought to take place not in the countryside but in the *cities* and their streets.

At a time when, in the UK and elsewhere, democratically elected governments were instituting increasingly draconian surveillance apparatuses and laws restricting civil liberties,[9] the campaigns of RTS and other similar groups took the form of increasingly evanescent sinsigns, which either were not covered by the news media or were represented in ways that reduced their campaigns to the dicent symbols of stereotypical anarchy: the destruction of public spaces or private property. Sympathetic coverage by independent media of communication on the Internet such as Indymedia provided alternative representations that, at least at the time this book was being completed, remained free to offer sharply dissenting discourses, but still struggled to overcome the hegemony of the predominant forms of mass mediation, and, as part of this, mass distribution.

These and other forms of environmental activism remained very much in flux by the middle of the first decade of the twenty-first century. Two things nonetheless seemed clear: first, the success or failure of the campaigns of the different groups was and would continue to be a matter of mass mediation, and that their fate would ultimately reside not just in the strength of their arguments but in the manner in which they engaged with these processes. One of the factors that made mass mediation more difficult and complex by the beginning of the twenty-first century was that it involved a growing proliferation of forms of communication for increasingly 'distracted' publics – or at least publics needing to attend to a growing number of 'personal' media – even as new forms of observation continued to emerge that required, indeed *demanded*, increasingly concentrated forms of attention. Jonathan Crary (1999) both historicizes and sums up this contradiction when he suggests on the one hand that, since the mid-1800s, perception has been 'fundamentally characterized by experiences of fragmentation, shock, and dispersal'; but on the other hand that, since the later nineteenth century, there has also been 'an imperative of a concentrated attentiveness' as a function of the disciplinary organization of labour, education, mass consumption and, we might add, mass mediation. Perhaps the medium that best exemplified this trend was the Internet, that heterotopia of heterotopias, but also that great devourer of attentive space–time.

Second, at the very moment when the category of material nature seemed to be becoming obsolete, events occurred that appeared to preserve the logic that I have described in terms of the dedoubling of nature. On the one hand, and most obviously, it remained the case that a variety of natural events could quite literally erupt as dicent sinsigns but also as dicent symbols of a nature not reducible – or 'productible' – to the categories of hybridity. But, equally if not more significantly, even in the contexts that best lent themselves to an analysis of the kind proposed by postmodern scholars, it remained both possible and necessary to speak of a nature that was not simply a 'third nature', and whose material forces remained very much the forces that they had always been. The possibility, for example, of herbicide-resistant superweeds such as were reportedly discovered by the Centre for Ecology and Hydrology in the UK[10] might well be interpreted as a sign of the continuing importance of something akin to first nature – a nature of possibility, and i-mediacy – even in the processes most extensively transformed by human intervention. Indeed, the concern with biotechnological processes going amok suggested, however paradoxically, that there *was* a certain continuity between the pre- and post-GM organisms – albeit not the one that the GM scientists desired, or indeed the one that the emergent industry would wish to highlight: a continuity in the capacity of the otherwise fundamentally different organisms to cross-pollinate or indeed cross-contaminate each other.

In so far as this is a valid assessment, it is possible to return to the Ndoki and to interpret it from a rather different perspective from the one introduced in the first chapters. Far from being an anachronism in the negative sense of this term, the Ndoki may be interpreted as a dicent symbol of a process that in some respects is at least as old as the oil palm nuts that Fay finds in the region's rivers. The process in question involves the human intervention in natural spaces which admittedly become something other than purely 'natural space', but whose human transformations may, in the fullness of time, become little more than specks in the context of the sublimity of forces that are far more powerful than anything that scientists might conjure.

In saying this I do not mean to deny the power of biotechnology or indeed of what now clearly seems a devastating human-induced form of climate change. Nor do I wish to justify, dismiss or somehow legitimize what remains a fundamentally domineering form of relating to nature among the vast majority of modern subjects. Rather, the point is to qualify the tendency to dismiss the space of the nature, the material nature, by suggesting that the nature that has reclaimed the Ndoki's plantations remains very much that: a *nature* whose capacity to rewild remains, at least for the time being, undiminished and fundamentally undetermined by the interventions of humankind.

Appendix

THE NATURE OF PEIRCE

Mediating Nature offers what I have described as a 'social semeiotic' problematization of the nature of mass mediation. The spelling of 'semeiotic' is deliberate, and refers to the work of Charles Sanders Peirce, in particular, his phenomenology and semeiotic theory. In the following pages I offer an introduction to his work.

Peirce's pragmatism

The decision to use Peirce's theory is based on two general considerations. The first of these involves the semeiotic character of at least some aspects of the process of mass mediation. Put simply, in so far as the mass mediation of nature involves representation, then it is necessary to explain the nature of representation. This point may seem banal or old-fashioned at a time when some researchers in cultural geography have called for the development of 'non-representational' theory (see for example, Thrift 1996, 1999), and when much research in media studies seems driven by audience research. In both fields, it has been apparent for some time that the pendulum has swung from what might be described as a form of 'semioticism' – an emphasis, or even overemphasis, on semiotic analyses of 'texts' – to what might be described as a form of neo-empiricism: an emphasis, or even an overemphasis on the 'lived' aspects of culture.

The critique of 'representationalist' approaches certainly has its merits. My own stance vis-à-vis this question is that, long before the present forms of empiricism came into vogue, Charles Sanders Peirce proposed a pragmatist or, as he eventually called it, a *pragmaticist* philosophy that employed the methods of logic – Peirce's general term for semeiotics – in order to discern the 'total' meaning of 'intellectual concepts' *in the course of habitual action*. I emphasize this last aspect because Peirce argued that the pragmatist ought to be concerned not so much with 'first conjectures' or 'experimental ideas' that a subject might produce in the course of her/his everyday life – what he called first logical interpretants – but rather with the sedimentation of such ideas into *habitual* forms of practice, the final or 'real' logical interpretant. Peirce defined habit as a 'readiness to act in a

241

certain way under given circumstances and when actuated by a given motive'; and he defined belief as 'a deliberate, or self-controlled, habit' (CP 5.480). It was this 'final' or 'real' logical interpretant that Peirce believed was the ultimate subject of study for the pragmatist. As he put it in his characteristically convoluted fashion, concepts, propositions or arguments might be logical interpretants, but not the *final* logic interpretants:

> the habit alone, which though it may be a sign in some other way, is not a sign in the way in which that sign of which it is the logical interpretant is the sign . . . The deliberately formed, self-analyzing habit – self-analyz-ing because formed by the aid of analysis of the exercises that nourished it – is the living definition, the veritable and final logical interpretant.
>
> (CP 5.491)

As I interpret Peirce's theory, it makes the case, quite radically, for what is at once a 'semioticist' theory *and* an 'empiricist' theory. Semiotics, or rather semeiot-ics, gives way to what might well be described as an anthropology of habit. In so far as this is the case, we can speak of a 'semeiotics of everyday habit' and, therefore, of an 'anthropological' semeiotic theory.

A second justification for using Peirce's semeiotics may seem to contradict this 'pragmaticist' orientation. But, as the analysis of the nature of nature in Chapter 1 begins to indicate, the researcher interested in problematizing nature is forced to grapple with truly *metaphysical* problems – problems concerning the fundamental nature of being and reality. Doing so is made difficult not just by the problems themselves but by the fact that, at the beginning of the twenty-first century, cul-tural theory continues to be dominated by the discourse of cultural materialism. In the context of studies of representation, this discourse is enacted in culturalist theories of representation which continue, despite numerous critiques, to appro-priate aspects of the theory of Ferdinand de Saussure (1983); in particular, aspects of his sign model, which to this day still provides many researchers with the predominant model of representation.

A brief account of this model begins to illustrate some of the issues at stake. Early in the twentieth century, Saussure, the founder of modern linguistics, is-sued a welcome challenge to naturalist theories of language by suggesting that representations are not direct analogons of an external reality. Signs, he suggested, are made up of the arbitrary conjunction a mental *signifier*, the 'material'[1] trace in the sounds of phonemes or the traces of writing, and a mental concept or *signified*, which the signifier may give rise to in the interpreter's mind. Using as an example the sign for 'tree', he suggested that:

> The linguistic sign is . . . a two-sided psychological entity . . . [whose] two elements are intimately linked and each triggers the other. Whether we are seeking the meaning of the Latin word *arbor* or the word by which Latin designates the concept 'tree', it is clear that only the connections

institutionalized in the language appear to us as relevant. *Any other connections there may be we set on one side*.

(Saussure 1983: 66–7, emphasis added)

Saussure argued that the conjunction of signified and signifier is arbitrary inasmuch as there is 'no internal connection, for example, between the idea "sister" [the signified] and the French sequence of sounds *s-ö-r* which acts as its signal [the signifier]' (1983: 67). Put differently, nothing 'naturally' connects one part of the sign with the other. Part of Saussure's evidence in making this argument was that every language would have at least a partly different word for sister, and every other term. Saussure did not take this to mean that a signal [or signifier] depended on the free choice of the speaker; in practice, individual speakers have no power, he argued, to alter a sign once it has become established in a linguistic community. On the contrary, 'arbitrary' meant that even if the sign is fundamentally 'unmotivated' in so far as it has no internal connection ('natural' or other) to reality (1983: 68–9), it is the result of something akin to a social contract rendered invisible by habitual linguistic practice.

As I began to note earlier, a number of scholars have critiqued this approach, and indeed have taken Saussure to task especially for the limitations of his structuralist stance (see, for example, Voloshinov 1973; Ricoeur 1974b; Hodge and Kress 1988). But a certain *culturalism* lingers in cultural theory in so far as researchers continue to employ Saussure's dyadic sign model without considering anything like a material *nature* 'in' linguistic (or other) signs. There may be good justifications for this; as I note in Chapter 1, many theories in the social sciences are only too willing to embrace uncritical forms of naturalism. Be that as it may, it seems clear that *cultural* materialism, as developed in much of the cultural theory, stands in an antithetical position to a broader materialism that considers the relation of culture to material *nature*.

I should reiterate that, in some respects, the Saussurean (or 'post-Saussurean') challenge is a welcome one in all those contexts where naturalism dominates the intellectual discourse, and where any 'equivocation' on the 'side' of 'nature' is enthusiastically taken as evidence that it is indeed 'nature all the way down'. But this concern might lead researchers to overlook an equally significant risk: that a silence over the question of nature – or indeed a less than dialectical account of the nature of nature – may well have given sociobiologists the freedom to develop radically naturalist accounts (see for example, Pinker 1994) to which there would appear to be few equally well publicized and debated alternatives.

One of my aims is thus to engage in a kind of 'archaeological' reminder of a philosopher whose theory appears to provide the kernel for a more dialectical account. By contrast to Saussure's theory, Peirce's philosophy developed what was, in his own terms, an 'ideal-realist' metaphysical doctrine which preserves the dimension of dedoubling that I describe in Chapter 1. Peirce was able to theorize this dimension because he was keen to address debates between nominalist and realist philosophers during the nineteenth century. He defined nominalism as

The doctrine that nothing is general but names; more specifically, the doctrine that common nouns, as man, horse, represent in their generality nothing in the real things, but are mere conveniences for speaking of many things at once, or at most necessities of human thought; individualism.

(Peirce quoted by Nathan Houser in EP 1.xxiv)

By contrast, he defined realism – or rather the realist – as 'A logician who holds that the essences of natural classes have some mode of being in the real things; in this sense distinguished as a scholastic realist; opposed to a nominalist' and as 'A philosopher who believes in the real existence of the external world as independent of all thought about it, or, at least, of the thought of any individual or any number of individuals (Peirce quoted by Nathan Houser in EP 1.xxiv).

A number of Peirce scholars have suggested that in the earlier stages of his life's work Peirce was a nominalist, whereas in the later he was a realist (see for example the account provided by Nathan Houser in the introduction to the first volume of *The Essential Peirce*). There are of course different forms of realism, and some dispute this account in the first place (see for example Hausman 1997). There does, however, seem to be widespread agreement that Peirce attempted to develop what was, by his own account, an 'ideal-realist' doctrine, i.e. a metaphysical doctrine that combined realism and *idealism*, the doctrine for which 'the real is of the nature of thought; the doctrine that all reality is in its nature psychical' (Peirce quoted by Nathan Houser in EP 1.xxiv).

In the present inquiry, Peirce's ideal-realist metaphysics arguably works at once to reconcile and to maintain a tension between an approach that privileges a nature of *signs* and one that that privileges the *nature* of signs. This tension is maintained in at least two aspects of his theory which I will now consider: Peirce's phenomenology and his semeiotic theory.

Peirce's phenomenology

In general, the task of phenomenology can be explained with reference to the ancient Greek meaning of *phainomenon*: 'thing appearing to view', as based on *phainein*, 'to show'. Accordingly, the task of a phenomenology is to provide an explanation of a phenomenon as it 'appears to the view', and, more generally, as it appears to human consciousness.

Peirce himself defined phenomenology in radically universalizing terms: as the process of ascertaining and studying 'the kinds of elements universally present in the phenomenon; meaning by the phenomenon, whatever is present at any time to the mind in any way'[2] (EP 2.259). 'The business of phenomenology', he explained, 'is to draw up a catalogue of categories[3] and prove its sufficiency and freedom from redundancies, to make out the characteristics of each category, and to show the relations of each to the others' (CP 5.43).

Peirce's phenomenological 'catalogue' involved just three categories: firstness, secondness, and thirdness.[4] In Peirce's words, 'Firstly come "firstnesses," or positive internal characters of the subject in itself; secondly come "secondnesses," or brute actions of one subject or substance on another, regardless of law or of any third subject; thirdly comes "thirdnesses," or the mental or quasi-mental influence of one subject on another relatively to a third' (CP 5.469).

A somewhat more detailed account of each of these terms benefits from an inversion of this order of presentation. Thirdness is called '*third*ness' because it involves a triadic relation, or a three-way relation between some *object of representation*; a *sign* or *representamen*; and an *interpretant*: the translation of the object of representation, as mediated by the representamen, into other signs. This point itself requires some elaboration. Any given thought is a sign in so far as it interrelates:

- an object of representation (real, imagined, past, present, future, factual or fictional), understood not only as an empirically verifiable object, but also as a quality, relation or fact, something thought to have existed or expected to exist. What constitutes the object of a sign is the fact that it is represented by the sign. This dimension institutes a first level of mediation insofar as it entails a classification – some *thing* or process is distinct enough to be treated as an object *of* representation – and in so far as that thing or process is *for* representation. In the sentence 'Chadwick was attacked by army ants', three examples of objects of representation are Chadwick, the army ants and the very act or process of the attack;
- a representamen, or the 'sign itself', an abstract quality or form of the sign, which presents its object as *an,* and as *that,* object, in some regard or respect. This aspect of the process of representation also entails mediation in so far as a representamen is ineluctably selective or 'partial'; it is a sign in *some* regard or respect. In the above example, each of the words ('Chadwick', 'was', 'attacked' and so forth) is a representamen, but so is the whole sentence;
- and, third, an interpretant, the 'interpretation' that the object of representation gives rise to, as mediated by the representamen. In practice, this process always entails a translation of the representamen into other signs, other representamens. Put differently, a matrix of signs must always be used in representation. The interpretant is not to be mistaken for the individual interpreter of the representamen; it is, more generally, any other sign or network of signs, into which a given sign must be translated in order to be meaningful. To return once again to the above example, the sentence 'Chadwick was attacked by army ants' can only be understood if the reader is able to translate each of the words, and the logic of the words strung together, into other signs by way of a process of more or less unselfconscious interpretation: Chadwick is a *National Geographic* writer, army ants are ants that engage in mass raids etc. All of these words, themselves signs, together constitute the interpretant.

We can say then that a sign is only a sign (or a 'mentality', as Peirce puts it elsewhere) in so far as it institutes this threefold relation, which may be represented diagrammatically as follows:

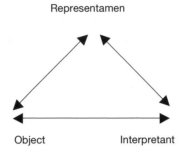

Representamen

Object   Interpretant

Figure 1 Peirce's triadic model of the sign.

Whereas Saussure proposed a dyadic model of signification (the sign as constituted by signified and signifier), and deliberatedly bracketed the question of reference, Peirce developed a triadic conception of signification, for which the question of reference was a central one. As far as Peirce was concerned – and anticipating by almost a century the critiques offered by poststructuralist scholars of Saussure's semiology – without an order of reference, there can be no information, no communication, and so any theory of representation that omits it must be fundamentally flawed.

Semiosis, one might note, is itself a matter of thirdness, just as thirdness is a matter of semiosis. But it is a thirdness that incorporates, and in some respects is produced by, secondness, which Peirce describes as a pre-semeiotic, or 'a-semeiotic', relationship between two entities that act and react with one another. As Peirce puts it in one of his papers:

> When a stone falls to the ground, the law of gravitation does not act to make it fall. The law of gravitation is the judge upon the bench who may pronounce the law till doomsday, but unless the strong arm of the law, the brutal sheriff, gives effect to the law, it amounts to nothing. True, the judge can create a sheriff if need be; but he must have one. The stone's actually falling is purely the affair of the stone and the earth at the time. This is a case of *reaction*. So is *existence* which is the mode of being of that which reacts with other things.
>
> (CP 8.330)

Secondness, by this account, is a matter of a dyadic or twofold relationship between entities that affect each other in a 'real' manner. The notion of the real here entails something akin to an unquestionable event; unquestionable in the twofold sense that it involves some kind of displacement, in time. It might thereby be thought that secondness is a matter of 'cause and effect'. But, as the quote I have just cited indicates, secondness *precedes* or is different from causality in so far as causality is, whatever its 'reality', itself a matter of interpretation: there are a number of different models of causality and, in any case, causality presupposes establishing an *order* of causality (the proverbial 'which came first, the chicken or the egg?'), which is itself, *as order*, a matter of intepretation or thirdness.

What, then, is firstness? This is in some respects Peirce's most slippery, but also his most fascinating category. From one perspective, firstness is a matter of 'monads': single, indivisible entities that nonetheless constitute an integral part of the phenomenological process. From a phenomenological perspective, firstness is a kind of *sine qua non*, a 'requirement' for observation and representation: to attend to something is to treat it, at least in some respects, as some thing, as that *(one) thing*.

There is, however, more to firstness. Peirce was intrigued by the role of chance and possibility in the universe, and became convinced that virtuality – understood not in the current sense of virtual reality in computing, but in the philosophical sense of something that might yet be embodied, emplaced and 'temporealized' – played a positive role in the universe. If the 'big bang' theory of the universe is correct, one might say that the universe was firstness before it 'banged'. But this principle might equally be applied to anything in the universe as it exists today: all kinds of entities are virtual in the sense that they are able to enter into relations with something else. Were this not the case, the universe would not be the universe, and change would not be possible. Firstness is, from this perspective, at once a kind of fundamental 'waiting-to-happen-ness' and an equally fundamental 'is-not-yet-determined-ness' which confounds both determinist forms of thought – the idea that things are determined from the start – and the kind of rationalism that silently informs much social (not to say physical) scientific theory.

Although Peirce was himself arguably very much a rationalist, the notion that his category of firstness critiques rationalism becomes clearer when it is considered that he privileged *feeling* as a matter of firstness. Peirce describes this well when he asks his readers to

> imagine, if you please, a consciousness in which there is no comparison, no relation, no recognized multiplicity (since parts would be other than the whole), no change, no imagination of any modification of what is positively there, no reflexion – nothing but a simple positive character. Such a consciousness might be just an odour . . . or it might be one infinite dead ache . . . it might be the hearing of a piercing eternal whistle. In short, any simple and positive quality of feeling would be something which our description fits that it is such as it is quite regardless of anything else. The quality of feeling is the true psychical representative of the first category of the immediate as it is in its immediacy, of the present

in its direct positive presentness. Qualities of feeling show myriad-fold variety, far beyond what the psychologists admit. This variety however is in them only insofar as they are compared and gathered into collections. But as they are in their presentness, each is sole and unique; and all the others are absolute nothingness to it – or rather much less than nothingness, for not even a recognition of absent things or as fictions is accorded to them. The first category, then, is Quality of Feeling, or whatever is such as it is positively and regardless of aught else.

(CP 5.44)

Peirce's semeiotics

I have thus far dwelt on Peirce's phenomenology. But Peirce's phenomenology can be said to be informed by his semeiotic theory – what Peirce also describes as a theory of logic – and vice versa. The semeiotic theory is informed by his phenomenology in so far as signs are thirdness, but 'carry' firstness and secondness 'within'. The opposite is however also true: Peirce's phenomenology is arguably inherently 'semeiotic' in so far as it has the logic of that semeiotic, and in so far as Peirce is an advocate of a pansemeiotic theory of the universe; as I note in Chapter 1, from Peirce's perspective, the universe is 'suffused' with signs.

It is possible to distinguish between two general aspects of Peirce's semeiotic theory: his 'grammar' of the sign and his sign typology. I have already provided an outline form of the 'grammar' by referring to Peirce's conception of the sign: signs are triadic entities constituted by an object of representation, a representamen, or 'the sign itself', and an interpretant. It is, however, necessary to both reiterate and specify various aspects of this grammar.

First, it cannot be emphasized enough that Peirce's notion of the object of representation is not abjectly empiricist, let alone positivist. As he puts it in one of his more lyrical passages, the object of a sign may be

> a single known existing thing or thing believed formerly to have existed or expected to exist, or a collection of such things, or a known quality or relation or fact, which single Object may be a mode of being, such as some act permitted whose being does not prevent its negation from being equally permitted, or something of a general nature desired, required, or invariably found under certain general circumstances.

(CP 2.232)

Second, any given sign by no means is necessarily or automatically tied to a single object, or vice versa. Peirce explains that a sign may have more than one object (CP 2.230); for example, the *National Geographic* article described in Chapter 1 begins with the sentence 'In a remote pocket of central Africa runs a river called Ndoki' (Allen 1995: 2). The sentence, written by the magazine's editor, is a sign. It has at least four objects: a remote pocket, central Africa, the river Ndoki and the fact that the river *runs*. In such situations, Peirce speaks of a 'complex Object' (CP 2.230).

Objects, whether complex or not, and this is the third point, are made more complex by the fact that they differ in kind: Peirce distinguishes between the 'immediate object', or the object as represented by the sign – in this case what might be described as the denotative features of each and every one of the objects mentioned in the above sentence – and the 'dynamical' object, what he describes as the 'really efficient but not immediately present Object' (CP 8.343). The latter, even more than the former, is, in many but by no means all contexts, a matter of interpretation: we might say, for example, that the dynamical object of Allen's first sentence (quoted above) is the 'Ndoki itself' as mediated by a conservationist discourse, and by the requirement of the magazine to sell as many copies as possible. This order of 'efficacy' might, of course, be inverted.

A fourth specification involves an analogous qualification vis-à-vis the character of the interpretant: Peirce also notes that it is necessary to distinguish between an 'immediate' interpretant – again, the interpretant represented or signified by the sign – and the 'dynamic' interpretant – the 'effect on the mind' 'actually produced' by the sign (CP 8.343). For good measure, Peirce adds to these the 'normal' interpretant, or 'the effect that would be produced on the mind by the Sign after sufficient development of thought' (CP 8.343).

I will now consider the question of a typology of signs. Peirce produced several different typologies of signs. In the following pages I provide an outline of the 1903 typology, which I adopt following the recommendation of Liszka (1996), and indeed the editors of Peirce's *Collected Papers*,[5] that this typology is the most thoroughly described and developed by Peirce.

This typology is usefully presented in the following diagrammatic form proposed by Winfried Nöth (1990).

Table 1 Peirce's 10-class Sign Typology

	Semeiotic		
Phenomenology	Sign as representation of object	Sign as representamen	Sign as interpretant
Firstness	Icon	Qualisign	Rheme
Secondness	Index	Sinsign	Dicent
Thirdness	Symbol	Legisign	Argument

Source: based on similar in Nöth (1990: 45).

Peirce proposes that any sign can be analysed from three trichotomic perspectives which correspond to the intersection of the three formal conditions of the sign (that any sign has an object, a representamen and an interpretant) with the three phenomenological categories of firstness, secondness and thirdness. Peirce used this grid to propose a typology made up of 10 types of signs. I use a number of these types throughout the book and define them at the first point of use. I also provide a definition and an example in the glossary of Peircian terms that appears below.

There are a number of rules that must be explained in order to clarify how Peirce meant to use this typology to *classify* signs. The following is James Liszka's (1996) account of these rules:

- *Composition Rule*: Signs are, by definition, constituted by triadic relations; it follows that every sign must partake of each of the three 'dimensions' or aspects just described. It also follows that all signs must be classified and indeed be classifiable in relation to each of the three central trichotomies.
- *Qualification Rule*: Although Peirce privileges semeiotics, he considers semeiotics to be subordinate to phenomenology. His phenomenology, which itself has a trichotomy as its basis – the categories of firstness, secondness and thirdness – establishes a hierarchy whereby a first can only determine a first, and a third a third. According to Peirce, qualisigns, icons and rhemes are phenomenologically typed as firsts; sinsigns, indexes and dicents as seconds; while legisigns, symbols and arguments are typed as thirds. Consequently, the total number of permutations suggested by the first rule – 27 – is in fact reduced to 10. The following are the 'corollaries' that result from this rule:
  - qualisigns will always represent their objects iconically;
  - qualisigns will always be interpreted rhematically;
  - icons will always be interpreted rhematically;
  - arguments can only represent their objects symbolically.
- *Dominance Rule*: every sign requires an element from each of the three trichotomies, but some subset of these will predominate over the others. For example the fact that a sign is an icon may be more important to one community than the fact that it is also a symbol.
- *Instantiation Rule*: all signs, to be signs, must be instantiated, and therefore each must be a sinsign. This, however, does not mean that a sign will necessarily be interpreted as being *primarily* a sinsign.
- *Inclusion Rule*: Finally, given the principles derived from the phenomenological hierarchy of signs, thirdness always incorporates secondness, and secondness firstness. Symbols are always to some extent iconic and indexical; arguments 'contain' rhemes and dicents; legisigns are to some extent qualisigns and sinsigns.

Especially the last rule suggests the possibility that that the typology becomes so blurred as to be rendered useless. This seems particularly surprising in the light of Peirce's realism. We must not forget, however, that Peirce described himself as an 'ideal-realist', and this fundamental tension comes through quite clearly in this context: on the one hand, Peirce readily engaged in the optimistically realistic task of naming all the names (signs) in the world. But even as he did so, and as if foreseeing the categorical scepticism of many postmodernist scholars, he suggested that all things might nonetheless be named with *all* the names he distinguished, effectively weakening the classifications. But, instead of opposing these two stances, Peirce strove to develop a semeiotic realism that almost seemed to rejoice in apparent contradiction of the two stances. Indeed, it is in keeping with Peirce's own semeiotic approach that any sign is at once primarily a certain kind of sign, even as it partakes of the rest of the types of signs. This play of sameness and difference perhaps characterizes culture, and nature, more generally.

Glossary of Peircian terms

Argument   A sign that, for its interpretant, 'is a Sign of law'; or a sign that 'is said to represent its Object in its character as sign' (CP 2.252). An example of an argument is its namesake, an argument or proposition, such that something is inductively, deductively or abductively (hypothetically) explained: in effect, a metasign in the sense that signs are used to explain signs.

Dicent   A sign that, for its interpretant, is a sign of existence, a sign that something 'does exist'. The animal at the zoo is at once meant to be an instance of the species and 'evidence' that the species does exist. As Peirce notes, a dicent (which he also describes as a 'dicisign' or 'proposition') involves a rheme which describes the fact that it is purportedly interpreting to exist. As he explains, it 'is a sign which distinctly indicates the Object which it denotes, called its *Subject*, but leaves its Interpretant to be what may' (CP 2.95).

Dicent indexical legisign   Any 'general type or law, however established, which requires each instance of it to be really affected by its Object in such a manner as to furnish definite information concerning that Object' (CP 2.260). I offer as examples the signs produced by way of thermometers and other devices designed to provide a conventional sign (legisign) (e.g. measurement with numbers) for the existence (dicent) of a real phenomenon (e.g. heat) by way of an indexical process.

Dicent sinsign   Any 'object of direct experience in so far as it is a sign, and, as such, affords information concerning its Object. This it can only do by being really affected by its Object; so that it is necessarily an Index. The only information it can afford is of actual fact' (CP 2.257).

Dicent symbol   A sign 'connected with its Object by an association of general ideas, and acting like a Rhematic Symbol, except that its intended interpretant represents the Dicent Symbol as being, in respect to what it signifies, really affected by its Object, so that the existence or law which it calls to mind must be actually connected with the indicated Object' (CP 2.262).

Entelechy   When a sign-object is at one and the same time its 'own' representamen and interpretant; in effect, the 'perfect' sign, a sign that is at once a sign and not a sign. Examples include all those objects which 'represent themselves', e.g. animals in zoos, landscapes and so forth. Of course, in one sense there can be no entelechy in so far as the interpretant is, by definition, a matter of translation into other signs. The notion is nonetheless a useful way of highlighting situations where, unlike 'conventional' signs, it is not possible to establish a clear distinction, an 'empirically verifiable' distinction, between the sign-object and the representamen, as occurs even in the 'quasi-entelechy' of naturalistic photography, film or television.

Icon   A sign which 'refers to the Object that it denotes merely by virtue of characters of its own, and which it possesses, just the same, whether any such Object actually exists or not' (CP 2.247). Examples are a photograph, a geometrical diagram, but also a metaphor or verbal simile. Anything, as Peirce explains, can be an icon of anything, 'in so far as it is like that thing and used as a sign of it' (CP 2.247). It follows that all signs must have an iconic dimension, however tenuous or non-obvious to the sign-user.

Iconic legisign   A 'type, in so far as it requires each instance of it to embody a definite quality which renders it fit to call up in the mind the idea of a like object' (CP 2.258). An example may be found in Wordsworth's reference to a topographical model of Switzerland. The type is the model, a conventional albeit highly iconic rendering of the landscape of the 'alpine country'.

Iconic sinsign   Any 'object of experience in so far as some quality of it makes it determine the idea of an object' (CP 2.255). As an example we might consider an encounter with any animal; the encounter, as performance, as event, is a sinsign, and of course the animal is a perfect icon of itself.

Index   A sign that refers to an object 'by virtue of being really affected by that Object'; it involves an icon 'of a peculiar kind' 'but it is not the mere resemblance of its Object, even in these respects which makes it a sign, but it is the actual modification of it by the Object' (CP 2.248). A classical example is smoke as a sign of fire. However, in so far as there is arguably always some kind of real relation between the sign and its object, then all signs must have an indexical dimension, however tenuous or non-obvious.

Interpretant   The third aspect of any sign, which entails the translation of the sign into other signs. Peirce suggested that a sign was a sign only in so far as it involved, amongst other aspects, its interpretation or, as I describe it, its transmediation into other signs. For example, the sign 'Ndoki' is only meaningful – and Peirce would say only a sign – in so far as it can be interpreted by way of other signs: the Ndoki is a rainforest, is located in central Africa, etc. The interpretant should not be confused with the interpre*ter*, the actual or empirical sign user. (See also Object/Sign-Object and Representamen.)

Legisign   A law that is a sign, and which is 'usually' established by humans. Every conventional sign, Peirce suggests, is a legisign, but significantly, the opposite is not true: not every legisign is a matter of convention. The word 'the' is an example of a legisign, but so is any sign that involves some kind of 'type'. By this account, 'Ndoki' is a legisign, but so is a characteristic type of rainforest, in so far as it is itself interpreted as a type. Legisigns require replicas for their instantiation (see Replica).

Object (or sign-object)   A quality, relation or fact, something thought to have existed or expected to exist. The object may be 'empirically verifiable', but might equally be a dream. What constitutes the object of a sign as object is the fact that it is represented by the sign, though it might also be said that what constitutes the sign of an object as sign is the fact that the object represents 'itself' by way of the sign. Objects can be simple or complex (multiple), may be immediate, 'dynamic' or part of an ongoing inquiry, and also 'final' in the sense that they are the object of habitual, conventional practice.

Qualisign   Any quality in so far as it is a sign. For example, the quality of 'untouched' wilderness is an example of a qualisign. In so far as any sign necessarily entails one or another quality, all signs must have a 'qualisignal' dimension.

Replica   The particular instantiation of any given sign. For example, the word 'the' written on this page is a replica of the legisign 'the'.

Representamen   The 'sign itself' or, more precisely, the abstract quality or form of the sign as sign, which presents its object as that object in some regard or respect. (See also Interpretant and Object/Sign-Object.)

Rhematic indexical legisign   Any 'general type or law, however established, which requires each instance of it to be really affected by its Object in such a manner as merely to draw attention to that object' (CP 2.259). An example is the code involving linear perspective, particularly as enacted by devices such as Brunelleschi's *tavoletta*, in which the use of silver paint allowed the painting to reflect the clouds and their motion.

Rhematic indexical sinsign   A replica of a rhematic indexical legisign (CP 2.259). (See Replica.)

Rhematic symbol   A 'sign connected with its Object by an association of general ideas in such a way that its Replica calls up an image in the mind which image, owing to certain habits or dispositions of that mind, tends to produce a general concept, and the Replica is interpreted as a Sign of an Object that is an instance of that concept' (CP 2.261). As an example we might cite a sign using the Linnaean system to classify a plant in a botanical garden. The sign – in itself a replica of the classification – is designed to call up an icon which in turn is associated with a general morphological feature which the plant is supposed to embody.

Rheme   A sign that 'is said to represent its object in its characters merely' (CP 2.252); it 'leaves its Object, and *a fortiori* its Intepretant, to be what it may' (CP 2.95). The rheme entails, in this sense, what appears to be a kind of 'degree-zero' interpretant. We might say, for example, that at least in one respect, an animal at a zoo is interpreted 'rhematically': it is regarded as a re/presentation of the species and, while it modifies the species *as species* by virtue of its individuality and sinsignical quality, it 'is' the species. A rheme or a rhematic sign is, in this sense, what I described as the 'presentation' aspect of 're/presentation'.

Sinsign   The actual 'event' or 'embodiment' of a sign. While qualisigns are abstract qualities, sinsigns are the actual *evenement* or 'performance' that is required to produce or enact the sign. By this account all signs must be 'sinsignical', even if that does not mean that they will necessarily be treated as such. In some cases, signs will be 'primarily' sinsigns in the sense that they will be evanescent signs, or signs which are signs by virtue of *becoming* signs. As examples of this, we might cite the call of a bird in so far as it *occurs*, and in so far as it makes the bird 'appear' to the birdwatcher.

Symbol A symbol is a sign 'which refers to the Object that it denotes by virtue of a law' which Peirce says causes the symbol 'to be interpreted as referring to that Object. It is thus itself a general type or law, that is, a Legisign' (CP 2.249). Examples are the category of 'rainforest', or indeed 'nature'. All signs that are a matter of habit or convention are necessarily symbolic in this sense of the term.

NOTES

INTRODUCTION

1 Most if not all technologies: if it is true that history offers innumerable examples of technologies which have not been appropriated by 'their' culture, it is also true that some modern cultural practices might well be read from the perspective of technologies which have, paradoxically, gone wild: wild in the sense that their 'evolution' cannot be simply explained in terms of human categories.

2 From another perspective, anachrony is arguably an ineluctable aspect of culture (and nature). For an account of this perspective, see Alfonso and Lindahl Elliot (2002).

3 'Problématisation ne veut pas dire représentation d'un objet préexistant, ni non plus création par le discours d'un objet qui n'existe pas. C'est l'ensemble des pratiques discursives ou non discursives qui fait entrer quelque chose dans le jeu du vrai et du faux et le constitue comme objet de pensée' (Foucault 1984: 18).

4 See for example, Williams (1980; 1983); Macnaghten and Urry (1998); or, for a cross-section of essays on the problem, Cronon (1996).

5 Deca-BDE is a flame retardant widely used in TVs, toasters, cushions and curtains. The most recent research suggests that, in fact, the most 'toxic animal' in the Arctic is now the killer whale. See http://news.bbc.co.uk/1/hi/sci/tech/4520104.stm (accessed 12 December 2005).

6 During a holiday in the southern Alps, Foucault's friend Jacqueline Verdeaux invited Foucault to survey magnificent landscapes along their travel route. Foucault 'made a great show of walking off towards the road, saying, "My back is turned to it"' (Eribon 1993: 46).

1 THE NATURE OF NATURE

1 See http://www.time.com/time/covers/0,16641,1101920713,00.html (accessed 12 December 2005).

2 Linden's account describes Fay as a botanist working for Wildlife Conservation International. Subsequent accounts describe him as an ecologist working for the WCS.

3 In September 2005, it was reported that gorillas had been sighted using sticks to test the depth of muddy waters in the Nouabalé-Ndoki Park (see http://news.bbc.co.uk/1/hi/sci/tech/4296606.stm, accessed 30 September 2005).

4 And indeed, not just *metaphorical* traps; see http://www.michaelnicknichols.com/article/camera_traps/ (accessed 25 September 2005).

5 By his own account, Wilson was an assiduous reader of the *National Geographic* whilst growing up in Alabama and in north Florida: 'I . . . thought that there could be no better life in this world than going on expeditions and seeing all of the wonderful things I saw and heard about in that magazine' (Wilson in www.edge.org/3rd_culture/wilson03/wilson03/wilson_p2.html, accessed 28 July 2005).

6 In this and the following chapters, I employ the following convention to cite Peirce: 'CP' refers to his *Collected Papers* (Peirce 1931–58), and the numbers that follow refer to the volume number and then the *paragraph* number. 'EP' refers to *The Essential Peirce* (Volume 1, Peirce 1992; Volume 2, Peirce 1998). The first number refers to the volume, while the second refers to the *page* number. These are conventions that are frequently employed by Peirce scholars.

7 Of course, 'action' and 'reaction' are themselves the beginning of 'thirdness'. More generally, it is true that the nature of 'facts' cannot be made intelligible without recourse to the nature of signs. However, after allowing for this proviso, the notion of 'actions' and 'reactions' comes closer to referring to a nature before representation.

8 It is also rationalist in so far as Peirce's pragmatism employs the model of the scientific experimenter to explain the nature of *all* cognition. For all its limitations, this is not necessarily a bad thing; a later chapter will consider the history by which 'the masses' have been reduced to an 'irrational mob'.

9 This is a reference to Friedrich Wilhelm Joseph von Schelling, the German philosopher who played a central role in the development of *Naturphilosophie*.

2 THE NATURE OF OBSERVATION

1 As begins to be evident from this account, and as Crary explains in a footnote, his form of engaging with the question of observation is itself 'genealogical' in the Foucaultian sense of this term. As such, it questions anything like the neat continuity of a subject that 'evolves through the course of history' (Foucault in Crary 1990: 6). If Foucault's work produces a genealogy of subjectivity in modern culture, Crary engages in an analogous, if rather more 'local' history with respect to what he describes as techniques of the observer.

2 While this is a hypothetical example, it is actually based on my own empirical research with hundreds of visitors to zoos, where I have noted again and again how the 'ways of seeing' – the modes of observation – were as much a result of what was 'there', 'in the zoo', as what the visitor 'brought', for the most part unselfconsciously, from 'elsewhere': from the media, from past learning experiences, and so forth. So it is, for example, that one child asked his parents why the zebra display at one zoo did not have any lions in it. In the course of the visit, it became clear that he was observing the zebras at least partly 'from elsewhere', and with reference to another time: the time of watching natural history documentaries at home, and the time, the temporality, of narratives in which, and for which, watching zebras was a matter of watching zebras being pursued by lions.

3 In his later work, Crary distinguishes between observation and attention (see Crary 1999). Although this is a useful conceptual distinction, the focus of the current study is on the history of modalities of observation.

4 This much was recognized years later, when a new series titled *Deep Jungle* was broadcast by Granada Television on UK television in 2005.

5 Here as in the rest of this book, the notion of the subject refers not to the autonomous 'person' as the beginning, origin or centre of social action, but to a certain form of individuality that is instituted by discourses and social contexts, and that both produces and is inhabited by individuals. One can say in one sense that it

is not so much that individuals have thoughts but that (social) thoughts have individuals. This, however, does not mean that individuality can be dispensed with, or should be dissolved into the sociality of discourse; if it is true that any particular subjectivity is always more than an individual, it is equally true that any particular individual is always more than a given subjectivity. I should perhaps also clarify that, here as elsewhere in this book, I understand discourse from a critical perspective, i.e. as a 'political' way of representing and relating to an aspect of the world. Not 'party political' – though discourses may also be party political – but in the sense that any given discourse produces the characteristic forms of classification and framing associated with both specific and generic institutions. Discourses, by this account, are both enabling and disabling, motivated and arbitrary, indispensable but questionable to those who reproduce them, that is to say, to their subjects. Subjects are, by this account, as much the 'products' of discourse as they are the producers of discourse. For more extended accounts of the concept of discourse, see Foucault (1971), Kress (1985a,b), Hall (1992b), Fairclough (1995) and Darier (1999). It might be assumed from this account that the category of the 'individual' – most notably, a 'genius' account of individuality – loses theoretical validity. In fact, in some respects the opposite case can be made: that even if discourse is, by definition, a matter of a practice that goes beyond an individual, individual 'geniuses' may be regarded as the 'sites' for particularly intense discursive activity.

6 A detailed consideration of this problem is beyond the scope of this book. I am acknowledging that, from one perspective, Bernstein's categories, which I introduce in the following paragraphs, tend to be informed by a notion of boundary that is itself dyadic: one thing is separated from another. However, any social semeiotic theory that fails to explain the dualisms of social practice itself – what Peirce readily describes as the elements of conflict, which might for example involve the contest and othering of one group by another – runs the risk of depoliticizing any given social practice.

7 Lefebvre is clearly aware of the implication that both levels involve triadic and not 'dyadic' relations: 'A triad: that is, three elements and not two. Relations with two elements boil down to oppositions . . . Philosophy has found it very difficult to get beyond such dualisms' (Lefebvre 1991: 39).

8 For an account of this distinction, see Alfonso and Lindahl Elliot (2002).

3 THE NATURE OF *MATHESIS*

1 Anachrony – being 'out of time' – can be not only 'forward looking' but also the beginning of change (Alfonso and Lindahl Elliot 2002).

2 As André Chastel puts it himself: 'La notion de l'art-science, c'est-à-dire d'un savoir enclos dans les structures figurees qui l'administrent, ouvre sur des problèmes peut-être encore plus remarquables' (Chastel 1970: 14).

3 Manetti describes this aspect of the painting as follows: 'e per quanto s'aveva a dimostrare di cielo, cioè che le muraglie del dipinto stampassono nella aria, messo d'ariento brunito, acciò che l'aria e' cieli naturali vi si specchiassono drento, e cosí e nugoli, che si veggono in quello airento essere menati dal vento, quand'e' trae' (Manetti 1976: 58).

4 To be sure, a similar point might be made with respect to Arab forerunners of the theory of vision in linear perspective; European elites, it seems, have long been good at inventing their own inventiveness.

5 Throughout the following chapters I will assume that the concept of the sign provides a more accurate way of describing the practices in question, if only because

'signs' allows for the possibility that some representations are not primarily 'symbolic' in nature.

4 THE NATURE OF COMMODIFICATION

1 William Leiss (1974) makes a similar point in *The Domination of Nature*.

2 The classical *epistéme* was contemporaneous with Descartes' mechanism, and indeed Foucault argues that the two knowledges were 'authorized by the same *epistéme*' (1970: 128), though he does not explain just how this is the case.

3 Grove speaks of Poivre and others as 'pioneers of modern *environmentalism*' and as 'romantic scientists', though he recognizes that the notion of 'pioneers of environmentalism' can be used only with the benefit of hindsight (1995: 9). A similar point can be made with respect to the notion of a 'scientist'.

4 See for example the succession of changes in http://darkwing.uoregon.edu/~helphand/englishpgsone/englishpg6.html (accessed 1 October 2005).

5 See http://www.wga.hu/frames-e.html?/html/g/gainsbor/ (accessed 1 October 2005).

6 In fact, this piece is atypical in showing its subjects not in the landscape garden but in the fields: see Bermingham on this point.

7 See http://www.modjourn.brown.edu/Image/Wilson/ThamesTwick-c1762.jpg (accessed 1 October 2005).

8 See http://www.the-athenaeum.org/art/by_artist.php?id=1315&msg=new (accessed 1 October 2005).

9 See http://www.abcgallery.com/C/constable/constable5.html (accessed 1 October 2005).

10 See http://www.tate.org.uk/servlet/ViewWork?cgroupid=999999961&workid=8667&searchid=15671 (accessed 1 October 2005).

5 THE NATURE OF INDUSTRIALIZATION

1 The discovery that suburbs in the UK may have a higher number of species than an industrial agricultural landscape does not contradict this point; we have only to think, for example, of what would happen if conservationists were to attempt to reintroduce the great bustard not in Salisbury Plain but in, say, Regent's Park.

2 The word is likely to have appeared in the fourteenth century, and is used in Chaucer's *Canterbury Tales*: '"Where dwelle ye? If it to telle be." "In the suburbs of a toun," quod he' (Chaucer in Dyos 1966: 20).

6 THE NATURE OF SUBLIMATION

1 Some suggest that, strictly speaking, the first such park was actually created in Arkansas by an Act of Congress of 20 April 1832 (Chapter 70, 4 Stat. 505) that provided 'that the hot springs in said territory, together with four sections of land including said springs, as near the center thereof as may be, shall be reserved for the future disposal of the United States, and shall not be entered, located, or appropriated, for any other purpose whatever.'

2 For an account of the debates by means of which the legislation was established, see Rives (1864). See also Rives *et al.* (1872).

3 For an analysis of these differences, see for example Oelschlaeger (1991).

4 There is a much older meaning of the term that may be derived from alchemy and is also found in modern science. In some alchemical treatises, sublimation (*sublimatio*) is regarded as one of the stages in the alchemical process: the process,

recognized by modern science, whereby a substance passes from the solid phase to the vapour phase without going through an intermediate (liquid) phase.

Carl Jung critiques Freud's use of the term as follows: 'Sublimation', Jung suggests, 'is not a voluntary and the forcible channeling of instinct into a spurious field of application . . . but an alchemical transformation for which fire and the black *materia prima* are needed. *Sublimatio* is a great mystery. Freud has appropriated this concept and usurped it for the sphere of the will, and the bourgeois, rationalistic ethos' (Jung 1973: 171).

5 See for example 'Yosemite in Spring' (http://www.sierraclub.org/john_muir_exhibit/frameindex.html?http://www.sierraclub.org/john_muir_exhibit/writings/yosemite_in_spring.html, accessed 4 December 2005), 'The treasures of the Yosemite' (http://www.sierraclub.org/john_muir_exhibit/frameindex.html?http://www.sierraclub.org/john_muir_exhibit/writings/the_treasures_of_the_yosemite/, accessed 4 December 2005), 'Features of the proposed Yosemite National Park' (http://www.sierraclub.org/john_muir_exhibit/frameindex.html?http://www.sierraclub.org/john_muir_exhibit/writings/features_of_the_proposed_yosemite_national_park/, accessed 4 December 2005).

6 The second medium, developed by Daguerre in France, became known as the daguerrotype and, despite offering an image with a higher resolution, eventually lost what might now be described as a kind of early mass-media 'battle of the formats'.

7 See http://www.foxtalbot.arts.gla.ac.uk/resources/opendoor.html, accessed 1 October 2005.

8 See http://www.nga.gov/exhibitions/watkinsimg.htm, accessed 1 October 2005.

9 See http://www.yosemite.ca.us/history/the_yosemite_book/plate_02.html, accessed 1 October 2005.

10 See http://www.yosemite.ca.us/history/the_yosemite_book/plate_10.html, accessed 1 October 2005.

11 It should nonetheless be noted that in this very indexicality lies one difference between the painted and the photographed panoramas. The various variations in the techniques of observation considered in this chapter worked to blur the boundary between the observer and the observed by naturalizing a certain subjective observational standpoint, and by framing this standpoint in ways that nevertheless objectified whatever was observed. However, the photographic naturalism of Watkins and other photographers took this tendency further in so far as their use of a naturalistic coding orientation foregrounded a relation of causal contiguity between the representation and the represented nature.

12 It is possible to question whether this conception of the horizon goes too far in the direction of culturalism; one might consider, for example, whether there is a biological link between horizon and perception that becomes apparent when someone suffers from illnesses or injuries to the vestibular system. If sufficiently severe, these can lead to the loss of equilibrium and in some cases a condition known as *oscillopsia*: the inability of the ocular system to maintain a stable horizon, described provocatively in some medical contexts as a 'jumbling of the panorama.'

13 In some respects, *dioramas* in zoos and natural history museums could.

7 THE NATURE OF INCORPORATION

1 Significant exceptions include Simon Winchester's *Krakatoa* (2003) and John B. Thompson's *The Media and Modernity* (1995).

2 As noted by Gramsci (1971), calling this a 'high wage' was in most respects

disingenuous. It was also a temporary phenomenon; once the logic of the market-place was reinstituted by the same conditions created by mass production, salary levels would fall.

3 Even the 'technical' aspects of the cinematographic sign differed from the camera obscura. The camera obscura can be described as being the technique of observation that perhaps comes closest to constituting an ideal index, that is, the one that comes closest to being like the weathervane, the thermometer and other forms of representation that involve what Peirce describes in terms of a causal relation of contiguity between the sign or representation and its object of representation. The gentleman of science observing a landscape in the camera obscura engaged, despite the mediation of the lens and the darkened chamber, in an activity that was remarkably close, at least in its temporal dimension, to the act of viewing 'nature itself'. In this sense, whatever its characteristic form of visual naturalism, the camera obscura produced scenes in the most real of real times. By contrast, the cinematic time was to become a matter of a spatial dis-contiguity, but also a *temporal linearity*. This linearity might be regarded as a kind of ultimate realism in a metaphysical sense (Deleuze argues that cinematography produces indirect 'glimpses' of the cosmic 'whole'), but at one and the same time emphatically a matter of social mediation in so far as it entailed the *assembly* of a *selection* of shots (Lindahl Elliot 2001).

4 Olmsted also played a role in the establishment of the Niagara Falls as a park.

5 For a discussion of these and other problems, see for example Scott (2000).

8 THE NATURE OF ENVIRONMENTALISM

1 The electronic signals were, and to this day continue to be, updated continuously by scanning devices. These created not so much 'frames' as continuously changing *fields*. Returning to the work of Deleuze (1986), we can say that television produced not 'any-instant-whatevers', but rather 'any-[electronic] *field*-whatevers'. The notion of field took the visual 'analysis' first performed by the cinematograph much further: if cinema produced relatively closed 'systems' of elements, we can say that the television camera produced relatively *open* and even more essentially dynamic systems of electronic elements which, to begin with at least, could not be 'frozen' into frames.

2 Television could be regarded, in Lefebvre's words, as a particularly appropriate medium in which the illusion of transparency made space appear 'luminous', a substance like air which gave action 'free reign' (1991: 27).

3 Without commercial breaks, the documentaries are between 45 and 50 minutes long.

4 Latin America has a long history of being regarded as being a continent without 'proper' animals. See Gerbi (1985) for a history of representations of nature in the 'New World'. This under-representation was addressed by one BBC series titled *Andes to Amazon* (2000).

5 Shooting in 'controlled conditions' was justified as follows by Colin Willock: 'Our view is simply this. Provided the "controlled shooting" exactly represents the behaviour of the creature in the wild and was obtained without harm to the animal or its environment, then the film-maker should not only use it but should use it without explanation, disclaimer or apology. We say this because we are certain that the viewer wants to see a fascinating piece of wildlife action, sharply defined and in close-up, and controlled shooting is sometimes the only way to guarantee this' (Willock 1978: 66).

6 An exception could be found in the programmes for children (e.g. the *Really Wild*

Show) that were structured along the lines of a more 'interactive' mode of representation (Nichols 1991). It might well be suggested that the blue-chip genre of natural history documentary constituted an amalgam of these three modes. Documentaries specializing in describing the *making* of blue-chip histories constituted a certain turn towards what Nichols (1991) describes as a reflexive mode of representation.

7 See for example the shots of a variety of arthropods in *Microcosmos* (1997).

8 An example of a similar dynamic involving the risk of racist and xenophobic circuits of anthropomorphism could be found in innumerable accounts of 'foreign invaders'. For example, one article in the *New Scientist* reported that 'In their natural habitats and hosts, phytophthoras do little harm. Transport them to new places and introduce them to species they've never encountered before and they can turn nasty. Mass movement of plants is responsible for a malevolent form of matchmaking, bringing together species of pathogen that would never normally meet' (Pain 2004: 41).

9 For an analysis of the changed market conditions, see Cottle (2004).

10 In the UK, the mainstreaming of this form of patriarchy was symbolized by the 'migration' of men's magazines from the top shelf to the middle shelves of shops. One example which I considered earlier was *FHM*; in 2004, the monthly format was joined by weekly magazines, an example of which was the new *Zoo* magazine. The new entry to what was itself an increasingly crowded market was promoted with a television advertisement that showed a group of men scampering up a hill like dogs towards a towering magazine.

11 To these we might add the later *Jonathan Livingston Seagull* (1973), and *Free Willy* (1993) films.

12 In the older *Birds* (1963), it is Melanie Daniels who seems to call out the 'curse' of birds and who is most viciously attacked by them after she succeeds in her 'flirtation' with Mitch Brenner.

13 It is also tempting to analyse the attacks in terms of the Cartesian 'cut' and the history considered throughout this book with respect to the lower body. Even in the case of animals that might be expected to attack from above (e.g. spiders) the tendency was for attacks (and the camera) to come *from below*, and to attack (or film) *the lower body*.

14 See for example Price (1996).

15 See for example Myers (1990).

EPILOGUE: CLIMACTIC CHANGE

1 See the Apollo Image Atlas at http://www.lpi.usra.edu/research/apollo/catalog/70mm/magazine/?148 (accessed 30 January 2006).

2 See http://www.nytimes.com/2006/01/29/science/earth/29climate.html?hp&ex=1138510800&en=0a858f5230677507&ei=5094&partner=homepage (accessed 29 January 2006).

3 For an example of this argument, see McComas and Shanahan (1999).

4 The main points agreed read as follows:

1. Resolves to engage in a dialogue, without prejudice to any future negotiations, commitments, process, framework or mandate under the Convention, to exchange experiences and analyse strategic approaches for long-term cooperative action to address climate change that includes, inter alia, the following areas:

(a) Advancing development goals in a sustainable way

(b) Addressing action on adaptation

(c) Realizing the full potential of technology

(d) Realizing the full potential of market-based opportunities;

2. Further resolves that the dialogue will take the form of an open and non-binding exchange of views, information and ideas in support of enhanced implementation of the Convention, and will not open any negotiations leading to new commitments.

(http://unfccc.int/files/meetings/cop_11/application/pdf/cop11_00_dialogue_on_long-term_coop_action.pdf, accessed 12 December 2005)

5 See http://www.ci.seattle.wa.us/mayor/climate/default.htm#cities (accessed 30 January 2006).

6 See, for example, 'Why we won't fly again' in http://observer.guardian.co.uk/travel/story/0,,1697188,00.html (accessed 30 January 2006).

7 See www.bseinquiry.gov.uk (accessed 31 January 2005) for the complete report.

8 For an analysis of the BSE crisis and its handling by MAFF, see for example Zwanenberg and Millstone (2005). As the authors explain, 'The food and agricultural policy regime into which BSE emerged in the mid-1980s was therefore a seemingly robust alliance between the productive sector and the public policy-makers, ostensibly stabilized by sound science. The policy community, and the networks of which it was comprised, saw themselves as serving a common set of interests. They also shared a common set of beliefs, including many about the nature and acceptability of possible risks from routine practices, and most of the participants in that community routinely represented their beliefs and judgements as sound science. That community, and the policy regime that it produced and sustained, took full advantage of the rules of official secrecy to ensure that it remained unaccountable and shielded from public scrutiny. Parliamentary scrutiny was consequently insubstantial and judicial oversight was non-existent' (Zwanenberg & Millstone 2005: 53–4).

9 See, for example, the analysis offered by George Monbiot in the *Guardian* on 4 October 2005 (http://www.guardian.co.uk/Columnists/Column/0,,1584140,00.html, accessed 6 January 2006).

10 See, for example, the report in http://news.bbc.co.uk/1/hi/sci/tech/4715221.stm (accessed 25 July 2005.) See also http://www.newscientist.com/channel/life/gm-food/dn7729 (accessed 26 July 2005).

APPENDIX: THE NATURE OF PEIRCE

1 The word 'material' is placed in inverted commas because Saussure was careful to note that even the signifier is a *mental* construction in so far as a sound is not the sound itself, but 'the hearer's psychological impression of a sound, as given to him [*sic*] by the evidence of his senses' (Saussure 1983: 66).

2 Peirce also coined the term *ideoscopy* to provide a rather more mundane account of phenomenology: '*Ideoscopy* consists in describing and classifying the ideas that belong to ordinary experience or that naturally arise in connection with ordinary life' (CP 8.328).

3 By his own account, Peirce understood 'category' in much the way that Aristotle, Kant and Hegel did, that is as 'an element of phenomena of the first rank

of generality'; 'it naturally follows', he argued, 'that the categories are few in number, just as the chemical elements are' (CP 5.43).

4 Peirce was aware of the dangers of phenomenological reductionism. As he explained to Lady Welby, 'This sort of notion is as distasteful to me as to anybody; and for years, I endeavoured to pooh-pooh and refute it' (CP 8.328). But Peirce was an advocate of scholastic realism. In the work of Scotus Erigena, scholastic realism was the doctrine that generality is a natural trait of reality. Generality, Peirce argued, is 'an indispensable ingredient of reality; for mere individual existence or actuality without any regularity whatever is a nullity. Chaos is pure nothing' (CP 5.431).

5 The editors of Peirce's *Collected Papers* date this typology to *c*. 1897 (see CP 2.227).

BIBLIOGRAPHY

Adler, J. (1989) 'Origins of sightseeing', in *Annals of Tourism Research,* 16: 7–29.

Adorno, T.W. (1941) 'On popular music', in *Studies in Philosophy and Social Science*, 9: 17–48.

Alberti, L.B. (1972) *On Painting and On Sculpture*, edited and translated by C. Grayson, London: Phaidon.

Alfonso, C. and Lindahl Elliot, N. (2002) 'Of hallowed spacings', in J. Arthurs and I. Grant (eds) *Crash Cultures*, London: Intellect, pp. 153–74.

Allan, S. (1999) *News Culture,* Buckingham: Open University Press.

Allan, S. (2002) *Media, Risk, and Science*, Buckingham: Open University Press.

Allan, S., Adam, B. and Carter, C. (2000) *Environmental Risks and the Media*, London: Routledge.

Allen, W.L. (1995) Editor's introduction to 'Ndoki: last place on earth', in *National Geographic*, 188(1): 2–46.

Ananthaswamy, A. (2004) 'Beware the ecotourist', *New Scientist*, 6 March, 6–7.

Anderson, B. (1991) *Imagined Communities: Reflections on the Origin and Spread of Nationalism*, London: Verso.

Anderson, N. (1991) '"The kiss of enterprise": the western landscape as symbol and resource', in W.H. Truettner (ed.) *The West as America: Reinterpreting Images of the Frontier, 1820–1920*, London: Smithsonian Institution Press, pp. 237–84.

Attenborough, D. (2002) *Life on Air,* London: BBC Books.

Bakhtin, M. (1984) *Rabelais and His World*, translated by H. Iswolsky, Bloomington, IN: Indiana University Press.

Barthes, R. (1985a) 'The photographic message', in *The Responsibility of Forms: Critical Essays on Music, Art, and Representation*, translated by R. Howard, New York: Hill and Wang, pp. 3–20.

Barthes, R. (1985b) 'Rhetoric of the Image', in *The Responsibility of Forms: Critical Essays on Music, Art, and Representation*, translated by R. Howard, New York: Hill and Wang, pp. 21–40.

Baudrillard, J. (1994) *Simulacra and Simulation*, translated by S.F. Glaser, Ann Arbor, MI: University of Michigan Press.

Beck, U. (1992) *Risk Society*, translated by M. Ritter, London: Sage Publications.

Beck, U. (1995) *Ecological Politics in an Age of Risk*, translated by A. Weisz, Cambridge: Polity.

Benjamin, W. (1999) 'The work of art in the age of mechanical reproduction', in H. Arendt (ed.) *Illuminations*, translated by H. Zohn, London: Pimlico, pp. 211–44.

Bermingham, A. (1986) *Landscape and Ideology: The English Rustic Tradition, 1740–1860*, London: University of California Press.

Bernstein, B. (1990) *The Structuring of Pedagogic Discourse*, London: Routledge.

Bernstein, B. (1996) *Pedagogy, Symbolic Control, and Identity*, London: Taylor & Francis.

Bettetini, G. (1984) *La Conversación Audiovisual*, translated by V. Ponce, Madrid: Cátedra.

Bordwell, D., Staiger, J. and Thompson, K. (1985) *The Classical Hollywood Cinema*, London: Routledge and Kegan Paul.

Bourdieu, P. (1991) *Language and Symbolic Power*, translated by G. Raymond and M. Adamson, Cambridge: Polity Press.

Bowles, S. (1869) *Our New West: Records of Travel between the Mississippi River and the Pacific Ocean*, New York: Hartford Publishing Company.

Braun, M. (1992) *Picturing Time: The Work of Etienne-Jules Marey (1830–1904)*, Chicago, IL: Chicago University Press.

Brown, M. and May, J. (1991) *The Greenpeace Story*, 2nd revised edition, London: Dorling Kindersley.

Bunnell, L.H. (1990) *Discovery of the Yosemite*, Yosemite National Park, CA: Yosemite Association.

Burch, N. (1990) *Life to Those Shadows*, London: British Film Institute.

Burke, E. (1998) *A Philosophical Enquiry Into the Origin of Our Ideas of the Sublime and the Beautiful*, London: Penguin Classics.

Calabrese, O. (1992) *Neo-Baroque: A Sign of the Times*, translated by C. Lambert, Princeton, NJ: Princeton University Press.

Carson, R. (1962) *Silent Spring*, London: Penguin Books.

Casetti, F. (1989) *El Film y su Espectador*, translated by A.L. Giordano Gramegna, Madrid: Cátedra.

Casetti, F. (1995) 'Face to face', in W. Buckland (ed.) *The Film Spectator: From Sign to Mind*, Amsterdam: Amsterdam University Press, pp. 118–39.

Cassirer, E. (1955) *The Philosophy of Symbolic Forms*, vol. 2, translated by R. Manheim, New Haven, CT: Yale University Press.

Castel, R. (1994) '"Problematization" as a mode of reading history', in J. Goldstein (ed.) *Foucault and the Writing of History*, translated by P. Wissing, Oxford: Blackwell, pp. 237–52.

Castoriadis, C. (1987) *The Imaginary Institution of Society*, Cambridge: Polity Press.

de Certeau, M. (1984) *The Practice of Everyday Life*, translated by S. Rendall, Berkeley, CA: University of California Press.

Chadwick, D.H. (1995) 'Ndoki: last place on Earth', in *National Geographic*, 188(1): 2–46.

Chanan, M. (1980) *The Dream that Kicks*, London: Routledge & Kegan Paul.

Chandler, Alfred D. (1977) *The Visible Hand: The Managerial Revolution in American Business*, London: Harvard University Press.

Chastel, A. (1970) 'Présentation', in R. Klein (ed.) *La Forme et l'intelligible: Écrits sur la renaissance et l'art moderne,* Paris: Gallimard.

Clarke, G. (1992) 'The moving temples of Stowe: aesthetics of change in an English landscape over four generations', in *Huntingdon Library Quarterly*, 55(3): 501–12.

Columbus, C. (1988) *The Four Voyages of Christopher Columbus*, translated and edited by C. Jane, New York: Dover.

Comment, B. (1999) *The Panorama*, London: Reaktion Books.

Conrad, J. (1973) *Heart of Darkness*, London: Penguin Books.

Cottle, S. (2004) 'Producing nature(s): on the changing production ecology of natural history TV', in *Media, Culture and Society*, 26(1): 81–102

Crary, J. (1990) *Techniques of the Observer*, London: MIT Press.

Crary, J. (1999) *Suspensions of Perception: Attention, Spectacle and Modern Culture*, Cambridge, MA: MIT Press.

Cronon, W. (ed.) (1996) *Uncommon Ground: Rethinking the Human Place in Nature*, London: W.W. Norton.

Crowther, B. (1995) 'Towards a feminist critique of television natural history programmes', in P. Florence and D. Reynolds (eds) *Feminist Subjects, Multimedia*, Manchester: Manchester University Press, pp. 127–46.

Curtis, H. (1995) 'Greenpeace mobilizes DTV action', in *Business Video*, 2(4): 18–21.

Damisch, H. (1994) *The Origin of Perspective*, translated by J. Goodman, London: MIT Press.

Damisch, H. (2002) *A Theory of/Cloud/*, translated by J. Lloyd, Stanford, CA: Stanford University Press.

Darier, E. (ed.) (1999) *Discourses of the Environment*, Oxford: Blackwell.

Dawkins, R. (1974) *The Selfish Gene*, Oxford: Oxford University Press.

Debord, G. (1995) *The Society of Spectacle*, New York: Zone Books.

Deleuze, G. (1986) *Cinema 1: The Movement Image*, London: Athlone.

Desmond, K. (1995) *Kew: The History of the Royal Botanic Gardens*, London: Harvill Press.

Dobbs (1991) *The Janus Faces of Genius: The Role of Alchemy in Newton's Thought*, Cambridge: Cambridge University Press.

Douglas, M. (1983) *Purity and Danger*, London: Routledge.

Drayton, R. (2001) *Nature's Government: Science, Imperial Britain and the 'Improvement' of the World*, Cambridge: Cambridge University Press.

Drouin, J.M. (1995) 'From Linnaeus to Darwin: naturalists and travellers', in M. Serres (ed.) *A History of Scientific Thought*, Oxford: Blackwell, pp. 401–421.

Dürer, A. (1977) *The Painter's Manual: A Manual of Measurement of Lines, Areas and Solids by Means of Compass and Ruler*, translated by W.L. Strauss, New York: Abaris Books.

Dyos, H.J. (1966) *Victorian Suburb: A Study in the Growth of Camberwell*, Leicester: Leicester University Press.

Eagleton, T. (2000) *The Idea of Culture*, Oxford: Blackwell.

Edwards, D. (1998) 'Can we learn the truth about the environment from the media?', in *The Ecologist*, 28(1): 18–22.

Eisenstein, E. (1979) *The Printing Press as an Agent of Change*, Cambridge: Cambridge University Press.

Ellis, J. (1992) *Visible Fictions*, revised edition, London: Routledge.

Emerson, R.W. (1906) 'Nature', in G. Sampson (ed.) *The Works of Ralph Waldo Emerson*, vol. 2, London: George Bell and Sons, pp. 371–416.

Erb, C. (1998) *Tracking King Kong: A Hollywood Icon in World Culture*, Detroit, MI: Wayne State University Press.

Éribon, D. (1993) *Michel Foucault*, translated by B. Wing, London: Faber and Faber.

Fairclough, N. (1995) *Critical Discourse Analysis: The Critical Study of Language,* London: Longman.

Febvre, L. and Martin, H.J. (1976) *The Coming of the Book*, translated by D. Gerard, London: Verso.

FHM (2004) 'Manimal!', in *FHM*, August, 18–19.

Foucault, M. (1970) *The Order of Things*, London: Tavistock.

Foucault, M. (1971) 'The order of discourse', translated by R. Sawyer, in *Social Science Information* 10(April): 7–31.

Foucault, M. (1984) 'Le Souci de la vérité', in *Magazine Littéraire,* 207(May): 18–23.

Foucault, M. (1986) 'Of other spaces', translated by J. Miskowiec, in *Diacritics*, 16(2): 22–7.

Foucault, M. (1988) 'Technologies of the self', in L.H. Martin, H. Gutman and P.H. Hutton (eds) *Technologies of the Self: A Seminar with Michel Foucault*, London: Tavistock, pp. 16–49.

Foucault, M. (1998) 'Nietzsche, genealogy, history', translated by D.F. Brouchard and S. Simon, in J.D. Faubion (ed.) *Essential Works of Michel Foucault, Vol. 2: Aesthetics, Method, Epistemology*, pp. 369–91.

Freeman, M. (1999) *Railways and the Victorian Imagination,* London: Yale University Press.

Gartman, D. (1994) *Auto Opium: A Social History of American Automobile Design*, London: Routledge.

Genette, G. (1980) *Narrative Discourse*, translated by J.E. Lewin, Ithaca, NY: Cornell University Press.

Genette, G. (1988) *Narrative Discourse Revisited*, translated by J.E. Lewin, Ithaca, NY: Cornell University Press.

Gerbi, A. (1985) *Nature in the New World: From Christopher Columbus to Gonzalo Fernández de Oviedo*, translated by J. Moyle, Pittsburgh, PA: University of Pittsburgh Press.

Giddens, A. (1985) *The Nation State and Violence*, Cambridge: Polity Press.

Glacken, Clarence J. (1967) *Traces on the Rhodian Shore: Nature and Culture in Western Thought from Ancient Times to the End of the Eighteenth Century*, Berkeley, CA: University of California Press.

Goddard, D. (ed.) (1995) *Saving Wildlife: A Century of Conservation*, New York: Harry Abrams Inc. and The Conservation Society.

Godlovitch, S., Godlovitch, R. and Harris, J. (eds) (1972) *Animals, Men and Morals: An Enquiry into the Maltreatment of Non-Humans*, London: Taplinger.

Gould, S.J. (1980) *Ever Since Darwin*, London: Penguin Books

Gramsci, A. (1971) *Selections from the Prison Notebooks*, edited and translated by Q. Hoare and G. N. Smith, New York: International Publishers.

Grant, B.K. (1996) (ed.) *The Dread of Difference*, Austin, TX: Texas University Press.

Grove, R. (1995) *Green Imperialism: Colonial Expansion, Tropical Edens and the Origin of Environmentalism 1600–1860*, Cambridge: Cambridge University Press.

Gutman, H. (1988) 'Rousseau's *Confessions*: a technology of the self', in L.H. Martin,

H. Gutman and P.H. Hutton (eds) *Technologies of the Self: A Seminar with Michel Foucault*, London: Tavistock, pp. 99–121.

Hall, S. (1992a) 'Introduction', in S. Hall and B. Gieben (eds) *Formations of Modernity*, Cambridge: Polity Press, pp. 1–16

Hall, S. (1992b) 'The west and the rest: discourse and power', in S. Hall and B. Gieben (eds) *Formations of Modernity*, Cambridge: Polity Press, pp. 275–323.

Halliday, M.A.K. (1978) *Language as Social Semiotic: The Social Interpretation of Language and Meaning*, London: Edward Arnold.

Hammond, S.H. (1857) *Wild Northern Scene*, New York: Derby and Jackson.

Hancocks, D. (2001) *A Different Nature*, London: University of California Press.

Hansen, A. (ed.) (1993) *The Mass Media and Environmental Issues*, Leicester: Leicester University Press.

Hanson, E. (2002) *Animal Attractions*, Princeton, NJ: Princeton University Press.

Haraway, D. (1989) *Primate Visions: Gender, Race and Nature in the World of Modern Science*, London, Routledge.

Haraway, D. (1991) 'A cyborg manifesto: science, technology, and socialist-feminism in the late twentieth century', in *Simians, Cyborgs, and Women: The Reinvention of Nature*, London: Free Association Books, pp. 149–81.

Harvey, D. (1989) *The Condition of Postmodernity*, Oxford: Oxford University Press.

Hausman, C.R. (1997) *Charles S. Peirce's Evolutionary Philosophy*, Cambridge: Cambridge University Press.

Held, D. (1992) 'The development of the modern state', in S. Hall and B. Gieben (eds) *Formations of Modernity*, Cambridge: Polity Press and Open University, pp. 71–126.

Hetherington, K. (1998) *Expressions of Identity: Space, Performance, Politics*, London: Sage.

Hobbes, T. (1968) *Leviathan*, Harmondsworth: Pelican Classics.

Hochschild, A. (1998) *King Leopold's Ghost*, New York: Houghton Mifflin Company.

Hodge, R. and Kress, G. (1988) *Social Semiotics*, Cambridge: Polity.

Holmberg, J. and Sandbrook, R. (1992) 'Sustainable development: what is to be done?', in J. Holmberg (ed.) *Policies for a Small Planet*, London: Earthscan, pp. 19–38.

Hoy, S. (1995) *Chasing Dirt: The American Pursuit of Cleanliness*, New York: Oxford University Press.

Humboldt, A. (1995) *Personal Narrative*, London: Penguin Books.

Hunter, R. (2004) *The Greenpeace to Amchitka: An Environmental Odyssey*, Vancouver: Arsenal Pulp Press.

Ingold, T. (1997) 'Life beyond the edge of nature?', in J.D. Greenwood (ed.) *The Mark of the Social*, London: Routledge, pp. 231–52.

Jenkins, V.S. (1994) *The Lawn: A History of An American Obsession*, Washington, DC: Smithsonian Books.

Johns, A. (1998) *The Nature of the Book: Print and Knowledge in the Making*, Chicago: University of Chicago Press.

Jung, C.G. (1973) *Letters of C.G. Jung, Vol. I: 1906–1950*, selected and edited by G. Adler with A. Jaffé, and translated by R.F.C. Hull and J.A. Pratt, London: Routledge & Kegan Paul.

Kant, I. (1987) *The Critique of Judgement,* translated by W.S. Pluhar, Cambridge: Hackett Publishing Company.

Kean, M. (1998) *Animal Rights: Political and Social Change in Britain Since 1800*, London: Reaktion Press.

Kingsley, M. (1993) *Travels in West Africa*, London: Everyman.

Kress, G. (1985a) *Linguistic Processes in Sociocultural Practice*, Oxford: Oxford University Press.

Kress, G. (1985b) 'Discourses, texts, readers and pro-nuclear arguments', in P. Chilton (ed.) *Language and the Nuclear Arms Debate*, London: Frances Pinter.

Kress, G. and van Leeuwen, T. (1996) *Reading Images*, London: Routledge.

Lamb, R. (1996) *Promising the Earth*, London: Routledge.

Lasdun, S. (1991) *The English Park: Royal, Private, and Public*, London: André Deutsch.

Lear, L. (1997) *Rachel Carson: Witness for Nature*, New York: Henry Holt and Company.

Lefebvre, H. (1991) *The Social Production of Space*, Oxford: Blackwell.

Lefort, C. (1986) 'Outline of the genesis of ideology in modern societies', in J.B. Thompson (ed.) *Claude Lefort: The Political Forms of Modern Society*, Cambridge: Polity Press.

Leggett, J. (ed.) (1990) *Global Warming: The Greenpeace Report*, Oxford: Oxford University Press.

Leiss, W. (1974) *The Domination of Nature*, New York: Beacon Press.

Leitch, V.B. (ed.) (2001) *The Norton Anthology of Theory and Criticism*, London: W.W. Norton & Company.

Lindahl Elliot, N. (2001) 'Signs of anthropomorphism: the case of natural history documentaries', in *Social Semiotics* 11(3): 289–305.

Lindahl Elliot, N. (2006) 'See it, sense it, save it: economies of multisensuality in contemporary zoos', in *Sense and Society*, 1(2): 203–24.

Linden, E. (1992) 'The last Eden', in *Time*, July 13, 140(2): 62–8.

Liszka, J.J. (1996) *A General Introduction to the Semeiotic of Charles Sanders Peirce*, Bloomington, IN: Indiana University Press.

Lovelock, J. (1979) *Gaia: A New Look at Life on Earth*. Oxford: Oxford University Press.

Lutz, C. and Collins, J. (1993) *Reading National Geographic*, Chicago, IL: Chicago University Press.

McCarry, C. (1988) 'Three men who made the magazine', in *National Geographic*, September, 174(3): 287–316.

McClelland, L. (1998) *Building the National Parks,* London: Johns Hopkins University Press.

McComas, K. and Shanahan, J. (1999) 'Telling stories about global climate change: measuring the impact of narratives on issue cycles', in *Communication Research* 26(1): 30–57.

Mackenzie, S. (1988) *The Empire of Nature*, Manchester: Manchester University Press.

Macnaghten, P. and Urry, J. (1998) *Contested Natures*, London: Sage.

Manetti, A. (1976) *Vita di Filippo Brunelleschi*, edited by Domenico de Robertis, Milan: Edizioni Il Polifilo.

Marsh, G.P. (1847) 'Address delivered before the Agricultural Society of Rutland

County', Rutland, VT: Herald Office in *The Evolution of the Conservation Movement, 1850–1920*, http://lcweb2.loc.gov/cgi-bin/query/r?ammem/consrv:@field(DOCID+@lit(amrvgvg02div1)) (accessed 12 March 2004).

Martín-Barbero, J. (1993) *Communication, Culture, and Hegemony*, translated by E. Fox and R.A. White, London: Sage.

Marx, K. (1974) *The Capital: A Critical Analysis of Capitalist Production*, translated by S. Moore and E. Aveling, edited by F. Engels, London: Lawrence & Wishart.

Merchant, C. (1980) *The Death of Nature*, New York: Harper San Francisco.

Merchant, C. (1992) *Radical Ecology*, London: Routledge.

Miele, C. (1999) 'From aristocratic ideal to middle-class idyll: 1690–1840', in *London Suburbs*, London: Merrell Holberton with English Heritage, pp. 31–60.

Mitchell, W.J.T. (ed.) (1994) *Landscape and Power*, London: Chicago University Press.

Mitman, G. (1999) *Reel Nature: America's Romance with Wildlife on Film*, London: Harvard University Press.

Morin, E. (2001) *El Cine o el Hombre Imaginario*, Barcelona: Paidós Comunicación.

Muchembled, R. (1985) *Popular Culture and Elite Culture in France, 1400–1750,* Baton Rouge, LA: Louisiana State University Press.

Muir, J. (1997) *The Mountains of California*, New York: Penguin Books.

Muir, J. (1996) 'A thousand-mile walk to the Gulf', in *John Muir: The Wilderness Journeys*, Edinburgh: Canongate Classics.

Mullan, B. and Marvin, G. (1999) *Zoo Culture*, 2nd edition, Chicago, IL: University of Illinois Press.

Musser, C. (1990) *The Emergence of Cinema: The American Screen to 1907*, Berkeley, CA: University of California Press.

Myers, D. (1999) *Mr. Zoo: The Life and Legacy of Dr. Charles Schroeder*, San Diego, CA: Zoological Society of San Diego.

Myers, K. (1990) 'Selling green', in C. Squiers (ed.) *The Critical Image*, London: Lawrence & Wishart, pp. 193–201.

National Geographic Society (1888a) 'Certificate of incorporation', in *National Geographic Magazine*, 1(1): 89.

National Geographic Society (1888b) 'Announcement', in *National Geographic Magazine*, 1(1): i–ii.

Nichols, B. (1991) *Representing Reality*, Bloomington, IN: Indiana University Press.

Nichols, M. (1996) 'Introduction', in M. Nichols *et al.*, *Keepers of the Kingdom: The New American Zoo*. Charlottesville, VA: Lickle Publishing, pp. 9–17.

Nickel, D.R. (1999) 'The art of perception', in D.R. Nickel (ed.) *Carleton Watkins: The Art of Perception*, San Francisco, CA: Harry N. Abrams Publishers, pp. 18–35.

Nöth, W. (1990). *Handbook of Semiotics*, Bloomington, IN: Indiana University Press.

Oelschlaeger, M. (1991) *The Idea of Wilderness*, London: Yale University Press.

Oettermannn, S. (1997) *The Panorama: History of a Mass Medium*, New York: Zone Books.

Olmsted, F. (1865) *The Yosemite Valley and the Mariposa Big Tree Grove,* report on the management of the Yosemite first published in *Landscape Architecture,* 1952, 43:12–25.

Pain, S. (2004) 'Felled by fungus', in *New Scientist*, 5 June, 41.

Palmquist, P.E. (1999) 'Chronology', in D.R. Nickel (ed.) *Carleton Watkins: The Art of Perception*, San Francisco: Harry N. Abrams Publishers, pp. 216–19.

Panofsky, E (1997) *Perspective as Symbolic Form*, New York: Zone Books.

Pearce, F. (2003) 'A greyer shade of green', in *New Scientist*, 21 June, 41–3.

Pearce, F. (2004) 'Flame retardant shows up in Arctic', in *New Scientist*, 12 June, 10–11.

Peirce, C.S. (1931–58) *Collected Papers*, 8 vols, edited by C. Hartshorne and P. Weiss, Cambridge, MA: Harvard University Press.

Peirce, C.S. (1992) *The Essential Peirce: Selected Philosophical Writings*, vol. 1, edited by N. Houser and C. Kloesel, Bloomington, IN: Indiana University Press.

Peirce, C.S. (1998) *The Essential Peirce: Selected Philosophical Writings*, vol. 2, edited by N. Houser, J.R. Eller, A.C. Lewis, A. De Tienne, C.L. Clark and D.B. Davis, Bloomington, IN: Indiana University Press.

Pinker, S. (1994) *The Language Instinct*, London: Penguin.

Poggi, G. (1978) *The Development of the Modern State*, London: Hutchinson.

Poggi, G. (1990) *The State: Its Nature, Development, and Prospects*, Cambridge: Polity Press.

Pratt, M.L. (1992) *Imperial Eyes*, London: Routledge.

Price, J. (1996) 'Looking for nature at the mall: A field guide to the Nature Company', in W. Cronon (ed.) *Uncommon Ground: Rethinking the Human Place in Nature*, London: W.W. Norton, pp. 186–203.

Prince, G. (1991) *A Dictionary of Narratology*, London: Scolar Press.

Prince, H. (1988) 'Art and agrarian change, 1710–1815', in D. Cosgrove and S. Daniels (eds) *The Iconography of Landscape*, Cambridge: Cambridge University Press, pp. 98–118.

Rabinbach, A. (1990) *The Human Motor: Energy, Fatigue and the Origins of Modernity*, Berkeley, CA: University of California Press.

Radio Times (1993) 'Antarctica, the last true wilderness on Earth', in *Radio Times*, 13–19 November, BBC West/Wales edition, 68.

Reichenbach, H. (1996) 'A tale of two zoos: the Hamburg Zoological Garden and Hagenbeck's Tierpark', in R. Hoage and W. Deiss (eds) *New Worlds, New Animals: From Menagerie to Zoological Park in the Nineteenth Century*, London: Johns Hopkins University Press, pp. 51–62.

Rice, T. (2000) *Voyages of Discovery: Three Centuries of Natural History Exploration*, London: Scriptum Editions.

Ricoeur, P. (1974a) 'The tasks of the political educator', in D. Stewart and J. Bien (eds) *Paul Ricoeur: Political and Social Essays*, Athens, OH: Ohio University Press, pp. 271–93.

Ricoeur, P. (1974b) *The Conflict of Interpretations*, Evanston, IL: Northwestern University Press.

Ritvo, H. (1987) *The Animal Estate*, Cambridge, MA: Harvard University Press.

Ritvo, H. (1996) 'The order of nature', in R. Hoage and W. Deiss (eds) *New Worlds, New Animals: From Menagerie to Zoological Park in the Nineteenth Century*, London: Johns Hopkins University Press, pp. 43–50.

Rorty, R. (1980) *Philosophy and the Mirror of Nature*, Oxford: Blackwell Publishers.

Rothfels, N. (2002) *Savages and Beasts: The Birth of the Modern Zoo*, London: John Hopkins University Press.

Rousseau, J.J. (1979a) *Emile*, translated by A. Bloom, London: Penguin Books.

Rousseau, J.J. (1979b) *Reveries of the Solitary Walker*, translated by P. France, London: Penguin Books.

271

Rowell, A. (1996) *Green Backlash: Global Subversion of the Environment Movement*, London: Routledge.

Rupert, M. (1995) *Producing Hegemony: The Politics of Mass Production and American Global Power*, Cambridge: Cambridge University Press.

de Saussure, F. (1983) *Course in General Linguistics*, translated by R. Harris, London: Duckworth.

Sax, J.L. (1980) *Mountains Without Handrails: Reflections on the National Parks*. Ann Arbor, MI: University of Michigan Press.

Schivelbusch, W. (1977) *The Railway Journey: The Industrialization of Time and Space in the 19th Century*, Leamington Spa: Berg Publishers.

Schudson, M. (1978) *Discovering the News: A Social History of American Newspapers*, New York: Basic Books.

Scott, A. (2000) 'Risk society or angst society? Two views of risk, consciousness, and community', in B. Adam, H. Beck, and J. Van Loon (eds) *The Risk Society and Beyond*, London: Sage, pp. 33–46.

Showalter, W.J. (1923) 'The automobile industry: An American art that has revolutionized methods in manufacturing and transformed transportation', in *National Geographic*, October, 44(4): 337–414.

Singer, P. (1976) *Animal Liberation: A New Ethics for our Treatment of Animals*, London: Cape.

Sivulka, J. (2001) *Stronger than Dirt: A Cultural History of Advertising Personal Hygiene in America, 1875 to 1940*, New York: Humanity Books.

Skinner, Q. (1978) *The Foundations of Modern Political Thought*, 2 vols, Cambridge: Cambridge University Press.

Slater, C. (1995) 'Amazonia as Edenic narrative', in W. Cronon (ed.) *Uncommon Ground: Rethinking the Human Place in Nature*. London: W.W. Norton & Company, pp. 114–31.

Smith, A. (1970) *The Wealth of Nations*, London: Penguin.

Sontag, S. (1977) *On Photography*, London: Penguin.

Soper, K. (1995) *What is Nature?*, Oxford: Oxford University Press.

Soper, K. (2003) 'Humans, Animals, Machines', in *New Formations*, 49: 99–109.

Stam, R. (1992) *New Vocabularies in Film Semiotics*, London: Routledge.

Stanley, H.M. (1874) *Life and Finding of Dr. Livingstone: Containing the Original Letters Written by H.M. Stanley, to the 'New York Herald'*. London: Dean and Son.

Stanley, H.M. (1878) *Through the Dark Continent*, London: Sampson Low.

Sutter, P.S. (2002) *Driven Wild*, London: University of Washington Press.

Symons, G.J. (ed.) (1888) *The Eruption of Krakatoa and Subsequent Phenomena: Report of the Krakatoa Committee of the Royal Society*, London: Trübner & Company.

Talbot, H.F. (1992) 'The pencil of nature', in M. Weaver (ed.) *Henry Fox Talbot: Selected Texts and Bibliography*, Oxford: Clio Press, pp. 75–104.

Thompson, E.P. (1991) *The Making of the English Working Class*, London: Penguin.

Thompson, E.P. (1997) *The Romantics: England in a Revolutionary Age*, London: Merlin.

Thompson, J.B. (1990) *Ideology and Modern Culture*, Cambridge: Polity Press.

Thompson, J.B. (1995) *The Media and Modernity*, Cambridge: Polity Press.

Thoreau, H.D. (1863) 'Walking', in *Excursions*, Boston: Ticknor and Fields, pp. 161–214.

Thrift, N. (1996) *Spatial Formations*, London: Sage.

Thrift, N. (1999) 'Steps to an ecology of place', in D. Massey, J. Allen, and P. Sarre (eds) *Human Geography Today*, Cambridge: Polity Press, pp. 295–322.

Todorov, T. (1984) *The Conquest of America: The Question of the Other*, New York: Harper Perennial.

Towner, J. (1985) 'The Grand Tour: a key phase in the history of tourism', in *Annals of Tourism Research*, 12: 297–333.

Tudor, A. (1989) *Monsters and Mad Scientists,* Oxford: Blackwell.

Turney, F. (1998) *Frankenstein's Footsteps: Science, Genetics, and Popular Culture*, New Haven, CT: Yale University Press.

Urry, J. (2002) *The Tourist Gaze*, 2nd edition, London: Sage.

Voloshinov, V.N (1973) *Marxism and the Philosophy of Language*, New York: Seminar Press.

Weaver, M. (ed.) (1992) *Henry Fox Talbot: Selected Texts and Bibliography*, Oxford: Clio Press.

Welton, D. (ed.) (1999) *The Body*, Oxford: Blackwell.

Whatmore, S. (2002) *Hybrid Geographies: Natures Cultures Spaces*, London: Sage Publications.

White, H. (1978) 'The forms of wildness: archaeology of an idea', in *The Tropics of Discourse: Essays in Cultural Criticism*, Baltimore, MD: Johns Hopkins University Press, pp. 150–82.

White, R. (1996) '"Are you an environmentalist or do you work for a living?" Nature and work', in W. Cronon (ed.) *Uncommon Ground: Rethinking the Human Place in Nature*, London: W.W. Norton, pp. 171–86.

Williams, R. (1973) *The Country and the City*, London: Chatto & Windus.

Williams, R. (1977) *Marxism and Literature*, London: Verso.

Williams, R. (1980) 'Ideas of nature', in *Problems in Materialism and Culture*, London: Verso, pp. 67–85.

Williams, R. (1983) 'Nature', in *Keywords: A Vocabulary of Culture and Society*, revised edition, London: Fontana.

Willock, C. (1978) *The World of Survival*, London: André Deutsch.

Wilson, A. (1992) *The Culture of Nature*, Oxford: Blackwell Publishers.

Wilson, E.O. (1980) *Sociobiology*, Cambridge, MA: Harvard University Press.

Wilson, E.O. (1992) *The Diversity of Life*, Cambridge, MA: Belknap Press.

Wilson, E.O. (1998) *Consilience*, London: Little, Brown.

Wilson, K. (2002) 'Forecasting the future: how television weathercasters' attitudes and beliefs about climate change affect their cognitive knowledge on the science', in *Science Communication* 24(2): 246–68.

Winchester, S. (2003) *Krakatoa: The Day the World Exploded*, New York: Viking.

Winter, J. (1999) *Secure from Rash Assault*, Berkeley, CA: California University Press.

Wöfflin, H. (1971) *The Art of Albrecht Dürer*, translated by A.H. Grieve, London: Phaidon.

Wolf, W. (1996) *Car Mania: A Critical History of Transport*, translated by G. Fagan, London: Pluto Press.

Wordsworth, W. (1977) *Guide to the Lakes*, Oxford: Oxford University Press.

World Commission on Environment and Development (WCED) (1987) *Our Common Future*, Oxford: Oxford University Press.

Wykes, M. (2000) 'The burrowers: news about bodies, tunnels and green guerrillas', in S. Allan, B Adam and C. Caxter (eds) *Environmental Risks and the Media*, London: Routledge, pp. 73–90.

Young, R. (1985) *Darwin's Metaphor: Nature's Place in Victorian Culture*, Cambridge: Cambridge University Press.

Zettl, H. (1990) *Sight–Sound–Motion: Applied Media Aesthetics*, 2nd edition, London: Wadsworth.

van Zwanenberg, P. and Millstone, E. (2005) *BSE: Risk, Science, and Governance*, Oxford: Oxford University Press.

INDEX

275